Routledge Revivals

Disaggregation in Econometric Modelling

In this book, first published in 1990, leading theorists and applied economists address themselves to the key questions of aggregation. The issues are covered both theoretically and in wide-ranging applications. Of particular interest is the optimal aggregation of trade data, the need for micro-modelling when important non-linearities are present (for example, tax exhaustion in modelling company behaviour) and the use of a micro-model to stimulate labour supply behaviour in a macro-model of the Netherlands.

Disaggregation in Econometric Modelling

Edited by
Terry Barker
and
M. Hashem Pesaran

Routledge
Taylor & Francis Group

First published in 1990
by Routledge

This edition first published in 2011 by Routledge
2 Park Square, Milton Park, Abingdon, Oxon, OX14 4RN

Simultaneously published in the USA and Canada
by Routledge
270 Madison Avenue, New York, NY 10016

Routledge is an imprint of the Taylor & Francis Group, an informa business

Publisher's Note
The publisher has gone to great lengths to ensure the quality of this reprint but
points out that some imperfections in the original copies may be apparent.

Disclaimer
The publisher has made every effort to trace copyright holders and welcomes
correspondence from those they have been unable to contact.

A Library of Congress record exists under LC Control Number: 90032516

ISBN 13: 978-0-415-61658-4 (hbk)
ISBN 13: 978-0-415-61663-8 (pbk)

Disaggregation in econometric modelling

Disaggregation in econometric modelling

Edited by Terry Barker and
M. Hashem Pesaran

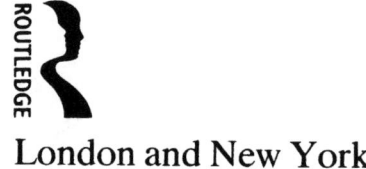

London and New York

First published 1990 by Routledge
11 New Fetter Lane, London EC4P 4EE

Simultaneously published in the USA and Canada by Routledge
a division of Routledge, Chapman and Hall, Inc.
29 West 35th Street, New York, NY 10001

Typeset by Leaper & Gard Ltd, Bristol, England

Printed in Great Britain by
Billings and Sons Limited, Worcester

British Library Cataloguing in Publication Data

Disaggregation in econometric modelling.
1. Economics. Models
I. Barker, Terry *1941*– II. Pesaran, Hashem *1946*–
330.011

ISBN 0–415–00918–9

Library of Congress Cataloging in Publication Data

Disaggregation in econometric modelling / edited by T.S. Barker and
M.H. Pesaran.
p. cm.
Includes bibliographical references (p.
ISBN 0-415-00918-9
1. Econometric models. I. Barker, Terry. II. Pesaran, M.
Hashem, 1946– .
HB141.D47 1990
330′.01′5195–dc20
90-32516
CIP

Contents

Contents

Tables

Tables

Figures

List of contributors

T.S. Barker — Department of Applied Economics, University of Cambridge, UK

A. Colin Cameron — Department of Economics, University of California, Davis, USA

Gopa Chowdhury — Department of Economics, Northeastern University, Boston, Mass., USA

Edwin Deutsch — University of Technology, Vienna, Austria

Mario Forni — Department of Political Economy, University of Modena, Italy

Clive W.J. Granger — Institute of Empirical Macroeconomics, Federal Reserve Bank of Minneapolis *and* University of California, San Diego, USA

Christopher Green — Cardiff Business School, University of Wales, UK

Peter ten Hacken — Department of Economics, Tilburg University, The Netherlands

Chris Higson — London Business School, London, UK

Sean Holly — London Business School, London, UK

Pekka Ilmakunnas — Research Institute of the Finnish Economy, Helsinki, Finland

Arie Kapteyn — Department of Economics, Tilburg University, The Netherlands

Edward E. Leamer — University of California, Los Angeles, USA

K. Lee — Department of Applied Economics, University of Cambridge, UK

Marco Lippi — Department of Political Economy, University of Modena, Italy

G. Meeks — Faculty of Economics, University of Cambridge, UK

David Miles — Bank of England, London, UK

M.H. Pesaran   Trinity College, Cambridge, UK *and* University of California, Los Angeles, USA

R.G. Pierse   Department of Applied Economics, Cambridge, UK

Kurt Rodler   University of Technology, Vienna, Austria

Thomas Sterner   Department of Economics, University of Gothenburg, Sweden

E.K.A. Van Doorslaer   Institute for Medical Technology Assessment, University of Limburg, The Netherlands

R.C.J.A. van Vliet   Department of Health Services Administration, Erasmus University, Rotterdam, The Netherlands

Preface

This book arose out of the desire to make the main contributions of an international conference on disaggregation held in Queens' College, Cambridge, in April 1987, available to a wider audience. However, it is not the proceedings of the conference. Those who presented papers were asked to revise their contributions for publication and others, not able to attend the conference, were invited to contribute to the book.

Our aim has been to provide one source which covers the main work in progress in the area of disaggregation in econometric modelling, both theoretical and applied.

Kath Wilson, Secretary of the Department of Applied Economics, University of Cambridge, organized the conference with efficiency and good nature and we are very grateful to her. We also wish to thank all those who have contributed to the conference and the book for their patience in rewriting papers and their contribution of new papers. A special thanks goes to Ann Newton, the Publications Secretary of the Department, who organized the contributions and editing.

The Editors
April 1989

Chapter one

Disaggregation in econometric modelling – an introduction

T.S. Barker and M.H. Pesaran*

1.1 The aggregation problem

In much economic theory and most applied work in economic modelling, there is a problem of aggregation. Economic theories generally focus on the behaviour of individuals (consumers or entrepreneurs) or groups such as owners of capital and labour, while empirical economic research is concerned primarily with the relationships between groups. Nearly every study must aggregate over time, over individual people, firms, or agents, over products and techniques, and over space, usually over most of these dimensions. Take the analysis of consumer expenditure as an example of a widely researched area in applied econometrics. Most studies use national expenditure data derived in part from household surveys. The analysis, if time-series, invariably involves temporal aggregation over months, quarters, or years; it will cover large numbers of decision-making units in the form of households and individuals; even if disaggregated, the product groups may cover many thousands of goods (defined as items of value, two equal quantities of which are completely equivalent as regards all characteristics, including location, for each seller and buyer); and the analysis will usually assume that all spending is located at one point in space. Similar considerations also apply to the analysis of firms, and even public institutions.

Despite the pervasiveness of aggregation in economics, and apart from the early contributions of Leontief (1947), Theil (1954), Malinvaud (1956), Gorman (1959), and Grunfeld and Griliches (1960), the aggregation problem is rarely addressed explicitly in mainstream economics.[1] Instead it is usually concealed through the use of terms and concepts such as industry, the economy,

* We are grateful to Tony Lawson, Ron Smith and Arnold Zellner for helpful comments and suggestions on an earlier version of this chapter. M.H. Pesaran gratefully acknowledges financial support from the ESRC and the Newton Trust.

1

labour, and capital which, if they are to have any empirical relevance, correspond to broad categories, or are brushed aside by resorting to the Marshallian concept of the 'representative' agent.[2] Neither response, however, is satisfactory if we are to retain the connection between micro and macro behaviour.[3] A proper understanding of the aggregation problem and the particular method chosen for its resolution is of crucial importance for the interpretation and evaluation of applied research in economics.

Unfortunately, a satisfactory resolution of the aggregation problem is not, in general, possible. For example, in the case of aggregation over individual agents, valid aggregation requires *a priori* knowledge of the distribution of the explanatory or predictor variables across the micro units. Aggregation over commodities also involves special assumptions concerning functional separability that are often highly restrictive, and unlikely to hold in practice. Similarly, restrictive assumptions are also required in the case of aggregation over time and space. The main issue in applied econometrics is not, however, whether consistent aggregation is possible, but rather at what level of aggregation or disaggregation the analysis should be carried out. What is needed is a framework for choosing the appropriate level of disaggregation in particular economic applications.

1.2 Which level of aggregation?

The factors influencing the choice of level of aggregation or disaggregation can be summarized under the following broad headings:

- the purpose of the exercise,
- the specification errors involved,
- the data available,
- the attitude of the investigator towards the postulates of simplicity and parsimony.

The purpose of the exercise

The purpose of the exercise is paramount. If the purpose is pedagogical, if the aim is to describe or to understand the underlying mechanisms at work, then the stripping out of inessential detail is important. Aggregation becomes a simplifying technique permitting a clearer understanding of the nature of the forces at work. A good example of this is provided by Leamer in chapter 7 below. If the purpose is policy formulation, for example the appropriate structure of an indirect tax, then disaggregation of policy instruments is essential and disaggregation of the revenue base into its major components is advisable. If it is forecasting, then the decisions which rely on the forecast will determine the minimum level of disaggregation required: aggregate macro variables such as GDP may suffice for the overall management of the economy, whilst the corporate planner may require sectoral forecasts of industrial markets.

The specification errors involved

In addition to the purpose behind the econometric exercise, the choice of level of disaggregation also depends on the relative magnitudes of the error of aggregation and the error of misspecification in the disaggregate model (see Pesaran *et al.*, 1989). For example, as shown by Ilmakunnas in chapter 4, a disaggregated forecasting model distinguishing between housing and non-housing constructions may be more appropriate, especially for long forecast horizons, even if the purpose is to forecast the aggregate level of construction activity.

The data available

The limited amount of disaggregated data available and the high costs of collecting and processing new data place further constraints on the level of disaggregation which can be employed in particular applications. Although macroeconomic data are usually derived from disaggregated sources (only a few series such as banks' base rates or some tax rates remain fixed over periods of time and do not involve aggregation over products or space), the costs of maintaining large databanks in a consistent manner at a disaggregated level are high and often prohibitive for individual researchers. Much of the data published by government agencies rely on a few conventional disaggregations by industrial sectors or regions, largely determined by official requirements rather than by considerations of economic research. The limited amount of disaggregated data which are available are also often of doubtful quality, further constraining the extent of disaggregation contemplated by researchers. There is clearly an urgent need for a general improvement in economic measurements, but meanwhile the quantity and the quality of the disaggregated data available will be an important factor in the choice between the aggregated and the disaggregated models.

Simplicity and parsimony

Another important consideration in the choice of level of dis-aggregation in applied econometrics is the notion of 'simplicity' and the overwhelming aversion that seems to exist towards complex hypotheses. Other things being equal, simple hypotheses or models are often regarded as being preferable to more complex ones. The preference for simple hypotheses, referred to by Jeffreys (1937) as the 'Simplicity Postulate', is deep-rooted in human psychology and is often justified by appeal to Occam's razor.[4] According to Jeffreys, '... the simpler hypothesis holds the field; the onus of proof is always on the advocate of the more complicated hypothesis' (1937, p. 252). A similar point of view is also expressed by Zellner (1971). The application of this postulate to the choice between the aggregated and the disaggregated model is, however, far from straightforward. The difficulty partly lies with the formalization of the concept of 'simplicity' or 'complexity' and the method used to quantify it. For example, Jeffreys (1948, p. 100) initially adopts a measure of the complexity of a hypothesis in terms of the number of its 'adjustable parameters', which was proposed earlier by himself and Dorothy Wrinch (1921). Later, in the third edition of his *Theory of Probability*, he abandons this definition in favour of a more general one, applicable to any hypothesis expressible by differential equations. He defines the complexity of a differential equation by 'the sum of the order, the degree and the absolute values of the coefficients' (1961, p. 47). Popper (1959, chapter 7), taking a different methodological stand, identifies the simplicity of a hypothesis with its falsifiability. He writes: 'The epistemological questions which arise in connection with the concept of simplicity can all be answered if we equate this concept with *degree of falsifiability*' (1959, p. 140). Different conclusions can clearly emerge from the application of these concepts to aggregated and disaggregated models. But even if it is accepted that aggregated models are simpler than their disaggregated counterparts, it does not necessarily follow that they are less probable or less likely to be true. The simplicity postulate on its own is unlikely to provide a justification for the choice of aggregated models over the less aggregated ones. The choice of the appropriate level of disaggregation needs to be made empirically and in the context of particular applications.

1.3 The case for aggregation

When the disaggregated model is correctly specified and the available data are free from measurement errors, then the investigator could not do worse (whether for explaining facts or in predicting future behaviour) by adopting a disaggregated approach as compared to an aggregated one; and he or she may do better. The use of aggregated data and models in these circumstances is only justified for educational purposes, to make particular points and as an aid to understanding. The conditions under which aggregation is justified appear to be so restrictive that in nearly every case it would seem that the more disaggregated the analysis the better.[5] Yet there are good reasons why the aggregated approach may be justified. The best known, set out by Grunfeld and Griliches (1960), is that the model specification may be less subject to errors at the macro level, rather than at the micro level as assumed by Theil.[6] In such a case the macro relationship may provide a better explanation (goodness of fit) and better predictions than the micro relationships. But, if the mis-specification is such that the micro equations omit macro influences, then the remedy may be to respecify the micro equations to include macro variables.

Another reason for analysing at the macro level is that there are errors in variables at the micro level which may roughly cancel out when the micro variables are added together (cf. Aigner and Goldfeld, 1974). Examples of such errors are those caused by misclassification, when an item is classified to one disaggregated group when it should be in another. This is especially damaging in time-series analysis when the misclassification occurs in some time periods and not in others.

A further possible justification is that individual equations have unobserved influences which may cancel out in the aggregate. This will lead to a better fit for the macro equation, and can lead to better predictions if the unobserved influences continue to cancel each other in the prediction period.

The most potent reason for macro analysis, however, is again the availability of data: the investigator often has no choice in the matter, given limited resources for the collection and processing of data.

The usual procedure in applied work, demonstrated by the papers below, is to start at one or other end of the spectrum. If one starts with a macro analysis, the questions arise: what are the benefits of disaggregation and how can they be established at reasonable cost? Starting from a micro model and micro data, the questions are: what are the costs of aggregating in the sense of loss of information, and is aggregation necessarily bad?

1.4 The case for disaggregation

It is worth bringing together the arguments for the disaggregation of macro relationships as they emerge from several chapters in this book.

More information

When reliable disaggregated data are available, then in principle it should be possible to use the extra information in the data to develop and apply more powerful tests to the hypotheses of interest. Difficulties arise in maintaining consistency of definition at the disaggregated level and in the availability of data for the same time period.

Better predictions

With more reliable disaggregated information and a better understanding of micro behaviour, one would expect the disaggregated model to predict better than the aggregated model. The applications of the prediction criterion proposed by Grunfeld and Griliches (1960) so far suggest that there is not much to be gained from disaggregation when the problem is one of predicting macro variables. But the Grunfeld–Griliches criterion has been generally applied to cases where the equations in the disaggregated model all have the same specification. It is important that the possibility of different specifications across micro units be allowed for in the comparison of the predictive performance of the aggregated and the disaggregated model. In fact one of the advantages of disaggregation is that the specification can be varied across micro units to suit the circumstances. For example, in the case of the determination of imports, some commodities such as oil or basic foodstuffs may behave as if the imports were residual supplies whilst others would require a specification more suited to demand for differentiated products. An elementary case of different specification for disaggregated equations occurs when different macro variables are dropped from the micro equations according to economic relevance or statistical significance.

Better parameter estimates

Estimates of parameters from macro equations can be seriously misleading for understanding the mechanisms at work or for formulating policy, because they rely on a particular aggregation structure. For example, the chapter below by Lee, Pesaran, and Pierse (chapter 6) reports a wage elasticity estimated from disaggregated equations for UK industrial employment of −0.54, whilst that estimated from the aggregated counterpart is −0.97. This has the strong policy implication that reductions in real wage rates, by whatever means, may result in rather less impressive effects on employment demand than previous studies, based on aggregated results, have indicated.

The rest of this book is divided into two parts. Part I contains those chapters which are concerned with the question of optimal aggregation and the effects of aggregation on parameter estimates and predictive performance. The chapters which address the practical problems of introducing micro or disaggregated data into macro models or macro equations are included in Part II of the book. This covers the problems of linking macro and micro models and the use of disaggregated data in macro models.

1.5 A summary of chapters in part I

Part I of the book starts with a chapter by Granger who surveys the literature on cross-sectional and temporal aggregation in the case of univariate time-series models, such as the autoregressive-moving-average (ARMA) models. He distinguishes between 'small-scale' and 'large-scale' aggregation and in the case of the latter shows that very different results can follow depending on whether or not the micro relations contain common factors.[7] This chapter also discusses the issues of 'causality' and 'cointegration' under both cross-sectional and temporal aggregation. It shows that both types of aggregation can be disruptive of causal relationships. Aggregation can introduce important feedbacks at the aggregate level not present at the disaggregate level. Similar ambiguities also arise with respect to the cointegration property under cross-sectional aggregation. Reviewing a recent paper by Gonzalo (1988) on the subject, Granger concludes that it is possible to have cointegration at the aggregate level without any evidence of cointegration at the disaggregate level and vice versa. There seems to be no general rule that could be applied. In each case the matter needs to be settled empirically.

The chapter by Lippi and Forni (chapter 3) considers the forecasting problem discussed briefly in chapter 2, and extends the results for the cross-sectional aggregation of ARMA models to time-series econometric models with stationary 'exogenous' or 'forcing' variables, known as ARMAX models. Lippi and Forni show that in general the dynamic specification of the aggregated

model can be far more complicated than the dynamic specifications of the underlying disaggregated models. For example, in
the absence of micro-homogeneity, the aggregated model may
have a complicated ARMAX form even when the disaggregated
equations contain no dynamic effects. This is an important result
for empirical analysis of the relative predictive performance of the
aggregated and the disaggregated models. It is, however, important
to note that, since Lippi and Forni assume that the disaggregated
model is correctly specified, then in general the disaggregated
model cannot do worse than the aggregated model, even if the
latter is specified to have a much richer dynamic specification.

The issue of the relative predictive performance of the aggregated and the disaggregated model is taken up by Ilmakunnas in
chapter 4, but now in an empirical context. Ilmakunnas considers
the problem of forecasting the total volume of construction activity
in Finland using ARIMA models as well as distributed lag
relations between starts and construction volumes. He investigates
two levels of disaggregation: a partial disaggregation where total
construction is split into housing and other buildings, and a more
detailed one where non-housing construction is further disaggregated into nine sub-groups. The lag weights in the distributed lag
models are computed directly from information on the average
construction times and costs of different types of building. The
results for forecasting the total volume of construction are mixed
and depend on the type of model employed (i.e. ARIMA or distributed lag models) and the length of the forecast horizon. The
aggregated models generally do better for short forecast horizons
while the disaggregated models perform best for long forecast
horizons. It is interesting to see whether this result holds in other
applications.

In their contribution Deutsch and Rodler (chapter 5) estimate
simultaneous models of wage formation and employment demand
for different types of labour in the Austrian economy. The model
has a recursive structure with real wages influencing employment
demand with no feedbacks from employment to the real wage
formation equation. The analysis distinguishes between low-skill
and high-skill workers and low-rank and high-rank employees, and
considers a number of different aggregation schemes. The authors
investigate the existence of aggregates for different labour types by
testing the hypothesis of micro homogeneity along the lines
suggested by Zellner (1962). They also use the Grunfeld and
Grilches (GG) (1960) goodness-of-fit criterion in their choice of
aggregation scheme, although strictly speaking the application of
the GG criterion has so far been justified only for single equation

disaggregated models. The results suggest that aggregation is much more of a problem in the labour demand equations than in the wage formation equations.

Chapter 6 deals with the issue of aggregation bias, and extends some of the results obtained in Pesaran, Pierse, and Kumar (1989) (PPK). In this chapter Lee, Pesaran, and Pierse (LPP) provide new estimates of employment functions for the UK economy disaggregated into forty industries. These estimates differ from those already reported in PPK in two important respects. First, the functions allow for a longer lagged effect of output on employment which empirically proves to be important. Second, to avoid some of the problems associated with the use of time trends as a proxy for technical change, LPP experiment, with some success, with a measure of embodied technological change based on the current and past movements of *gross* investment (*à la* Kaldor, 1961), in place of the simple time trend. LPP then carry out statistical tests of the aggregation bias in the estimates of the long-run wage and output elasticities, comparing the average of micro elasticities with their corresponding estimates based on the aggregated model. The results indicate a wide diversity in the responsiveness of labour demand to different influences across industries, and provide significant evidence of aggregation bias in the estimates of the long-run real wage elasticity based on the aggregated model. However, there does not seem to be any statistically significant evidence of aggregation bias in the long-run estimates of output and technological change elasticities.

The chapter by Leamer (chapter 7) considers the problem of optimal aggregation as a method of simplification, to aid understanding and communication. Here the aim is not to predict macro variables from the micro equations, but to replace a high dimensional micro system by a lower dimensional one, with a minimal loss of information. As Leamer puts it, 'This is like the problem of constructing an optimal language: An optimal vocabulary trades off miscommunication from too many words with miscommunication from too few'. Building on the work of Fisher (1969) and Chipman (1976), Leamer sets up an optimization framework for the aggregation problem at hand and suggests a simple computer algorithm which gives a local solution to the optimization problem. The procedure is then applied to a system of trade equations explaining net exports of fifty-six commodity groups in terms of measured factor supplies such as land, labour, and capital for the years 1958 and 1975 separately. The chapter contains a number of results of special interest to the students of international trade. For example, it is shown that a locally optimal aggregation scheme with nine aggregates is more accurate (in the quadratic loss sense) by a wide margin than the one-digit SITC classification. The primary reason for this seems to be that the one-digit SITC combines cereals (SITC-04) with coffee, tea, cocoa, spices, etc (SITC-07), while the data suggest that these two classifications are significantly different as far as the sources of their comparative advantages are concerned.

Sterner in chapter 8 compares own-price and substitution elasticities estimated for five inputs into Mexican production at three levels of aggregation: eighteen four-digit groups, four three-digit groups, and the total. He finds that there is little analytical value in the official grouping of the data, which may be more geared to end-use than to technique of production. His main result is that his aggregate elasticities do not relate systematically to the weighted averages of the component industries' elasticities; in those cases where there is a relationship, the reason for it is not obvious. His results strongly emphasize the need for caution before generalizing results across different levels of aggregation.

Chapter 9 by van Vliet and Van Doorslaer compares the results of a micro model of demand for hospital care in the Netherlands with those from macro studies. The two approaches yield substantially different policy conclusions, so this is an area in which the level of aggregation in econometric analysis could have a significant social impact. The authors find that their results at both levels of aggregation support the micro approach, but conclude that differences from other published results may be due to biases in the selection of the samples used and that further investigation is required. They examine inconsistent aggregation, omission of micro variables in the macro equation, and a simultaneous system of equations, but find these of little consequence for the estimated coefficients. The most important finding for micro-macro analysis is that, for reliable estimates of the effects of micro variables, such as family size, compared with those of regional variables, such as number of hospital beds, disaggregated data are indispensable.

The last chapter in this part of the book (chapter 10) is by Cameron, who examines the aggregation problem in discrete choice models and gives a brief account of the problem of non-linear aggregation in general. The focus of this literature is the non-linearity of the micro equations and it is usually assumed that the micro parameters are the same across the micro equations. This is to be contrasted with the literature on linear aggregation, where the micro equations are assumed to be linear but the micro coefficients are allowed to vary freely across the micro equations. Cameron reviews the work of Kelejian (1980) and Stoker (1984) on the existence of complete aggregation structures, and in the case of discrete choice models discusses alternative procedures for deriving macro equations from the knowledge of the underlying micro equations and the probability distribution of the conditioning variables in the micro model. One important application of this literature has been to the problem of predicting macro behaviour from micro equations, using aggregated data only. This problem is also discussed by Cameron who, by means of simulation experiments, shows that substantial loss of accuracy in macro predictions can result if data on micro variables are unavailable.

1.6 A summary of the chapters in part II

Part II of the book is mainly concerned with the problems of linkage, although there is some overlap with the topics covered in part I in that several of the papers examine the effects of aggregation on parameter estimation.

The chapter by Higson and Holly (chapter 11), which opens part II, covers some of the main issues in linking microeconomic models, estimated on cross-section or pooled data, with macroeconomic models of national economies. They concentrate on areas where the underlying economic behaviour might be expected to display non-linearities or discontinuities, areas where macro equations may be particularly biased. Micro models of the UK personal tax and benefit system and the UK corporation tax system are reviewed, with particular stress on the treatment of tax exhaustion. They point out that a noticeable feature of the micro models is that they are almost entirely calibrated or arithmetical, with very few behavioural responses and often no dynamics. Furthermore, the modellers generally do not try to ensure that all the variables not actually explained by the model are strictly exogenous.

The chapter considers four responses by the modellers to the issues involved in linking micro and macro models. The first is to use the micro results to impose coefficients on the macro equation; this is better than nothing, but does not allow the macro model to incorporate the detailed policy analysis available in the micro model. The second response is to solve the micro and macro models in tandem; the problem here is the possible linkages between the micro models, e.g. links between a micro model of household labour supply and one of personal taxation, which would be ignored. The third response is to use the micro models to generate measures of unobservable factors such as corporate tax exhaustion or income distribution which can then be introduced into the macro model. This may be the direction in which macro models will go; but micro models are essential to identify which compositional factors are important and how they are to be defined. The fourth response is to suggest that the macro models should be replaced by a set of integrated micro models; however, given the costs of data collection and the difficulties involved in linking cross-section sample data and time-series macro data, this response is considered unlikely to succeed.

Chapter 12 by ten Hacken and Kapteyn is an example of the second response. It is a detailed account of the linking of a micro model (in this case one of household labour supply) with a macro model, the quarterly model developed by the Netherlands Central Planning Bureau. The micro model replaces the aggregate equation in providing labour supply to the macro model; the macro model supplies average wages, the demand for labour, production, and income to the micro model. The two models are fully integrated by means of an interactive solution. The equations of the micro model cannot be aggregated exactly, but the solution for the numbers of hours worked can be obtained for the sample and grossed up to give the labour supply for the population. This procedure links the demographic and social structure of a particular year (the micro model is estimated on a survey done in 1985) with a time-series macro model. Thus the much richer structure of the micro model brings with it the problem that the micro relationships have to be assumed to be static and time-invariant. The investigators also face another common problem in that the grossed-up sample measure of labour supply does not correspond with the published totals. A simulation of the micro model gives annual results for 1981-4 consistently below the actual numbers of person-years in labour supply, employment, and unemployment. The chapter demonstrates the benefits for policy making of disaggregation in a critical area. The micro model is able to identify the responses of labour supply to changes in real wages and unemployment benefits which are missing in the macro model.

Chapter 13 by Barker considers the problem of disaggregating a particular variable in a macro model, where disaggregated data are available for the variable. He considers four methods of disaggregating, both with and without constraints being imposed to force the components to add up to the total. This represents one extreme approach to linkage, that of forcing the aggregate results of the micro model to fit with the results of the macro model, and is to be contrasted with the other extreme of replacing the macro model equation with the micro model results, illustrated by ten Hacken and Kapteyn (in chapter 12). Barker compares the predictive performance of the four methods, using quarterly data on UK production, and concludes that the simple share method produces surprisingly good results, perhaps because it gives maximum weight to the most recent observation.

Green, Chowdhury, and Miles (GCM) in chapter 14 compare the explanations of bank borrowing and liquid lending by UK companies given by aggregate equations with those given by a disaggregated study of a sample of 694 medium and large quoted non-financial companies over the period 1971–83. There are several features in this chapter which are worth summarizing. First, there is the question of why the company sector should simultaneously borrow and lend liquid assets on a large scale. The aggregate equations cannot help much here because they cannot differentiate between a situation in which some companies are borrowing and other companies are lending, because of the nature of their business, and one in which individual companies are lending and borrowing at the same time. This issue is critical in any explanation of the phenomenon and is a general issue in aggregated behaviour when there are large two-way flows, e.g. intra-industry trade. GCM find that the net lending by companies is bimodal but not strongly so, suggesting that indeed some companies borrow and others lend.

A second feature of the GCM paper is the introduction of specific company variables in disaggregate equations. They find that changes in bank borrowing are explained by large but conflicting pressures, with a very important contribution made by company size, but with smaller effects from other company-specific variables. The paper demonstrates the substantial increase in information gained by a disaggregated analysis, and suggests valuable directions for the analysis of aggregate borrowing behaviour by showing the importance of modelling *net* borrowing rather than borrowing and lending separately.

Chapter 15 by Meeks is also concerned with disaggregating the UK company sector. He argues that 'even if all companies were identical in their response to market stimuli, threshold effects could still make disaggregation the most efficient route to aggregate conclusions'. By threshold effects he means substantially different responses depending on whether a company lies on one side or another of a statutory or institutional threshold. Three areas are explored: tax exhaustion, dividend payments during periods of incomes policy, and the effects of company failure. The importance of these micro effects is illustrated by micro models estimated on UK data. He reports estimated company taxation as much as 14 per cent higher from the micro model than from the macro model. In the case of dividend payments in the 1970s, at least a quarter of the sample are estimated to have paid smaller dividends, though in the absence of controls. Finally, he reports striking non-linearities in the death rates for companies in response to different exchange rate appreciations or depreciations.

Notes

1   Some notable exceptions are the work of Muellbauer (1975, 1976), Sonnenschein (1972), Lau (1980, 1982), Kelejian (1980), Stoker (1984, 1986), and Pesaran *et al.* (1989).
2   Following Zellner (1966), some investigators have also adopted the random coefficient framework to deal with the aggregation problem. This approach results in considerable simplification of the aggregation problem in linear models, but its validity depends crucially on the assumption that differences in micro parameters can be satisfactorily characterized by a stable probability distribution.
3   The view expressed here about the desirability of a connection between micro and macro theory is not uncontroversial. Proponents of a holistic approach see no point in insisting that there need be any such links (see, for example, Peston, 1959).
4   It appears that the rule known as Occam's razor was first given in its usual Latin form *Entia non sunt multiplicanda sine necessitate* (entities should not be multiplied unnecessarily) by John Ponce in 1639 (see Jeffreys, 1937, p. 264).
5   The conditions for perfect aggregation in the case of linear models are set out by Theil (1954), and for certain classes of non-linear problems they are given, for example, by Gorman (1959), Kelejian (1980), and Stoker (1984).
6   We assume for the discussion which follows that 'macro' means 'aggregated' and 'micro' means 'disaggregated'; the terms macro and micro are usually used to refer to relationships and variables at the level of the economy and the individual agent or goods, with no satisfactory term for those relationships and variables that may be postulated between the two, e.g. concerning industries or goods aggregated into broad commodity groupings or institutions into sectors.
7   These results, however, depend crucially on the assumption that the coefficients of the macro variables in the micro equations remain fixed as the number of the micro units is allowed to increase without bound.

Part I

Chapter two

Aggregation of time-series variables: a survey

Clive W.J. Granger

Introduction

The first three sections of this chapter will consider three types of aggregation that occur in the context of the analysis of time series: (a) 'small-scale' aggregation, (b) 'large-scale' aggregation, and (c) temporal aggregation. An example of small-scale aggregation is if X_t is generated by an AR(1) equation, such as

$$X_t = \alpha_1 X_{t-1} + \varepsilon_{1t}$$

and similarly Y_t is AR(1)

$$Y_t = \alpha_2 Y_{t-1} + \varepsilon_{2t}$$

where ε_{1t}, ε_{2t} are each white noises and if X_t, Y_t are independent, so that ε_{1t}, ε_{2t} are independent, then what model does

$$S_t = X_t + Y_t$$

obey? The answer is found usually to be ARMA(2,1). Small-scale aggregation involves sums of a few time-series variables, which are not necessarily independent. A clear practical conclusion is that mixed models, i.e. ARMA(p, q), are likely to arise from small-scale aggregation.

'Large-scale' aggregations will involve the sums of very many variables, such as total US consumption, which is the sum of the consumptions by the many million individual families that make up the consumers in the economy. One may expect special properties for aggregates over very large numbers of components.

Temporal aggregation occurs when a variable is generated over a month, by some model such as an AR(1) process, but is only observed quarterly, for example. The question arises, what model will the temporally aggregated data obey? The answer will depend on whether the variable is a stock or a flow and is discussed in section 2.3.

The other sections of the survey consider special topics that are particularly relevant for the time-series context, section 2.4 is on forecasting, section 2.5 on causation and section 2.6 on co-integration.

2.1 Small-scale aggregation

Many of the results concerning aggregation of univariate series rely on the following simple result (from Granger and Morris, 1976):

Theorem 1

If X_{1t}, X_{2t} are MA(q) processes, generated by

$$X_{jt} = \sum_{k=0}^{q} a_{jk}\varepsilon_{j(t-k)}$$

where the innovation processes are individually white noise (i.e., $\text{cov}(\varepsilon_{jt}, \varepsilon_{js}) = 0$, $t \neq s$, $j \neq k$) then the sum

$$S_t = X_{1t} + X_{2t}$$

is also an MA(q) process, and it will have a representation

$$S_t = \sum_{k=0}^{q} b_k \eta_{t-k}$$

where η_t is a white noise. There seems to be no simple relationship between the b_j and the component coefficients a_{jk}, $k = 1, 2$.

As the result holds for the sum of a pair of moving averages it clearly holds for the sum of any number of MA(q) variables. If ε_{1t}, ε_{2t} are correlated other than contemporaneously, the sum may be MA(q^*) for any finite q^*. For example, if

$$X_{1t} = \varepsilon_{1t} + b\varepsilon_{1(t-1)}$$
and

$$X_{2t} = \varepsilon_{1(t-3)} + c\varepsilon_{1(t-4)}$$

18

then each series is MA(1) but the sum is MA(4). In the case of only contemporaneous correlation between innovations, the theorem should strictly state that S_t is MA(q^*), where $q^* < q$. For example, if

$$X_{1t} = \varepsilon_{1t} + b\varepsilon_{1(t-1)}$$

$$X_{2t} = \varepsilon_{2t} + c\varepsilon_{2(t-1)}$$

and $\text{cov}(\varepsilon_{jt}, \varepsilon_{ks}) = 0$ all $t \neq s$ and when $k \neq j$ then $\text{cov}(S_t, S_{t-1}) = \text{cov}(X_{1t}, X_{1(t-1)}) + \text{cov}(X_{2t}, X_{2(t-1)}) = b \, \text{var}(\varepsilon_1) + c \, \text{var}(\varepsilon_2)$ and clearly this *can* be zero, making S_t a white-noise series. However, if $\text{cov}(S_t, S_{t-1})$ is zero it may be thought of as a coincidental or low-probability event.

Darroch, Jirina, and McDonald (1986) have shown that if the moving averages each has a unit root, so that

$$X_{1t} = (1 - B)a_1(B)\varepsilon_{1t}$$

$$X_{2t} = (1 - B)a_2(B)\varepsilon_{2t}$$

where $a_j(B), j = 1, 2$, are polynomials in B of order $q - 1$, then, S_t will also contain a unit root and be of the same form. Thus, if the components are non-invertible moving averages, of this particular kind, then so will be their sum.

A univariate series X_{1t} will be said to be ARMA(p_1, q_1) if it is generated by

$$a_1(B)X_{1t} = b_1(B)\varepsilon_{1t}$$

where ε_{1t} is white noise, $q_1(B)$ is a polynomial of order p_1, $b_1(B)$ is a polynomial of order q_1 and $a_1(B)$, $b_1(B)$ have no common roots. The immediate generalization of the theorem for moving averages is:

Theorem 2
If

$$X_{1t} \sim \text{ARMA}(p_1, q_1)$$

$$X_{2t} \sim \text{ARMA}(p_2, q_2)$$

and $(\varepsilon_{1t}, \varepsilon_{2t})$ is a bivariate white noise, then

$$S_t = X_{1t} + X_{2t}$$

is ARMA(m, n) where

$$m \leq p_1 + p_2$$

$$n \leq \max(p_1 + q_2, p_2 + q_1)$$

(proved in Granger and Morris, 1976). Thus, for example, if X_{1t} ~ AR(1), X_{2t} ~ AR(1) then generally S_t is ARMA(2.1) but in special cases these orders can be lower. If S_t is given by

$$a_s(B)S_t = b_2(B)\eta_t$$

then $a_s(B)$ will consist of the product of $a_1(B)$ multiplied by all the roots of $a_2(B)$ that are not also in $a_1(B)$. It follows that aggregates may 'usually' be expected to have ARMA models rather than the simpler AR models. In particular, if X_t is AR(p) but is observed with a white-noise measurement error, the observed series will be ARMA(p, p), from this theory.

A particularly important consequence of these results is that if *any* component series contains a unit root (and thus is $I(1)$) so that $a_1(B) = (1 - B)\alpha_1(B)$, for example) then the sum S_t will also be $I(1)$.

Some generalizations of theorem 2 have been provided for the multivariate case by Peiris (1987) who proves:

Theorem 3

If X_{1t} is a multivariate series with N components generated by

$$A_1(B)X_{1t} = C_1(B)\varepsilon_{1t}$$

where $A_1(B)$ is an $N \times N$ matrix in the lag operator B, each component of this matrix being a polynomial of order p_1 in B, and similarly the matrix $C_1(B)$ consists of polynomials of order q_1, then X_{1t} ~ ARMA(p_1, q_1). If also X_{2t} ~ ARMA(p_2, q_2), and if the stacked vector $(\varepsilon_{1t}, \varepsilon_{2t})$ is a $2N$ white-noise vector (so that components are at most correlated contemporaneously), *and* if the matrix $A_1(B)A_2(B)$ is symmetric, then

$$S_t = X_{1t} + X_{2t}$$

is ARMA(m, n), with m, n as given in theorem 2. In particular, the sum of two MA(q) vectors will also be MA(q). The symmetry condition is rather a stringent one and it is unclear what occurs when it does not hold.

A caveat about these results and some of those in later sections is that, although they are correct in theoretical situations, they are of somewhat limited value in practice when analysing an actual data series. One may assume that an ARMA(p, q) model is appropriate but the values of p and q have to be identified either using the methods proposed by Box and Jenkins (1970) or model-size selection criteria such as AIC. In practice, the true p, q may be very large – as suggested by the aggregation results, for instance – but low values of p and q may provide an adequate approximate model. This suggests that researchers should not completely believe their identified models, and so should not be surprised if the results from aggregation theory do not work perfectly with estimated models.

2.2 Large-scale aggregation

Many of the most important variables in macroeconomics are simple, unweighted sums or aggregates of very large numbers of components. Thus, for example, consumption of non-durable goods in the US is the sum of this quantity over 80 million households and total corporate profits are the sum of profits for 2.5 million individual firms. If the components are all AR(1), with different parameters, *and are independent,* their sum will be ARMA(N, $N-1$) using the results in the previous section when there are N independent components. When N is the millions, the number of parameters will be unreasonably large. Clearly, a model with fewer parameters will provide an adequate approximation, perhaps because individual AR(1) models will have similar parameter values and because roots may (almost) cancel for the AR and MA polynomials in B of the aggregate series. A different approach is to assume that the AR(1) parameters are drawn from some distribution, and then some curious results can occur. Consider the case where the jth component is AR(1), generated by

$$X_{jt} = \alpha_j X_{j(t-1)} + \varepsilon_{jt}$$

where ε_{jt} is a zero-mean white noise, with variance $(\varepsilon_{jt}) = \sigma^2$ and the vector $(\varepsilon_{jt}, j = 1, \ldots, N)$ consists of independent components. The spectrum of the sum

$$S_t = \sum_{j=1}^{N} X_{jt}$$

will be the sum of the individual spectra. If the α_j are assumed to be independently drawn from a distribution $F(\alpha)$, the spectrum of S_t will be approximately

$$\bar{f}(\omega) = \frac{N}{2\pi} \sigma^2 \int \frac{1}{|1 - \alpha z|^2} \, dF(\alpha) \tag{2.1}$$

where $z = e^{i\omega}$. (The assumption that all ε_{jt} have the same variance is easily relaxed and is of little consequence.) A reasonable assumed distribution for the α's is the beta distribution of the form

$$dF(\alpha) = \frac{2}{B(p, q)} \alpha^{2p-1}(1 - \alpha^2)^{q-1} d\alpha$$

$$= 0 \text{ elsewhere}$$

$$0 \le \alpha \le 1, \quad p, q > 0$$

each α_j lies in the region zero to one and so, each X_{jt} is stationary, with probability one. It is shown in Granger (1980b) that in this case S_t will be $I(d)$, where $d = 1 - q/2$. Thus, $(1 - B)^d S_t$ has a stationary MA(∞) representation. Note that d will not be a positive integer as $q > 0$, and so S_t generally will be fractionally integrated. If $0 < q \le 1$, S_t will have an asymptotically infinite variance but if $q > 1$, S_t will have a finite variance. The point of this example is that series with unusual long-memory properties can arise from the aggregation of independent components. Some of the simplifying assumptions in this example can be relaxed without changes in the basic result. However, if $0 < \alpha_j < \bar{\alpha} < 1$ for all j, so that there is an upper bound to the α_j values, which is strictly less than one, then the fractional integration result is lost.

A more general result is found if the independence assumption is removed. The model considered is

$$X_{jt} = \alpha_j X_{j(t-1)} + \beta_j W_t + \varepsilon_{jt}$$

where again the α_j are from the distribution $F(\alpha)$, the β_j are from some distribution with non-zero mean $\bar\beta$, and the common factor W_t is $I(d_\omega)$. It is then found that

$$S_t \sim I(d)$$

where d is the largest of the two terms, $1 - q + d_\omega$ (from the W component), and $1 - q/2$ (from the ε component). In particular, if W_t is stationary, so that $d_\omega = 0$, then $d = 1 - q/2$ as before.

It is perhaps interesting that S_t will not be $I(1)$, as so frequently 'observed' with macro variables from aggregation of this form and with the beta distribution as here assumed. It is unclear if $I(d)$ aggregates can occur with other distributions, having the property $\text{Prob}(\alpha \geq 1) = 0$. However, the result that S_t is $I(1 - q/2)$ has to be interpreted with some care, as

$$S_t = \left(\sum_j \frac{\beta_j}{1 - \alpha_j B} \right) W_t + \sum_j \frac{1}{(1 - \alpha_j B)} \varepsilon_{jt}$$

and the first term can be approximated by

$$N\bar\beta[\int \frac{1}{1 - \alpha B} \, dF(\alpha)] W_t \tag{2.2}$$

It follows that, provided $\bar\beta \neq 0$, the first term will have variance of order N^2 whereas the second term has variance of order N, as seen from (2.1). Thus, for large N, the first term will dominate in size but the second term will provide the larger value of d, provided $d_\omega < q/2$. In this analysis, W_t is a 'common factor', that occurs in the generating process for (almost) all components and because of this it provides the dominant component of the aggregate.

The implications of the existence of common factors in aggregation was studied in Granger (1987). Simple regressions are investigated and the time-series properties are not given particular attention. The potential importance of common factors can be illustrated from the very simple case

$$Y_{jt} = x_{jt} + cz_t$$

where x_{jt} is independent of x_{kt}, $j \neq k$, and x_{jt} is also independent of

z_t. Thus the observed value of a variable for the jth unit, y_{jt}, consists of a common factor cz_t and an independent component x_{jt}. All series will be taken to be stationary and for this example, suppose also that $\mathrm{var}(y_j) = 1$, $\mathrm{var}(z) = 1$, so that $\mathrm{var}(x_j) = 1 - c^2$. Denote

$$S_{xt} = \sum_{j=1}^{N} x_{jt}$$

and similarly S_{yt} is the sum of the y's, then

$$S_{yt} = S_{xt} + Ncz_t$$

so that

$$\mathrm{var}(S_{yt}) = N(1 - c^2) + N^2 c^2$$

Two extreme cases can be considered: (i) z_t is observable but the x_{jt} are not. Thus, at the micro level y_{jt} is explained by just z_t and at the macro level S_{yt} is also explained by z_t, and (ii) the x_{jt} are observed, but z_t is not, so the micro regression explains y_{jt} by x_{jt} and at the macro level S_{yt} is explained by just S_{xt}. At the macro level it will always be assumed that only macro (aggregate) variables are available, not their components. The R^2 values for the case where $c^2 = 0.001$ and N is one million are as follows:

	Case 1	Case 2
	z observed x not observed	x observed z not observed
micro R^2	0.001	0.999
macro R^2	0.999	0.001

It is seen that a very high R^2 can be observed at the micro level but a very small R^2 at the macro level (in case 2), or vice versa. In this example, the common factor is of very minor relevance at the micro level and so could be found insignificant in an analysis of micro data, yet it dominates the macro relationship, having variance of order N^2 compared to a variance of order N from the S_x component. In a sense, the macro relationship is simpler than the micro relationships, if essentially irrelevant terms are ignored. This is still true when both x's and the common factor z_t are observed.

A variety of different models are considered in Granger (1987) but the main result can be illustrated by the following micro relationship

$$y_{jt} = x_{jt} + \beta_j z_t + \gamma_j w_t + \varepsilon_{jt}$$

where z_t, w_t are common factors and x_{jt}, ε_{jt} are independent components. Thus, at the macro level

$$S_{yt} = S_{xt} + \bar{\beta} z_t + \bar{\gamma} w_y$$

The first component has a variance of order N and the other two have variances of order N^2 provided $\bar{\beta}$, $\bar{\gamma}$ are not zero. Some simple cases are:

(i) No common factors, z_t, $w_t \equiv 0$, R^2 at the macro level can take any value but S_{xt}, S_{yt} and the residual $S_{\varepsilon t}$ are all perfectly normally distributed, owing to the effect of central limit theorem, unless ε_{jt} have extraordinary distributions.

(ii) Both z_t, w_t are present and observed R^2 will be very near to one.

(iii) Both common factors present, z_t observed, w_t not observed, macro R^2 takes any value, depending on the relative importance of the two common factors, residuals not necessarily Gaussian.

(iv) One or both common factors present, neither observed, R^2 will be very nearly zero.

As case (iii) seems to be the most likely to be observed (if all series are stationary rather than $I(1)$), one can conclude that common factors are present but are not all observed. It is interesting to ask what these common factors are, particularly the unobserved ones.

The results of this section provide an implied criticism of the 'typical decision-maker' theory used to suggest macroeconomic relationships from a micro theory. A behavioural equation for a typical consumer, say, is derived from basic micro theory, all consumers are considered to be identical and so the macro relationship is just N times the micro one. It is seen that a badly misspecified macro relationship can occur.

It is also suggested in Granger (1987) that non-linear micro relations may become effectively linear relationships between observed aggregates. Consider the simple case where

$$y_{jt} = \alpha_0 + \alpha_1 x_{jt} + \beta(x_{jt}^2 - \sigma_x^2)$$

so that all micro relationships have the same coefficient, $E[x_{jt}] = 0$ and so there are no common factors and $\sigma_x^2 = \text{var}(x_{jt})$ is the same for all x_{jt}. In the aggregate

$$S_{yt} = \alpha_0 + \alpha S_{xt} + \beta \, \text{sum}(x_{jt}^2 - \sigma_x^2)$$

but the last term is not observed, in general, and is poorly estimated by the observed quantities S_{xt}, $(S_{xt})^2$ – as a variance is little related to means or means squared. Thus, the final term becomes part of the residual in the equation, which is effectively linear.

The type of model considered here is rather different from that of the classical literature, as exemplified by Theil (1954). The question considered is the effect of aggregation on some 'true' micro relationship; with an endogenous variable explained by a set of 'exogenous' variables, possibly including lagged values of the dependent variable. The residuals may or may not be interdependent between micro unit relationships. However, the time-series properties of the variables are not specifically considered, although a stationarity assumption seems to be usual. The effects of common factors in the residuals are also not considered. The classical theory is generally concerned with the relationships between the macro parameters and micro parameter values rather than with the effects on the specification of the macro relationships given micro relationships. The two sets of results are thus complementary rather than competitive.

2.3 Temporal aggregation and systematic sampling

The discussion in this section follows Weiss (1984) which contains references to important work in this area. Suppose that the basic time interval for which a series is generated is unity, but that observations occur every k units ($k > 1$), then the series may be said to have been 'systematically sampled'. For example, some prices may be determined monthly but only recorded – or observed – quarterly, so that $k = 3$. Systematic sampling may be viewed as a type of temporal aggregation appropriate for 'stock' variables. For a 'flow' variable, a summation will occur over the k units before systematic sampling. An example is automobile production, which can be observed monthly or quarterly, the quarterly figure being the sum of the component monthly production figures.

Consider initially the ARMA(p, d, q) series Y_t generated by

$$a(B)(1 - B)^d Y_t = b(B)\varepsilon_t$$

and suppose that

$$a(B) = \prod_{j=1}^{P} (1 - \delta_j B)$$

where $|\delta j| < 1$, for all j.

If now the series is systematically sampled every k units (for some integer $k > 1$), then the new observed series obeys an ARMA(p, d, r) model where

$$r = [(p + d) + (q - p - d)/k]$$

and $[x]$ represents the integer part of x. Further, the AR polynomial for the sampled series is $a_k(B) = \prod_{j=1}^{P} (1 - \delta_j^k B^k)$, where B is the unit lag operator. For example if Y_t is generated by the AR(1) model

$$Y_t = \alpha Y_{t-1} + \varepsilon_t \qquad (2.3)$$

on the unit interval, where $\mathrm{cov}(\varepsilon_t, \varepsilon_{t-j}) = 0$, $j \neq 0$, the sampled process on k intervals, Y_t^k will appear to be generated by

$$Y_T^k = \alpha^k Y_{T-1}^k + \varepsilon_T^k$$

where $T = kt$ and

$$\mathrm{cov}(\varepsilon_t^k, \varepsilon_{T-j}^k) = 0, \quad j \neq 0$$

If $|\alpha| < 1$, then as k increases α^k will become small and Y^k will become nearly a white noise. It is generally true that, if a stationary series is systematically sampled, its memory will decline. However, if Y_t is a random walk, so that $\alpha = 1$ in (2.3), the sampled process Y_T^k will also be a random walk. More generally, the ARMA(p, d, q) process becomes approximately an MA($d, d - 1$) model for k large.

Somewhat similar results occur with temporal aggregation. An ARMA(p, d, q) process becomes ARMA(p, d, r) where

$$r = [(p + d + 1) + (q - p - d - 1)/k]$$

For example, an AR(1) process, becomes ARMA(1,1) and a

random walk becomes an IMA(1,1) process. An early result in this area comes from Working (1960), who showed that for $k \geq 4$, the MA component was

$$\varepsilon_T + 0.25\, \varepsilon_{T-1}$$

to a close approximation.

For both cases it is seen that, if the process is generated over small time intervals compared to the observation period, so that k is large, the AR component of the generating mechanism becomes unimportant, the unit root components remain unchanged and the moving average component simplifies but can remain relevant.

Weiss (1984) also considers a temporal aggregation of models with seasonal components and ARMAX models. (For detailed results, see that paper.) The ARMAX model considered is

$$a(B)(1 - B)^d Y_t = c(B)(1 - B)^f X_t + b(B)\varepsilon_t$$

$$D(B)(1 - B)^f X_t = F(B)e_t$$

with $C(0) = 0$, so that X_t causes Y_t but not vice versa and there is no instantaneous relationship between X_t and Y_t. After systematic sampling and temporal aggregation, equations for the maximum lag of the independent variable are provided by Weiss (1984) and are generally rather complicated. As k becomes large the relationship between Y_T^k and X_T^k takes the form

$$(1 - B^k)^d Y_T = (1 - B^k)^f X_T + a_T \qquad (2.4)$$

where a_T is MA($d - 1$) for systematic sampling (stock variables) and is MA(d) for temporal aggregation (flow variables). Again, simplification occurs when k is large and it may be particularly noted that temporal aggregation has produced a contemporaneous relationship.

2.4 Forecasting

A univariate stationary series Y_t has optimum (least-squares) one-step forecast $f_{t-1,1}$ based on the information set I_{t-1} given by

$$f_{t-1,1} = \mathrm{E}[Y_t | I_{t-1}]$$

In this survey, just linear, one-step forecasts are considered. The forecast error is

$$e_{t-1,1} = Y_t - f_{(t-1)1}$$

and a natural measure of (one-step) forecastability is

$$R^2 = 1 - \frac{\text{var}(e)}{\text{var}(Y)}$$

If Y_t is integrated, then it is assumed that appropriate differencing is applied to produce a stationary series before forecasting is attempted. A convenient notation is to use $f^{(j)}$ for the optimum one-step forecast of Y_{jt}, based on the information set $I^{(j)}$ available at time $t - 1$. If

$$S_{yt} = \sum_{j=1}^{N} Y_{jt}$$

then the optimum forecast of S_t is

$$f^{(s)} = \sum_{j=1}^{N} f^{(j)}$$

assuming that the union of all the individual information sets $I^{(u)} = \bigcup_j I^{(j)}$ is available. In this rather extreme case, in a sense nothing is lost by the aggregation, although R^2 for S may take almost any value depending on the extent to which the $e^{(j)}$ are intercorrelated. However, the more typical case is that the full information set is not available after aggregation and so some forecasting ability will be lost. For example, it is clear from the result of the previous section that temporal aggregation generally reduces forecastability.

For ordinary small-scale aggregation, Kohn (1982) has obtained necessary and sufficient conditions for no loss of forecasting ability. Suppose that the component series Y_{jt} are written as a vector Y_t which is generated by the k-order vector autoregression.

$$Y_t = \sum_{j=1}^{P} A_j Y_{t-j} + \varepsilon_t$$

where ε_t is a vector white noise, and let S_{yt} be the sum of these components, so that

$$S_{yt} = i' X_t$$

where i is a vector of ones. S_{yt} can be forecast either from $I^{(1)}_{t-1}$: $Y_{t-j}, j \geq 1$, or from $I^{(2)}_{t-1}$: $S_{y(t-j)}, j \geq 1$. Thus, in the first information set all information is available, in the second only lagged sums are available. Kohn proves that the two forecasts are identical only if there exists a sequence of constants α_j such that

$$i' A_j = \alpha_j i' \tag{2.5}$$

and in this case, S_{yt} obeys the AR(p) model

$$S_{yt} = \sum_{j=1}^{P} \alpha_j S_{y(t-j)} + e_t$$

(2.5) is a very stringent set of conditions which is unlikely to hold exactly, so that usually S_{yt} will be forecast less well if the smaller information set is available rather than the larger one.

However, these results are less clearly relevant when large-scale aggregation occurs with common factors. The results of section 2.2 show that virtually all of the forecasting ability of the full information set is available if just the common factors are available.

The results given in this section are theoretical. In practice, where models have to be identified and estimated, relative forecasting abilities of different information sets can be less clean cut, as shown by the simulation results of Lütkepohl (1985).

2.5 Causation

A definition of 'causation' that has found wide-spread application says that x_t causes y_{t+1} if y_{t+1} is better forecast from the information set $I^{(1)}_t$: $y_{t-j}, w_{t-j}, x_{t-j}, j \geq 0$ than from the information set $I^{(2)}_t$: $y_{t-j}, w_{t-j}, j \geq 0$. Thus, x_{t-j} contains information that is helpful in forecasting y_{t+1} and which is not in $I^{(2)}_t$. Strictly, x_t is a prima facie cause of y_{t+1} in mean with respect to the information set $I^{(2)}_t$. The definition is discussed in Granger and Hatanaka (1964), Granger (1980a), and elsewhere. As the definition is based on forecastability, aggregation can be disturbing as information sets are deformed.

With ordinary small-scale aggregation the following rules generally hold:

(i) If at the disaggregate level x_{jt} does not cause $y_{j(t+1)}$ *and y_{jt}*

does not cause $x_{j(t+1)}$ for most j then S_{xt} will not cause $S_{y(t+1)}$.

(ii)   If x_{it} causes $y_{i(t+1)}$ but y_{jt} does not cause $x_{j(t+1)}$ for most j, then S_{xt} will generally cause $S_{y(t+1)}$ and S_{yt} may appear to cause $S_{x(t+1)}$. Thus correct causality is still found but a spurious feedback may occur because of aggregation. However, aggregation may weaken the correct causality, as found for forecastability in section 4.

(iii) If there is feedback at the disaggregate level it will theoretically occur at the aggregate level, in general.

To illustrate the statements in (ii) consider the simple situation where there are two micro units and for each a pair of variables, X, Y are measured, these being related by

$$Y_{it} = a_i \varepsilon^X_{i(t-1)} + \varepsilon^Y_{it}, \quad i = 1, 2$$

$$X_{it} = \varepsilon^X_{it} + b_i \varepsilon^X_{i(t-1)}, \quad i = 1, 2$$

where ε^X, ε^Y are independent (2×1) vector white-noise processes. If $S_y = y_1 + y_2$, and using a similar notation for other variables, then

$$S_{yt} = a' \varepsilon^X_{t-1} + S_{\varepsilon Yt}$$

$$S_{xt} = S_{\varepsilon xt} + b' \varepsilon^x_{t-1}$$

where $a' = (a_1, a_2)$, $\qquad \varepsilon^x = \begin{pmatrix} \varepsilon^x_1 \\ \varepsilon^x_2 \end{pmatrix}$, $\qquad b' = (b_1, b_2)$

Causality will be found at the macro level if

$$E[S_{y(t+1)} S_{xt}] \neq 0$$

which will be true if

$$a_1(\sigma_1^2 + p\sigma_1\sigma_2) + a_2(\sigma_2^2 + p\sigma_1\sigma_2) \neq 0 \qquad (2.6)$$

where

$$\sigma_1^2 = \text{var}(\varepsilon^x_1), \qquad \sigma_2^2 = \text{var}(\varepsilon^x_2)$$

$$\text{cov}(\varepsilon^x_1, \varepsilon^x_2) = p\sigma_1\sigma_2$$

31

Clearly (2.6) will usually occur (but need not), so that the causation that occurs at the micro level will be found at the macro level. However, it will also be generally true that $E[S_{x(t+1)}, S_{yt}] \neq 0$ as it is a perfect linear combination of $S_{yt} - S_{\varepsilon xt} = a'^x_{t-1}$ and $S_{\varepsilon x(t-1)}$ which is a component of $S_{x(t-1)}$. Thus although there is no causation from Y_{jt} to $X_{j(t+1)}$ at the micro level, it does occur at the macro level.

It is hardly surprising that temporal aggregation can be disruptive of causal relations as past and future values get mixed up, part of one aggregate will occur both before and after part of another aggregate. If at the unit interval there is one-way causation between a pair of series, after temporal aggregation a feedback or two-way causation may be found. As k, the number of time units being aggregated over becomes large, stationary series appear to be just contemporaneously related and so actual causality can be lost.

2.6 Cointegration

A pair of $I(1)$ series X_t, Y_t are said to be cointegrated if there exists a linear combination

$$z_t = X_t - A Y_t$$

which is stationary (or $I(0)$). This will occur if X_t, Y_t both possess a common $I(1)$ factor, with all other components being $I(0)$, so that

$$X_t = A W_t + \bar{X}_t$$

$$Y_t = W_t + \bar{Y}_t$$

where $W_t \sim I(1)$, $\bar{X}$, $\bar{Y}$ both $I(0)$. If the series are cointegrated there will always exist an error-correction mechanism of the form

$$\Delta X_t = -\rho_1 z_{t-1} + \text{lagged } \Delta X_t, \Delta Y_t + \text{residual}$$

$$\Delta Y_t = -\rho_2 z_{t-1} + \text{lagged } \Delta X_t, \Delta Y_t + \text{residual}$$

where at least one of ρ_1, ρ_2 is non zero.

As integrated series remain integrated under temporal aggregation, it is clear that cointegration remains true for series which are so aggregated. However, the form of the error-correction models may be altered.

The effects of small-scale cross-sectional aggregation has been studied by Gonzalo (1988). For convenience, denote a pair of series X_{jt}, Y_{jt} for 'state' j, which are aggregated into

$$S_{xt} = \sum_j X_{jt}$$

and similarly S_{yt}.

To show that a variety of results can occur it should be noted that: (i) there can be cointegration at the aggregate level but not at the disaggregated states and (ii) there can be cointegration at the states but not at the aggregate level. To illustrate (i), suppose there are just two states ($j = 1, 2$), that S_{xt}, S_{yt} are cointegrated and that $X_{1t} = S_{xt}$, $X_{2t} = 0$ all t, $Y_{1t} = 0$ all t and $Y_{2t} = S_{yt}$. More generally, X_{2t} and Y_{1t} can both be $I(0)$. To illustrate (ii), suppose that all X_{1t}, Y_{it}, $i = 1, 2$, are $I(1)$, $z_{1t} = X_{1t} - A_1 Y_{1t}$, $Z_{2t} = X_{2t} - A_2 Y_{2t}$ are both $I(0)$ with $A_1 \neq A_2$, then

$$S_{xt} - \alpha S_{yt} = z_{1t} + z_{2t} + (A_1 - \alpha) Y_{1t} + (A_2 - \alpha) Y_{2t}$$

so that S_{xt}, S_{yt} are cointegrated only if both $A_1 = \alpha$ and $A_2 = \alpha$ and this occurs only if $A_1 = A_2$, which is excluded by assumption. This result would not hold if Y_{1t}, Y_{2t} are cointegrated.

Gonzalo (1988) has sufficient reasons for cointegration at one level of cointegration to imply cointegration at another (higher or lower) level. For example, suppose that all X_{it}, Y_{it} and $I(1)$ with Wold representations

$$(1 - B)X_{it} = X_{xi}(B)\varepsilon_{it}$$

$$(1 - B)Y_{it} = C_{yi}(B)\eta_{it}$$

stacking all the residuals produces a $2N \times 1$ vector

$$r'_t = (\varepsilon_{1t}, \eta_{1t}, \varepsilon_{2t}, \eta_{2t}, \ldots, \varepsilon_{Nt}, \eta_{Nt})$$

with covariance matrix $E[r_t r'_t] = \Sigma$.

If S_{xt}, S_{yt} are cointegrated it is shown that a sufficient condition for all X_{1t}, Y_{1t} to be cointegrated is that Σ be of full rank. This result assumes no cointegration of components across states. If, for example, Y_{it}, Y_{jt} are cointegrated for some i, j there are more possibilities.

A simple case has been considered by Lippi (1987b) for which Y_{it}, Y_{jt} are cointegrated for all i, j, and X_{it}, Y_{it} are cointegrated for all i; it follows that X_{it}, X_{jt} are cointegrated for all i, j. Thus, there is a single common $I(1)$ factor causing all X_{it}, Y_{it} components to be $I(1)$. In this case S_{xt}, S_{yt} will also be $I(1)$ because of this common factor and so will be cointegrated.

Conclusion

Cross-sectional aggregation generally produces more complicated time-series models but, in certain circumstances, important simplifications occur. The sum of a few independent AR(1) models will produce a mixed ARMA model, for example. However, the sum of many AR(1) models with different parameters can produce a fractional integrated model, which is a parsimonious model but one that in practice is difficult to use. The effects of aggregation over large numbers of components is substantially different from that over just a few components.

Quite different results also occur when the input innovations contain common factors across individuals from when those inputs do not have common factors. In the first case, considerable simplications can occur, when irrelevant components are dropped. It is possible for the number of relevant explanatory variables to be reduced, for non-linearity to become less important and similarly for time-varying parameters and heteroscedasticity.

Temporal aggregation will also generally produce simpler models and relationships, although integration and cointegration are not affected.

The extent to which an aggregated variable is forecastable from other aggregate variables depends on the time-series structures of the component variables and on the presence or not of common factors.

Aggregation will often confuse causal relationships, either weakening the strength of the causation or introducing a weak form of bi-causal (feedback) relation from what was originally a one-way causality.

The preservation or not of cointegration under cross-sectional aggregation depends on where cointegration occurs at the disaggregate level. No general rules seem to apply. It is possible to have cointegration at the aggregate level but at no disaggregate level, for example.

An area where further work is required is on the aggregation of non-linear time-series models, with and without common factors.

Chapter three

On the dynamic specification of aggregated models

Marco Lippi and Mario Forni*

Introduction

The problem dealt with in this paper can be outlined simply. Assume we wish to compare the performances of a linear disaggregated versus a linear aggregated model in predicting the aggregated variable $Y_t = \Sigma y_{it}$. Assume further that at the disaggregated level the following model has been specified, estimated, and (successfully) tested

$$y_{it} = a_i x_{it} + u_{it} \qquad (3.1)$$

where u_{it} is a white noise for any i. Now suppose that, on the basis of a naïve idea about the micro-macro relationship, the macro model is specified as

$$Y_t = aX_t + E_t \qquad (3.2)$$

where Y_t is defined as above, while $X_t = \Sigma x_{it}$. Throughout this chapter, boldface characters will denote vectors, matrices, and also all aggregate scalars.

The question is whether using specification (3.2) we may get the predictor of Y_t giving the minimum-variance prediction error within the class of all predictors which are linear in X_t and past values of X_t and Y_t. The answer is affirmative in the following cases: (c_1) the a_i's are equal across individual equations, (c_2) compositional stability of the x_{it}'s (i.e. x_{it}/x_{jt} is independent of t for any i and j), (c_3) the x_{it}'s are white noises. But if none of these conditions hold, then *in general* – i.e. with the exception of particular values for the micro parameters – the solution lies outside specification (3.2), even if we allow for an autocorrelated E_t;

* We wish to thank M.H. Pesaran and an anonymous referee for very useful comments and criticism. Financial support from CNR and Ministero della Pubblica Istruzione is gratefully acknowledged.

35

precisely, the variance of the prediction error may be reduced if the macro model, in spite of naïvely reproducing the micro equations, contains lagged values of both X_t and Y_t.

Such results may be extended to micro models that are less simple than (3.1), i.e. to micro equations containing lagged values of both dependent and explanatory micro variables. Under suitable assumptions which are set up below, the macro model is

$$\alpha(L)Y_t = \beta(L)X_t + \gamma(L)E_t \qquad (3.3)$$

where $\alpha(L)$, $\beta(L)$, $\gamma(L)$ are polynomials in the lag operator L, $\alpha(0) = \gamma(0) = 1$, while E_t is a white noise. The dynamic shape of (3.3) may be classified according to many typologies, corresponding to distinct economic and/or econometric viewpoints. The following is a classification in order of increasing complication in the lag profile; assuming that there are no polynomial factors common to $\alpha(L)$, $\beta(L)$, $\gamma(L)$:

(s_1) static: $\alpha(L) = \gamma(L) = 1$; $\beta(L)$ has degree zero;
(s_2) finite distributed lag: $\alpha(L) = \gamma(L) = 1$;
(s_3) finite distributed lag with ARMA disturbance: $\alpha(L)$ is a factor of $\beta(L)$;
(s_4) rational distributed lag with white-noise disturbance: $\alpha(L) = \gamma(L)$;
(s_5) unrestricted ARMAX: none of the above restrictions hold.

Now – this is our result – if cases (c_1), (c_2) (suitably restated) and (c_3) are excluded, then in general the macro model dynamic shape will be (s_5), i.e. that of an unrestricted ARMAX, *independently of the class to which the micro model belongs*. Such a 'dynamization', as we shall see in detail, is due to the fact that the macro coefficients result from a mixture of both the coefficients of the micro equations and the coefficients of the processes generating the x_{it}'s.

Cases (c_1) and (c_2) above are well-known conditions for consistent aggregation. Hence, we might rephrase our results in the following way: when consistent aggregation is not possible, then, provided the x_{it}'s are not white noises, not only will an aggregation error arise but also the dynamic shape will be altered, passing from micro to macro equations. This is a fairly faithful statement of the central point of the paper; unfortunately, an intricate variety of cases will prevent such a clear cut terminology.

It is worth highlighting two issues which are closely related to our results. First, as regards the economic interpretation of macro equations, the dynamic complications due to aggregation cast serious doubts on intertemporal optimization-based direct derivation of macro equations from microeconomic models (this point will not be dealt with in detail in this chapter; see, however, subsections 3.3.2 and 3.3.3 below).

Second, as regards the relationship with empirical work, it must be pointed out that here the processes and equations generating the disaggregated data are assumed to be known. This entails that no specification error affects the micro equations, nor are we taking into account the consequences of using estimated (instead of true) coefficients in small samples.[1] Therefore, it is hardly surprising that in the present paper aggregation will result as 'necessarily bad'. However, when actual data and estimated models are concerned, so that the aggregated model is not necessarily worse (because of the aforementioned possibilities), then our results on the dynamic shape of the aggregated model can be translated into the following recommendation: in order to give a fair chance to the aggregated model, the specification of the latter should allow for a more complicated dynamic as compared to the dynamic specification of the micro model. The mere reproduction of the micro model dynamic shape (even allowing for an auto-correlated error term) does not fully exploit, in general, aggregated information.

Lastly, though we shall deal with only one explanatory variable (at all possible lags), our methods and results may be extended fairly easily to micro equations containing more than one explanatory variable, common macro variables, dummies, time trends. This, however, is left to further work.

In section 3.1 we give the definition of the aggregated model, given the micro model, and analyse the error term of the former: this is shown to be decomposable into the sum of the disaggregated errors plus an aggregation error. Sufficient conditions for the latter being non zero are established. In sub-section 3.1.5 a brief account is given of different approaches to aggregation. The main results are presented in section 3.2, where the dynamic shape of the aggregated equation is compared to the micro equations under simple assumptions on the latter. It is shown that not only does the mere reproduction of the micro equations lead to misspecification, but the introduction of an autoregressive (or even ARMA) disturbance term in the macro model, while reproducing the micro model for all other aspects, also gives an unsatisfactory specification. Results obtained after dropping the simplifying assumptions are also reported. In section 3.3, among miscellaneous observations, the degree of the aggregated model and the issue of economic interpretation of aggregated macro models are briefly analysed. The mathematical appendix contains statements and references on well-known results on vector stochastic processes.

3.1 Aggregated model and aggregation error

3.1.1 Assumptions on the disaggregated model

Let us begin by formally stating our assumptions on the micro model.

Assumption I

There are n micro equations, $n > 1$:

$$\alpha_i(L)y_{it} = \beta_i(L)x_{it} + \gamma_i(L)u_{it} \tag{3.4}$$

where u_{it} is a white-noise orthogonal to $x_{j(t-k)}$, $y_{j(t-h)}$, $h > 0$, for any j and k; $\alpha_i(L)$, $\beta_i(L)$, $\gamma_i(L)$ are polynomials in L; $\alpha_i(0) = \gamma_i(0) = 1$. Moreover, we shall assume that there is no polynomial factor common to $\alpha_i(L)$, $\beta_i(L)$, $\gamma_i(L)$, and that all roots of $\alpha_i(L)$ and $\gamma_i(L)$ are of modulus greater than one (for the sake of simplicity we do not consider constant terms in equations (3.4)).

Before we go on with definitions and assumptions, a short comment on the orthogonality condition between u_{it} and $x_{j(t-k)}$ is called for. As k is not restricted to being positive, this condition implies absence of Granger-causality running from the y_{it}'s to the x_{jt}'s. In fact, as the y_{jt}'s are linear combinations of the $x_{i(t-k)}$'s and the $u_{i(t-k)}$'s $k \downarrow 0$, and since these latter give no help in predicting the x_{jt}'s, then past values of the y_{jt}'s give no additional help in predicting the x_{jt}'s once the information contained in the past values of the x_{jt}'s has been fully exploited. The above assumption on micro feedback will allow a simplified treatment. Many of the results proved below may however be shown to be independent of this assumption.

The aggregated variables are defined as:

$$X_t = \sum_{i=1,n} x_{it}, \qquad Y_t = \sum_{i=1,n} y_{it}$$

The aggregated model is defined as the linear equation linking Y_t to X_{t-k}, Y_{t-h}, $k \geq 0$, $h > 0$, that provides the best predictor, i.e. the minimum-variance prediction error, among all predictors which are linear in X_t and past values of X_t and Y_t.[2]

We shall restrict ourselves to the following case.

Assumption II

The vector $x_t = (x_{1t}, x_{2t}, \ldots, x_{nt})$ is stationary (i.e. the x_{it}'s are co-stationary) and has rational spectral density.

This is a convenient simplification to obtain existence and uniqueness for the aggregated model. However, the results obtained and methods employed below are easily extendible to cases of non-stationarity such as those of integrated variables or variables containing time trends.[3]

Assumption II implies that x_t possesses an ARMA representation or, equivalently, a rational Wold representation, that is

$$x_t = B(L)\chi_t$$

in which $B(L)$ is a matrix of rational functions having no poles of modulus smaller than or equal to one, $\det(B(L))$ has no roots of modulus smaller than one, $B(0) = I$; while χ_t is an n-dimensional white-noise vector, so that $\chi_t \perp x_{t-h}, h > 0$.[4]

It must be noted that the equations of the Wold representation of x_t are not to be interpreted as structural equations. The Wold representation is a merely mathematical entity bearing a one-to-one correspondence with the covariance matrices $\Sigma_x(k)$, whose coefficients are $E(x_{it} x_{j(t-k)})$, for $k \geq 0$. In general, the coefficients of the Wold representation will be complicated functions of the structural parameters.

3.1.2 Derivation of the aggregated equation

Let us now proceed to the derivation of the aggregated model. As a first step we shall establish the Wold representation for the aggregated vector whose components are Y_t and X_t. Under assumptions I and II, it is easily seen that:

(i) the vector

$$(x_{1t}, x_{2t}, \ldots, x_{nt}, y_{1t}, y_{2t}, \ldots, y_{nt})$$

is stationary with rational spectral density;

(ii) the two-dimensional vector $Z_t = (Y_t, X_t)$ is stationary and has rational spectral density. Let its Wold representation be

$$\begin{pmatrix} Y_t \\ X_t \end{pmatrix} = D(L)v_t = \begin{pmatrix} d_{11}(L) & d_{12}(L) \\ d_{21}(L) & d_{22}(L) \end{pmatrix} \begin{pmatrix} v_{1t} \\ v_{2t} \end{pmatrix} \tag{3.5}$$

Disaggregation in econometric modelling

where $D(L)$ and v_t fulfil the conditions listed above for $B(L)$ and χ_t respectively; in particular: $D(0) = I$.

Our last assumption will be:

Assumption III

The determinant of $D(L)$ has no unit modulus roots, i.e. $D(L)$ is invertible (for a discussion of this assumption, see appendix 3A, section 3).

As a second step, rewrite equations (3.5) as

$$\begin{pmatrix} d_{22}(L) & -d_{12}(L) \\ -d_{21}(L) & d_{11}(L) \end{pmatrix} \begin{pmatrix} Y_t \\ X_t \end{pmatrix} = \det(D(L)) \begin{pmatrix} v_{1t} \\ v_{2t} \end{pmatrix} \quad (3.5')$$

that is

$$\begin{aligned} d_{22}(L)Y_t - d_{12}(L)X_t &= \det D(L)v_{1t} \\ -d_{21}(L)Y_t - d_{11}(L)X_t &= \det D(L)v_{2t} \end{aligned} \quad (3.5'')$$

(this is obtained by multiplying both sides of (3.5) by the adjoint of $D(L)$).

Now note that the first of equations (3.5″) can be used as a predictor of Y_t using the past of Y_t and the past of X_t (remember $D(0) = I$, so that $d_{22}(0) = 1$, while $d_{12}(0) = 0$). To bring also the simultaneous value of X_t into the first equation, define $K = \text{cov}(v_{1t}, v_{2t})/\text{var}(v_{2t})$, then multiply the second of equations (3.5″) by K and subtract from the first. We get

$$[d_{22}(L) + Kd_{21}(L)]Y_t = [Kd_{11}(L) + d_{12}(L)]X_t + \det(D(L))E_t \quad (3.6)$$

where $E_t = v_{1t} - Kv_{2t}$. Then let us eliminate denominators from (3.6) (remember that the coefficients of $D(L)$ are rational functions) by multiplying by the least common multiple; finally, eliminate common polynomial factors. We get

$$\alpha(L)Y_t = \beta(L)X_t + \gamma(L)E_t \quad (3.7)$$

where $\alpha(L)$, $\beta(L)$, $\gamma(L)$ are polynomials, $\alpha(0) = \gamma(0) = 1$. The process E_t is a white noise (since it is a linear combination of v_{1t}, v_{2t}, the vector v_t being white noise) and is orthogonal to X_{t-k}, Y_{t-h}, $k \geq 0$, $h > 0$, since the v_{it}'s are orthogonal to such processes. Moreover, $E_t \perp X_t$, owing to the definition of K. Finally the

40

assumptions above on the roots of $\det(D(L))$ imply that the polynomial $\gamma(L)$ has all its roots outside the unit circle and is therefore invertible.

We claim that equation (3.7) is the aggregated model. To prove this, consider the Hilbert space H generated by the stochastic variables y_{it} and x_{it} when t runs from $-\infty$ to $+\infty$, $\text{cov}(\cdot)$ being the inner product. Let us call H' the sub-space spanned by X_{t-k}, Y_{t-h}, $k \geq 0$, $h > 0$. Now, as $\gamma(L)$ is invertible, we may write

$$Y_t = P_t + E_t \tag{3.8}$$

where

$$P_t = \left(1 - \frac{\alpha(L)}{\gamma(L)} \right) Y_t + \frac{\beta(L)}{\gamma(L)} X_t$$

We have $E_t \perp H'$, and since P_t lies in H', (3.8) is the decomposition of Y_t into its orthogonal projection on H' and the residual. It is well known that E_t has minimum length (minimum variance) within the set of all the vectors $Y_t - W_t$, for $W_t \in H'$. Since vectors W_t are all possible linear combinations of X_t and past values of X_t and Y_t, then P_t is the best predictor that we were seeking.

Two observations are necessary before we go on with the analysis of equation (3.7). First, in order to avoid a possible misunderstanding, it must be pointed out that, owing to the assumptions $u_{it} \perp x_{j(t-k)}$, $u_{it} \perp y_{j(t-h)}$, any $i, j, k, h > 0$, micro model (3.4) provides the best predictor of Y_t within the class of all predictors which are linear in $x_{i(t-k)}$, $y_{i(t-h)}$, $k \geq 0$, $h > 0$. Therefore, the micro and the macro model obey the same definition. Their differences are: (i) the different sets of variables used in prediction, (ii) starting, as we are doing, with the micro model given in explicit form (equation (3.4)), the macro model can be defined implicitly by the minimum-variance condition, but its explicit form is usually difficult to attain, and is in general – this is the main point we shall develop below – quite different from the micro model form.

Second, the parameters in (3.7) depend on the parameters in representation (3.5). The latter, in turn, depend on the micro parameters in (3.4) and on the coefficients of $B(L)$. In general, the relationship between the coefficients of (3.5) and the micro parameters is complicated and difficult to model. In section 3.2 we shall establish explicitly such relationship in a simplified case.

Disaggregation in econometric modelling

3.1.3 Decomposition of the aggregated model error

Let us define: $U_t = \sum\limits_{i=1,n} u_{it}$. Then consider $A_t = E_t - U_t$ and let us

demonstrate that A_t is orthogonal to U_t. First, we rewrite Y_t as

$$Y_t = \sum_{i=1,n} y_{it} = \tilde{Y}_t + U_t$$

where

$$\tilde{Y}_t = \sum_{i=1,n} \left(1 - \frac{\alpha_i(L)}{\gamma_i(L)} \right) y_{it} + \sum_{i=1,n} \frac{\beta_i(L)}{\gamma_i(L)} x_{it}$$

Note that $\tilde{Y}_t$ is the best linear predictor of Y_t in the space H'' spanned by micro variables $y_{i(t-k)}$, $x_{i(t-h)}$, $k > 0$, $h \geq 0$, $i = 1, 2, \ldots, n$. In fact, $\tilde{Y}_t$ belongs to H'', while U_t is orthogonal to H''.

Next, consider the orthogonal projection of $\tilde{Y}_t$ on H': $\tilde{Y}_t = \tilde{P}_t + A_t$. We have

$$Y_t = \tilde{P}_t + A_t + U_t$$

Since $\tilde{P}_t \in H'$, while $A_t + U_t$ is orthogonal to H', and since decomposition (3.8) is unique, then $\tilde{P}_t = P_t$ and $E_t = A_t + U_t$. Moreover, since A_t belongs to the space spanned by $y_{i(t-h)}$, $x_{i(t-k)}$, $k \geq 0$, $h > 0$, and since u_{it} is orthogonal to such a sub space, then U_t is orthogonal to A_t.

Thus the aggregated model error has been decomposed into U_t, i.e. the sum of the micro disturbance terms, and an orthogonal component, i.e. A_t. Since U_t is the prediction error of a model employing the disaggregated variables, A_t is precisely that part of E_t which arises from aggregation and will therefore be called *aggregation error*. If $A_t = 0$, the macro variables retain all information on Y_t contained in the micro variables, so that prediction of Y_t based on the micro relations (3.4) and prediction of Y_t based on macro relation (3.7) are the same. As we shall see in 3.1.5, the condition $A_t = 0$ is very strictly related to 'consistent aggregation'.

The results obtained so far on the aggregated model may be grouped within the following:

Theorem 1

Consider a micromodel fulfilling Assumptions I, II, and III. There exist polynomials $\alpha(L)$, $\beta(L)$, $\gamma(L)$, with $\alpha(0) = \gamma(0) = 1$ and $\gamma(L)$ invertible, and a white noise E_t orthogonal to X_{t-k}, Y_{t-h}, $k \geq 0$, $h > 0$, such that the model

$$\alpha(L)Y_t = \beta(L)X_t + \gamma(L)E_t$$

provides the best predictor (i.e. the one with the minimum variance) of Y_t among all predictors which are linear in X_t and past values of X_t and Y_t. Moreover $E_t = U_t + A_t$, where $U_t = \sum_{i=1,n} u_{it}$ and $A_t \perp U_t$.[5]

3.1.4 Conditions for a non-zero aggregation error

We shall now address the question of when the aggregation error A_t vanishes. Two well-known sufficient conditions were mentioned in the Introduction to this chapter – see cases (c_1) and (c_2), i.e. identical micro parameters across micro equations and compositional stability of the x_{it}'s – and will now be restated and discussed in detail. Unfortunately, such conditions are not necessary, i.e. A_t may be zero in spite of the fact that neither of them holds. We were not able to find any alternative elegant characterization of micro models yielding $A_t = 0$. However, some interesting results are grouped in theorem 2. On the other hand, we shall suggest in sub-sections 3.2.4 and 3.2.5 that cases in which $A_t = 0$ but neither (c_1) nor (c_2) hold are negligible from an economic point of view. Readers exclusively interested in the economic and econometric aspects of aggregation may therefore limit themselves to reading the presentation and statement of theorem 2 and then skip to section 3.2.

We shall proceed as follows: first, we aggregate over sub-groups of identical micro equations and define the rank of the vector of the explanatory variables; this will prove useful in order to establish conditions for $A_t \neq 0$. Second, we restate conditions (c_1) and (c_2). Third, an example is given in which neither (c_1) nor (c_2) holds but $A_t = 0$. Finally, theorem 2 is proved.

Without loss of generality, we may assume that there exists an $\hat{n}$, $1 \leq \hat{n} \leq n$, such that if i and j are smaller or equal to $\tilde{n}$ then at least one of the following inequalities holds: $\alpha_i(L) \neq \alpha_j(L)$, $\beta_i(L) \neq \beta_j(L)$, $\gamma_i(L) \neq \gamma_j(L)$; while if $j > \hat{n}$ then there exists an $i \leq \hat{n}$ such that corresponding micro parameters of micro equations j and i are equal.

Thus individual equations may be grouped into $\hat{n}$ sub-sets. Within each of the latter aggregation is immediate (corresponding

Disaggregation in econometric modelling

individual micro parameters being identical), so that the disaggregated system (3.4) becomes

$$\alpha_i(L)\hat{y}_{it} = \beta_i(L)\hat{x}_{it} + \gamma_i(L)\hat{u}_{it} \tag{3.4'}$$

where $i = 1, 2, \ldots, \hat{n}$, and where $\hat{y}_{it}$, $\hat{x}_{it}$, $\hat{u}_{it}$ are obtained by aggregating the corresponding micro variables within the ith group, i.e. aggregating over all j such that equation j is equal to equation i. Obviously

$$X_t = \sum_{i=1,\hat{n}} \hat{x}_{it}, \qquad Y_t = \sum_{i=1,\hat{n}} \hat{y}_{it}, \qquad U_t = \sum_{i=1,\hat{n}} \hat{u}_{it}$$

while for $i \neq j$ the corresponding micro equations in (3.4') are different at least for a micro parameter.

The vector $\hat{x}_t = (\hat{x}_{1t}, \hat{x}_{2t}, \ldots, \hat{x}_{\hat{n}t})$ is stationary and has rational spectral density. As a consequence it will admit a Wold representation

$$\hat{x}_t = \hat{B}(L)\hat{\chi}_t$$

with a rational $\hat{B}(L)$, where $\hat{\chi}_t$ is an $\hat{n}$-dimensional white noise.

Now let $\mu(\hat{\chi}_t)$ be the rank of the variance–covariance matrix of $\hat{\chi}_t$. Assuming $\hat{\chi}_t \neq 0$ we have $1 \leq \mu(\hat{\chi}_t) \leq \hat{n}$. As regards the mathematical meaning of $\mu(\hat{\chi}_t)$, it is easily seen (see also appendix 3A, section 1) that, though having dimension $\hat{n}$, $\hat{\chi}_t$ (and consequently $\hat{x}_t$) is driven by $\mu(\hat{\chi}_t)$ white noises, while the others are exact linear combinations of the former. For instance, if $\hat{x}_{it}/\hat{x}_{jt}$ is independent of t for any i and j, then $\mu(\hat{\chi}_t) = 1$, in which case all the $\hat{x}_{it}$'s are driven by only one white noise. As regards the economic meaning of $\mu(\hat{\chi}_t)$, see sub-section 3.2.5.

Let us now restate the most obvious conditions under which no aggregation error arises. The first is:

(A) Micro-homogeneity, i.e. corresponding micro parameters are equal across all equations (3.4); this obviously implies $\hat{n} = 1$.

Let us then restate condition (c_2). Rewrite (3.4') as

$$\frac{\alpha_i(L)}{\gamma_i(L)}\hat{y}_{it} = \frac{\beta_i(L)}{\gamma_i(L)}\hat{x}_{it} + \hat{u}_{it} \tag{3.4''}$$

(remember that invertibility of $\gamma_i(L)$ is included in assumption I). The condition is:

(B) For any i and j, $\hat{x}_{it}/\hat{x}_{jt}$ is independent of t (compositional stability of the $\hat{x}_{it}$'s), while $\alpha_i(L)/\gamma_i(L) = \alpha_j(L)/\gamma_j(L)$.

In case (A) aggregation is immediate. In case (B), as $\hat{x}_{it} = q_i X_t$ (where q_i is independent of t) and $\alpha_i(L)/\gamma_i(L) = \alpha(L)/\gamma(L)$ for any i, from $(3.4'')$ one obtains

$$\frac{\alpha(L)}{\gamma(L)} Y_t = \Sigma\, q_i \frac{\beta_i(L)}{\gamma_i(L)} X_t + U_t$$

Case (B) deserves some observations. First, note that (B) contains more than compositional stability. This allows easy aggregation without aggregation error when the polynomials $\alpha_i(L)$ and $\gamma_i(L)$ are non-trivial (as was the case in model (3.1)). Yet one may wonder why we limit ourselves to assuming $\alpha_i(L)/\gamma_i(L) = \alpha_j(L)/\gamma_j(L)$, for any i and j, and do not take into consideration the 'pure' case in which there is compositional stability both for the $\hat{x}_{it}$'s and the $\hat{y}_{it}$'s, while possibly $\alpha_i(L)/\gamma_i(L) \neq \alpha_j(L)/\gamma_j(L)$, for some i and j. In fact, in that case also aggregation error is immediately seen to be zero: since $\hat{y}_{it} = q_i' Y_t$, we have

$$\Sigma\, q_i' \frac{\alpha_i(L)}{\gamma_i(L)} Y_t = \Sigma\, q_i \frac{\beta_i(L)}{\gamma_i(L)} X_t + U_t$$

However, the following simple example should be sufficient to convince the reader that compositional stability of the $\hat{y}_{it}$'s is not a sensible assumption.[6] Consider the disaggregated model: $y_{it} = a_i y_{i(t-1)} + b_i X_t + u_{it}$ (compositional stability of the x_{it}'s is incorporated into the b_i's) for $n = \hat{n} = 2$. Moreover, assume the rank of the u_{it}'s is two. Compositional stability of the y_{it}'s implies that for a suitable $h \neq 0$

$$y_{1t} - hy_{2t} = a_1 y_{1(t-1)} - ha_2 y_{2(t-1)} + (b_1 - hb_2)X_t + u_{1t}$$
$$- hu_{2t} = 0$$

Orthogonality conditions between u_{it}'s and $x_{j(t-k)}$, $y_{j(t-h)}$, for $h > 0$, any j and k, imply that $u_{1t} - hu_{2t} = 0$. In turn, this implies that

45

Disaggregation in econometric modelling

$$X_t = -(b_1 - hb_2)^{-1}(a_1 y_{1(t-1)} - ha_2 y_{2(t-1)})$$

The latter relationship is void of any economic meaning, and will hold only by a fluke.

Second, it must be pointed out that condition (B) could hold for (3.4′) but not for (3.4). This result occurs when, roughly speaking, the x_{it}'s are different but uniformly distributed among different micro equations, so that ratios $\hat{x}_{it}/\hat{x}_{it}$ are independent of t. We shall return to this possibility in sub-section 3.2.5.

The following is an example in which $A_t = 0$ although neither (A) nor (B) hold. Consider the following disaggregated model: $n = 2$, $\alpha_i(L) = \gamma_i(L) = 1$, $\beta_i(L) = b_i$, $b_1 \neq b_2$, $u_{1t} = u_{2t} = \eta_t/2$, and $x_{it} = (1 + \theta_i L)v_t$, where η_t and v_t are scalar white noises. Finally, $\theta_1 \neq \theta_2$. In this case $\hat{n} = 2$ and $\mu(\hat{\chi}_t) = 1$. We have

$$X_t = 2(1 + \bar{\theta}L)v_t$$

where $\bar{\theta} = (\theta_1 + \theta_2)/2$. On the other hand

$$y_{it} = b_i(1 + \theta_i L)v_t + \frac{1}{2}\eta_t$$

so that

$$Y_t = [b_1(1 + \theta_1 L) + b_2(1 + \theta_2 L)]v_t + \eta_t$$

The aggregated equation is immediately obtained

$$(1 + \bar{\theta}L)Y_t = \frac{1}{2}[b_1(1 + \theta_1 L) + b_2(1 + \theta_2 L)]X_t \\ + (1 + \bar{\theta}L)\eta_t$$

Note that in this example, though no aggregation error arises, the dynamic shape of the aggregated model is different from that of the disaggregated one. Moreover, the coefficients of the former are not invariant with respect to the θ_i's. We shall come back to these points in section 3.2.

In the above example the condition $\mu(\hat{\chi}_t) = 1$ has permitted an easy demonstration that $A_t = 0$. Such a demonstration will be generalized – theorem 2, statement (a) – to a wide class of micro models for which $\mu(\hat{\chi}_t) = 1$. Unfortunately – see statement (b) – there also exists a wide class of micro models for which $\mu(\hat{\chi}_t) = 1$ but $A_t \neq 0$. In statement (c) we skip to the opposite extreme, i.e. $\mu(\hat{\chi}_t) = \hat{n}$, and prove that $A_t \neq 0$ under an additional assumption. No results are given in the intermediate case $1 < \mu(\hat{\chi}_t) < \hat{n}$, but the example following theorem 2 shows that $\mu(\hat{\chi}_t) > 1$ is not sufficient for $A_t \neq 0$.

Theorem 2

Let us assume that neither (A) nor (B) holds:

(a) If $\mu(\hat{\chi}_t) = 1$ and $\alpha_i(L)/\gamma_i(L) = \alpha_j(L)/\gamma_j(L)$ for any i and j, then $A_t = 0$.
(b) If (i) $\mu(\hat{\chi}_t) = 1$ but $\alpha_i(L)/\gamma_i(L) \neq \alpha_j(L)/\gamma_j(L)$ for some i and j; (ii) $\mu(\hat{u}_t) = \hat{n}$, where $\hat{u}_t = (\hat{u}_{1t}, \hat{u}_{2t}, \ldots, \hat{u}_{nt})$; then $A_t \neq 0$.
(c) If (i) $\mu(\hat{\chi}_t) = \hat{n}$; (ii) $\mu(\hat{u}_t) = \hat{n}$; then $A_t \neq 0$.

The proof of theorem 2 is contained in section 4 of appendix 3A. The following example shows that $\mu(\hat{\chi}_t) > 1$ could not replace $\mu(\hat{\chi}_t) = \hat{n}$ in statement (c). Consider: $y_{it} = a_i x_{it} + u_{it}$, for $n = 3$, the x_{it}'s being white noises, $x_{1t} \perp x_{2t}$, $x_{3t} = c x_{2t}$, $c \neq 0$. The term A in the regression

$$a_1 x_{1t} + a_2 x_{2t} + a_3 x_{3t} = a(x_{1t} + x_{2t} + x_{3t}) + A_t$$

vanishes if, for instance, $a_3 = 0$, $a_2 = (1 + c)a_1$.

3.1.5 Different approaches to aggregation

The approach adopted in the present paper may be summarized as follows: (1) stochastic micro equations, (2) the x_{it}'s are generated by a multivariate ARMA (or ARIMA) process, (3) the aggregate equation is defined as the best linear predictor of Y_t based on X_t *plus* all past values of X_t and Y_t.

The same set-up, with minor modifications, is used, for instance, in Granger (1980b), Lütkepohl (1984a and 1987), and also in works on temporal aggregation such as Sims (1970), and Tiao and Wei (1976). By contrast, most econometric literature on aggregation deals with finite samples instead of processes, while the definition of the aggregate equation is not uniform. The first difference will not be analysed here. As regards the second, let us mention, first, Theil's pioneering 1954 book, where the aggregated equation is defined by simply reproducing the micro equation shape (but see also, for instance, Grunfeld and Griliches, 1960, Boot and de Wit, 1960, Allen, 1963). Second, as representative of recent work, let us mention Jorgenson *et al.* (1982) and Stoker (1984), where the macro equation contains, in addition to the aggregated explanatory variable X_t, also those moments of the distribution of the x_{it}'s which may be useful for explanation of Y_t variation.

It may be useful to see the above definition and the one adopted in the present paper as two alternative attempts at recovering information lost through aggregation: by resorting to lagged variables in our definition; by resorting to distributional variables in the other. Linking the two definitions would be a most interesting development. At present we only know of an empirical result by Stoker (1986), where the introduction of a distributional variable in a macro equation is sufficient to destroy the (spurious) dynamics which had been previously estimated.

In spite of the differences outlined above, some detailed comparisons will provide clarification. As regards the aggregation error, we remind the reader that our A_t is the residual of the projection of $\tilde{Y}_t$, i.e. the best linear predictor of Y_t in the space H'' spanned by the micro variables, on the space spanned by the macro variables Y_{t-k}, X_{t-h}, $k > 0$, $h \geq 0$. This projection has in our framework the same role as the 'auxiliary equation' in Theil (1954, p. 13). However, our auxiliary equation contains X_t and all past values of X_t and Y_t, whereas Theil's contains only those lags of the macro variables that correspond to lags which are present in the micro equations.

The condition $A_t = 0$ is the dynamic equivalent of Theil's (1954) condition of 'perfect aggregation'. In fact, perfect aggregation is defined by Theil as consistency between the macro equation and the micro equations with respect to prediction of Y_t (see Theil, 1954, pp. 140–1).

Condition $A_t = 0$ is also very close to Green's (1964) 'consistent aggregation'. The latter is defined (p. 35) as the existence of aggregating functions (not necessarily consisting in summing) for the explanatory micro variables, and a macro equation (not necessarily linear) linking, without residual, Y_t to aggregated (via the aggregating functions) explanatory variables. In our case, if we include the u_{it}'s among the explanatory variables (to make our set-up comparable to Green's), then $A_t = 0$ implies that Y_t is linked, linearly and without residual, to X_t, U_t, plus possible lags of X_t, U_t and Y_t. Thus, the aggregating function consists of simple summing, while we also allow, unlike Green, for lags which may not appear in the micro equations.

Theorem 2(c), states that micro homogeneity, i.e. condition (A), is not only sufficient but also necessary for $A_t = \mathbf{0}$ when the variance-covariance matrices of the $\hat{\chi}_{it}$'s and of the $\hat{u}_{it}$'s are non-singular. Such a result is a generalization to the dynamic case of a well-known static result, stated for instance in Green (1964, theorem 7). In Green's theorem 7, the assumption that the x_{it}'s are 'free to take on all values' has the same role as our hypothesis on the variance-covariance matrices of the $\hat{\chi}_{it}$'s and the $\hat{u}_{it}$'s.[7]

The condition of 'compositional stability' contained in our case (B) is also well known in the literature on static aggregation and is discussed for instance in Theil (1954, pp. 17–19) and Boot and de Wit (1960, pp. 14–16).

Last, another aspect of the approach adopted here deserves some consideration. Let us note once more that in the present chapter the x_{it}'s are modelled as a joint ARMA process; this implies that each x_{it} is a stationary variable, while x_{it} and x_{jt} are co-stationary (remember that this may be true after suitable transformations of the x_{it}'s). It is useful to contrast this aspect of our set-up with the way the x_{it}'s are treated, for instance, in Stoker (1984). In that work no model is given for the individual x_{it}'s. Rather, the distribution of the x_{it}'s among the agents is directly modelled. So, to make an easy example, if the x_{it}'s are individual incomes, in our approach the parameters of the process driving the x_{it}'s are at the centre of the representation, whereas deriving mean and variance of the distribution of the x_{it}'s among agents at any one time would be fairly complicated. By contrast, in the alternative approach, mean and variance (and possibly other features) of such a distribution are the basic parameters, while there is no interest in time evolution of individual x_{it}'s. Our approach has the advantage of permitting an easy and large-scale employment of linear stochastic process techniques, i.e. spectral analysis and Wold representation. However, it must be observed that for the representation of the x_{it}'s as an ARMA process fully to make sense, the x_{it}'s (and consequently the y_{it}'s) must already be aggregated to some extent: indeed, it would be rather odd to assume that strictly individual incomes follow a joint ARMA process (this would imply, for instance, that given two individuals, the covariances of their incomes at any lag is independent of time). The alternative approach is definitely superior in this respect: permanent or smoothly varying features are assumed only for aggregates and not for individuals. We limit ourselves to these few observations, while noting that systematic integration of the above mentioned different approaches should be a source of great improvement in analysing aggregation.

3.2 The dynamic shape of the aggregated model

In section 3.1 we saw that when either (A) or (B) holds then aggregation error vanishes. It is also easily seen that in these cases no modification of dynamic shape is produced by aggregation. However, it is worth stressing that the condition $A_t = 0$ is neither necessary nor sufficient for identity between micro and macro dynamic shape. In fact, in sub-section 3.1.4 we saw an example in which dynamic complications occur but $A_t = 0$. On the other hand, assuming that the x_{it}'s are white noises, so that no dynamization effects arise (see case (c_3) in the Introduction to this chapter), examples for which $A_t \neq 0$ are easily found. Consider, for instance, $n = 2$, $x_{1t} \perp x_{2t}$, $y_{it} = a_i x_{it} + u_{it}$. The aggregation error is

$$A_t = a_1 x_{1t} + a_2 x_{2t} - KX_t = (a_1 - K)x_{1t} + (a_2 - K)x_{2t}$$

where K is defined as in sub-section 3.1.2. If $a_1 \neq a_2$ we have $A_t \neq 0$.

In this section we shall focus on the dynamization effects of aggregation. Models in which $\mu(\hat{\chi}_t) = 1$ allow a relatively elementary treatment: see once more the aforementioned example, but also the proof of statements (a) and (b) of theorem 2 in appendix 3A. Explicit expressions for the macro equation parameters are given in formulae (3.26) and (3.27). Simple inspection of (3.26) shows that if the micro equations are static or finite distributed lag then the macro equations are rational distributed lag with a white-noise disturbance.

In sub-sections 3.2.1, 3.2.2, and 3.2.3 we shall analyse the consequences of the assumption $\mu(\hat{\chi}_t) > 1$ (in theorem 2, statement (c), only the aggregation error has been considered). As this case is much more difficult we shall limit ourselves to a very simple disaggregated model. For possible directions of generalization see sub-section 3.2.4 below.

Consider the micro equations

$$y_{it} = a_i x_{it} + u_{it} \tag{3.9}$$

with $n = 2$, the x_{it}'s being generated by

$$\begin{pmatrix} 1 - b_1 L & 0 \\ 0 & 1 - b_2 L \end{pmatrix} \begin{pmatrix} x_{1t} \\ x_{2t} \end{pmatrix} = \begin{pmatrix} \chi_{1t} \\ \chi_{2t} \end{pmatrix} \tag{3.10}$$

with $\chi_{1t} \perp \chi_{2t}$, so that if $a_1 \neq a_2$ then $\mu(\hat{\chi}_t) = 2$. Moreover, we shall assume that $u_{it} \perp x_{j(t+k)}$, $k > 0$, i.e. the y_{it}'s do not Granger-cause the x_{it}'s, and that $\mu(u_t) = 2$, where $u_t = (u_{1t}, u_{2t})$. These assumptions imply that if $a_1 \neq a_2$ then $A_t \neq 0$ (theorem 2(c)).

We shall consider first the static specification for the aggregated model and show its inadequacy. Then we shall prove that a static specification with an ARMA error term is, in general, also inadequate. Finally, the equation

$$(1 - aL)Y_t = (K - K_1 L)X_t + (1 - cL)E_t \tag{3.11}$$

where in general $a \neq K_1/K$, $a \neq c$, will be seen to solve the problem of aggregated specification.

3.2.1 The same shape for aggregated and disaggregated models

Consider the specification

$$Y_t = KX_t + E_t \tag{3.12}$$

with E_t white noise. If specification (3.12) were correct then the spectral density of E_t should be constant. Now

$$E_t = Y_t - KX_t = \frac{a_1 - K}{1 - b_1 L}\chi_{1t} + \frac{a_2 - K}{1 - b_2 L}\chi_{2t} + U_t$$

so that the spectral density of E_t is a

$$G_E(z) = \frac{(a_1 - K)^2}{|1 - b_1 z|^2}s_1 + \frac{(a_2 - K)^2}{|1 - b_2 z|^2}s_2 + s$$

where $z = e^{-i\lambda}$, $s_1 = \text{var}(\chi_{1t})$, $s_2 = \text{var}(\chi_{2t})$ and $s = \text{var}(U_t)$. Now, $G_E(z)$ is constant as a function of λ if and only if either (i) $b_1 = b_2 = 0$, i.e. the x_{it}'s are white noises, or (ii) $a_1 = a_2 = K$, i.e. the micro equations have the same coefficients.

51

Disaggregation in econometric modelling

3.2.2 The same shape but an ARMA error term

Consider the specification

$$Y_t = KX_t + \frac{\gamma(L)}{\alpha(L)} E_t \tag{3.13}$$

with E_t white noise. An equation like (3.13) could be specified to take into account residual autocorrelation in (3.12). Actually (3.13) represents a step in the right direction, even though it is not a sufficient departure from the micro model shape.

If (3.13) is the aggregated model, E_t must be orthogonal to X_{t-k}, $k \geq 0$. Now put $\tilde{E}_t = (\gamma(L)/\alpha(L))E_t$. We can write[8]

$$\tilde{E}_t = \left(1 - \frac{\alpha(L)}{\gamma(L)}\right) \tilde{E}_t + E_t \tag{3.14}$$

Since E_t must be orthogonal to X_{t-k}, $k \geq 0$, (3.14) can be considered as the regression of $\tilde{E}_t$ on the past of both $\tilde{E}_t$ and X_t. Therefore X_t does not Granger-cause $\tilde{E}_t$. This, as is well known (see appendix 3A, section 2), is equivalent to saying that within the regression

$$X_t = h(L)\tilde{E}_t + e_t$$

of X_t on present, past, and future values of $\tilde{E}_t$, all coefficients corresponding to future values are zero, i.e. $h(L)$ does not contain terms in L^{-k}, $k > 0$. This latter statement may be checked by calculating $h(L)$. We have (see appendix 3A, section 2)

$$h(L) = \frac{G_{X\tilde{E}}(L)}{G_{\tilde{E}}(L)}$$

where $G_{X\tilde{E}}(z)$ is the cross-spectrum of X_t and $\tilde{E}_t$, $G_{\tilde{E}}(z)$ is the spectrum of $\tilde{E}_t$, while $h(L)$ is obtained by substituting $z = e^{-i\lambda}$ with L in the spectra. Using (3.9), (3.10) and $\dot{E}_t = Y_t - KX_t$ we get (see appendix 3A, section 2).

$$h(L) = \frac{(a_1 - K)G_{x_1}(L) + (a_2 - K)G_{x_2}(L)}{(a_1 - K)^2 G_{x_1}(L) + (a_2 - K)^2 G_{x_2}(L) + s} \tag{3.15}$$

52

where $G_{x_1}(L) = s_1/[(1 - b_1 L)(1 - b_1 F)]$, $G_{x_2}(L) = s_2/[(1 - b_2 L)(1 - b_2 F)]$, $F = L^{-1}$. We note first that $h(L) = h(F)$, so that $h(L)$ may be unilateral only if all its coefficients, except possibly the constant term, are zero. This is not true in general for (3.15). Sufficient conditions for (3.15) to be unilateral are: (*i*) $a_1 = a_2 = K$, (ii) $b_1 = b_2$, $K = (a_1 s_1 + a_2 s_2)/(s_1 + s_2)$. We shall see in sub-section 3.2.3 that either $a_1 = a_2$ or $b_1 = b_2$ is also necessary for unilaterality of $h(L)$, while in both such cases $K = (a_1 s_1 + a_2 s_2)/(s_1 + s_2)$.

3.2.3 An unrestricted dynamic shape

We shall now show that specification (3.11) is the solution to our problem. It will suffice to determine a, K, K_1, c, with $|c| < 1$, so that the process E_t implicitly defined is orthogonal to X_{t-k}, Y_{t-h}, $k \geq 0$, $h > 0$. This is tantamount to saying that the cross-spectrum $G_{EX}(z)$ must contain only negative powers of $z = e^{-i\lambda}$, and that $G_{YE}(z)$ must contain only non-positive powers of z. Let us write explicitly E_t, X_t and Y_t in terms of χ_{it} and U_t

$$E_t = \frac{(a_1 - K) - (a_1 a - K_1)L}{(1 - cL)(1 - b_1 L)} \chi_{1t} + \frac{(a_2 - K) - (a_2 a - K_1)L}{(1 - cL)(1 - b_2 L)} \chi_{2t}$$
$$+ \frac{1 - aL}{1 - cL} U_t$$

$$X_t = \frac{1}{1 - b_1 L} \chi_{1t} + \frac{1}{1 - b_2 L} \chi_{2t}$$

$$Y_t = \frac{a_1}{1 - b_1 L} \chi_{1t} + \frac{a_2}{1 - b_2 L} \chi_{2t} + U_t$$

For the cross-spectrum $G_{EX}(z)$ we have

$$G_{EX}(z) = \frac{(a_1 - K) - (a_1 a - K_1)z}{(1 - cz)(1 - b_1 z)(1 - b_1 z^{-1})} s_1 + \frac{(a_2 - K) - (a_2 a - K_1)z}{(1 - cz)(1 - b_2 z)(1 - b_2 z^{-1})} s_2$$
$$= \frac{[(a_1 - K) - (a_1 a - K_1)z]s_1 M_2(z) + [(a_2 - K) - (a_2 a - K_1)z]s_2 M_1(z)}{(1 - cz)(1 - b_1 z)(1 - b_1 z^{-1})(1 - b_2 z)(1 - b_2 z^{-1})}$$

53

where $M_i(z) = (1 - b_i z)(1 - b_i z^{-1})$. In order that $G_{EX}(z)$ contains only negative powers of z, it is necessary that the term $(1 - cz)(1 - b_1 z)(1 - b_2 z)$, appearing in the denominator, is compensated, i.e. the numerator vanishes when z is made equal to $1/b_1$, $1/b_2$, $1/c$. Substituting the first two values we obtain

$$aa_1 - K_1 = b_1(a_1 - K)$$
$$aa_2 - K_1 = b_2(a_2 - K) \tag{3.16}$$

that is

$$a = \frac{b_1(a_1 - K) + b_2(K - a_2)}{a_1 - a_2}$$

$$K_1 = \frac{a_2 b_1(a_1 - K) + a_1 b_2(K - a_2)}{a_1 - a_2} \tag{3.17}$$

Putting these expressions of a and K_1 into $G_{EX}(z)$ we get

$$G_{EX}(z) = \frac{(a_1 - K)(1 - b_2 z^{-1})s_1 + (a_2 - K)(1 - b_1 z^{-1})s_2}{(1 - cz)(1 - b_1 z^{-1})(1 - b_2 z^{-1})}$$

Lastly, equating the numerator to zero for $z = 1/c$ and solving for K

$$K = \frac{a_1 s_1(1 - cb_2) + a_2 s_2(1 - cb_1)}{s_1(1 - cb_2) + s_2(1 - cb_1)} \tag{3.18}$$

Now consider the cross-spectrum

$$G_{EY}(z) = \frac{(a_1 - K)(1 - b_2 z^{-1})a_1 s_1 + (a_2 - K)(1 - b_1 z^{-1})a_2 s_2}{(1 - cz)(1 - b_1 z^{-1})(1 - b_2 z^{-1})}$$

$$+ \frac{[1 - \dfrac{b_1(a_1 - K) + b_2(K - a_2)}{a_1 - a_2} z](1 - b_1 z^{-1})(1 - b_2 z^{-1})s}{(1 - cz)(1 - b_1 z^{-1})(1 - b_2 z^{-1})}$$

Substituting expression (3.18) for K and equating the numerator to zero for $z = 1/c$, we get the equation in c

$$(1 - b_1 c)(1 - b_2 c)[(a_1 - a_2)^2 s_1 s_2 c$$
$$- s[s_1(1 - b_2 c)(b_2 - c) + s_2(1 - b_1 c)(b_1 - c)]] = 0 \tag{3.19}$$

Among the roots of (3.19) we have to retain only those for which $|c| < 1$. Thus $1/b_1$ and $1/b_2$ must be discarded. The polynomial between braces, let us call it $p(c)$, has two reciprocal roots: in fact $p(c) = c^2 p(1/c)$. One of these will fulfil $|c| < 1$. The solution is obtained putting this value of c into (3.18) and (3.17).

Once the macro coefficients have been obtained let us first note that, as long as we remain in our simplified model, $a_1 \neq a_2$ is sufficient to have $A_t \neq 0$ even if the assumption $\mu(u_t) = 2$ is dropped. Actually, as χ_{1t}, χ_{2t} and U_t are mutually orthogonal, simple inspection of the expression given above for E_t shows that

$$\text{var}(E_t) = \text{var}(U_t) + (a_1 - K)^2 \text{var}(\chi_{1t}) + (a_2 - K)^2 \text{var}(\chi_{2t}) + \cdots$$

Second, note that equation (3.11) takes the form of a static equation with an ARMA error if and only if either $a_1 = a_2$, or $b_1 = b_2$: in fact if $a_1 \neq a_2$, putting $K_1 = aK$ in (3.16) we get $a = b_1 = b_2$; conversely, putting $b_1 = b_2 = b$ in (3.17) we get $a = b$, $K_1 = bK$ (thus the proposition stated in sub-section 3.2.2 is proved).

Third, consider another possible simplification of (3.11): that is $a = c$. In this case (3.11) may be written as a rational distributed lag model with a white-noise error term

$$Y_t = \frac{K - K_1 L}{1 - aL} X_t + E_t \tag{3.20}$$

Now, $a = c$ is equivalent to c being a solution of

$$s_1(1 - b_2 c)(b_2 - c) + s_2(1 - b_1 c)(b_1 - c) = 0 \tag{3.21}$$

as may be seen by putting K, as given by (3.18), into the

expression of $c = a$ given by the first of equations (3.17). Now, a real c which is a solution of both (3.19) and (3.21) will also be a solution of (3.21) and

$$\frac{s_1 s_2}{s} c = 0$$

(we are assuming, of course, $a_1 \neq a_2$). Therefore, in order to have $a = c$ we must have $c = 0$; in turn, $c = 0$ is a solution for (3.21) only if $s_1 b_2 + s_2 b_1 = 0$. This latter condition does not seem to have any particular meaning, except for the case $b_1 = b_2 = 0$. Note, however, that (3.21) becomes more and more compatible with (3.19) if $s_1 s_2 / s$ tends to zero, i.e. if the variance of U_t tends to become bigger and bigger with respect to the variances of the x_{it}'s. Therefore, as $s_1 s_2 / s$ tends to zero, the aggregated model tends to form (3.20).

Summing up the above results, starting with static micro equations we found that in general the aggregated model is an unrestricted ARMAX. It may be worth noting once more that if we start with the same static micro equations but $\mu(\hat{\chi}_t) = 1$, then the aggregated model is no more complicated than a rational distributed lag with a white-noise error term (see the beginning of this section).

As a further difference between micro and macro models, in general the aggregated variable Y_t will Granger-cause X_t, in spite of the unidirectional causation at the disaggregated level. In fact, consider the bilateral regression (i.e. the regression of Y_t on X_{t-h}, with h positive, zero and negative)

$$Y_t = k(L)X_t + w_t$$

We have

$$k(L) = \frac{G_{YX}(L)}{G_X(L)} = \frac{a_1(1 - b_2 L)(1 - b_2 F)s_1 + a_2(1 - b_1 L)(1 - b_1 F)s_2}{(1 - b_2 L)(1 - b_2 F)s_1 + (1 - b_1 L)(1 - b_1 F)s_2}$$

It is easily seen that $k(L) = k(F)$, and that $k(L)$ is constant if and only if either $a_1 = a_2$ or $b_1 = b_2$.

Moreover, the coefficients of the macro model, as given in (3.17) and (3.19), are not invariant with respect to changes in b_1, b_2, s_1, s_2, even though a_1 and a_2 are invariant with respect to such parameters. This is tantamount to saying that interventions on X_t affecting the parameters in (3.10), i.e. the model generating the x_{it}'s, affect the relation linking Y_t and X_t as well.

The above phenomena imply that X_t is neither strongly exogenous nor super exogenous in macro equation (3.11), even if the x_{it}'s are, respectively, strongly exogenous or super exogenous in the micro model.[9]

3.2.4 Generalization to any number of micro equations

The results obtained in this section may be generalized to models with any number of agents whatever, with any dynamic shape for the micro equations and for the processes generating explanatory micro variables. Detailed assumptions and demonstrations may be found in Lippi (1987a) and (1988a). Here we limit ourselves to briefly reporting the results and applying them to the present paper.

Assume that the micro parameters – i.e. the parameters of the micro equations and of the processes generating the x_{it}'s – are allowed to vary within an open convex set $\Gamma \subset R^q$, q being the number of micro parameters necessary to describe fully the disaggregated model (the set Γ may be the result of a re-parameterization obtained from the 'structural' parameterization). The basic result in Lippi (1987a) is that the parameters of the aggregated model are analytic functions of the micro parameters (points of Γ): this implies that if an algebraic relationship involving the macro parameters is given, then either such a relationship holds all over Γ or on a zero-measure subset of Γ. Stated differently, if the relationship does not hold for one point of Γ, then it holds only for a zero-measure subset of Γ.

The above proposition is easily applicable to the coefficients of the variance–covariance matrix of $\hat{\chi}_t$, so that: given the set Γ over which the micro model is defined, then either $\mu(\hat{\chi}_t) = 1$ all over Γ, or $\mu(\hat{\chi}_t) > 1$ all over Γ with the exception of a negligible subset.

Consider first the case $\mu(\hat{\chi}_t) > 1$. It is easily seen that specific dynamic shapes of the macro model correspond to algebraic equations being fulfilled by the macro parameters. For instance, the macro model will be a finite distributed lag with an ARMA disturbance term if polynomial $\alpha(L)$ divides polynomial $\beta(L)$, this entailing a number of algebraic relationships between the co-efficients of $\alpha(L)$ and $\beta(L)$. So, if there exists in Γ one point for which $\alpha(L)$ does not divide $\beta(L)$, then the same holds all over Γ, apart from a negligible subset. Or, if there is one point for which $A_t \neq 0$ (that is var$(A_t) \neq 0$), then $A_t \neq 0$ almost everywhere in Γ.

Disaggregation in econometric modelling

As regards the existence of such single points, let us reconsider the example we worked out in this section. Assume the micro model is that of (3.9) and (3.10), but drop the assumption $n = 2$. Γ will be a subset of R^{4n}, as four parameters are necessary for each i. Now, consider the point of Γ for which $a_i = a_1$, $b_i = b_1$, for $i = 1$, $2, \ldots, n - 1$, while $a_n \neq a_1$, $b_n \neq b_1$. Obviously, all the conclusions drawn in section 3.2.3 – both on the dynamic shape of the macro model and on A_t – are valid for such a point; therefore, the analyticity result reported above implies that such conclusions are valid all over Γ with the exception of a negligible subset. Similarly, if a micro model is given, and we are able to find a point in Γ for which the assumptions of statement (d) of theorem 2 are valid, then $A_t \neq 0$ almost everywhere in Γ.

Resorting to special points with $\hat{n} = 2$, jointly with the analyticity proposition, allows the treatment of rather complicated models in which $\mu(\hat{\chi}_t) > 1$ (see Lippi, 1988a). Explicit formulae for the macro parameters may be obtained only for these special points, while analyticity permits generalization to almost all points of Γ. Under reasonable assumptions, we may conclude that almost everywhere in Γ: $A_t \neq 0$, $\alpha(L)$ is not a factor of $\beta(L)$, nor is $\alpha(L) = \gamma(L)$, irrespective of whether the micro equations are static or not.

The case $\mu(\hat{\chi}_t) = 1$. If compositional stability of the x_{it}'s holds then aggregation is immediate. When this is not the case, conditions for $A_t = 0$ and for $A_t \neq 0$ have been obtained in theorem 2. Moreover, the explicit form for the aggregated equation may be obtained. Aggregation of static or finite distributed lag micro equations yields a rational distributed lag model with a white-noise error (theorem 2 (a)).

3.2.5 A short discussion of the assumptions about $\mu(\hat{\chi}_t)$

Let us now turn to a brief consideration of the economic meaning of $\mu(\hat{\chi}_t)$. The case of compositional stability of the x_{it}'s is of some economic interest: for instance, if the x_{it}'s are wage-rates faced by different firms, then $x_{it} = x_{jt}$, for any i and j, may be a good approximation in certain circumstances.[10]

However, in most economically interesting models, the explanatory micro variables will be affected in different ways by several causes, so that dynamically different x_{it}'s will result: i.e. the ratios x_{it}/x_{jt} are not independent of t. Even when such dynamic differences occur, we might find that $\hat{x}_{it}/\hat{x}_{jt}$ is independent of t, for any i and j (such an occurrence has already been considered in subsection 3.1.4; see the second observation on condition (B)).

Nevertheless, this seems to be rather a remote possibility. Consider, for instance, micro equations (3.1) as representing the pricing behaviour of different industries, y_{it} and x_{it} being, respectively, prices and costs, while the a_i's are mark-up factors. Now, there is no reason to assume that aggregating over industries having the same mark-up would give the same sub-aggregated variable. A similar consideration could be made if y_{it} and x_{it} were, respectively, consumption and income, the a_i's being individual propensities to consume.

Finally, it does not seem easy to find economically interesting examples in which $\mu(\hat{\chi}_t) = 1$, while the ratios $\hat{x}_{it}/\hat{x}_{jt}$ are not independent of t. Such cases appear therefore of exclusively mathematical interest.

Summing up, either there are economic reasons such that compositional stability appears to be a good approximation to reality, i.e. the model assumes that x_{it}/x_{jt} is independent of t for any i and j, for any point of Γ, and the same holds, consequently, for the ratios $\hat{x}_{it}/\hat{x}_{jt}$; or the model assumes $\mu(\hat{\chi}_t) > 1$ almost everywhere in Γ. Now, in both cases, if there exists a point such that $A_t \neq 0$, then the set on which $A_t = 0$ is negligible in Γ.[11] Therefore the subsets of Γ on which condition (A) or condition (B) hold are negligible, and the subset of Γ on which $A_t = 0$ while neither (A) nor (B) hold is also negligible. On the other hand, in the case in which $A_t = 0$ all over Γ, at least one of these possibilities must occur: (1) condition (A) is valid all over Γ, (2) condition (B) is valid all over Γ, (3) $A_t = 0$ all over Γ, but conditions (A) and (B) are valid only on negligible subsets. This third possibility appears to be a perverse case void of any economic meaning.

In conclusion, cases in which $A_t = 0$ but neither (A) nor (B) hold do not appear to be of economic interest.

3.3 Miscellaneous considerations

3.3.1 The degree of the aggregated equation

It is easy to show that the degree of the polynomials $\alpha(L)$, $\beta(L)$ and $\gamma(L)$ rises with the number of different micro equations. We do not intend to deal with this issue formally. Thus we limit ourselves to simple cases in which $\mu(\hat{\chi}_t) = 1$. Let n be the number of different individual equations, so that $n = \hat{n}$, let $(1 - \theta_i L)x_{it} = v_i$, v_i being a scalar white noise, be the micro processes generating the explanatory variables, and let the micro equations be $y_{it} = a_i x_{it} + u_{it}$. The macro equation, written in the distributed lag form is

$$Y_t = \frac{\sum\limits_{i=1,\,n} a_i G_i(L)}{\sum\limits_{i=1,\,n} G_i(L)} X_t + U_t$$

where $G(L) = \prod\limits_{i=1}^{n} (1 - \theta_i L)$, $G_i(L) = G(L)/(1 - \theta_i L)$

Another example is the following. Assume $x_{it} = X_t/n$, while the micro equations are: $(1 - \alpha_i L) y_{it} = a_i x_{it} + u_{it}$. We also assume that $u_{it} \perp X_{t+k}$, $k > 0$. The aggregated model is

$$H(L)Y_t = n^{-1} \left[\sum a_i H_i(L) \right] X_t + \gamma(L)E_t$$

$$\gamma(L)E_t = \sum H_i(L) u_{it}$$

where $H(L)$ and $H_i(L)$ are defined as $G(L)$ and $G_i(L)$ (replacing the θ_i's with the α_i's). Since the autocovariance of $\sum H_i(L)u_{it}$ dies at lag n, then $\gamma(L)$ has degree $n - 1$.[12] Thus, in this case, the polynomials of the aggregated model have degrees, respectively, n, $n - 1$, $n - 1$, while in the previous example we had $n - 1$, $n - 1$, $n - 1$.

In general, it is possible to show that the degrees of the polynomials in the macro equation

$$\alpha(L)Y_t = \beta(L)X_t + \gamma(L)E_t$$

rise linearly with the number of different micro equations. This result may appear to be in contrast with experience of commonly estimated macro equations, whose degrees, usually rather low, do not seem to bear any relationship to the number of underlying micro equations. However, it must be recalled first that actual dynamic specification processes normally make use of models like the following one:

$$\tilde{\alpha}(L)Y_t = \tilde{\beta}(L)X_t + \tilde{E}_t$$

where $\tilde{\alpha}(L)$ and $\tilde{\beta}(L)$ are polynomials, and second that such specification processes end when a balance has been reached between parsimony on the one hand, and, on the other, the non-rejection of a white-noise $\tilde{E}_t$ hypothesis. Estimated $\tilde{\alpha}(L)$ and $\tilde{\beta}(L)$ can therefore be considered as truncations of the Taylor expansions of, respectively, $\alpha(L)/\gamma(L)$ and $\beta(L)/\gamma(L)$, centered in $L = 0$, where the accuracy of the approximation is implicitly evaluated by means of the estimated correlogram of $\tilde{E}_t$.

Now, such truncations can provide good approximations, with respect to the above criterion, even for quite low degrees of $\tilde{\alpha}(L)$ and $\tilde{\beta}(L)$. Let us limit ourselves to the first of the examples above. In this case $\alpha(L)/\gamma(L) = 1$, while

$$\frac{\beta(L)}{\gamma(L)} = \frac{\sum\limits_{i=1,n} a_i G_i(L)}{\sum\limits_{i=1,n} G_i(L)} = K \frac{(1 - s_1 L)(1 - s_2 L)\ldots(1 - s_{n-1}L)}{(1 - \tilde{s}_1 L)(1 - \tilde{s}_2 L)\ldots(1 - \tilde{s}_{n-1}L)}$$

On the other hand

$$\frac{1 - s_i L}{1 - \tilde{s}_i L} = 1 + (\tilde{s}_i - s_i)L + \tilde{s}_i(\tilde{s}_i - s_i)L^2 + \tilde{s}_i^2(\tilde{s}_i - s_i)L^3 + \ldots$$

Therefore, the coefficients of the Taylor expansion of $\beta(L)/\gamma(L)$ may rapidly approach zero either if the roots of $\gamma(L)$ are small, or if they are near to the roots of $\beta(L)$ (i.e. the differences $\tilde{s}_i - s_i$ are small). In turn, the occurrence of one or both of these conditions does not depend on the number n, but on the joint distribution of the a_i's and the θ_i's. Thus a huge number of different micro equations may be reconciled with low-degree estimated polynomials. Further research is necessary to extend such considerations to less easy models, in which the roots of $\alpha(L)$, $\beta(L)$ and $\gamma(L)$ are complicated functions of the micro parameters.

3.3.2 Individual behaviour and aggregated equations

So far we have considered the comparison, on the basis of a prediction error criterion, of a disaggregated and an aggregated model. However, independently of whether micro data are available, our methods and results may be employed to discuss a rather different issue, namely the interpretation of estimated macro equations in terms of representative agents.[13]

Let us consider a simple example. Assume we have specified

Disaggregation in econometric modelling

and estimated the following model linking observable aggregated variables

$$Y_t - \alpha Y_{t-1} = aX_t + bX_{t-1} + E_t \qquad (3.22)$$

where E_t is a white-noise orthogonal to X_{t-k}, Y_{t-h}, for $k \geq 0$, $h > 0$. Usually, an explanation, or an interpretation, of equation (3.22) consists in deriving its principal features from the maximizing behaviour of a *single* agent. One starts with an intertemporal objective function; the equation eventually resulting from maximization, plus substitution of expected values according to the theory of expectations adopted, must reproduce, even though not exactly, equation (3.22). In our case, the presence of the lagged dependent variable should be obtained as a consequence of the objective function shape.[14]

Now, the results obtained in sections 3.1 and 3.2 above show that if neither identical micro equations nor compositional stability of the x_{it}'s are assumed, then the dynamic shape of micro and macro equations may be very different. In particular, we have seen in section 3.2 that the presence of lagged variables – both dependent and explanatory – is most likely in macro equations, even though it has not necessarily a correspondence in the micro equations. Such a dynamization, together with the usual resort to the representative agent, whose behaviour is assumed to be identical to the aggregated equation, constitutes in our opinion a powerful source of bias in favour of the idea that economic agents' behaviour follows a complicated dynamic.[15]

3.3.3 Unobserved components

It must be pointed out also that equations between observed disaggregated data may possess a complicated dynamic shape in spite of simple static behaviour on the part of agents. This will be the case when agents base their decisions on components of the explanatory variables that are observable by them, but not by the investigator. Consider the following micro model

$$\begin{aligned}
y_t &= a\tilde{x}_t + u_t \\
x_t &= \bar{x}_t + \tilde{x}_t \\
\tilde{x}_t &= x_{t-1} + \epsilon_t \\
\hat{x}_t &= c\hat{x}_{t-1} + v_t
\end{aligned} \qquad (3.23)$$

where u_t, ϵ_t and v_t are mutually orthogonal white noises, $0 < c < 1$. Equation (3.23) could represent the pricing behaviour of a firm, which sets its price y_t by charging a fixed mark-up on the trend component $\tilde{x}_t$ of the cost. Such a trend is assumed to be known to the firm, while the cost variable available to the investigator, $\bar{x}_t$, also contains a cyclical component $\tilde{x}_t$. Alternatively, y_t could represent employment in a firm, as a function of the output trend.

Model (3.23) can be dealt with using the method developed in section 3.2. The equation linking y_t and x_t will be dynamic although agents behave statically.[16]

Last we point out that dynamization effects similar to those shown above may also arise from: (*i*) errors both in explanatory and in dependent variables,[17] (*ii*) temporal aggregation,[18] (*iii*) linear specification of non-linear relationships, (*iv*) omission of relevant variables. All these cases can be dealt with within the analytical framework used in the present paper.

Concluding remarks

The aggregated model has been defined as the linear function of X_t and past values of X_t and Y_t that minimizes the prediction error variance. We have seen that in general the dynamic shape of the aggregated model can not be obtained just by reproducing the dynamic shape of the disaggregated model: the aggregated model is an unrestricted ARMAX, even when the micro equations are static or simple finite distributed lags.

The error variance of the aggregated model is never smaller, and almost always greater, than the disaggregated error variance. This result holds true under our assumption of a known micro model. The opposite outcome in empirical cases, i.e. better performance of the aggregated model, may be traced to micro misspecification and/or to the use of estimated (instead of true) coefficients in small samples. On the other hand, it is worth insisting that a better performance of the disaggregated model in comparison with its mere reproduction at the aggregated level is insufficient, both within our approach and in empirical cases, to draw a conclusion in favour of disaggregated modelling. Only by allowing for an unrestricted (relative to the disaggregated) dynamic shape at the aggregated level can we fully exploit the information contained in the past history of the aggregated variables.

Disaggregation in econometric modelling

Appendix 3A

1 The Wold representation

Let $\xi_t = (\xi_{1t}, \xi_{2t}, \ldots, \xi_{st})$ be a stationary s-dimensional stochastic process, and let $\Sigma_\xi(k) = E(\xi_t, \xi'_{t-k})$. The spectral density is defined as

$$G_\xi(z) = \sum_{k=-\infty}^{+\infty} \Sigma_\xi(k)z^{-k}$$

where $z = e^{-i\lambda}$, $-\pi \leq \lambda \leq \pi$. Let us assume that $G_\xi(z)$ is a matrix of rational functions in z, and let the rank of such a matrix be s for λ almost everywhere in $[-\pi, \pi]$. Then $G_\xi(z)$ may be decomposed in the following way

$$G_\xi(z) = B(z)\Sigma B'(z^{-1}) \tag{3.24}$$

where $B(z)$ is a matrix of rational functions in z, Σ is positive definite. Moreover, substituting ζ for z, where ζ is a complex variable, we have $B(0) = I$, $B(\zeta)$ has no poles of modulus smaller or equal to one, $\det(B(\zeta))$ has no roots of modulus smaller than one. Finally, substituting L for z, we have

$$\xi_t = B(L)\omega_t \tag{3.25}$$

where ω_t is a white-noise vector such that $E(\omega_t \omega'_t) = \Sigma$. Equation (3.25) is known as the Wold representation of ξ_t. It is worth noticing that ω_{it} is the residual of the orthogonal projection of ξ_{it} on the space spanned by $\xi_{j(t-k)}$, $k > 0$, $j = 1, 2, \ldots, s$.

The above results may be easily extended to the case in which $G_\xi(z)$ does not have maximum rank. We define $\mu(\xi_t) = \text{rank}(\Sigma_\xi(0))$. Its meaning is obvious: the vector ξ_t lies in a linear sub-space of R^s whose dimension is $\mu(\xi_t)$. If $\mu(\xi_t) = s'$, without loss of generality $(\xi_{1t}, \xi_{2t}, \ldots, \xi_{s't})$ is a vector of rank s', to which the above results are applicable. The remaining components may be treated as linear combinations of the first s'. Therefore representation (3.25) may be extended to cases in which $\mu(\xi_t) = s' < s$. We shall have $\mu(\omega_t) = s'$.[19]

2 Cross-spectrum and Granger-causation

Let $s = 2$. We have

$$G_\xi(z) = \begin{pmatrix} G_{\xi_1}(z) & G_{\xi_1\xi_2}(z) \\ G_{\xi_2\xi_1}(z) & G_{\xi_2}(z) \end{pmatrix}$$

The function $G_{\xi_1\xi_2}(z) = \overline{G_{\xi_2\xi_1}(z)}$ is called the cross-spectrum. Consider now the orthogonal projection of ξ_{1t} on the whole process ξ_{2t}

$$\xi_{1t} = \sum_{k=-\infty}^{+\infty} a_k \xi_{2(t-k)} + v_t$$

where $v_t \perp \xi_{2(t-k)}$, any k. We have

$$\sum_{k=-\infty}^{+\infty} a_k L^k = \frac{G_{\xi_1\xi_2}(L)}{G_{\xi_2}(L)}$$

where the right-hand side is obtained by substituting L for z in the corresponding spectral functions.

We recall that ξ_{1t} fails to Granger-cause ξ_{2t} if and only if $a_k = 0$ for any $k < 0$, i.e. for all k corresponding to future values of ξ_{2t}.[20]

Finally, if ξ_{1t} and ξ_{2t} are given as linear combinations of the components of a white-noise vector, then the spectral functions are easily obtainable. Assume

$$\xi_{it} = \sum_{j=1,m} b_{ij}(L) v_{jt}$$

where v_t is a white-noise m-dimensional vector, and that, for the sake of simplicity, $v_{ht} \perp v_{kt}$ for any h, k. We shall have

$$G_{\xi_i} = \sum_{j=1,m} |b_{ij}(z)|^2 \sigma_{vj}^2$$

$$G_{\xi_i\xi_k} = \sum_{j=1,m} b_{ij}(z) b_{kj}(\bar{z}) \sigma_{vj}^2$$

3 Unit roots

Consider the aggregated model (3.7). If in the Wold representation of $Z_t = (Y_t, X_t)$ the determinant of $D(L)$ has no unit modulus roots then $\gamma(L)$ will have no unit modulus roots either. In turn, thanks to decomposition (3.24) recalled just above, $\det(D(L))$ has no unit modulus roots if and only if the determinant of the spectral density of Z_t has this property.

To simplify the discussion let us assume that: (i) $u_{it} \perp x_{j(t+k)}$, $k > 0$, any i and j, i.e. there is no feedback from the y_{it}'s to the x_{it}'s (see the discussion of this point in sub-section 3.1.3 above), (ii) the u_{it}'s are mutually orthogonal, (iii) the x_{it}'s are mutually orthogonal. In such a case

$$
G_Z(z) = \begin{pmatrix} \displaystyle\sum_{i=1,n} \left| \frac{\gamma_i(z)}{\alpha_i(z)} \right|^2 \sigma_{u_i}^2 + \sum_{i=1,n} \left| \frac{\beta_i(z)}{\alpha_i(z)} \right|^2 G_{x_i}(z) & \displaystyle\sum_{i=1,n} \frac{\beta_i(z)}{\alpha_i(z)} G_{x_i}(z) \\[4mm] \displaystyle\sum_{i=1,n} \frac{\beta_i(\bar{z})}{\alpha_i(\bar{z})} G_{x_i}(z) & \displaystyle\sum_{i=1,n} G_{x_i}(z) \end{pmatrix}
$$

whose determinant is

$$
\left(\sum_{i=1,n} \left| \frac{\gamma_i(z)}{\alpha_i(z)} \right|^2 \sigma_{u_i}^2 \right) \left(\sum_{i=1,n} G_{x_i}(z) \right)
$$

$$
+ \frac{1}{2} \sum_{i \neq j} \left| \frac{\beta_i(z)}{\alpha_i(z)} - \frac{\beta_j(z)}{\alpha_j(z)} \right|^2 G_{x_i}(z) G_{x_i}(z)
$$

In order for the latter expression to be always positive for $-\pi \leq \lambda \leq \pi$, it is sufficient that $\gamma_i(L)$ does not have unit modulus roots for any i (as assumed in 1.1) and that at least one among the $G_{xi}(z)$'s is strictly positive for $-\pi \leq \lambda \leq \pi$. Another sufficient condition is that there exist i and j such that (i) $G_{xi}(z)$ and $G_{xj}(z)$ are both positive, and (ii) $|(\beta_i(z)/\alpha_i(z)) - (\beta_j(z)/\alpha_j(z))|^2$ is positive.

Now, it is important to point out that if the x_{it}'s and the y_{it}'s are obtained from non-stationary processes by differencing, then a unit modulus root may be intrinsic to $\det(G_Z(z))$. For instance, assume that the x_{it}'s are I(1) (i.e. the x_{it}'s are non-stationary while the Δx_{it}'s are stationary), and that the micro model is

$$\alpha_i(L)y_{it} = \beta_i(L)x_{it} + u_{it}$$

with $\beta_i(1) = \alpha_i(1)$ for any i, so that y_{it} and x_{it} are cointegrated.[21] Then, by differencing we get

$$\alpha_i(L)\Delta y_{it} = \beta_i(L)\Delta x_{it} + \gamma_i(L)u_{it}$$

with $\gamma_i(L) = 1 - L$. Since we have $\beta_i(1)/\alpha_i(1) = \beta_j(1)/\alpha_j(1) = 1$, then $\det(G_Z(z))$ will contain the term $|1 - z|^2$ and therefore $\gamma(L)$ will contain the factor $1 - L$.

It is possible to show (see Lippi, 1987a) that also in this case the aggregated model (3.7) solves our minimum problem. Moreover, as regards prediction, as soon as we go back to the levels (integrating the differenced variables), the unit root of $\gamma(L)$ may be eliminated together with the $1 - L$ in front of Y_t and X_t, so that the resulting polynomial, $\gamma(L)(1 - L)^{-1}$, may be inverted.

In conclusion, if the unit modulus roots are not intrinsic, then their presence appears to be very unlikely, i.e. conditions (i) and (ii) above are very easily fulfilled. If the unit modulus roots are intrinsic, as in the cointegrated case, a treatment is possible so as to get the same results obtained in their absence. This point deserves further investigation. In particular, the assumption of no feedback should be dropped.

4 Proof of theorem 2

Let us give the proof of theorem 2. For statements (a) and (b), since $\mu(\hat{\chi}_t) = 1$ we may write

$$\hat{x}_{it} = \theta_i(L)r_i v_t$$

v_t being a scalar white noise, while the $\theta_i(L)$'s are rational functions (all the $\hat{x}_{it}$'s are moving averages of the same white noise), with $\theta_i(0) = 1$. We have

$$X_t = \sum_{i=1,\acute{n}} \hat{x}_{it} = \left(\sum_{i=1,\acute{n}} r_i\theta_i(L) \right)v_t = \left(\sum_{i=1,\acute{n}} r_i \right)\bar{\theta}(L)v_t$$

67

Disaggregation in econometric modelling

where

$$\bar{\theta}(L) = \sum_{i=1,\dot{n}} \theta_i(L) / \sum_{i=1,\dot{n}} r_i$$

Notice that $\bar{\theta}(0) = 1$. Substituting in the disaggregated model we get

$$\hat{y}_{it} = \frac{\beta_i(L)}{\alpha_i(L)} \theta_i(L) v_t + \frac{\gamma_i(L)}{\alpha_i(L)} \hat{u}_{it} = \frac{1}{\dot{n}} \frac{\beta_i(L) \theta_i(L)}{\alpha_i(L) \bar{\theta}(L)} X_t + \frac{\gamma_i(L)}{\alpha_i(L)} \hat{u}_{it}$$

so that

$$Y_t = \frac{1}{\dot{n}\bar{\theta}(L)} \sum_{i=1,\dot{n}} \frac{\beta_i(L)\theta_i(L)}{\alpha_i(L)} X_t + \sum_{i=1,\dot{n}} \frac{\gamma_i(L)}{\alpha_i(L)} \hat{u}_{it} \quad (3.26)$$

If $\gamma_i(L)/\alpha_i(L) = \gamma_j(L)/\alpha_j(L)$, any i and j, then, putting $E_t = U_t = \sum_{\dot{u}\dot{u}}$, the aggregated equation is immediately obtained from (3.26), eliminating denominators and common factors, and (a) is proved. Under the assumptions of statement (b) let us consider the Wold representation of the scalar process $\sum(\gamma_i(L)/\alpha_i(L))\hat{u}_{it}$. We have

$$\sum_{i=1,\dot{n}} \frac{\gamma_i(L)}{\alpha_i(L)} \hat{u}_{it} = r(L)E_t$$

where $\tau(L)$ is a rational function with no poles or zeros of modulus smaller or equal to one,[22] $\tau(0) = 1$, while E_t is a white noise. Since E_t lies in the space generated by the $\hat{u}_{it}$'s, then E_t is orthogonal to X_{t-k}, any k. Now rewrite (3.26) as:

$$Y_t = \frac{1}{\dot{n}\bar{\theta}(L)} \left(\sum_{i=1,\dot{n}} \frac{\beta_i(L)\theta_i(L)}{\alpha_i(L)} \right) X_t + \tau(L)E_t. \quad (3.27)$$

Since E_t is orthogonal to X_{t-k} and to E_{t-h}, $k \geq 0$, $h > 0$, then E_t is also orthogonal to Y_{t-k}, $k > 0$, so that the aggregated model is immediately obtained from (3.27). Now consider

$$E_t = \sum_{i=1,\acute{n}} f_i(L)\,\hat{u}_{it}, \qquad f_i(L) = \tau(L)^{-1}\,\frac{\gamma_i(L)}{\alpha_i(L)}$$

We have

$$E_t = U_t + A_t, \qquad A_t = \sum_{i=1,\acute{n}} (f_i(L) - 1)\,\hat{u}_{it}$$

Then rewrite A_t as

$$A_t = (g_1(L) \quad g_2(L) \ldots g_{\acute{n}}(L)) \begin{pmatrix} \hat{u}_{1t} \\ \hat{u}_{2t} \\ \vdots \\ \hat{u}_{\acute{n}t} \end{pmatrix}$$

where $g_i(L) = f_i(L) - 1$. If it were true that $A_t = \mathbf{0}$, then by multiplying by $\hat{u}_{t-k}$, $k \ge 1$, we would get

$$(g_1^k \quad g_2^k \cdots g_{\acute{n}}^k)\ \Sigma_{\hat{u}} = 0$$

for any $k \ge 1$, where $\Sigma_{\hat{u}}$ is the variance–covariance matrix of $\hat{u}_t$, while g_i^k is the coefficient of $g_i(L)$ that corresponds to lag k. As $\Sigma_{\hat{u}}$ is non-singular we get $f_i(L) = 1$, i.e. $\gamma_i(L)/\alpha_i(L) = \tau(L)$, for any i, contrary to the assumption. Thus $A_t \ne \mathbf{0}$.

Let us now come to statement (c). Assume $A_t = \mathbf{0}$, so that $E_t = U_t$, namely

$$0 = E_t - U_t = \frac{a(L)}{\gamma(L)} \sum_{i=1,\acute{n}} \hat{y}_{it} - \frac{\beta(L)}{\gamma(L)} \sum_{i=1,\acute{n}} \hat{x}_{it} - \sum_{i=1,\acute{n}} \hat{u}_{it}$$

$$= \sum_{i=1,\acute{n}} \left(\frac{\beta_i(L)a(L)}{\alpha_i(L)\gamma(L)} - \frac{\beta(L)}{\gamma(L)} \right) \hat{x}_{it}$$

$$+ \sum_{i=1,\acute{n}} \left(\frac{\gamma_i(L)a(L)}{\alpha_i(L)\gamma(L)} - 1 \right) \hat{u}_{it}$$

$$= \phi(L)\hat{B}(L)\hat{\chi}_t + \psi(L)\hat{u}_t$$

Disaggregation in econometric modelling

where $\phi(L)$ is the row vector whose components are

$$\frac{\beta_i(L)a(L)}{a_i(L)\gamma(L)} - \frac{\beta(L)}{\gamma(L)}$$

$\psi(L)$ is the row vector whose components are

$$\frac{\gamma_i(L)a(L)}{a_i(L)\gamma(L)} - 1$$

Multiplying by $\hat{u}_{t-k}$, $k \geq 1$ (remember that $\hat{u}_{t-k} \perp \hat{\chi}_{t-h}$, for any k and h), we get

$$\psi^k \Sigma_{\hat{u}} = 0$$

for any $k \geq 1$, ψ^k being the vector of k-lag coefficients of $\psi(L)$. As $\Sigma_{\hat{u}}$ is non-singular, $\psi(L) = 0$, i.e.

$$\frac{\gamma_i(L)}{a_i(L)} = \frac{\gamma(L)}{a(L)} \qquad\qquad \text{--} \qquad (3.28)$$

for any i. Then, multiplying by $\hat{\chi}_{t-k}$, $k \geq 0$, we get

$$(\phi^k + \phi^{k-1} \hat{B}^1 + \ldots + \phi^0 \hat{B}^k) \Sigma_{\hat{\chi}} = 0$$

for $k \geq 0$. As $\Sigma_{\hat{\chi}}$ is non-singular, this entails $\phi^k = 0$, for $k \geq 0$ (this may be easily checked recursively starting with $k = 0$). Thus

$$\frac{\beta_i(L)}{a_i(L)} = \frac{\beta(L)}{a(L)} \qquad\qquad (3.29)$$

for any i. Equations (3.28) and (3.29), taken together, imply that all individual equations are equal. Thus $A_i = 0$ leads to a contradiction and the theorem is proved.

Notes

1　See Pesaran *et al.* (1989) for a discussion of this point. See also Lütkepohl (1987, chapter 5).

2　The treatment below can be immediately adapted to the case when macro variables are defined by averaging instead of summing.

3　This observation parallels the one contained in the Introduction concerning the micro equations. For a treatment of non-stationary cases, see Lippi (1988a).

4　On the Wold representation of rational spectrum stochastic vectors see appendix 3A, section 1.

5　The ratios $\alpha(L)/\gamma(L)$ and $\beta(L)/\gamma(L)$ are uniquely determined by the micro model: see Lippi (1988a, proposition 1).

6　When models with more than one explanatory variable are considered, identity of micro parameters across micro equations for some of the micro variables, together with compositional stability for the remainders, give rise to a variety of mixed cases in which $A_t = 0$ (see, for example, Pesaran *et al.*, 1989, section 5).

7　See Green, 1964, p. 36 and the comments on pp. 40–1.

8　In the present case invertibility of $\gamma(L)$ is a consequence of the assumptions made on the x_{it}'s.

9　As regards the exogeneity concepts above, see Engle *et al.* (1983). The relationship between aggregation and exogeneity is dealt with in detail in Forni (1987).

10　Note that in this case X_t is not defined as Σx_{it} but as $n^{-1} \Sigma x_{it}$.

11　Remember that compositional stability alone does not necessarily imply $A_t = 0$; if the ratios $\alpha_i(L)/\gamma_i(L)$ are different across micro equations we may have $A_t \neq 0$; see theorem 2, statement (b).

12　See Lütkepohl (1984a).

13　For a more extensive treatment of this issue, see Lippi (1988b).

14　The pervasiveness of the attitude described above – namely the attribution of the features of a macro equation to the behaviour of a single agent – may be assessed by reading through important review articles on dynamic equations in econometrics as: Nerlove (1972), Sims (1974), Hendry *et al.* (1984).

15　In empirical work the possibility of dynamic macro models in spite of static micro behaviour has been recently considered in Stoker (1986b) and Blanchard (1987).

16　Thus, for instance, the presence of the lagged dependent variable in the disaggregated equations used in Pesaran *et al.* (1989, section 7) to model employment as a function of the wage rate and output, need not necessarily be interpreted in terms of an objective function containing an adjustment cost. Static behaviour based on a trend component of output could explain the dynamics of the disaggregated equations. Moreover, it must be pointed out that industry data used by Pesaran *et al.* are still aggregated over firms. As the latter might face different outputs (as stochastic processes), and react with different coefficients, the dynamization effects described in sections 3.1 and 3.2 could be an explanation for the dynamics at the industry level.

71

17 For the possibility of dynamization effects due to unobserved components or errors in variables, see Nerlove *et al.* (1979, pp. 167–8).
18 See Sims (1970), Tiao and Wei (1976).
19 For a treatment of rational spectrum stochastic vectors, see Hannan (1970), Rozanov (1967).
20 See Sims (1972).
21 See Engle and Granger (1987).
22 The fact that $\tau(L)$ has no unit modulus roots is a consequence of the $\gamma_i(L)$'s having no unit modulus roots.

Chapter four

Aggregation *versus* disaggregation in forecasting construction activity

Pekka Ilmakunnas

1 Introduction

Construction in any given period consists of construction projects started during the same period and ones begun in past periods. Therefore a forecasting model of construction activity could be based on two sub-models: a distributed lag from starts to volume of construction, and a forecasting model for started construction. This chapter reports on aggregated and disaggregated distributed lag forecasting models of construction activity in Finland. Forecasting starts is not discussed.

The volume index of construction and information on starts are published in Finland for ten groups (types) of buildings. Our main interest here, however, is in forecasting the volume of total building construction. Also of interest are the largest group, construction of housing (group 0), and the aggregate of the other groups, construction of other buildings (groups 1–9). One has to decide whether to forecast the aggregate index directly or to form disaggregate forecasts for the sub-groups which are then aggregated. The traditional argument is that there is a loss of information in aggregation. In the present case, there is reason to believe that the sub-group lag patterns contain information that is lost if only an aggregate lag pattern is determined. On the other hand, there is some tradeoff between aggregation and disaggregation since some of the sub-group volume indices have very wide variations, which seem difficult to forecast. The aggregate index is, in contrast, much smoother and therefore perhaps easier to forecast.

For the sub-groups it has been possible to use information on average construction times and costs to calculate the lag weights. This has improved forecasts for the individual groups. For the aggregate series it is possible to calculate a lag structure which is consistently aggregated from the sub-group lags. An alternative approach is to obtain the aggregate forecast from the sub-group forecasts without having to determine the aggregate distributed lag.

In section 4.1 the calculation of the lag weights and a consistently aggregated lag are explained, in section 4.2 the final forecasting models are described and in section 4.3 the forecasting performance is studied.

4.1 Calculation of the lag weights

4.1.1 Disaggregate lag weights

Information on average construction times and costs of different types of buildings are used in the calculation of the lag weights. In practice the lengths and costs of projects vary within the groups of buildings. If data on individual projects were available, distributed lags for different projects and the size distribution of the projects could be used for determining the distributed lags by group (see Merkies and Bikker, 1981, Trivedi, 1985). In the terminology of Trivedi, the lag distribution is a kernel and the size distribution a compounder. Since the necessary data are not available and the published volume indices are in any case based on the average times and costs, this aggregation issue is not discussed here. Instead, the chapter concentrates on aggregation of the group distributed lags.

Assume that a total of s_{im} cubic metres of construction are started in group i during month m. On average, these projects last a total of m_i months. The real value (volume) accrued from the projects during the total construction time is

$$Q_{i/m} = \sum_{j=0}^{m_i} p_{ij} s_{im} \qquad (4.1)$$

where p_{ij} is the average real cost per cubic metre of buildings in group i in the stage of construction under way when j ($j = 0, \ldots, m_i$) months have passed from the start of construction. The data on p_{ij} and m_i can be used for determining the distributed lag from starts to volume in a certain period. Van Alphen and Merkies (1976) have used a related method for calculating a distributed lag for the value of housing construction in the Netherlands.

We have information on the costs per cubic metre of different phases of construction and on the average lengths of these phases in months (see Tahvanainen and Lindqvist, 1983). Assume that, within a phase, each month has the same share of the cost of the phase. This gives the monthly costs p_{ij}. It is further assumed that no volume accrues at the start of the project, so that $p_{i0} = 0$.

The next step is to determine how the volume accrued during a month depends on construction started in past months. During month m the real value of construction in group i is

$$q_{im} = \sum_{j=1}^{m_i} p_{ij} s_{i(m-j)} \tag{4.2}$$

Hence at the monthly level the distributed lag weights are simply the monthly real construction costs per cubic metre.

The monthly weights still have to be converted to quarterly weights, since the data on the volume and starts are published only quarterly. It is known how many cubic metres of construction are started during a quarter, but not how the starts are distributed within the quarter. If it is assumed that starts are evenly distributed, the probability of starts S_{it} (we use upper case letters to denote quarterly figures) to have taken place during any single month of the quarter is $\frac{1}{3}$.

The expected volume accrued in quarter t from projects started during the same quarter is, remembering that $p_{i0} = 0$

$$[\frac{1}{3}(p_{i0} + p_{i1} + p_{i2}) + \frac{1}{3}(p_{i0} + p_{i1}) + \frac{1}{3} p_{i0}] S_{it}$$

$$= \frac{1}{3}(2p_{i1} + p_{i2}) S_{it} \equiv w_{i0} S_{it}$$

Similarly, during quarter t projects started at $t - 1$ produce expected volume

$$[\frac{1}{3}(p_{i3} + p_{i4} + p_{i5}) + \frac{1}{3}(p_{i2} + p_{i3} + p_{i4}) + \frac{1}{3}(p_{i1} + p_{i2}$$

$$+ p_{i3})] S_{i(t-1)}$$

75

$$= \frac{1}{3}(p_{i1} + 2p_{i2} + 3p_{i3} + 2p_{i4} + p_{i5})S_{i(t-1)} \equiv w_{i1}S_{i(t-1)}$$

In general form the lag weights are

$$w_{i0} = \frac{1}{3}(2p_{i1} + p_{i2})$$

$$w_{ij} = \frac{1}{3}(p_{i(3j-2)} + 2p_{i(3j-1)} + 3p_{i3j} + 2p_{i(3j+1)}$$

$$+ p_{i(3j+2)}), \quad j = 1, \ldots \tag{4.3}$$

In the tail of the lag distribution the weights decline because we can assume that $p_{i(3j+k)} = 0$ ($k = -2, -1, 0, 1, 2$) when $3j + k >$ m_i, i.e. no volume accrues after the end of the average construction time. The weight w_{ij} is zero when $3j - 2 > m_i$ or $j > (m_i + 2)/3$. The total lag length in quarters, T_i, is the smallest integer value of j for which this inequality holds, minus one. For example, if average construction time is ten months, volume accrues from construction started in the five quarters $t, t - 1, \ldots, t - 4$ and the lag length is four quarters. The sum of the lag weights is $\sum_{j=0}^{T_i} w_{ij} =$ $\sum_{j=1}^{m_i} p_{ij}$, i.e. the total construction cost per cubic metre for a typical project in group i. The volume of construction in quarter t can be expressed as a distributed lag

$$Q_{it} = \sum_{j=0}^{T_i} w_{ij}S_{i(t-j)} \tag{4.4}$$

which can be used for forecasting future values of Q_i when relevant forecasts of S_i are given.

In most sub-groups the volume index is actually based on a slightly more detailed disaggregation to different types of buildings and a few size classes for each type. The volume index and amount of starts are published only for the ten sub-groups. Hence in forecasting it is not possible to use more disaggregated distributed lags. After calculating the weights w_{ij} for all size and type classes within each group, these weights in each group were aggregated using the shares of the sub-classes in completed buildings (in m^3) in 1982–4.

4.1.2 Aggregate lag weights

To forecast the total volume of construction activity, it would be desirable to derive a distributed lag from total starts to total volume. In this way only the forecast of total starts would be needed when total volume is forecast. However, this would ignore variations in the lag patterns between the sub-groups, and it is therefore better to start from a consistent aggregate of the sub-group distributed lags. This gives an idea of the probable size of error caused by ignoring inter-group variation.

Since the group volumes are measured by real value, they can be added to obtain the total volume in quarter t

$$Q_t = \sum_{i=0}^{9} Q_{it} = \sum_{i=0}^{9} \sum_{j=0}^{T_i} w_{ij} S_{i(t-j)} \tag{4.5}$$

As discussed above, after $j > T_i$, we can set the weights w_{ij} equal to zero. Therefore $T = \max(T_i)$ is used as the common lag length for all groups. This allows the total volume to be written as

$$Q_t = \sum_{j=1}^{T} \sum_{i=0}^{9} w_{ij} S_{i(t-j)}$$

$$= 10 \sum_{j=1}^{T} \bar{w}_j \bar{S}_{t-j} + 10 \, \text{cov}_j(w_{ij}, S_{i(t-j)}) \tag{4.6}$$

where $\bar{w}_j = \dfrac{1}{10} \sum_i w_{ij}$, $\bar{S}_{t-j} = \dfrac{1}{10} \sum_i S_{i(t-j)}$ and

$$\text{cov}_j = \frac{1}{10} \sum_j \sum_i (w_{ij} - \bar{w}_j)(S_{i(t-j)} - \bar{S}_{t-j}).$$

Disaggregation in econometric modelling

This kind of decomposition is sometimes used in aggregation theory (see, e.g. van Daal and Merkies, 1984). The first term can be written in the form $\sum_i \bar{w}_j S_{t-j}$, where $S_{t-j} = \sum_i S_{i(t-j)}$ is total starts in period $t - j$. This gives a distributed lag from total starts to total volume, where lag weights are averages of the group lag weights. The second term measures the error caused by omission of between group variations. This term would tend to be large when the greatest number of starts is always in groups where construction costs are highest. There seems to be no reason for this to be always true so that the error from using only the first term may in practice be small.

A second way of decomposing the aggregate volume is

$$Q_t = T \sum_{i=0}^{9} \bar{w}_i \bar{S}_i + T \operatorname{cov}_i(w_{ij}, S_{i(t-j)}) \tag{4.7}$$

where $\bar{w}_i = \dfrac{1}{T} \sum_j w_{ij}$, $\bar{S}_i = \dfrac{1}{T} \sum_j S_{i(t-j)}$ and

$$\operatorname{cov}_i = \frac{1}{T} \sum_i \sum_j (w_{ij} - \bar{w}_i)(S_{i(t-j)} - \bar{S}_i)$$

The first term can be written as $\sum_i w_i \bar{S}_i$, where $w_i = \sum_j w_{ij}$ is the sum of the lag weights. This is an approximate intertemporal aggregate of the distributed lag, whereas above there was an approximate contemporaneous aggregate. The average of past starts in a group is weighted by the total cost per cubic metre of a typical project in that group. The covariance term now measures the impact of intertemporal variations. In practice using the first term of (4.7) as an approximation of the lag is not useful, since starts for all ten groups would still have to be forecasted.

There are several alternative ways of forecasting the aggregate volume. First, the individual group forecasts can be aggregated. If the lag patterns derived above are used as such in forecasting, this yields the same result as when the consistently aggregated lag (4.5) is used. Second, the lag can be approximated by the first term in (4.6). Third, one could try to estimate directly a distributed lag from total starts to total volume without using the weights w.

78

4.1.3 The adequacy of the calculated weights

In principle it would be possible to use the calculated lag weights directly to forecast the volume of construction. The only necessary adjustment in this case would be to scale the forecasts in each group by the average quarterly volume in 1980 in that group. In this way the forecasts would be in index form with 1980 as the base year. The group forecasts could then be aggregated using 1980 volume shares as weights. For various reasons this procedure proved not to be entirely satisfactory.

The fitted volume from a distributed lag deviates from the volume calculated by Finnish Central Statistical Office for various reasons.

First, the actual construction times of different projects deviate from the historical group averages. If projects progress consistently faster than or more slowly than these averages, then the actual lag profile differs from the one used here. Differing total construction times have an impact on the tail of the distributed lag; actual lags may be shorter or longer than the average ones. It would be possible to study the distributed lag from starts to completions to see how the actual lag lengths vary (cf. Borooah, 1979).

Second, the shares of the size classes within a group may vary. For example, shifts towards classes with longer construction times or higher costs would change the actual lag.

Third, the distribution of starts within the quarters may not be uniform. If the actual distribution is concentrated mostly at the beginning (end) of a quarter, the actual lag in quarters is shorter (longer) than the one used here.

Fourth, there may be systematic (seasonal, cyclical, or trendlike) changes in the ratio of the volume and the fit from a distributed lag. Seasonality in the ratio may arise from buildings of different sizes being started systematically at different times of the year, or from confinement of starts to certain months, e.g. because of holidays. Seasonality was found also by van Alphen and Merkies (1976) in a distributed lag model of Dutch housing construction. Cyclical variations can be caused by adjustment of construction times to economic conditions. For example, an increase in industrial output may hasten the construction of industrial buildings so that the total construction time is shorter than average and also the lag profile changes. This kind of effect was found in van Alphen and Merkies (1976) and Borooah (1979) in models of housing construction. Trendlike changes in the ratio may result from technical progress which systematically shortens construction times.

Fifth, there are breaks in the available statistics. It was possible to derive time series of starts and volume for 1975–85. However, breaks in the way the Finnish Central Statistical Office has calculated the basic data may have changed the relationships of the volume series and the fits from the distributed lags.

The above deficiencies in the calculated lag weights show up as an error term in the models. If the error is completely random, it may not matter in forecasting. However, it is likely that in some cases the error is systematically different from zero and autocorrelated, and has therefore to be taken into account in the forecasting models.

In some groups the lag weights were changed. The volume index was regressed on the fitted distributed lag and some additional lagged starts. It turned out that in a few cases the lags should be longer than the average construction times had indicated and that more weight should be given to the tail of the lag. This seems to reflect delays in construction, which show up as a peak at the end of the lag profile. The lag weights were corrected in five of the ten groups, so that the sum of the weights in each group was kept unchanged.

Seasonality in the lags was taken into account by taking 4-quarter differences of the indices and the fitted lags in the final forecasting models. In the cases where a visual inspection showed that the fit/volume ratio had changed when there were breaks in the statistics, the estimation period of the forecasting models was shortened. To take into account other changes in the fit/volume ratio, an error correction term was added into the forecasting models. Finally, the inclusion of business cycle variables was tried, but this did not improve the fit of the models.

4.2 Forecasting models

Denote the final, corrected, lag weights by w_{ij}^*. The corresponding fit of the distributed lag is $Q_{it}^* = \sum_j w_{ij}^* S_{i(t-j)}$. The volume index we want to forecast is $IQ_{it} = 100\ Q_{it}/Q_{i80}$, where Q_{i80} is the average quarterly volume of group i in 1980. The estimated models were in the form

$$\Delta_4\ IQ_{it} = a\Delta_4 Q_{it}^* + b((Q_{i(t-4)}^*/IQ_{i(t-4)}) - Z_t) + u_t \qquad (4.8)$$

where Z_t is the 'target' value of the ratio Q_i^*/IQ_i. It is defined as the ratio of the 8-quarter moving averages of lagged values of Q_i^* and IQ_i, centred at $t - 4$. The Q_i^*/IQ_i-ratio adjusts in this model to past values of the ratio. The correction term helps to smooth seasonality and errors caused by varying construction times etc. It also accounts for trend-like changes in the Q_i^*/IQ_i ratio.

Models of this kind were estimated with OLS for all ten subgroups and for the aggregates total building construction and other-than-housing construction. For the aggregates the model was estimated both using the consistently aggregated distributed lag (4.5) and the approximation that ignores the covariance term in (4.6). (In the case of non-housing, $i = 0$ is not included.)

As a comparison to the models with *a priori* determined lag weights, transfer function models were estimated as well. In these the lag weights are freely determined. These models have the general form

$$A(L)\Delta_4 IQ_{it} = B(L)\Delta_4 S_{it} + C(L)e_t \tag{4.9}$$

where L is a lag operator, $A(L)$, $B(L)$ and $C(L)$ are lag polynomials and e_t is an error term. The orders of the polynomials were identified using cross correlations of the differenced volume indices and starts, and using the corner method (see Liu and Hanssens, 1982). The final models were estimated using the Maximum Likelihood method. Since in most sub-groups the estimated lag patterns were not reasonable, only the transfer function models for total building construction, housing construction, and construction of other buildings were used. Best forecasting results were obtained when these models did not include contemporaneous starts (i.e. lag 0).

In addition, ARIMA models were estimated for all ten subgroups, non-housing construction and total construction. These have the form

$$A(L)\Delta_4 IQ_{it} = C(L)e_t \tag{4.10}$$

so that the forecasts are based only on past values of the volume indices. The models were identified using the autocorrelation, partial autocorrelation, and extended autocorrelation functions of the volume indices (see Liu, Hudak *et al.*, 1983). The identified models were estimated using Maximum Likelihood. In both transfer function and ARIMA models the out-of-sample forecasting performance was also used as a model choice criterion. This helped in rejecting over-parameterized models which had a good

81

fit in the estimation period but did not forecast well.

The transfer function and ARIMA models are used here mainly to compare them with the models with calculated lag weights. However, it is also interesting to study the choice between aggregate and disaggregate forecasting in these models. Theoretically, it can be shown that aggregating disaggregate ARIMA forecasts leads to a smaller mean squared error than forecasting an aggregate time series directly.

It would also be justifiable to forecast the disaggregate models as a vector ARMA system, where the contemporaneous correlation of the errors is taken into account (see Lütkepohl, 1984a). However, in practice, when the parameters and the orders of the lag polynomials are unknown, disaggregation or system estimation do not necessarily improve forecasting performance (see Lütkepohl, 1984b). The identification and estimation of a 10-equation vector ARMA model would also be a difficult task. For these reasons the models have been estimated separately.

In all models the estimation period was 1975.1–1983.4. The actual number of observations in the estimates varied depending on the length of the lags used. The period 1984.1–1985.4 was left for out-of-sample forecasting comparisons. Details on the estimated models are given in Ilmakunnas and Lassila (1988).

4.3 Forecasting comparisons

No attempts were made to discriminate between aggregation and disaggregation in the estimation period, for instance by using tests suggested by Pesaran, Pierse, and Kumar (1986). Instead, the choice of the forecasting model and the level of aggregation is based on the out-of-sample forecasting performance of the models.

Three aggregation levels were compared. Total building construction can be forecasted directly, forecasts for housing and non-housing can be aggregated, or forecasts for all ten sub-groups can be aggregated.

Volume shares in 1980 were used as weights when disaggregated forecasts of volume indices were aggregated. Since in some sub-groups the forecasts were quite poor it might actually be possible to change the weights so that groups with better forecasts had more weight. Some alternatives are studied in Ilmakunnas (1986).

Tables 4.1 and 4.2 present the forecasting results. Four criteria were used in the comparisons, root mean squared error (RMSE), mean error (ME), mean absolute error (MAE), and mean absolute percentage error (MAPE).

Table 4.1 Forecasting results for distributed lag models

	Forecast horizon		
	0	*1*	*2*
Forecast of total construction using consistently aggregated lag			
RMSE	2.88	2.80	7.56
ME	0.36	0.13	−1.49
MAPE	2.38	2.60	6.72
MAE	2.39	2.64	6.73
Forecast of total construction using approximate lag			
RMSE	2.72	2.89	7.13
ME	−0.24	−0.36	−1.25
MAPE	2.31	2.56	6.14
MAE	2.29	2.53	6.26
Aggregation of forecasts for housing and non-housing; consistently aggregated lag for non-housing			
RMSE	2.61	2.68	5.84
ME	−0.26	−0.32	−0.69
MAPE	2.21	2.38	5.42
MAE	2.31	2.42	5.60
Aggregation of forecasts for housing and non-housing; approximate lag for non-housing			
RMSE	2.96	2.95	3.67
ME	0.02	−0.01	−1.21
MAPE	2.45	2.45	3.30
MAE	2.55	2.54	3.29
Aggregation of forecasts for ten sub-groups			
RMSE	3.08	3.10	3.82
ME	−0.41	−0.46	−1.85
MAPE	2.31	2.36	2.86
MAE	2.45	2.47	2.97

Since the models require forecasts of starts as inputs, two types of forecasts were made. In the first type, it is assumed that in the forecast period starts can be perfectly forecasted. This is denoted as forecast horizon 0 in table 4.1. In the second type, it is assumed that a 'no change' forecast of starts is used. In this case in forecast horizon 1, one-period-ahead forecasts are made, forecasting $\Delta_4 S_{i(t+1)}$ to be zero. In forecast horizon 2, two-period-ahead forecasts are made, using forecasts $\Delta_4 S_{i(t+1)} = 0$ and $\Delta_4 S_{i(t+2)} = 0$. Given these naïve forecasts of starts, the forecasting performance of the models rapidly deteriorates when the forecast horizon is lengthened. However, the results for forecast horizon 0 can be

Table 4.2 Forecast results for transfer function and ARIMA models

	Forecast horizon	
	1	*2*
Transfer function models		
Forecast of total construction		
RMSE	2.55	2.61
ME	0.97	−0.21
MAPE	1.80	2.10
MAE	1.92	2.11
Aggregation of forecasts for housing and non-housing		
RMSE	3.08	3.90
ME	0.06	−1.52
MAPE	2.60	2.80
MAE	2.68	2.87
ARIMA models		
Forecast of total construction		
RMSE	3.14	3.64
ME	−0.93	−1.26
MAPE	2.70	3.10
MAE	2.66	3.02
Aggregation of forecasts for housing and non-housing		
RMSE	2.63	3.18
ME	−1.01	−1.26
MAPE	1.90	2.30
MAE	1.94	2.39
Aggregation of forecasts for ten sub-groups		
RMSE	2.74	3.32
ME	−0.98	−1.45
MAPE	2.40	2.90
MAE	2.45	2.90

used as a comparison to see what can be gained from improving the forecasts of starts. In Ilmakunnas and Lassila (1988) some forecasting models for construction starts are estimated, but in general they do not perform very well.

Since the transfer function models do not include current period starts as explanatory variables, results for forecast horizons 0 and 1 are the same. In forecast horizon 2 it was again assumed that $\Delta_4 S_{i(t+1)} = 0$. The ARIMA models are based on only the past volumes so that the starts need not be forecasted.

As may be seen in table 4.1, there is not much difference between the volume forecasts when starts are perfectly forecasted and when the forecast horizon is short. With a forecast horizon of two quarters, aggregation of the forecasts for the two main groups, housing and non-housing construction, and aggregation of all the ten sub-group forecasts give the best results.

When the total volume of construction is directly forecasted, there is not much difference between using the consistently aggregated lag and using an approximate lag structure. This shows that the covariance term in (4.6) is probably small enough so that it can be left out without worsening the forecasting performance of the model. For forecast horizon 2 the approximate lag is slightly better, which probably reflects the effect of having to forecast starts for all the sub-groups when the consistently aggregated lag is used.

When forecasts for housing and non-housing construction are aggregated, there is again not much difference between using the consistent lag structure and using the approximate lag for non-housing construction. However, if the forecast horizon is 2 periods the approximate lag gives smaller forecast errors. Again this reflects poor forecasts of starts.

Table 4.2 gives the forecast results for the transfer function and ARIMA models. The aggregate transfer function models gives slightly better results than the distributed lag models for total construction. Hence free estimation of the weights gives better forecasts than the calculated weights. The lag patterns are clearly different, since the transfer function model that was used in obtaining the results includes only starts lagged one and two periods. When the forecast horizon is 2, the transfer function is clearly better than the other models. This may partly be due to the fact that current period starts are not included in the transfer function models.

Combination of the transfer function forecasts for housing and non-housing gives worse results than using the aggregate transfer function forecasts.

Finally, in the ARIMA models the combination of forecasts for housing and non-housing construction is best and the aggregate ARIMA model worst in terms of forecast errors for both forecast horizons. This gives some support to the theoretical results mentioned above, although the optimal level of disaggregation is in this case between the aggregate and completely disaggregate specifications. The forecast performance of the ARIMA models is in general fairly similar to that of the transfer function and distributed lag models.

Conclusion

Alternative forecasting models for construction activity in Finland have been formulated and compared at different levels of aggregation. The optimal level of aggregation varies from one model to another. For distributed lag models in which the weights are based on *a priori* information about the way the volume index of construction is calculated, disaggregate forecasting is preferable only for a long forecast horizon. In transfer function models the aggregate model has the best forecast performance. In ARIMA models aggregation of disaggregate forecasts is slightly preferable to aggregate forecasting.

In all, the results show that, when the goal is to forecast the aggregate volume of construction, good results may be obtained with fairly simple, even ARIMA, models, and there is not much loss in using aggregate models for forecasting. When the goal is to obtain forecasts for the individual sub-groups of construction, the models with calculated lag weights improved forecasting performance, in some cases considerably, compared to ARIMA forecasts. Detailed results are presented in Ilmakunnas and Lassila (1988).

However, combining good sub-group forecasts does not necessarily give good forecasts of total construction, since the sub-group forecast errors may not cancel each other out in the average. Also, the aggregate series has relatively less quarter-to-quarter variation and its changes are therefore more predictable than the disaggregate series. The performance of the combination of disaggregate forecasts may be improved by taking into account the correlations between the error terms of the groups. The good results obtained by combining forecasts of the two main groups, housing and non-housing, may also reflect the fact that when one sub-group (housing) is large compared to the other groups and therefore dominates the movements of the aggregate, there is little gain from further disaggregation of the residual group.

Chapter five

Aggregation problems in a model of wage formation and employment demand

Edwin Deutsch and Kurt Rodler

Introduction

The contribution of this paper is to discuss the problems introduced by the aggregation of labour in a model of wage formation and employment demand. For this purpose, a simultaneous equation system is estimated and tested on data for Austrian industry. The model is designed to capture bargaining procedures and market forces in the institutional setting of Austrian incomes policies. Since effects of incomes policies usually differ between various labour types, the choice of appropriate levels of labour aggregates is critical. In this respect, two mutually related problems of aggregation are considered:

(i) The analyst faces the problem of information losses when aggregated observations and models are used instead of disaggregated ones. This is the well-known question of whether aggregation is necessarily bad. It is dealt with in statistical aggregation approaches, for instance on the lines of Grunfeld and Griliches (1960) and Zellner (1962). In the following, Zellner's test for the existence of aggregates based on the micro-homogeneity property will prove to be useful.

(ii) In the course of political decision-making, the problem arises of how to manage economic performance in various segments of society when the number of signals and decision instruments is limited. The incomes policies which are dealt with here provide a typical example. To some extent, this problem is related to the axiomatic approach of aggregation of preferences, technologies, and derived demand systems along the lines of Gorman (1968). However, bargaining procedures add specific features which are beyond the scope of received aggregation theory.

As will be made clear below, both points of view lead to the same inverse problem of aggregation: How accurately may disaggregated phenomena be predicted by aggregated data? And, if full aggregation has to be rejected, is there an intermediate stage of aggregation which permits parsimonious model building?

By means of observations drawn from Austrian industry, it is shown that information losses in the aggregation of wages are considerably lower than those occurring in the aggregation of employment. This result is obtained by applying statistical methods in the context of problem (i) above. In the context of problem (ii), this result suggests (provided of course that the model is a true picture of reality) that Austrian incomes policies exert more control on wage developments than on employment. Patterns of employment differ greatly between various types of labour.

The likely existence of wage aggregates and the non-existence of employment aggregates is derived from a test for micro homogeneity in a system of equations. The test implies equality restrictions for coefficients belonging to same regressors in the disaggregated model. As shown in detail below, this amounts to testing for perfect aggregates conditional upon a set of exogenous regressors, for which we suggest the term *conditional perfect aggregation*.

However, the positive test result obtained for wages has to be considered with caution. Aggregated observations on wages are Divisia-indices calculated from disaggregated data on wages and employment. If the true parameter values in related disaggregated equations differ only slightly, the hypothesis on wage aggregates is accepted at seemingly sufficient levels of significance, although estimates in aggregated wage equations may be biased.

One conclusion of this paper is that the full aggregation of labour entails considerable losses of information. This fact deserves attention. Often, econometric model builders deal with aggregation problems in the context of sectoral classifications of markets and technologies, while leaving aside the problem of the disaggregation of labour. It is our purpose to show that, whenever available, employment data should at least be classified according to levels of qualification.

The plan of the paper is as follows. Section 5.1 describes the specific model of wage formation and employment demand in Austrian industry, together with a full account of labour types and aggregates. Section 5.2 presents unrestricted estimates in disaggregated, partial and fully aggregated models. Section 5.3 deals with the tests for conditional perfect aggregation derived from restricted estimates. Section 5.4 draws some conclusions on optimal aggregation levels. For convenience, estimation procedures, tests, and related formal problems are discussed in appendix 5A. The list of variables, some data, and additional estimates are to be found in appendix 5B.

5.1 The model

The model outlined here is designed for the analysis of real wage formation and employment demand in the Austrian economy. This gives a specific flavour to the analysis, although essential features of the model easily apply to other economies as well.

Austrian incomes policy is the outcome of autonomous bargaining procedures between representatives of firms and trade unions. Its principle feature is to provide an informal platform for wage negotiations and price controls. Its objective is to stabilize wages, prices, and employment. In this respect, it does not depend on the operation of public authorities, although it is supported by fiscal and monetary policies (see Arndt, 1982).

The following model is an attempt to capture some features of the process of wage negotiation and its effects on various types of labour. The object of study is Austrian manufacturing industry in the years from 1966 to 1984. During this period, Austrian industry faced important challenges, among them a tendency towards increased foreign trade, structural changes brought about by technological innovations and growing uncertainty within markets, and a steady decline of less-qualified employment. Until about 1980, Austrian incomes policies were successful in preventing unemployment and in stabilizing wages. Despite many conflicts, there was consensus in maintaining purchasing power and full employment. Since then, however, international competition and budgetary deficits have put increasing pressure on the working of the negotiation system, and the distribution of incomes has widened. Real average wages became stagnant, and unemployment rose. But, various regional and sectoral problems notwithstanding, it can be stated that the more flexible and qualified a worker, the better his/her job opportunities and prospects of higher wages in Austrian industry. This and other reasons stimulated the investigation of labour types in a disaggregated scheme.

Given this background, the following model should be self-explanatory. It consists of three parts:

 (i) determination of nominal wage floors in centralized collective wage negotiations (referred to as collective wages),
 (ii) decentralized formation of real wages in firms,
(iii) realization of employment demand in firms.

The model reflects the dynamics of subsequent centralized and decentralized decision making (in fact, the dynamics result from specification tests which are not given here). The formal sub-models (i) to (iii) are outlined here, while empirical results follow in the next section and details on estimation are discussed in appendix 5A. A list of variables is given in appendix table 5B.1. In appendix table 5B.5, additional regressors capturing labour supply conditions are found. These regressors are left aside now. The discussion focuses on the variables relevant to aggregation procedures.

The endogenous variables collective wages C, real (effective) wages Y and employment X are indexed by $i = 1, \ldots, m$. This means that m labour types with corresponding equations are considered.

All variables are one-period growth rates (except for unemployment rates) and refer to the period of observation 1966–84. The time index t is omitted for convenience.

Collective wages C

$$C_i = a_{i1} P_{-1} + a_{i2} Q_{-1} + a_{i3} U_{-1} \qquad (5.1)$$

Negotiations on nominal wages are influenced by signals on the inflation rate P, on real full-capacity industrial output Q and on (first differences of) the overall unemployment rate U. All signals are lagged for one period; this reflects some dynamics of the process of wage formation. Some expectational patterns are included by full-capacity output signals which smooth out short-run variations in capacity utilization. The latter are substituted by the rate of unemployment. Although trade unions aim at achieving real wage increases, the negotiated outcome is formulated in nominal terms. This is the reason for taking nominal values C.

Real effective wages Y

$$Y_i = \beta_{i1} C_i + \beta_{i2} P + \beta_{i3} Q + \beta_{i4} EX + \beta_{i5} CU \qquad (5.2)$$

Nominal collective wages form a wage floor. Payments of wages above this floor are customary, but they vary and usually increase with qualification. Equation (5.2) accounts for possible over payments in decentralized decisions of firms. In (5.2), nominal values C are deflated by the inflation rate P in order to get real figures. The amount of deflation is assumed to be a behavioural, price-setting phenomenon. Additional signals in (5.2) are real full-capacity output Q, the export share EX in industrial GDP, and the rate of capacity utilization CU.

Employment X

$$X_i = \gamma_{i0} Y_i + \gamma_{i1} + \gamma_{i2} Q + \gamma_{i3} EX + \gamma_{i4} CU \qquad (5.3)$$

Employment decisions taken by firms are assumed to depend on real wages Y, real full-capacity output Q, the export quota EX and the rate of capacity utilization CU. The constant γ_1 reflects some unexplained long-term rates of labour saving due to innovations. Only own-wage effects induced by Y_i are considered: in (5.3), demand for labour type i does not depend on the real wages of other types. For further discussion of this topic see the next section and appendix 5A.

The essential feature of the model is the characterization of labour types. In Austria (and also in Germany) the labour force is institutionally classified into workers (*Arbeiter*), employees (*Angestellte*) and civil servants (*Beamte*). Civil servants are not employed in industry and are excluded from consideration. Workers and employees roughly correspond to blue-collar and white-collar work.

The distinction between workers and employees is expressed in laws and customs. Under existing laws, employees still enjoy various advantages over workers. These advantages refer to terms of payment (monthly in advance instead of weekly afterwards), quality of social security, promotion according to agency, and severance payments in case of dismissal. Trade unions consider these advantages to be discriminatory. In recent times they have succeeded in narrowing several of the gaps in working conditions between workers and employees.

Workers and employees are represented by different trade unions. The trade unions bargain on collective wages separately, and the outcome of wage negotiations is settled in separate wage contracts. Nevertheless, the trade unions are tied to a trade union board whose strategy is to claim equal pay for equal work and to synchronize real wage developments in the economy.

For our study we used additional information about qualification levels. Thus at the disaggregated level, four types of labour are considered: low-skill workers H, high-skill workers F, low-rank employees D, and high-rank employees E (see figure 5.1).

At an intermediate stage, partial aggregates can be formed. Two possibilities are considered:

Disaggregation in econometric modelling

1 Aggregation of (*HF*) to workers *W*, and of (*DE*) to employees *A*, yielding the aggregates (*WA*). This aggregation method conforms to the institutionalized classification into workers and employees.

2 Aggregation of (*HD*) to less-qualified labour *L*, and of (*FE*) to qualified labour *Q*, yielding the aggregates (*LQ*) (the symbol *Q* should not be confused with output; see the note to Figure 5.1). This aggregation method refers to the level of qualification and to prevailing labour supply and demand patterns.

At the stage of full aggregation, (*HFDE*), (*WA*), and (*LQ*) are aggregated to total labour *B*.

Observations on collective wages appear as intermediate aggregates *CW* and *CA*, or as the full aggregate *CB*, because collective wage contracts do not distinguish between levels of qualification.

This aggregation scheme will be investigated further below.

Figure 5.1 Labour types and aggregation scheme (with German equivalents)

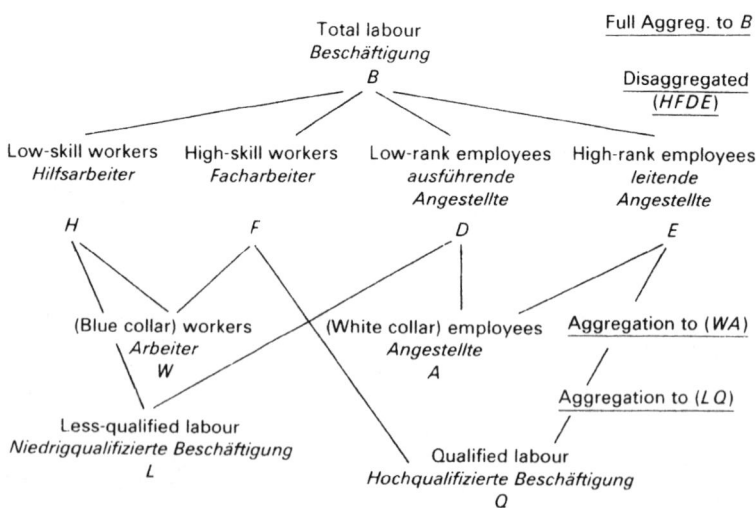

Note: In the definition of variables, symbols defined above will be preceded by:
   C for nominal collective wage floors, i.e., *CB*, *CW*, *CA*;
   Y for real effective hourly wages, i.e., *YB*, *YH*, etc.;
   X for employment, i.e., *XB*, *XH*, etc.

5.2 Empirical results for Austrian industry, 1966–84

This section presents unrestricted (IV) – estimates of the model
(5.1)–(5.3), first for the disaggregated model $(HFDE)$, then for
partial aggregates (WA) and (LQ), and finally for the full aggregate (B). Insignificant coefficients are dropped from the estimation. Note that the set of instruments consists of the whole set
of exogenous regressors and is identical in **all** the models considered below. Minor differences in estimated coefficients which
appear in equations of the same endogenous variable are due to

Table 5.1 Disaggregated model $(HFDE)$, 1966–84 (IV-estimates)

Nominal collective wages

$$CW = \underset{(0.08)}{1.16*P_{-1}} + \underset{(0.07)}{0.34*Q_{-1}} - \underset{(0.65)}{1.32*U_{-1}}$$
$$s = 1.12 \qquad (5.1.1)$$

$$CA = \underset{(0.07)}{1.18*P_{-1}} + \underset{(0.07)}{0.30*Q_{-1}} - \underset{(0.64)}{1.31*U_{-1}}$$
$$s = 1.27 \qquad (5.1.2)$$

Real effective wages

$$YH = \underset{(0.07)}{0.66*CW} - \underset{(0.11)}{0.68*P} + \underset{(0.05)}{0.16*Q} + \underset{(0.04)}{0.16*EX} - \underset{(0.08)}{0.17*CU}$$
$$s = 1.40 \qquad (5.1.3)$$

$$YF = \underset{(0.07)}{0.62*CW} - \underset{(0.11)}{0.70*P} + \underset{(0.05)}{0.19*Q} + \underset{(0.04)}{0.22*EX} - \underset{(0.09)}{0.21*CU}$$
$$s = 1.27 \qquad (5.1.4)$$

$$YD = \underset{(0.13)}{0.88*CA} - \underset{(0.19)}{0.82*P} + \underset{(0.06)}{0.09*EX} - \underset{(0.11)}{0.18*CU}$$
$$s = 1.47 \qquad (5.1.5)$$

$$YE = \underset{(0.10)}{0.92*CA} - \underset{(0.16)}{0.89*P} + \underset{(0.05)}{0.08*EX} - \underset{(0.10)}{0.19*CU}$$
$$s = 1.46 \qquad (5.1.6)$$

Employment

$$XH = -\underset{(0.40)}{2.03} - \underset{(0.12)}{0.68*YH} + \underset{(0.08)}{0.78*Q} - \underset{(0.05)}{0.16*EX} + \underset{(0.12)}{0.87*CU}$$
$$s = 1.38 \qquad (5.1.7)$$

$$XF = \underset{(0.04)}{0.09*EX_{-1}} + \underset{(0.11)}{0.43*CU}$$
$$s = 1.19 \qquad (5.1.8)$$

$$XD = -\underset{(0.50)}{2.67} + \underset{(0.07)}{0.66*Q} + \underset{(0.07)}{0.18*EX}$$
$$s = 1.62 \qquad (5.1.9)$$

$$XE = \underset{(0.06)}{0.72*Q} + \underset{(0.13)}{0.35*CU}$$
$$s = 1.55 \qquad (5.1.10)$$

Notes: s: Root mean square prediction error in %.
Standard errors of parameter estimates in parentheses.

Table 5.2 Reduced form in model (*HFDE*), stationary exogenous
variables (calculated for $P = P_{-1}$, $Q = Q_{-1}$, $EX = EX_{-1}$)

Real effective wages

$$YH \ = \quad 0.09*P \qquad + 0.38*Q \quad + 0.16*EX \ - 0.16*CU \ - 0.87*U \tag{5.2.1}$$

$$YF \ = \quad 0.03*P \qquad + 0.40*Q \quad + 0.22*EX \ - 0.21*CU \ - 0.82*U \tag{5.2.2}$$

$$YD \ = \quad 0.20*P \qquad + 0.27*Q \quad + 0.09*EX \ - 0.18*CU \ - 1.15*U \tag{5.2.3}$$

$$YE \ = \quad 0.18*P \qquad + 0.28*Q \quad + 0.18*EX \ - 0.19*CU \ - 1.20*U \tag{5.2.4}$$

Employment

$$XH \ = \ - 2.03 \ - 0.05*P + 0.52*Q \qquad - 0.27*EX \ + 0.98*CU \ + 0.59*U \tag{5.2.5}$$

$$XF \ = \qquad\qquad\qquad\qquad\qquad\quad + 0.09*EX \ + 0.43*CU \tag{5.2.6}$$

$$XD \ = \ - 2.67 \qquad\quad + 0.66*Q \quad + 0.18*EX \tag{5.2.7}$$

$$XE \ = \qquad\qquad\qquad + 0.72*Q \qquad\qquad\quad + 0.35*CU \tag{5.2.8}$$

Note: All coefficients in reduced form significant at 5% level of significance.

the use of one-step iterated instrumental estimation, i.e. they result from different covariance structures (compare, for instance, equations (5.1.1) and (5.3.1)).

We first examine the basic model (*HFDE*). The estimates are given in table 5.1. Consider first some economic aspects. Collective wages *C* in (5.1.1) and (5.1.2) are well explained by lagged regressors. The negative elasticity with respect to the rate of un-employment indicates that trade unions reduce their wage claims when unemployment rises.

Equations (5.1.3) to (5.1.6) show that real collective wages exert a strong influence on real effective wages, but that they are not fully transmitted; the elasticities are below one. The residual explanatory power is split between full-capacity output *Q*, export share *EX* and capacity utilization *CU*. The elasticities with respect to *CU* are negative. This seemingly paradoxical result is brought about by hiring additional and therefore cheaper labour in times of business peaks. To some extent, this effect is offset by positive elasticities with respect to *EX*. These estimates can be interpreted in the sense of wage incentives which stimulate workers' efficiency in increasingly export-oriented industries.

The estimates for employment (5.1.7) to (5.1.10) differ much more among labour types than those in preceding equations. A strong labour-saving tendency is to be noted for less-qualified

Table 5.3 Partial aggregation model (*WA*), 1966–84 (IV-estimates)

Nominal collective wages

$$CW = \underset{(0.08)}{1.15 * P_{-1}} + \underset{(0.07)}{0.34 * Q_{-1}} - \underset{(0.66)}{1.39 * U_{-1}}$$

$$s = 1.13 \qquad (5.3.1)$$

$$CA = \underset{(0.09)}{1.17 * P_{-1}} + \underset{(0.08)}{0.29 * Q_{-1}} - \underset{(0.75)}{1.34 * U_{-1}}$$

$$s = 1.26 \qquad (5.3.2)$$

Real effective wages

$$YW = \underset{(0.08)}{0.79 * CW} - \underset{(0.12)}{0.83 * P} + \underset{(0.05)}{0.11 * Q} + \underset{(0.04)}{0.14 * EX} - \underset{(0.07)}{0.11 * CU}$$

$$\bar{s} = 1.34 \qquad (5.3.3)$$

$$YA = \underset{(0.12)}{0.99 * CA} - \underset{(0.18)}{0.92 * P}$$

$$\bar{s} = 1.44 \qquad (5.3.4)$$

Employment

$$XW = \underset{(0.37)}{-1.55} - \underset{(0.11)}{0.56 * YW} + \underset{(0.07)}{0.58 * Q} + \underset{(0.10)}{0.70 * CU}$$

$$\bar{s} = 1.12 \qquad (5.3.5)$$

$$XA = \underset{(0.41)}{-0.94} + \underset{(0.07)}{0.66 * Q} + \underset{(0.11)}{0.20 * CU}$$

$$\bar{s} = 1.34 \qquad (5.3.6)$$

Notes: s: Root mean square prediction error (disaggregated), in %.
$\bar{s}$: Root mean square prediction error (intermediate aggregation), in %.
The symbols $\bar{s}$ must be replaced by s when values are compared with table 5.5.
Standard errors of parameter estimates in parentheses.

labour types H and D: the autonomous rate of yearly decline is more than 2 per cent. A structural effect is possibly captured for low-skill workers: the negative elasticity w.r.t. *EX* indicates an average decline of low-skill employment when export shares increase. Employment for high-skill workers F depends mostly on capacity utilization, but also on labour supply conditions (see table 5B.5). Finally, consider the interpretation in the sense of neo-classical production models. Except for high-skill workers, output elasticities are significant, possibly indicating increasing returns to labour. Own-wage effects are significant only in the case of low-skill workers. This does not mean that labour costs are irrelevant for other types. It means that changes in real wages are immediately triggered to demand only in the case of low-skill workers. Here it has to be noted that the employment quota of low-skill workers started at 55 per cent in 1966 and declined to 45 per cent in 1984. Thus the wage bill paid to low-skill workers was nevertheless considerable. As far as other labour types are concerned, unit labour costs or other measures do of course affect their employment

Table 5.4 Partial aggregation model (LQ), 1966-84 (IV-estimates)

Nominal collective wages

$$CB = \underset{(0.08)}{1.19*P_{-1}} + \underset{(0.08)}{0.29*Q_{-1}} - \underset{(0.68)}{1.46*U_{-1}}$$

$$\bar{s} = 1.09 \qquad (5.4.1)$$

Real effective wages

$$YL = \underset{(0.12)}{0.68*CB} \underset{(0.17)}{-0.72*P} + \underset{(0.07)}{0.10*Q} + \underset{(0.05)}{0.15*EX} - \underset{(0.10)}{0.15*CU}$$

$$\bar{s} = 1.50 \qquad (5.4.2)$$

$$YQ = \underset{(0.11)}{0.68*CB} - \underset{(0.16)}{0.71*P} + \underset{(0.07)}{0.14*Q} + \underset{(0.05)}{0.17*EX} - \underset{(0.10)}{0.19*CU}$$

$$\bar{s} = 1.42 \qquad (5.4.3)$$

Employment

$$XL = - \underset{(0.41)}{1.69} \underset{(0.15)}{-0.93*YL} + \underset{(0.08)}{0.74*Q} + \underset{(0.12)}{0.53*CU}$$

$$\bar{s} = 1.26 \qquad (5.4.4)$$

$$XQ = \qquad + \underset{(0.04)}{0.28*Q} + \underset{(0.10)}{0.45*CU}$$

$$\bar{s} = 1.00 \qquad (5.4.5)$$

Notes: s: Root mean square prediction error (disaggregated), in %.
$\bar{s}$: Root mean square prediction error (intermediate aggregation), in %.
The symbols $\bar{s}$ must be replaced by s when values are compared with table 5.5.
Standard errors of parameter estimates in parentheses.

levels, but rather in the longer term or indirectly via development of output or exports. If output rises, firms may simply afford higher wage bills for qualified labour, as the example of type E in (5.1.10) may indicate (see also Deutsch, 1988 for further discussion).

Additional interesting results can be seen from the reduced form in table 5.2, the coefficients of which are calculated for constant exogenous variables. There is practically no money illusion in the case of workers; the elasticities w.r.t. P are almost zero. The corresponding elasticities for employees are low. This means that trade unions do not push for higher wages, but are concerned with maintaining or improving real purchasing power. This conforms to their publicly stated goals. To be noted also is the positive elasticity w.r.t. U in (5.2.5). This means that, if the rate of unemployment rises, the wage claims of trade unions are tuned to stabilize employment. In fact, this conforms to a tendency towards an increasingly restrictive wage policy which has been pursued by trade unions over the last decade. The major reason for this restrictive policy was the overall decline in the growth rate of output demand. But even with declining real wages after 1980,

Table 5.5 Fully aggregated model (*B*), 1966–84 (IV-estimates)

Nominal collective wages

$$CB = \begin{array}{ccc} 1.24*P_{-1} & + 0.26*Q_{-1} & - 1.65*U_{-1} \\ (0.09) & (0.08) & (0.70) \end{array}$$

$$\hat{s} = 1.08 \qquad (5.5.1)$$

Real effective wages

$$YB = \begin{array}{cccc} 0.82*CB & - 0.79*P & + 0.16*EX & - 0.19*CU \\ (0.11) & (0.18) & (0.05) & (0.10) \end{array}$$

$$\bar{s} = 1.54 \qquad (5.5.2)$$

Employment

$$XB = \begin{array}{cccc} - 1.43 & - 0.49*YB & + 0.59*Q & + 0.57*CU \\ (0.35) & (0.12) & (0.06) & (0.10) \end{array}$$

$$\bar{s} = 0.89 \qquad (5.5.3)$$

Notes: $\bar{s}$: Root mean square prediction error (full aggregates), in %.
Standard errors of parameter estimates in parentheses.

trade unions and therefore income policies were unable to stabilize employment by means of wage formation. The estimates presented here provide a partial explanation for this loss of control. Output demand proves to be the main source for employment demand.

The statistical properties of the equations

The estimated coefficients in table 5.1 are significant. (*IV*)-estimates without iteration yield R squares between 0.85 and 0.95. The root mean square prediction errors s range between 1.2 and 1.6. Compare this with the data shown in table 5B.2. It has to be noted that up to 50 per cent of the values s are generated by prediction errors in 1972 and 1973, a period of inflation and economic turmoil. Thus the root mean squares appear satisfactory.

The statistical properties of the aggregated models are now considered. Estimates for models (*WA*), (*LQ*), and (*B*) are given in tables 5.3, 5.4, and 5.5. At first glance, the statistical properties of these models are also satisfactory: all coefficients are significant, root mean square errors s, $\bar{s}$ are in the same range as before or even lower. But various aspects call for caution.

The first aspect is related to the inverse problem of aggregation: how well do aggregated predictors approximate disaggregated data? In order to answer this question, corresponding root mean square errors are derived in (5A.13) (see appendix 5A and table 5B.4). For real wages, the values of $\bar{s}$ are still in the same range as before. But for employment, several values are considerably higher, and especially so in the case of the fully aggregated model

(*B*). In that case, $\bar{s}$ ranges between 1.95 (for low-skill workers) and 4.17 (for high-rank employees). Thus employment patterns are fairly divergent and will not be captured by fully aggregated models.

This corresponds to the twofold aspect of the aggregation problem mentioned at the beginning. Collective wage negotiation policies exert some control over wage patterns, but are themselves limited in the extent to which they stabilize employment. Successful stabilization has to be based on other instruments as well.

These other aspects are related to the problem of the existence of (partial) aggregates, and are dealt with in the next section.

5.3 Tests for the existence of aggregates

The micro-homogeneity property requires equality of coefficients in equations which are selected for testing the existence of aggregates. This necessitates the same set of regressors within a group of equations selected for the test. This is done here by obeying the following rule: if a regressor yields significant estimates in at least one equation within the group, it is included in all equations within the group.

The results of the test procedure are shown in table 5.6. All the disaggregated and partially aggregated models of section 5.1 are tested. The test statistic evaluated here is the Wald statistic, labelled ψ. It is asymptotically $\chi^2(m)$ distributed, with m degrees of freedom. The number of degrees of freedom corresponds to the minimal number of restrictions necessary for testing the null.

If the null is not rejected, the corresponding endogenous aggregates are said to exist in the sense of conditional perfect aggregation: for any given but fixed set of exogenous values z_t, no information losses on conditional expectations of endogenous variables are entailed if aggregates are predicted by means of the corresponding aggregated (sub-) system (for details see appendix 5A).

The test statistics yield positive results for almost all collective and real wages. The existence of aggregates CB (collective wages) and YW, YA (real effective wages for workers and employees) is significant at the 5 per cent level. However, the existence of employment aggregates must be rejected throughout. Therefore one has also to reject the hypothesis that all restrictions hold true simultaneously (see the first and the last columns in table 5.6).

Consider now the case of aggregated real wages, for instance in model (*WA*), workers and employees, table 5.3. There the elasticities w.r.t. collective wages CW and CA are 0.79 and 0.99

Table 5.6 Wald test statistics ψ for conditional perfect aggregation

Aggregation scheme	Hypothesis H_0 $\alpha_{W_i} = \alpha_{A_i}$* $\beta_{ij} = \beta_{kj}$ $\gamma_{ij} = \gamma_{kj}$ (all restr.)	Hypothesis H_0 $\alpha_{W_i} = \alpha_{A_i}$ (restr. w.r.t. nom. coll. wages)	Hypothesis H_0 $\beta_{ij} = \beta_{kj}$ (restr. w.r.t. real eff. wages)	Hypothesis H_0 $\gamma_{ij} = \gamma_{kj}$ (restr. w.r.t. employment)
$(HFDE) \rightarrow$ $\rightarrow (WA)$ $(i,k \in \{H,F\})$ $\vee (i,k \in \{D,E\})$	$\psi(17) = 142.3$		$\psi(9) = 3.3$	$\psi(8) = 133.8$
$(HFDE) \rightarrow$ $\rightarrow (LQ)$ $(i,k \in \{H,A\})$ $\vee (i, k \in \{F, E\})$	$\psi(21) = 405.2$	$\psi(3) = 2.1$	$\psi(10) = 25.6$	$\psi(8) = 272.3$
$(HFDE) \rightarrow (B)$ $i,k \in \{H,F,D,E\}$	$\psi(33) = 653.4$	$\psi(3) = 2.1$	$\psi(15) = 14.9$	$\psi(15) = 370.7$
$(WA) \rightarrow (B)$ $i,k \in \{W,A\}$	$\psi(12) = 198.9$	$\psi(3) = 2.3$	$\psi(5) = 7.3$	$\psi(4) = 151.1$
$(LQ) \rightarrow (B)$ $i,k \in \{L,Q\}$	$\psi(9) = 109.7$		$\psi(5) = 10.0$	$\psi(4) = 80.7$

degr. of freedom	3	4	5	8	9	10	12	15	17	21	33
5% lev.	7.8	9.5	11.1	15.5	16.9	18.3	21.0	25.0	27.6	32.7	47.4
1% lev.	11.4	13.3	15.1	20.1	21.7	23.2	26.2	30.6	33.4	38.9	54.8

Notes: *Restriction dropped in $(WFDE) \rightarrow (WA)$ and $(LQ) \rightarrow (B)$.
Degrees of freedom of Wald statistic ψ in parentheses: For m restrictions,
$\psi(m) \sim \chi_m^2$.

respectively. Now, both estimates are higher than the corresponding estimates in the disaggregated model $(HFDE)$: for low-skill and high-skill workers in equations (5.1.3) and (5.1.4), one obtains the estimates 0.66 and 0.62 (<0.79); for low-rank and high-rank employees in equations (5.1.5) and (5.1.6), one obtains the estimates 0.88 and 0.92 (<0.99). Thus the estimates obtained from the aggregated model (WA) are biased relative to the disaggregated estimates. The reason suggested here is that the true parameter values in the disaggregated model $(HFDE)$ differ only slightly, so that the null of equality may be accepted (compare

$\psi(9) = 3.3$ in table 5.6). Nevertheless, the differences entail some specification bias in the aggregated equations (5.3.3) and (5.3.4). The details of this argument are worked out in appendix 5A.

Thus, assuming a true structure in the disaggregated model, partially or fully aggregated models may be sensitive to specification errors even if aggregates are assumed to exist in the sense of the micro-homogeneity property.

It remains to ask which aggregation strategy should be chosen if various reasons suggest parsimonious model building? Is there some optimal intermediate level of aggregation?

In fact, there is no simple answer to the problem: the strategy depends on the scope of the investigation. This can be demonstrated by means of the models considered here.

The appendix 5A derives the root mean square error $\tilde{s}$ for the case of forward aggregation (see formula (5A.15)). It is a measure of goodness of fit: how well do weighted sums of disaggregated predictors approximate aggregated data? (In the case of growth rates considered here, weighted sums are needed for aggregating the predictors.) Along the lines of the Grunfeld-Griliches approach, comparison of $\tilde{s}$ with the root mean square error $\bar{s}$ obtained for the aggregated model yields a tentative selection criterion: choose the disaggregated model if $\tilde{s}$ is lower than $\bar{s}$ (see also (5A.16)).

Now, consider the crucial case of employment. The $\tilde{s}$ values for model ($HFDE$) are given in table 5B.3: for workers XW, it is 0.93; for employees XA, 1.32; for less-qualified labour XL, 1.26; for qualified labour XQ, 1.02.

These values of $\tilde{s}$ are to be compared with the corresponding $\bar{s}$ values given in tables 5.3 and 5.4. These are 1.12 and 1.34 (see (5.3.5) and (5.3.6)) in model (WA); and in model (LQ), they are 1.26 and 1.00 (see (5.4.4) and (5.4.5)).

If economic reasoning calls for choice of (WA)-aggregates, i.e. for classification according to workers and employees, a comparison of $\tilde{s}$ and $\bar{s}$ suggests one should stay at the disaggregated level ($HFDE$). If it calls for choice of (LQ)-aggregates, i.e. for classification according to levels of qualification, the aggregated model (LQ) might be chosen.

Nevertheless, the case of full aggregation deserves attention: for employment, the value $\bar{s} = 0.89$ according to table 5.5 is lower than all corresponding values of $\tilde{s}$ in table 5B.3, column XB. There is no similar result for wages: the value $\bar{s} = 1.54$ is not lower than the corresponding values of $\tilde{s}$ in table 5B.3, column YB. Acceptance or rejection of the micro-homogeneity hypothesis finds no clear-cut analogue in the measures of goodness-of-fit.

5.4 Conclusions

The results presented in this article show the intricate connection between the statistical and the economic features of the aggregation problem. It is demonstrated that the search for definite statistical criteria might fail in particular cases: the answer to the question of how to choose an optimal level of aggregation depends on the economic point of view as well as the statistical one.

Nevertheless, statistical criteria are essential and have to be evaluated with care. By means of an econometric system based on observations in growth rates it has been shown that several criteria have to be investigated. For instance, acceptance of the micro-homogeneity property does not necessarily prevent specification biases; the problem of information losses has to be investigated from different angles, if some 'best' aggregation strategy is to be chosen for the problem at hand. For that purpose, we suggested a test for 'conditional perfect aggregation', and compared the test results with a simple root mean square measure along the lines of Grunfeld–Griliches.

Although empirical data were available over a rather short period of observation only, it seems worth while drawing attention to the following result: the test for conditional perfect aggregates accepted the existence of wage aggregates, but rejected the existence of employment aggregates. However, the root mean square criterion did not yield the same ranking of aggregation alternatives and it is unclear whether the measure of goodness-of-fit used here is appropriate in the case of Divisia-aggregation of growth rates. Several unresolved problems in this respect are mentioned in appendix 5A.

Appendix 5A Estimation procedures and tests

The discussion of methods is confined to real wage and employment equations. Collective wage formation is left aside.

Consider an industry with m labour types. Let these types be indexed with $i \in M$, $M = \{1, \ldots, m\}$. Denote their real wage levels by Y_{it}, their employment levels by X_{it}, where t denotes time, $t = 0, \ldots, T$. Observations on stochastic one-period growth rates y_{it} and x_{it} are obtained from

$$y_{it} \equiv \frac{Y_{it} - Y_{i(t-1)}}{Y_{i(t-1)}}, \qquad x_{it} \equiv \frac{X_{it} - X_{i(t-1)}}{X_{i(t-1)}}, \qquad t = 1, \ldots, T \tag{5A.1}$$

Disaggregation in econometric modelling

Let z_{jt}, $j = 1, \ldots, K$ be the set of non-stochastic exogenous variables. For the period of observation $t = 1, \ldots, T$, the model maintains linear relations of the following form

$$y_{it} = \sum_{j=1}^{K} \beta_{ij} z_{jt} + u_{yit}, \quad i = 1, \ldots, m \qquad (5A.2)$$

$$x_{it} = \gamma_{i0} y_{it} + \sum_{j=1}^{K} \gamma_{ij} z_{jt} + u_{xit}, \quad i = 1, \ldots, m \qquad (5A.3)$$

The coefficients β and γ are elasticities. Some of them may be restricted to zero.

The coefficients γ_{i0} are own-wage elasticities for labour type i. Cross-wage elasticities do not appear. Under the assumption of profit maximization or cost minimization, this implies a locally additive separable technology.

The model (5A.2), (5A.3) is recursive in the sense that there is no simultaneous feedback from employment to wages. This does not restrict the scope of discussion. The following reasonings are extended to models with simultaneous feedbacks.

Random effects at time t are captured by m-dimensional vectors $u_{y \cdot t}$ and $u_{x \cdot t}$. Define the $2m$-dimensional random variable u_t by

$$u_{\cdot t} \equiv (u'_{y \cdot t}, u'_{x \cdot t})', \quad t = 1, \ldots, T \qquad (5A.4)$$

Let the random variable u_t be i.i.d. with

$$\mathrm{E}[u_t] = 0, \quad \mathrm{E}[u_t u'_t] = \Sigma, \quad \mathrm{E}[u_t u'_\tau] = 0 \quad \forall \, t \neq \tau \quad (5A.5)$$

where Σ denotes a positive definite $2m \times 2m$ variance–covariance matrix. Let second-order moments of regressors converge asymptotically to a finite and positive definite matrix.

By means of these assumptions, the model (5A.2), (5A.3) can be estimated consistently with (IV): instrumental variables. The estimates presented below are evaluated with (IV) in one iteration, thereby exhausting information on Σ by calculating covariances of residuals from the first step of instrumental estimation. The instrumental approach chosen here uses the full set of exogenous variables z in all models. Hence (IV)-estimation in the system (5A.2), (5A.3) is numerically equivalent to $2SLS$ (without iteration) and to one-step $3SLS$ (with iteration) (see for instance Fomby *et al.*, 1984, p. 481).

Denote (IV)-estimates by $\hat{\beta}$ and $\hat{\gamma}$. Conditional expectations of endogenous variables $\hat{x}$ and $\hat{y}$ are calculated by means of the estimated reduced form

$$\begin{pmatrix} \hat{y}_i \\ \hat{x}_i \end{pmatrix} = Z \cdot \hat{\Pi}_i, \quad i = 1, \ldots, m \tag{5A.6}$$

where some self-evident ordering of vectors and coefficients is used. A $2m$-dimensional vector of residuals conforming to the random vector u_t is denoted by e_t. By definition, the residuals are **always** calculated from the reduced form. Hence, using (5A.6), reduced-form residuals are

$$e_t = \begin{pmatrix} y_{1t} \\ \vdots \\ y_{mt} \\ x_{1t} \\ \vdots \\ x_{mt} \end{pmatrix} - \begin{pmatrix} \hat{y}_{1t} \\ \vdots \\ \hat{y}_{mt} \\ \hat{x}_{1t} \\ \vdots \\ \hat{x}_{mt} \end{pmatrix} \tag{5A.7}$$

A simple root mean square statistic s serves as measure of goodness-of-fit

$$s_k = \left(\frac{1}{T} \sum_{t=1}^{T} e_{kt}^2 \right)^{\frac{1}{2}} \quad k = 1, \ldots, 2m \tag{5A.8}$$

For notational convenience, the $2m$-vector s is split into the first m components s_{yi} related to wages, and into the second m components s_{xi} related to employment.

Consider now the process of aggregation. Real-wage and employment observations of m labour types are aggregated into aggregate observations by following Divisia-index rules. Real wages y_{it} are aggregated into $\bar{y}_t$ by means of wage-bill shares v_{it} in the total industrial wage bill

$$\bar{y}_t = \sum_{i=1}^{m} v_{it} y_{it} \tag{5A.9}$$

Disaggregation in econometric modelling

Growth rates of employment x_{it} are aggregated into $\bar{x}_t$ by means of shares w_{it} which represent employment quotas of labour types i in total industrial employment

$$\bar{x}_t = \sum_{i=1}^{m} w_{it} x_{it} \tag{5A.10}$$

The weights are assumed to be non-stochastic. In the context of the model considered here, this assumption cannot be maintained exactly, since growth rates of wages and employment are endogenous. But in rather short finite samples it may be maintained as an approximation, since in contrast to growth rates the time series of weights are rather smooth.

Given these definitions and assumptions, the aggregated model is now

$$\bar{y}_t = \sum_{j=1}^{K} \bar{\beta}_j z_{jt} + \bar{u}_{yt}$$

$$\bar{x}_t = \bar{\gamma}_0 \bar{y}_t + \sum_{j=1}^{K} \bar{\gamma}_j z_{jt} + \bar{u}_{xt} \tag{5A.11}$$

Maintaining similar assumptions as before, this model can again be estimated consistently by (IV) in one-step iteration. Denote estimates of (5A.11) by $\hat{\bar{\beta}}$ and $\hat{\bar{\gamma}}$, and reduced-form residuals by $\bar{e}_{yt}$, $\bar{e}_{xt}$. The root mean square statistic is then

$$\bar{s}_k = \left(\frac{1}{T} \sum_{t=1}^{T} \bar{e}_{kt}^2 \right)^{\frac{1}{2}} \quad k = y, x \tag{5A.12}$$

Denote *ex post* predictors of the aggregate model (5A.11) by $\hat{\bar{y}}_t$, $\hat{\bar{x}}_t$, and consider the inverse procedure of aggregation. How well do aggregated predictors approximate disaggregated observations? This yields the following backwards root mean square statistics

$$\bar{s}_{yi} = \left(\frac{1}{T} \sum_{t=1}^{T} (y_{it} - \hat{\bar{y}}_t)^2 \right)^{\frac{1}{2}}, \qquad \bar{s}_{xi} = \left(\frac{1}{T} \sum_{t=1}^{T} (x_{it} - \hat{\bar{x}}_t)^2 \right)^{\frac{1}{2}},$$

$$i = 1, \ldots, m \tag{5A.13}$$

Forward aggregation of residuals is obtained as follows. Take the reduced-form residuals e_t from (IV) – estimates of the disaggregated model (5A.2), (5A.3), and the weights v_{it} and w_{it} defined above. Then calculate aggregated residuals $\tilde{e}_y$ for wages and $\tilde{e}_x$ for employment by applying the weighting rule

$$\tilde{e}_{yt} = \sum_{i=1}^{m} v_{it} e_{it}, \qquad \tilde{e}_{xt} = \sum_{i=1}^{m} w_{it} e_{kt}, \quad k = i + m, \quad t = 1, \ldots, T$$

$$(5A.14)$$

Then root mean square statistics are obtained

$$\tilde{s}_k = \left(\frac{1}{T} \cdot \sum_{t=1}^{T} \tilde{e}_{kt}^2 \right)^{\frac{1}{2}}, \quad k = y, x \tag{5A.15}$$

Comparison of (5A.12) and (5A.15) yields the following choice criterion: prefer the disaggregated model, if

$$\tilde{s}_y \leq \bar{s}_y \quad \text{and} \quad \tilde{s}_x \leq \bar{s}_x \tag{5A.16}$$

with at least one strict inequality; prefer the aggregated model, if the inequalities are reversed.

No strict test for this decision problem is developed here. Instead we only make some conjectures. The well-known (GG) approach of Grunfeld–Griliches (1960) refers to the problem of information loss in prediction when aggregated observations are used instead of disaggregated ones. In the (GG) context, aggregated data are the sums of the corresponding disaggregated data. The disaggregated equations and the aggregate equation are of identical structure; the coefficients may be different. All equations are evaluated with (OLS) by definition. The sum of the squares of the sum of disaggregated residuals is compared with the sum of the squares of the aggregated residuals. This yields the testable (GG) criterion which is analogous to (5A.16). Recently, Pesaran, Pierse, and Kumar (1989) have investigated the problem of (SURE)-estimation of the disaggregated equations. They admit non-identical sets of regressors in disaggregated equations and assume i.i.d. errors with covariance matrix $\Omega = \Sigma \oplus I_T$, Σ being non-diagonal. In the context of aggregation by summation they show that the (GG) criterion is biased in small samples, but the bias may be eliminated by appropriate correction terms (see Pesaran *et al.*, 1989, formula (4.6)).

For the system considered here, the following can be stated: by applying a well-known transformation, the original system of equations can be transformed in a reduced form system such that

Disaggregation in econometric modelling

(2SLS)- and (3SLS)-estimates are obtained by equivalent-(SURE)-estimation; the estimates are consistent, but in general biased in small samples (see again Fomby *et al.*, 1984, pp. 480, 500). The reduced-form residuals defined in (5A.7) are obtained from estimates of that (SURE)-system. We do not solve the problem whether the (GG) criterion can indeed be applied to these residuals. For this purpose one must show that the transformation mentioned above applies to the (GG) criterion, at least in sufficiently large samples, and if only aggregation by summation with constant weights were considered.

In the context considered here there arises the additional problem that aggregation of observations is formed by Divisia-index rules with time-varying weights. This problem can be reduced to simple summation by considering the modified disaggregated system

$$v_{it}y_{it} = \sum_{j=1}^{K} \beta_{ij} v_{it} z_{jt} + v_{it} u_{yit}, \quad i = 1, \ldots, m$$

$$w_{it}x_{it} = \gamma_{i0} w_{it} y_{it} + \sum_{j=1}^{K} \gamma_{ij} w_{it} z_{jt} + w_{it} u_{xit}, \quad i = 1, \ldots, m \,(5A.17)$$

Since the weights are assumed to be non-stochastic, the variables in the modified system (5A.17) consist of the products $v_{it}y_{it}$, etc. This system is heteroscedastic with known heteroscedasticity, but simultaneity is clearly lost. The system can be estimated by some appropriate Aitken-estimator. Aggregation reduces to simple summation. The sums of residuals of (5A.17) have to be compared with the residuals of the corresponding aggregate equation (5A.11). As a conjecture, a modified (GG) criterion along the lines of Pesaran *et al.* (1989) should be attainable. Further research in that direction is needed.

For the moment, let the validity of criterion (5A.16) in the context of the simultaneous (albeit recursive) system be maintained as the tentative proposition: criterion (5A.16) which is based on reduced-form residuals serves as valid test criterion in large samples provided that the time series of weights are smooth and approximately stationary.

In contrast to the previous discussion, strict tests are considered in the context of microhomogeneity. The hypothesis of micro-homogeneity is applied to the disaggregated model and requires equality of coefficients belonging to the same regressors. This in turn requires that the same set of regressors is used in all equations selected for the test. The following discussion centres upon the suggested concept of conditional perfect aggregation.

The null hypothesis $H_0(W)$ of microhomogeneity applied to the wage equations (5A.2) is

$$H_0(W): \beta_j = \beta_{ij} = \beta_{kj}, \quad \forall \quad j = 1, \ldots, m, \text{ and } \forall \ i, k \in M$$

$$(5A.18)$$

The corresponding $H_0(E)$ applied to the employment equations (5A.3) is

$$H_0(E): \gamma_j = \gamma_{ij} = \gamma_{kj}, \quad \forall \quad j = 0, \ldots, m \text{ and } \forall \ i, k \in M$$

$$(5A.19)$$

The combined hypothesis $H_0(C)$ is of special interest

$$H_0(C): \beta_j = \beta_{ij} = \beta_{kj}, \quad j = 1, \ldots, m$$

$$\gamma_j = \gamma_{ij} = \gamma_{kj}, \quad j = 0, \ldots, m, \text{ and } \forall \ i, k \in M \quad (5A.20)$$

Consider first the case where the true parameter values β and γ are known. Then it is easy to see that under $H_0(C)$ conditional expectations on growth rates of disaggregated wages $\hat{y}_{it}$ and employment $\hat{x}_{it}$ coincide. Consider any given but fixed Z_t. By (5A.2) and $H_0(W)$

$$\hat{y}_{it} = \mathrm{E}[y_{it}|Z_t] = \sum_j \beta_{ij} z_{jt} = \sum_j \beta_j z_{jt} \equiv \hat{y}_t \qquad (5A.21)$$

By (5A.3), (5A.21), and $H_0(E)$

$$\hat{x}_{it} = \mathrm{E}[x_{it}|Z_t] = \gamma_{i0}\hat{y}_{it} + \sum_j \gamma_{ij} z_{jt} = \gamma_0 \hat{y}_t + \sum_j \gamma_j z_{jt} \equiv \hat{x}_t$$

$$(5A.22)$$

It is also true that these conditional expectations coincide with the aggregated conditional expectations. From (5A.11), (5A.9), and (5A.10), (5A.2), and (5A.3)

$$\bar{y}_t = \sum_i \sum_j v_{it}\beta_{ij} z_{jt} + \sum_i v_{it} u_{yit}$$

$$\bar{x}_t = \sum_i w_{it}\gamma_{i0} y_{it} + \sum_i \sum_j w_{it}\gamma_{ij} z_{jt} + \sum_i w_{it} u_{xit} \qquad (5A.23)$$

Disaggregation in econometric modelling

Since the weights sum up to unity for every t, microhomogeneity $H_0(C)$ yields

$$\bar{y}_t = \sum_j \beta_j z_{jt} + \epsilon_{yt}, \qquad \bar{x}_t = \gamma_0 \sum_i w_{it} y_{it} + \sum_j \gamma_j z_{jt} + \epsilon_{xt} \quad (5A.24)$$

with appropriate heteroscedastic error terms ϵ_t.

It is clear that the structure of the disaggregated system (5A.2), (5A.3) does not carry over to (5A.24). $\bar{y}_t = \sum_i w_{it} y_{it}$ only under the very restrictive condition $v_{it} = w_{it}$. Perfect aggregation in the usual sense does not prevail, but it is clear that conditional expectations coincide. By inserting (5A.21) and (5A.22), (5A.24) yields

$$\hat{\bar{y}}_t = E[\bar{y}_t | Z_t] = \sum_j \beta_j z_{jt} = \hat{y}_t$$

$$\hat{\bar{x}}_t = E[\bar{x}_t | Z_t] = \gamma_0 \hat{y}_t + \sum_j \gamma_j z_{jt} = \hat{x}_t \quad (5A.25)$$

Thus, conditional upon the choice of Z_t, the aggregated variables $\bar{y}_t$ and $\bar{x}_t$ can be predicted by the aggregate model without loss of information, if the combined microhomogeneity hypothesis $H_0(C)$ holds true. For this type of aggregation, the authors suggest the term conditional perfect aggregation. This notion receives its meaning in the context of the simultaneous equation structure at hand.

It must be noted that conditional perfect aggregation has been defined for known coefficients. So far the notion has nothing to do with the problems of bias, consistency, and efficiency which appear in estimating unknown coefficients.

For instance, in our case: for the disaggregated model (5A.2), (5A.3), let the assumption (5A.5) hold true together with the asymptotic condition that $Z'Z/T$ converges to a positive definite non-stochastic matrix. Then disaggregated (IV)-estimates and predictors are consistent. However, (IV)-estimates of the aggregated equations (5A.11) are consistent only if the weights form a process which converges to a positive constant in quadratic mean such that the second order moment matrix of weighted exogenous variables converges as well. But even in that case aggregate (IV)-estimates based on (5A.5) are not efficient (compare (5A.17) and (5A.24)). In the main text, consistency and efficiency of the aggregate models follow from hypotheses which are maintained independently.

The last topic discussed in this appendix deals with the economic content of the microhomogeneity property and with related questions arising from aggregation bias.

Consider the case where $H_0(E)$ holds true. Among others, output elasticities in employment equations are equal. Hence, in the framework of profit maximization or cost minimization, the underlying technology has to be homothetic. This characteristic adds to local additive separability. Furthermore, equality of own-wage elasticities implies even more stringent conditions on technology and feasible allocations.

Now, consider the case of interest: Let $H_0(W)$ in (5A.18) hold true, while rejecting $H_0(E)$ in (5A.19), and assume sufficient conditions for consistent estimation of coefficients. Then, as stated before, the recursive structure of the model guarantees that estimation of aggregated wages in (5A.11) is consistent with the process of data generation. This follows immediately from (5A.24).

In practice, however, true coefficients belonging to the same regressors in disaggregated equations (5A.2) may still differ slightly. Since the hidden Divisia-index identity (5A.9) does not appear in (5A.11), changes in exogenous variables z_t will change the proportions among real wages y_{it}. Hence specification biases in estimating aggregated coefficients (5A.11) are to be expected. This holds true *a fortiori* in models where feedbacks from employment to real wages are admitted. Then, by construction of aggregated data in (5A.9) and (5A.10), it is easy to see that estimates of the aggregated models will be biased if the combined hypothesis $H_0(C)$ does not hold true.

To some extent, this assertion depends on the specification of the model presented here. Indeed, the case of the micro-homogeneity hypothesis is often considered to be unduly restrictive. Perfect aggregates may exist also if the microhomogeneity property fails. On the lines of Gorman (1968), one might use wage and employment equations based on perfect aggregation in the sense of two-stage budgeting (see also Blackorby *et al.*, 1978). In such a fully fledged model, cross-elasticity effects are added. However, systems of this type usually suffer from over-parameterization. Moreover, since the period of observations is rather short, they do not leave enough degrees of freedom when the number of endogenous variables exceeds two or three. Therefore the somewhat simpler model with own-wage effects is used here.

Appendix 5B List of variables, data and additional estimates

Table 5B.1 List of variables, observations, 1966–84

Endogenous variables		
CW	Nominal collective wages: Workers	
CA	Nominal collective wages: Employees	
CB	Nominal collective wages: Full aggregate	$W + A$
YH	Real effective wages: Low-skill workers	
YF	Real effective wages: High-skill workers	
YD	Real effective wages: Low-rank employees	
YE	Real effective wages: High-rank employees	
YW	Real effective wages: Workers	$H + F$
YA	Real effective wages: Employees	$D + E$
YL	Real effective wages: Less-qualified	$H + D$
YQ	Real effective wages: Qualified	$F + E$
YB	Real effective wages: Full aggregate	$H + F + D + E$
XH	Employment: Low-skill workers	
XF	Employment: High-skill workers	
XD	Employment: Low-rank employees	
XE	Employment: High-rank employees	
XW	Employment: Workers	$H + F$
XA	Employment: Employees	$D + E$
XL	Employment: Less-qualified	$H + D$
XQ	Employment: Qualified	$F + E$
XB	Employment: Full aggregate	$H + F + D + E$
Exogenous variables		
P	GDP-deflator of total Austrian economy	
Q	Real gross industrial full capacity output (potential GDP)	
U	Austrian unemployment rate (first differences)	
EX	Share of industrial exports in industrial GDP	
CU	Industrial capacity utilization rate	

Note: All variables: one period growth rates (except for U).

Table 5B.2 Partial and full aggregates: real wages and employment, 1966–84

			(one period growth rates)							
	YW	*YA*	*YL*	*YQ*	*YB*	*XW*	*XA*	*XL*	*XQ*	*XB*
1966	3.5	4.1	3.9	3.6	4.2	−1.7	4.0	−1.7	2.3	−0.5
1967	5.1	6.1	5.4	6.8	6.1	−4.6	3.1	−3.4	−2.0	−3.0
1968	1.6	3.8	2.1	1.8	2.2	−1.1	−2.5	−1.9	−0.5	−1.5
1969	4.0	1.5	3.4	3.2	3.2	3.5	4.2	4.0	2.7	3.6
1970	5.3	2.6	2.4	3.1	2.7	2.8	5.6	3.7	3.0	3.4
1971	4.6	5.0	4.5	5.3	5.1	1.4	5.6	1.9	3.3	2.4
1972	2.4	1.4	0.5	2.4	1.5	1.5	5.5	2.2	3.1	2.5
1973	3.8	3.5	4.1	3.9	4.1	1.1	5.4	1.7	3.0	2.2
1974	6.1	5.6	6.2	6.8	6.7	−2.3	4.8	−1.1	0.7	−0.5
1975	12.0	9.8	9.0	9.5	10.2	−7.6	1.5	−7.8	0.0	−5.2
1976	4.3	5.0	3.9	4.4	4.7	−1.8	−0.6	−3.1	1.6	−1.5
1977	2.9	3.3	2.3	2.6	2.6	0.9	0.8	0.4	1.7	0.9
1978	0.2	−0.0	−0.1	0.1	0.4	−2.3	0.0	−2.8	0.3	−1.7
1979	1.2	0.8	1.1	0.4	1.1	−0.6	0.2	−1.5	1.6	−0.4
1980	1.0	1.3	0.9	1.0	1.0	1.3	0.6	0.9	1.5	1.1
1981	1.3	2.0	1.4	1.5	1.8	−2.7	−1.1	−3.3	−0.4	−2.2
1982	0.3	1.0	0.8	0.4	0.9	−4.7	−2.7	−5.0	−2.8	−4.1
1983	1.7	2.2	1.2	1.2	1.9	−4.6	−3.0	−6.6	−0.4	−4.1
1984	−1.2	−0.3	−1.2	−0.9	−1.1	−0.2	−1.3	−0.3	−1.0	−0.6

Table 5B.3 Root mean square errors $\bar{s}$ for weighted predictors (forwards)

From model to	*YW*	*YA*	*YL*	*YQ*	*YB*	*XW*	*XA*	*XL*	*XQ*	*XB*
(*HFDE*)	1.32	1.45	1.56	1.41	1.43	0.93	1.32	1.26	1.02	0.94
(*WA*)					1.55					1.04
(*LQ*)					1.48					0.98

Note: See also formula (5A.15) above.

Table 5B.4 Root mean square errors $\bar{s}$ from aggregated predictors (backwards)

From model to	*YH*	*YF*	*YD*	*YE*	*XH*	*XF*	*XD*	*XE*
(*WA*)	1.45	1.33	1.64	1.56	1.61	2.52	2.19	1.92
(*LQ*)	1.54	1.30	1.59	1.66	1.51	1.98	3.32	3.01
(*B*)	1.61	1.54	1.75	1.65	1.95	2.28	2.66	4.17

Note: See also formula (5A.13) above.

Disaggregation in econometric modelling

Table 5B.5 Additional regressors in model (*HFDE*) (IV-estimates)

Nominal collective wages					
CW	=	......	+ 1.15*RW		
			(0.08)		(5.1.1)
Real effective wages					
YE	=	......	+ 0.35*RW		
			(0.10)		(5.1.6)
Employment					
XH	=	......	− 5.94*DS	+ 4.30*DF	
			(0.90)	(0.89)	(5.1.7)
XF	=	......	+ 0.94*IQ	+ 0.02*SA	
			(0.21)	(0.01)	(5.1.8)

Note: Standard errors of parameter estimates in parentheses.

Exogenous variables	
RW	Regular (normal) working time. Declined stepwise from 48 hours/week and 2 weeks vacation time in early sixties to 40 hours/week and 4 weeks vacation in early eighties. In available statistics, *RW* is already accounted for in *CA*, *YH* and *YF*. *RW* appears in the wage equations listed in table 5B.5.
DS	1966 – Dummy for general introduction of ninth school year. In 1966, a complete labour vintage remained in school and did not enter the market.
SF	1969 – Dummy for liberalization of labour market restrictions with respect to foreign labour, in majority less skilled workers from South-East Europe.
IQ	Investment quota: Share of real industrial investment in industrial *GDP*.
SA	Labour supply variable: Successfully completed apprenticeships.

Note: all variables: one period growth rates.
Data sources: Bundeskammer der Gewerblichen Wirtschaft, Austrian Statistical Institute, Austrian Institute for Economic Research, own additional calculations.

Chapter six

Aggregation bias in labour demand equations for the UK economy*

K. Lee, M.H. Pesaran, and R.G. Pierse

Introduction

The responsiveness of employment to changes in real wages is an issue of considerable importance, particularly for policy analysis, and over the past decade a number of studies have been devoted to this issue in the UK. Notable examples include the papers by Nickell (1984), Symons (1985), Wren-Lewis (1986), and Burgess (1988) for the manufacturing sector, and by Beenstock and Warburton (1984), Layard and Nickell (1985, 1986) for the private sector and the economy as a whole. In contrast to the earlier work by Godley and Shepherd (1964), Brechling (1965), and Ball and St Cyr (1966), these recent studies find a significant and quantitatively important effect for real wages on employment. The point estimates of the long-run wage elasticity obtained in these studies vary widely depending on the coverage of the data (whether the data set used is economy-wide or just manufacturing), and on the specification of the estimated equations. A recent review of these studies by HM Treasury (1985) concludes that the estimate of long-run wage elasticity most likely falls in the region -0.5 to -1 although, under the influence of Layard and Nickell's important contributions, for the economy as a whole the 'consensus' estimate of this elasticity in the UK currently seems to centre on the figure of -1.[1] All these studies are, however, carried out using highly aggregated data, either at the level of the whole economy or the manufacturing sector, and given the significance of their results for macroeconomic policy it is important that the robustness of their results to the level of aggregation chosen are carefully investigated.

*   We are grateful to Ed Leamer and Franco Peracchi for helpful comments and suggestions. Financial support from the ESRC and the Newton Trust is gratefully acknowledged.

113

Disaggregation in econometric modelling

This paper extends the empirical work described in Pesaran, Pierse, and Kumar (1989) (PPK), and examines the effect of aggregation on the estimates of long-run wage and output elasticities of demand for employment in the UK. The aggregate and the disaggregate employment functions analysed in this paper differ from those in PPK in two respects. First, the functions allow for a longer lagged effect of output on employment. Second, in order to deal with some of the econometric difficulties associated with the use of the time trend as a proxy for technical change in estimating the employment functions,[2] the time trend will be replaced by a measure of embodied technological change based on the current and past movements of *gross* investment, à la Kaldor (1957, 1961). This measure of technological change is both statistically less problematic than a simple time trend and more satisfactory from a theoretical standpoint.

The paper also applies the statistical methods recently developed for the analysis of aggregation by PPK and Lee, Pesaran, and Pierse (1989) (LPP) to employment equations for the UK. Specifically, the aggregation bias in the estimates of the long-run wage and output elasticities will be tested statistically, and the possibility of misspecification of the disaggregate employment equations will be investigated by means of the Durbin-Hausman type test developed in LPP. The adequacy of the aggregate model (relative to the disaggregate specification) will also be investigated by means of the goodness-of-fit criteria and the test of perfect aggregation proposed in PPK.

The plan of the paper is as follows. Section 6.1 sets out the disaggregate employment functions and discusses the theoretical rationale that underlies them. Section 6.2 motivates the use of a distributed lag function in *gross* investment as a proxy for technological change. Section 6.3 reviews the various statistical methods to be applied. Section 6.4 presents the empirical results, and the final section provides a summary of the main findings of the paper.

6.1 Industrial employment functions: theoretical considerations

In specifying the employment demand functions we follow the literature on derivation of dynamic factor demand models and suppose that the employment decision is made at the industry level by identical cost minimizing firms operating under uncertainty in an environment where adjustment can be costly. We assume that in the absence of uncertainty and adjustment costs the industry's employment function is given by

114

$$h_t^* = f(w_t, y_t, a_t) + v_t, \tag{6.1}$$

where

h_t^* = the desired level of man-hours employment (in logs),
w_t = the real wage rate (in logs),
y_t = the expected level of real demand (in logs),
a_t = an index of technological change,
v_t = mean zero serially uncorrelated productivity shocks.

The actual level of employment, h_t, measured in logarithms of man-hours employed in the industry is then set by solving the following optimization problem

$$\min_{h_t, h_{t+1}, \ldots,} E \left\{ \sum_{\tau=0}^{\infty} \beta^\tau [(h_{t+\tau} - h_{t+\tau}^*)^2 + \frac{1}{2}\phi_1(\Delta h_{t+\tau})^2 \right.$$

$$\left. + \frac{1}{2}\phi_2(\Delta^2 h_{t+\tau})^2] \mid \Omega_t \right\} \tag{6.2}$$

where $\Omega_t = (h_t, h_{t-1}, \ldots, w_t, w_{t-1}, \ldots, y_t, y_{t-1}, \ldots, a_t, a_{t-1}, \ldots, u_t, u_{t-1}, \ldots,)$ represents the information set of the firm at time t, Δ is the first difference operator, and $0 \leq \beta < 1$ is the real discount factor. The first term in (6.2) measures the cost of being out of equilibrium, and the second and the third terms stand respectively for the costs of changing the level and the *speed* with which changes in employment are put into effect. The inclusion of the last term in (6.2) is proposed in Pesaran (1988) and generalizes the familiar adjustment cost–rational expectations models discussed, for example, by Sargent (1978) and Kennan (1979), and is of some interest as it provides a theoretical justification for the inclusion of h_{t-2} in the employment function.[3] In practice, the speed of adjustment coefficients ϕ_1 and ϕ_2 could vary with the state of the labour market as argued, for example, by Smyth (1984) and Burgess (1988). Here, however, we shall assume that they are fixed. The unique solution to the above optimization problem is derived in Pesaran (1988) and is given by

$$h_t = \psi_1 h_{t-1} + \psi_2 h_{t-2} + \sum_{j=0}^{\infty} \theta_j E(h_{t+j}^* \mid \Omega_t) \tag{6.3}$$

Disaggregation in econometric modelling

where

$$\psi_1 = \mu_1' + \mu_2' > 0, \qquad \psi_2 = -\mu_1'\mu_2' < 0$$
$$\theta_j = (\mu_1^{-j-1} - \mu_2^{-j-1}) / [\phi_2(\mu_2 - \mu_1)]$$

and μ_1, μ_2, μ_1' and μ_2' are the roots of

$$\alpha_2 x^2 + \alpha_1 x + \lambda_1 x^{-1} + \lambda_2 x^{-2} = 1$$

The reduced-form parameters α_1, α_2, λ_1, and λ_2 are defined in terms of the structural parameters, β, ϕ_1 and ϕ_2 (see, Pesaran, 1988). It is important to note that for plausible values of the structural parameters the theory suggests a negative value for the coefficient of h_{t-2} in (6.3). Adopting a linear approximation for (6.1), and assuming that conditional expectations of w_{t+j}, $yt+j$, and a_{t+j} with respect to Ω_t are formed rationally on the basis of an rth order vector autoregressive (VAR) system, the decision rule (6.3) becomes

$$h_t = \text{intercept} + \psi_1 h_{t-1} + \psi_2 h_{t-2} + c_{r-1}'(L)z_t + u_t \qquad (6.4)$$

where $u_t = (1 - \psi_1 - \psi_2)(1 - \psi_1/\beta - \psi_2/\beta^2)v_t$, $z_t = (a_t, y_t,$

$w_t)'$, and $c_{r-1}(L) = \sum\limits_{i=1}^{r} c_i L^{i-1}$ is a 3×1 vector of lag polynomials

of order $r - 1$ in the lag operator L. In the case where the variables y_t, w_t and a_t have univariate $AR(r_i)$, $i = y, w, a$ representations, (6.4) simplifies to

$$h_t = \text{intercept} + \psi_1 h_{t-1} + \psi_2 h_{t-2} + \left(\sum_{i=1}^{r_y} \gamma_{iy} L^{i-1} \right) y_t$$

$$+ \left(\sum_{i=1}^{r_w} \gamma_{iw} L^{i-1} \right) w_t + \left(\sum_{i=1}^{r_a} \gamma_{ia} L^{i-1} \right) a_t + u_t, \qquad (6.5)$$

which is a generalization of the aggregate employment function (7.2) in PPK.[4] Under the rational expectations hypothesis (REH), the coefficients c_i in (6.4), and γ_{iy}, γ_{iw}, γ_{ia} in (6.5) will be subject to $3r - 4$ and $(r_y + r_w + r_a) - 4$ cross-equation restrictions, respectively. However, given our concern with the problem of aggregation, in the present study we do not consider imposing these

116

restrictions, and employ instead the unrestricted version of (6.5) as our maintained hypothesis.[5] We then choose the orders of the lag polynomials on h_t, y_t, w_t, and a_t empirically. The validity of the RE restrictions at the industry level and the problem of aggregation bias in the context of RE models is beyond the scope of the present paper.

6.2 Modelling and measurement of technological change

In the empirical analysis of labour demand, technological change, broadly defined to include new scientific, engineering, and electronic discoveries and inventions, is generally assumed to occur exogenously, evolving independently of market conditions and government policy interventions. It is inferred either indirectly as a residual using a production function approach, or is represented by linear, piece-wise linear, or non-linear functions of time. Neither procedure is satisfactory. The former approach, employed, for example, by Layard and Nickell (1985), assumes an *a priori* knowledge of the production possibilities and involves circular reasoning, while the latter is devoid of a satisfactory theoretical rationale and is adopted by most researchers as a 'practical' method of dealing with a very difficult problem (Arrow, 1962).[6]

Ideally, what we need are direct reliable measures of technological change, and there are some data such as expenditure on research and development (R&D) and the number of patents and product designs granted over a given period that can be used. In the absence of suitable direct measures of technological change, here we adopt an indirect approach and following Kaldor (1957, 1961) postulate a distributed lag relationship between the a_t, the technological change index, and the rate of *gross* investment, GI_t,

$$a_t = \text{intercept} + \sum_{j=0}^{\infty} \lambda_j \log(GI_{t-j}) \qquad (6.6)$$

A static version of this relationship when used in a linear version of (6.1) yields a log linear approximation to Kaldor's 'technical progress function', which relates the rate of change of productivity per worker to the rate of change of gross investment.[7] According to this model technological progress is 'embodied' in the process of capital accumulation and takes place primarily through *gross* capital formation by the infusion of new equipment and machines, embodying the most up-to-date technology into the economy. The

117

Disaggregation in econometric modelling

formulation (6.6) can also be justified along the lines suggested by Arrow (1962) in his seminal paper on 'learning by doing'. Arrow (1962, p. 157) himself uses cumulative gross investment as an index of experience, which is closely related to the distributed lag function in (6.6).

The technological progress function (6.6) is more than a theoretical postulate. It is also based on direct empirical support. Schmookler (1966) in his pioneering work, using patents as a measure of technological change, showed there exist strong positive correlations between gross investment and patents in railroads, petroleum refining, and building industries over the period 1873–1940. He also obtained similar results using cross-section data. While there is some doubt about the direction of causation in Schmookler's findings, there is little dispute about the existence of a close relationship between gross investment and technological change.[8] Since our aim here is not to explain the causes of technological change but to estimate its impact on employment demand, we feel that the controversy over the causality of the investment-patents relationship has little bearing on our analysis.

The coefficients λ_j, $j = 1, 2, \ldots$ measure the impact of past investments on the current state of technological advance, and it is reasonable to assume that they are a decreasing function of the lag length, $j = 1, 2, \ldots$ The likely rate of decline of λ_j depends on the importance of the learning-by-doing component of a_t. Under a pure learning story, $\{\lambda_j\}$ will be fixed or show a very slow rate of decline. The rate of decline of $\{\lambda_j\}$ is likely to be much higher if one adopts Kaldor's idea. Here, for the purpose of empirical analysis we assume the following geometrically declining pattern for λ_j

$$\lambda_j = \alpha(1 - \lambda)\lambda^j, \quad j = 0, 1, 2, \ldots \quad \alpha, \lambda > 0$$

and write (6.6) as

$$a_t = \text{intercept} + \alpha d_t(\lambda) \tag{6.7}$$

where $d_t(\lambda)$ satisfies the following recursive formula

$$d_t(\lambda) = \lambda d_{t-1}(\lambda) + (1 - \lambda)\log(GI_t) \tag{6.8}$$

Substituting (6.7) in (6.5) now yields

$$\begin{aligned} h_t = \text{intercept} &+ \psi_1 h_{t-1} + \psi_2 h_{t-2} + \gamma_y(L)y_t \\ &+ \gamma_w(L)w_t + \alpha\gamma_a(L)\,d_t(\lambda) + u_t \end{aligned} \tag{6.9}$$

118

where $\gamma_y(L)$, $\gamma_w(L)$, and $\gamma_a(L)$ are lag operator polynomials of orders $r_y - 1$, $r_w - 1$ and $r_a - 1$, respectively. It is clear that in general α is not identifiable, although the decay coefficient, λ, can in principle be estimated from the data. We shall return to the issue of the estimation of (6.9) in section 6.4, but first we briefly review the econometric issues concerning testing for aggregation bias and the relative predictive performance of aggregate and disaggregate models.

6.3 The aggregation problem: econometric considerations

Suppose that, for a given value of the decay parameter λ, the variables in (6.9), namely h_i, y_i, w_i, and $d_i(\lambda)$, are observed over the period $t = 1, 2, \ldots, n$ for each of the m firms (industries), $i = 1, 2, \ldots, m$. Then the disaggregate employment equations can be written in matrix notation as

$$H_d : h_i = X_i\beta_i + u_i, \quad i = 1, 2, \ldots, m \qquad (6.10)$$

where h_i is the $n \times 1$ vector of observations on the log of man-hours employment in the ith firm (industry), X_i is the $n \times k$ ($k = r_y + r_w + r_a + 3$) matrix of observations on the regressors in (6.9) for the ith firm (industry). β_i is the $k \times 1$ vector of the coefficients associated with columns of X_i, and u_i is the $n \times 1$ vector of disturbances for the ith firm (industry). The aggregate equation associated with (6.9) is given by

$$H_a : h_a = X_a b_a + v \qquad (6.11)$$

where

$$h_a = \sum_{i=1}^{m} h_i, \qquad X_a = \sum_{i=1}^{m} X_i$$

and b_a is the $k \times 1$ vector of macro parameters.

The aggregation problem arises when the disaggregate model (6.10) holds but the investigator decides to base his/her analysis on the aggregate specification (6.11). The econometric implications of aggregation in linear models have been discussed in the literature in some detail.[9] The principal issues concern the accuracy of predictions and the bias in the parameter estimates. For the analysis of the predictive performance of models (6.10) and (6.11), PPK propose using a modified version of the Grunfeld and Griliches criterion which compares the sums of squared errors of predicting h_a using the aggregate and disaggregate models, adjusting for the differences in the degrees of freedom (see section 4 of PPK). They also propose a test of perfect aggregation which tests the hypothesis that

$$\underset{\sim}{\xi} = \sum_{i=1}^{m} X_i \beta_i - X_a b = 0$$

To test for aggregation bias, two approaches are possible. The first is the method employed in Zellner (1962) and involves testing the micro homogeneity hypothesis

$$H_\beta : \beta_1 = \beta_2 = \ldots = \beta_m$$

However, as is pointed out in LPP, as a test of aggregation bias this approach is unduly restrictive. Instead they propose testing the hypothesis of zero aggregation bias directly by comparing an average of the estimates of the micro coefficients, or a function thereof, with the aggregate counterpart. In the case of the present study, the parameters of interest are the long-run output and wage elasticities, which, assuming $r_y = r_w = 2$ in (6.10), are given (in terms of the elements of β_i) for the ith industry by

$$\epsilon_{iy} = \frac{\beta_{i4} - \beta_{i5}}{1 - \beta_{i2} - \beta_{i3}}$$

and

$$\epsilon_{iw} = \frac{\beta_{i6} + \beta_{i7}}{1 - \beta_{i2} - \beta_{i3}}$$

respectively.[10] The null hypothesis we wish to test is that aggregation bias is zero, i.e.

$$\eta_g = g(b) - \frac{1}{m} \sum_{i=1}^{m} g(\beta_i) = 0 \tag{6.12}$$

where $g(\underset{\sim}{\beta_i})$ is an $s \times 1$ vector of parameters of interest from the disaggregate model (6.10) and $g(b)$ is the corresponding vector from the aggregate model. In the case of our application

$$g(\beta_i) = (\epsilon_{iy}, \epsilon_{iw})' \tag{6.13}$$

Following LPP we distinguish two situations: (i) where $g(b)$ is given *a priori* (for example by a consensus view) and (ii) where $g(b)$ is estimated from the aggregate model (6.11).

Two corresponding statistics are derived

$$q_1^* = \left[g(b) - \frac{1}{m} \sum_{i=1}^{m} g(\hat{\beta}_i) \right]'$$

$$\hat{\Omega}_n^{-1} \left[g(b) - \frac{1}{m} \sum_{i=1}^{m} g(\hat{\beta}_i) \right] \underset{\sim}{a} \chi_s^2 \tag{6.14}$$

and

$$q_2^* = n^{-1} \hat{\eta}_g' \hat{\Phi}_n^{-1} \hat{\eta}_g \underset{\sim}{a} \chi_s^2 \tag{6.15}$$

where

$$\hat{\eta}_g = g(\hat{b}) - \frac{1}{m} \sum_{i=1}^{m} g(\hat{\beta}_i) \tag{6.16}$$

and $\hat{\Omega}_n$ and $\hat{\Phi}_n$ are estimated covariance matrices defined in LPP.[11]

These tests of aggregation bias assume that the disaggregate model H_d holds and it is important that this assumption is also tested. To this end LPP derive a Durbin–Hausman-type mis-specification test which examines the statistical significance of the difference between the estimates of the parameters of the aggregate model based on the disaggregate and aggregate specifications respectively. If this difference turns out to be significant then it is likely that the disaggregate model is misspecified and the aggregation bias tests may be misleading.

6.4 Empirical results

In this section the theoretical considerations on employment functions of sections 6.1 and 6.2 and the statistical methods outlined in section 6.3 are brought together in the estimation of disaggregate and aggregate employment functions for the UK and the analysis of aggregation bias. The data employed are taken from the Cambridge Growth Project Databank, and full details are provided in appendix 6A. Figures are available annually for the period 1954–84 and, except for some public sector services, the whole of the UK economy is covered, with data provided on a 41-industry basis. As in PPK, industry 4 (mineral oil and natural gas) is excluded from the analysis, and both the disaggregate and the aggregate specifications are based on the remaining 40 industry groups (i.e. $m = 40$). Although our data set start in 1954, all the equations are estimated over the period 1956–84, and the data for the years 1954 and 1955 are used to generate the lagged values of employment, output, and real wages that are included in the employment function (see equation 6.9)). For the technical change variable $d_t(\lambda)$, we employed the recursive formula given by (6.8), for $t = 1955, 1956, \ldots, 1984$ and experimented with different methods of initializing the recursive process. We also experimented with different estimates of the decay rate, λ.

6.4.1 Initialization of the $d_t(\lambda)$ process

We tried two methods for generating the initial value, $d_{1954}(\lambda)$. In one set of experiments we derived $d_{1954}(\lambda)$ assuming that the process generating $\log(GI_t)$ in the pre-1954 period can be characterized by a random walk and that on average $E[\log(GI_{1954})] = E[\log(GI_{1953})] = \ldots = \log(\bar{GI})$, where we estimate $\bar{GI}$ by the average of gross investment over the 1954–8 period. Under these assumptions, the estimate of $d_{1954}(\lambda)$, which we denote by $\hat{d}_{01}$, is given by[12]

$$\hat{d}_{01} = \log(\bar{GI}) \tag{6.17}$$

As an alternative procedure we followed the backward forecasting procedure proposed in Pesaran (1973), and derived the following alternative estimate for $d_{1954}(\lambda)$

$$\hat{d}_{02} = \left\{ \frac{\hat{\rho}\lambda}{\hat{\rho} - (1 - \lambda)} \right\} \log(GI_{1954}) \tag{6.18}$$

This estimate assumes that in the pre-1954 period $\log(GI_t)$ follows the first-order autoregressive process

$$\log(GI_t) = \rho \log(GI_{t-1}) + \epsilon_t, \quad t = 1954, 1953, \ldots$$

and that ρ can be estimated consistently by the OLS method using data over the period 1954–84.

6.4.2 Estimation of the decay rate parameter, λ

In the initial experiments we assumed a decay rate of $\lambda = 0.10$ and estimated the employment equations under both methods of initializing the $d_t(\lambda)$ process described above. We found that the technological variable, $d_t(\lambda)$ showed significantly in about half of the industries, and of these the majority demonstrated the better fit using $\hat{d}_{01}$ (i.e. had the larger log likelihood value, LLF) as opposed to $\hat{d}_{02}$. The difference between LLF obtained in most industries was well below 1, and in only two cases did the difference exceed 2. In both of these $\hat{d}_{01}$ proved to be the more satisfactory measure. In view of these preliminary results we decided to initialize the $d_t(\lambda)$ process with $\hat{d}_{01}$. However, we note that, apart from the size of the coefficient on the constant in the estimated equations, there was little qualitative difference between results obtained using either of the two initialization methods.

Using $\hat{d}_{01}$ we also estimated the industrial employment equations by the grid search method, for values of λ in the range (0.0, 0.30). Again restricting attention to those industries with significant technological change effects, we found for about half of these industries the maximum likelihood estimates of λ fell within this interval, with many of the rest located on the $\lambda = 0.0$ bound. In general, however, we found the results to be qualitatively robust to the choice of the decay parameter in the range (0.0, 0.30). In the absence of any strong evidence of a more appropriate estimate of λ, therefore, we decided to maintain our original choice of $\lambda = 0.10$ in the remainder of the empirical work.

6.4.3 The estimated equations

The most general set of equations that we considered are presented in table 6.1. This includes among the explanatory variables two lagged dependent variables, h_{t-1} and h_{t-2}, and current and lagged values of industry output, wages, and technological change ($y_t, y_{t-1}, y_{t-2}, w_t, w_{t-1}, d_t, d_{t-1}$).[13] This equation follows from the theoretical discussion of sections 6.1 and 6.2, by setting r_y

Table 6.1 Unrestricted industrial labour demand equations

		inpt/40	y_t	y_{t-1}	y_{t-2}	h_{t-1}	h_{t-2}	w_t	w_{t-1}	y_{tu}	$\dot{y}_{t-1u}$	d_t	d_{t-1}	R^2 (LLF)	σ
1	Agriculture, etc.	-8.3291 (101.8650)	0.3996 (0.1641)	0.3135 (0.1996)	-0.2215 (0.1442)	0.5188 (0.2661)	0.0008 (0.1542)	-0.5179 (0.1006)	0.0399 (0.1511)	-0.1477 (0.1740)	-0.1409 (0.1704)	0.4305 (0.4127)	0.3869 (0.3583)	0.9982 (90.1369)	0.0141
2	Coal mining	-99.6698 (66.1970)	0.3380 (0.0499)	-0.5043 (0.0953)	0.1258 (0.1254)	1.3944 (0.2044)	-0.3702 (0.2355)	-0.2331 (0.0369)	-0.0772 (0.0777)	0.0075 (0.1254)	0.1290 (0.1402)	-0.4265 (0.2022)	0.3679 (0.2374)	0.9986 (86.5871)	0.0160
3	Coke	-426.9027 (183.1692)	0.4256 (0.1479)	0.2996 (0.2329)	0.1716 (0.2395)	0.0496 (0.2288)	0.1848 (0.1285)	-0.6430 (0.1066)	0.0465 (0.1225)	0.2449 (0.3889)	0.1604 (0.4312)	-1.3583 (0.4749)	1.8793 (0.5582)	0.9710 (53.1491)	0.0506
4	Mineral oil and natural gas														
5	Petroleum products	69.7436 (233.7634)	0.7333 (0.4544)	-0.0163 (0.4349)	0.0576 (0.2395)	0.6440 (0.2651)	-0.0224 (0.2815)	-0.4099 (0.1412)	0.0223 (0.1804)	0.1563 (0.8680)	-1.0622 (0.8383)	0.5526 (0.3451)	-0.6812 (0.3579)	0.8841 (44.8866)	0.0672
6	Electricity, etc.	-26.1434 (51.5244)	0.0030 (0.1887)	0.3339 (0.2606)	-0.2057 (0.1605)	0.8984 (0.2033)	-0.3624 (0.1964)	-0.1186 (0.0768)	-0.1291 (0.0845)	0.0347 (0.1893)	0.3182 (0.2049)	0.6020 (0.2726)	-0.7048 (0.2477)	0.9917 (87.3926)	0.0155
7	Public gas supply	184.9195 (131.9965)	-0.1753 (0.2299)	0.6582 (0.2748)	-0.6325 (0.2016)	0.5349 (0.1630)	0.0739 (0.2029)	-0.3584 (0.0857)	0.2904 (0.0858)	-0.2904 (0.2853)	0.1382 (0.2625)	0.2513 (0.1922)	-0.1382 (0.2368)	0.9779 (69.6787)	0.0286
8	Water supply	-187.1010 (93.4028)	1.0830 (0.4370)	0.2506 (0.5354)	-0.4169 (0.4807)	0.5300 (0.1454)	0.0286 (0.1480)	-0.4472 (0.1069)	0.3289 (0.1258)	-0.0699 (0.3251)	0.7324 (0.2887)	-2.8566 (0.7126)	2.0447 (0.5450)	0.9594 (67.4242)	0.0309
9	Minerals and ores n.e.s.	79.1062 (171.5604)	0.2078 (0.1627)	-0.0659 (0.1775)	-0.1183 (0.1319)	0.5591 (0.2462)	0.2587 (0.1974)	-0.1445 (0.0952)	0.0586 (0.1142)	-0.5481 (0.4423)	0.4380 (0.6235)	-0.2124 (0.3888)	0.1637 (0.4321)	0.9706 (63.7009)	0.0351
10	Iron and steel	-114.7884 (76.2388)	0.3066 (0.1046)	0.2143 (0.1108)	-0.1191 (0.1014)	0.5330 (0.2617)	0.1296 (0.1655)	-0.1959 (0.1471)	-0.0661 (0.1674)	0.2340 (0.3665)	-0.2408 (0.3609)	0.4557 (0.1928)	-0.2938 (0.2185)	0.9923 (69.8891)	0.0284
11	Non-ferrous metals	-31.6300 (33.2585)	0.2543 (0.1174)	-0.1371 (0.1294)	-0.0952 (0.1154)	1.0529 (0.1748)	-0.2393 (0.1712)	-0.1066 (0.0465)	-0.0500 (0.0576)	0.6953 (0.2225)	-0.6961 (0.1985)	0.2762 (0.1125)	-0.0547 (0.1306)	0.9906 (78.8431)	0.0208
12	Non-metallic mineral products	-412.1530 (163.0320)	0.3213 (0.1825)	0.0723 (0.1916)	-0.1101 (0.1668)	0.4784 (0.2423)	0.4562 (0.2947)	-0.3170 (0.1253)	-0.1929 (0.1451)	0.5393 (0.3488)	0.2921 (0.4147)	-0.0472 (0.4862)	-0.2831 (0.4049)	0.9932 (82.9853)	0.0181
13	Chemicals and mm fibres	-185.8193 (45.5295)	0.0643 (0.1694)	0.0698 (0.1161)	-0.0238 (0.0925)	0.0445 (0.2309)	0.4134 (0.1742)	-0.3640 (0.0978)	-0.0953 (0.1229)	0.3515 (0.3008)	0.2586 (0.2523)	0.4584 (0.2036)	-0.3184 (0.2028)	0.9819 (89.0752)	0.0146
14	Metal goods n.e.s.	54.6916 (125.6580)	0.2179 (0.1241)	0.0515 (0.1540)	-0.1951 (0.1097)	0.5656 (0.2116)	0.1800 (0.1728)	-0.2192 (0.1143)	0.0742 (0.1190)	0.1296 (0.3236)	-0.2402 (0.3611)	1.1805 (0.6468)	-1.0864 (0.4716)	0.9893 (83.2485)	0.0179
15	Mech. engineering	-61.0479 (69.0331)	0.4429 (0.1756)	-0.2644 (0.1849)	0.0449 (0.1384)	0.4550 (0.2231)	-0.0847 (0.2248)	-0.1736 (0.1317)	-0.3027 (0.1531)	-0.1211 (0.1878)	0.4252 (0.2083)	0.6855 (0.4794)	-0.5910 (0.5108)	0.9917 (90.3325)	0.0140

No.	Industry														
16	Office machinery, etc.	-469.2709 (238.0055)	0.3130 (0.1262)	-0.1861 (0.1643)	0.2028 (0.1074)	1.0064 (0.2490)	0.1025 (0.2770)	-0.6552 (0.2125)	-0.0961 (0.2181)	0.4731 (0.3203)	0.2497 (0.3034)	-0.7454 (1.1230)	0.3020 (1.1174)	0.9331 (71.1734)	0.0272
17	Elect. engineering	116.3987 (26.1750)	0.3691 (0.0762)	-0.0526 (0.1130)	0.0530 (0.0950)	0.1906 (0.1719)	0.1288 (0.1140)	-0.2311 (0.0838)	0.0905 (0.0842)	-0.0759 (0.1322)	0.5089 (0.1589)	0.5176 (0.2558)	-1.3098 (0.2954)	0.9894 (99.4433)	0.0102
18	Motor vehicles	-26.1567 (88.6237)	0.5670 (0.0721)	-0.2497 (0.1452)	-0.0747 (0.1808)	0.8065 (0.1991)	0.0150 (0.2676)	0.1033 (0.1286)	-0.2076 (0.1413)	0.2030 (0.2125)	-0.0142 (0.2216)	-0.0786 (0.3168)	-0.2601 (0.3650)	0.9868 (81.3391)	0.0191
19	Aerospace equipment	222.3672 (112.9182)	0.0106 (0.0956)	0.0719 (0.0983)	-0.0980 (0.0900)	0.8612 (0.2301)	-0.3314 (0.2567)	-0.0477 (0.1001)	-0.1448 (0.1029)	-0.2439 (0.2800)	0.2692 (0.2864)	-0.0317 (0.5831)	-0.6019 (0.4519)	0.9837 (67.3423)	0.0310
20	Ships and other vessels	-234.0763 (75.5925)	0.5828 (0.1078)	-0.1889 (0.1700)	-0.3240 (0.1530)	1.0843 (0.1868)	0.1554 (0.2188)	0.0276 (0.0654)	0.0009 (0.0839)	0.8235 (0.2530)	-0.4509 (0.2490)	-0.8088 (0.5227)	0.8595 (0.3407)	0.9881 (72.3533)	0.0261
21	Other vehicles	-168.3526 (135.2829)	0.2968 (0.1062)	0.1114 (0.1206)	-0.0248 (0.1278)	1.0604 (0.2377)	-0.1252 (0.2550)	-0.1545 (0.0741)	0.1153 (0.0652)	0.2878 (0.2332)	-0.1187 (0.2443)	0.9568 (0.4453)	-0.8510 (0.3900)	0.9968 (72.1643)	0.0262
22	Instr. engineering	467.8993 (122.7449)	0.0551 (0.1390)	0.1219 (0.1263)	0.3384 (0.1302)	0.2943 (0.1752)	-0.2474 (0.1310)	-0.1954 (0.0850)	0.2810 (0.0897)	-0.0956 (0.2179)	0.1420 (0.2458)	0.9770 (0.4345)	-2.4352 (0.5578)	0.9727 (87.4193)	0.0155
23	Manufactured food	-96.1864 (138.7636)	0.7245 (0.3199)	-0.3829 (0.2337)	0.1395 (0.2045)	0.4446 (0.1915)	0.2049 (0.1648)	-0.1728 (0.0757)	-0.0398 (0.1034)	-0.0032 (0.1593)	0.2371 (0.1614)	0.6892 (0.4081)	-1.0381 (0.3510)	0.9862 (88.2687)	0.0151
24	Alcoholic drinks, etc.	-106.2884 (190.7833)	0.4993 (0.5409)	0.0207 (0.5076)	-0.3969 (0.5117)	1.0974 (0.2355)	-0.1643 (0.3246)	-0.1113 (0.1279)	0.0734 (0.1178)	0.0755 (0.6244)	0.2879 (0.4363)	-0.5152 (0.6288)	0.2831 (0.5310)	0.9033 (68.1601)	0.0301
25	Tobacco	150.7833 (238.0243)	1.3370 (0.4483)	-0.4851 (0.4499)	-0.5259 (0.4688)	0.6519 (0.2355)	1.0220 (0.3253)	0.0061 (0.0687)	-0.1805 (0.0846)	-2.0127 (0.5811)	0.0303 (0.5378)	1.6853 (0.9638)	-0.6736 (0.7384)	0.8996 (56.2608)	0.0454
26	Textiles	-163.5445 (110.9788)	0.4008 (0.1809)	0.0199 (0.1746)	-0.3391 (0.1335)	0.3040 (0.2162)	0.1939 (0.1579)	-0.4269 (0.0869)	-0.1452 (0.1585)	0.2241 (0.2388)	0.1107 (0.3882)	-0.1934 (0.3831)	0.5008 (0.3380)	0.9984 (86.4858)	0.0160
27	Clothing and footwear	-50.6793 (62.0796)	0.5050 (0.1060)	0.0437 (0.1899)	-0.0218 (0.1111)	0.5797 (0.2890)	-0.0361 (0.1783)	-0.4216 (0.0871)	0.0527 (0.1505)	-0.1067 (0.1944)	-0.0706 (0.1993)	-0.0193 (0.3359)	0.1237 (0.2419)	0.9980 (94.1785)	0.0123
28	Timber and furniture	57.3350 (83.7562)	0.2824 (0.1185)	0.0633 (0.1490)	0.0163 (0.1127)	0.3392 (0.2469)	0.0730 (0.1428)	-0.2734 (0.0935)	0.0580 (0.0981)	0.0904 (0.2622)	-0.0689 (0.3858)	0.3085 (0.3788)	-0.4176 (0.3563)	0.9851 (89.4445)	0.0145
29	Paper and board	92.5460 (49.1811)	0.1240 (0.2041)	0.1082 (0.1692)	0.0645 (0.1207)	0.3571 (0.2419)	0.3316 (0.1362)	-0.1795 (0.0769)	0.1637 (0.1279)	0.4807 (0.3626)	0.1567 (0.3013)	0.1453 (0.4445)	-1.5894 (0.4768)	0.9942 (84.5039)	0.0171
30	Books, etc.	116.8745 (38.6891)	0.2547 (0.1161)	0.0013 (0.1355)	-0.0353 (0.0777)	0.8079 (0.2747)	-0.2086 (0.2297)	-0.0864 (0.0590)	-0.0626 (0.0617)	-0.1167 (0.1828)	-0.2457 (0.1840)	0.7865 (0.3149)	-0.5611 (0.2934)	0.9427 (96.8764)	0.0112

Note: n.e.s. – not elsewhere specified

	inpt: 40	y_t	y_{t-1}	y_{t-2}	h_{t-1}	h_{t-2}	w_t	w_{t-1}	$\dot{y}_{iu}$	$\dot{y}_{(t-1)u}$	d_t	d_{t-1}	$\bar{R}^2$ (LLF)	$\hat{\sigma}$
31 Rubber and plastic pr.	-114.0693 (68.7654)	0.3664 (0.2515)	-0.0228 (0.2248)	-0.3178 (0.1387)	0.4959 (0.2956)	0.3564 (0.2238)	-0.2941 (0.2183)	0.0733 (0.1284)	0.0953 (0.4141)	0.0950 (0.4318)	0.1452 (0.7177)	0.0405 (0.6053)	0.9795 (82.5569)	0.0183
32 Other manufactures	157.9064 (71.7964)	0.3169 (0.0739)	0.0061 (0.1356)	0.0167 (0.1194)	0.6974 (0.1986)	-0.0339 (0.2011)	-0.1025 (0.0938)	0.0520 (0.0909)	0.1378 (0.2044)	-0.6710 (0.2084)	0.5953 (0.2537)	-0.4945 (0.1999)	0.9918 (91.1621)	0.0136
33 Construction	0.1708 (72.0577)	0.3346 (0.1097)	-0.4336 (0.1464)	0.1650 (0.0958)	1.1032 (0.1785)	-0.2506 (0.1212)	-0.3106 (0.0893)	0.4361 (0.1073)	0.3935 (0.1970)	0.0579 (0.1980)	-0.4806 (0.3877)	0.1353 (0.3364)	0.9804 (89.9104)	0.0142
34 Distribution, etc.	165.8094 (89.2530)	-0.0730 (0.2295)	0.6536 (0.3158)	-0.1662 (0.1553)	0.7386 (0.2320)	-0.2110 (0.1739)	-0.1118 (0.1285)	-0.0537 (0.1296)	-0.0828 (0.1893)	-0.5416 (0.2348)	0.6452 (0.5798)	-0.4648 (0.4992)	0.9548 (88.7516)	0.0148
35 Hotels and catering	42.4162 (100.6322)	0.3120 (0.2517)	0.3603 (0.4124)	-0.2291 (0.3271)	0.5370 (0.3275)	0.0360 (0.2834)	-0.3282 (0.1593)	0.1610 (0.1738)	-0.0757 (0.2217)	-0.1791 (0.2135)	-0.1462 (0.3011)	0.2173 (0.2850)	0.8996 (77.6065)	0.0218
36 Rail transport	120.7537 (103.6046)	0.3027 (0.1210)	0.4311 (0.1312)	-0.0013 (0.1354)	0.4013 (0.1979)	-0.1819 (0.1413)	-0.1381 (0.1133)	-0.0703 (0.1043)	-0.1976 (0.2297)	-0.3762 (0.2246)	1.1548 (0.2405)	-0.7263 (0.1962)	0.9979 (84.8173)	0.0170
37 Other land transport	191.4749 (77.5060)	-0.0685 (0.1657)	0.2417 (0.1952)	-0.2581 (0.1712)	0.9714 (0.2405)	-0.3262 (0.2238)	0.0266 (0.0591)	0.0380 (0.0650)	0.0908 (0.1671)	-0.0147 (0.1733)	0.3518 (0.2886)	-0.4643 (0.2605)	0.9740 (85.5580)	0.0165
38 Sea, air and other	63.4575 (132.3929)	0.2006 (0.1897)	-0.5264 (0.2355)	-0.1053 (0.1519)	1.1557 (0.2143)	-0.5003 (0.2906)	-0.2569 (0.1420)	0.2130 (0.1521)	-0.0463 (0.2573)	0.6873 (0.3391)	-0.3834 (0.4332)	0.3880 (0.3686)	0.9196 (76.7924)	0.0224
39 Communications	259.2154 (82.2347)	0.5147 (0.2695)	-0.4403 (0.4696)	-0.2152 (0.3093)	0.6941 (0.2071)	-0.3138 (0.2094)	-0.1371 (0.1147)	0.1954 (0.1024)	-0.1709 (0.2188)	0.1549 (0.1711)	0.7280 (0.3443)	-0.5472 (0.2974)	0.9416 (84.0346)	0.0174
40 Business services	354.3580 (95.7801)	0.0441 (0.1496)	0.1689 (0.1514)	-0.1074 (0.1404)	0.3361 (0.2678)	-0.1646 (0.2481)	0.0769 (0.0859)	-0.1400 (0.0939)	-0.0283 (0.1137)	-0.2971 (0.1173)	0.9987 (0.3955)	-0.7970 (0.3127)	0.9942 (93.5970)	0.0125
41 Miscell. services	-248.5543 (145.5570)	0.4159 (0.1826)	-0.2700 (0.1973)	0.2990 (0.1843)	1.0218 (0.2370)	0.0167 (0.2849)	-0.2817 (0.1605)	0.1537 (0.1468)	0.0955 (0.2302)	0.1960 (0.2065)	-0.1665 (0.4956)	-0.1150 (0.4013)	0.9483 (76.1713)	0.0229

Notes: $\hat{\sigma}$ is equation standard errors.

LLF is the maximized value of log-likelihood function.

Standard errors in brackets, $\bar{R}^2$ is adjusted multiple correlation coefficient.

Source: For source of data see the Appendix.

Labour demand equations for the UK economy

$= 3$ and $r_w = r_a = 2$ in (6.9). Also included in the list of explanatory variables are current and lagged aggregate output measures,

$\bar{y}_{ta}$ and $\bar{y}_{t-1,a}$ $\left(\bar{y}_{ta} = \dfrac{1}{m} \sum\limits_{i=1}^{m} y_{ti} \right)$. These variables were shown to be

important in the empirical work of PPK, and it is clearly necessary to consider their influence here also. Their inclusion can be justified on the grounds that agents could use this aggregate information in the formation of their conditional expectations of y_{t+j}, w_{t+j} which we have shown to be important in explaining current employment. This unrestricted model differs from that in PPK by excluding the time trend, and by including y_{t-2}, d_t and d_{t-1}. Replacing the time trend by d_t and d_{t-1} alone caused a serious deterioration in the performance of many of the industrial equations, and in particular many became unstable. The inclusion of a second lagged output term remedied this in most of the equations, however, and table 6.1 represents a satisfactory set of results. The fit of most of the equations is satisfactory, with $\bar{R}^2$ falling below 0.90 only for industry 5 (Petroleum products). Short-run elasticities of employment with respect to wages, employment, and technological change are generally of the expected sign, although as the standard errors of the coefficients (shown in brackets) indicate, the equations are in many cases over-parameterized.

For this reason, a specification search was carried out on these equations to obtain a more parsimonious set of results, and these are presented in tables 6.2 and 6.3. Coefficients with t-values less than one (in absolute value) were omitted. Some *a priori* incorrectly signed coefficients were also constrained to zero where the constraints were not violated by the data. Specifically, we expect the coefficients on h_{t-2}, and the long-run wage and technological change effects to be negative. The χ^2 statistic for testing the validity of linear restrictions imposed on the parameters of the unrestricted equations to obtain the results of table 6.2 are given in the second column in table 6.3. It can be seen that the imposed restrictions are not rejected for any industry, at the conventional levels of significance.

The overall performance of the equations in table 6.2 is good and in line with those of PPK. Real wages show up significantly (and negatively) in most industries, with no long-run wage effect found only in industries 22, 33, 37, and 40. The output variable also performed well, showing significantly and positively in all but three industries (6, 20, 38), the last one of which shows a strong

Table 6.2 Restricted industrial labour demand equations

	inpl/40	y_t	y_{t-1}	y_{t-2}	h_{t-1}	h_{t-2}	w_t	w_{t-1}	y_{iw}	$y_{i(t-1)w}$	d_t	d_{t-1}
1 Agriculture, etc.	5.9025 (57.5851)	0.4080 (0.1365)	0.3215 (0.1440)	-0.1981 (0.1169)	0.4782 (0.0669)		-0.5134 (0.0836)		-0.3886 (0.0480)			
2 Coal mining	-24.6379 (10.1993)	0.2845 (0.0338)	-0.4268 (0.0716)	0.2247 (0.0957)	1.3624 (0.1359)	-0.4332 (0.1680)	-0.2194 (0.0297)				-0.1226 (0.0326)	
3 Coke	-81.9147 (66.9629)	0.3733 (0.1351)	0.5137 (0.2122)		0.1876 (0.1151)		-0.4294 (0.0790)		-0.1354 (0.1158)		-1.4606 (0.4225)	1.4606 (0.4225)
4 Mineral oil and nat. gas												
5 Petroleum products	-92.6973 (88.2755)	0.3475 (0.1847)			0.7915 (0.1253)		-0.2882 (0.1086)					
6 Electricity, etc.	42.7381 (26.8282)		0.5112 (0.1342)	-0.3648 (0.1475)	1.1202 (0.1862)	-0.4619 (0.1803)	-0.1490 (0.0746)				0.3281 (0.2698)	-0.5234 (0.2702)
7 Public gas supply	112.7709 (44.4602)		0.4462 (0.1803)	-0.5338 (0.1653)	0.6934 (0.1060)		-0.2975 (0.0681)	0.2300 (0.0774)			0.2793 (0.2408)	-0.3007 (0.1838)
8 Water supply	-167.9418 (62.5607)	1.4846 (0.3476)			0.4752 (0.1039)		-0.4094 (0.0976)	0.1846 (0.1085)	-0.5337 (0.2560)		-3.0775 (0.6623)	2.4681 (0.5508)
9 Minerals and ores nes	172.9158 (79.1246)	0.2655 (0.1265)			0.6931 (0.0790)		-0.1494 (0.0622)					
10 Iron and steel	-155.7089 (20.5070)	0.3796 (0.0562)	0.1997 (0.0711)		0.5533 (0.0854)		-0.3402 (0.0596)					0.1489 (0.0636)
11 Non-ferrous metals	-21.3448 (27.8342)	0.2912 (0.1040)	-0.1825 (0.1138)		1.0929 (0.1544)	-0.3288 (0.1229)	-0.1061 (0.0439)	-0.0520 (0.0496)	0.6320 (0.2043)	-0.7019 (0.1920)	0.2278 (0.0572)	
12 Non-metallic min. pr.	-236.8126 (65.3042)	0.3842 (0.1125)			0.8437 (0.0450)		-0.2505 (0.1029)	-0.1262 (0.1188)	0.3674 (0.2118)			-0.2609 (0.1336)
13 Chemicals and mm fibres	-99.1032 (28.1020)				0.5831 (0.0710)		-0.2735 (0.0329)		0.5764 (0.0769)		0.2720 (0.1678)	-0.2720 (0.1678)
14 Metal goods nes	-51.0504 (67.1158)	0.2663 (0.1006)			0.6006 (0.0653)		-0.2355 (0.0763)		0.2716 (0.2663)		0.4410 (0.3831)	-0.6038 (0.3240)
15 Mech. engineering	-101.2152 (51.8451)	0.4909 (0.0750)	-0.3408 (0.1484)	0.1184 (0.0960)	0.5996 (0.2087)	-0.2925 (0.1792)	-0.1979 (0.1133)	-0.3348 (0.1163)		0.4802 (0.1746)		
16 Office machinery, etc.	-67.1178 (75.6691)			0.2278 (0.0600)	0.8571 (0.0721)		-0.2389 (0.1049)		0.2548 (0.1399)		1.0366 (0.5489)	-1.5206 (0.5314)
17 Elect. engineering	106.1219 (25.5818)	0.3463 (0.0462)			0.3886 (0.0646)		-0.2592 (0.0771)	0.1351 (0.0637)		0.3684 (0.1099)	0.2694 (0.1979)	
18 Motor vehicles	-74.0164 (48.8105)	0.5451 (0.0470)	-0.2618 (0.1197)		0.8395 (0.1614)	-0.1165 (0.0909)		-0.2102 (0.0666)	0.2625 (0.1099)		-0.2471 (0.0892)	-0.9762 (0.2051)
19 Aerospace equipment	246.9802 (75.2084)				1.1388 (0.1495)	-0.6421 (0.1727)		-0.1737 (0.0720)			-0.6598 (0.2197)	
20 Ships and other vessels	-0.7667 (0.3086)	0.4809 (0.1171)	-0.4809 (0.1171)		1.4717 (0.1543)	-0.4717 (0.1543)			0.5103 (0.2000)	-0.5103 (0.2000)		

	(1)	(2)	(3)	(4)	(5)	(6)	(7)	(8)	(9)	(10)	(11)	(12)
21 Other vehicles	−165.4705 (58.7346)	0.3896 (0.0706)			0.9154 (0.0419)		−0.1680 (0.0552)	0.1064 (0.0564)	0.2078 (0.1235)		0.7687 (0.3109)	−0.7687 (0.3109)
22 Instr. engineering	423.2630 (55.7285)		0.2115 (0.0825)	0.3539 (0.0987)	0.3177 (0.1267)	−0.2486 (0.1064)	−0.2377 (0.0581)	0.2377 (0.0581)			1.2396 (0.3043)	−2.6097 (0.3537)
23 Manufactured food	−172.9101 (63.0103)	0.5982 (0.1660)			0.4844 (0.1266)	0.3037 (0.1327)	−0.2337 (0.0581)				0.6483 (0.3462)	−0.8005 (0.3177)
24 Alcoholic drinks, etc.	−96.0446 (69.2247)				1.1312 (0.1750)	−0.3072 (0.2359)	−0.0956 (0.0705)		0.4479 (0.1457)			−0.1047 (0.0868)
25 Tobacco	155.5488 (182.3643)	1.3459 (0.4049)	−0.4827 (0.4058)	−0.5240 (0.3982)	0.6473 (0.2205)	1.0209 (0.2796)		−0.1781 (0.0668)	−2.0136 (0.5337)		1.7244 (0.6965)	−0.6987 (0.6201)
26 Textiles	−69.3333 (39.2933)	0.3637 (0.0675)	−0.2759 (0.0871)		0.5652 (0.0657)				0.0882 (0.1207)			0.2960 (0.1265)
27 Clothing and footwear	−68.9489 (11.9600)	0.4514 (0.0372)			0.5364 (0.0411)		−0.4337 (0.0753)					
28 Timber and furniture	27.5732 (13.7004)	0.3925 (0.0352)	0.1880 (0.0929)		0.5144 (0.0572)		−0.3756 (0.0284)	0.1108 (0.0681)			−0.1174 (0.0282)	
29 Paper and board	39.4291 (31.8083)	0.4375 (0.0640)	−0.2040 (0.0681)		0.4661 (0.0659)		−0.2885 (0.0595)		−0.2125 (0.1434)		−0.5252 (0.1523)	
30 Books, etc.	96.1742 (32.3071)	0.4094 (0.0946)			1.3273 (0.1955)	−0.6121 (0.1602)	−0.2130 (0.0477)	−0.0578 (0.0477)				
31 Rubber and plastic pr.	−81.7005 (16.8687)	0.4581 (0.0427)		−0.2463 (0.0729)	0.5365 (0.1198)	0.3160 (0.1195)	−0.2692 (0.0700)					
32 Other manufactures	56.9103 (51.0746)	0.2992 (0.0602)			0.7367 (0.0902)		−0.0805 (0.0810)		0.4048 (0.1692)	−0.6459 (0.1125)		
33 Construction	3.3516 (27.4087)	0.3475 (0.0858)	−0.3710 (0.1167)	0.1345 (0.0835)	0.9814 (0.0957)	−0.2355 (0.0955)	−0.3435 (0.0704)	0.3435 (0.0704)	0.3916 (0.1500)		−0.2830 (0.0705)	
34 Distribution, etc.	141.2744 (41.2202)		0.7842 (0.1615)	−0.2726 (0.1207)	0.6360 (0.0917)		−0.0409 (0.0356)			−0.5717 (0.1527)		
35 Hotels and catering	−58.7494 (44.4425)	0.3544 (0.1150)			0.7096 (0.1022)		−0.3876 (0.1191)	0.1959 (0.1094)				
36 Rail transport	−50.9886 (25.3141)	0.1307 (0.0894)	0.3372 (0.1055)		0.5187 (0.0978)		−0.2545 (0.0718)				0.8608 (0.2211)	−0.6958 (0.1953)
37 Other land transport	118.4359 (34.6439)		0.2123 (0.1302)	−0.2016 (0.1434)	1.0003 (0.1803)	−0.2638 (0.1884)					0.4509 (0.2304)	−0.5162 (0.1937)
38 Sea, air and other	67.2451 (92.1103)	0.1608 (0.1269)	−0.3506 (0.1263)		1.2952 (0.1460)	−0.6002 (0.1863)	−0.2432 (0.1204)	0.1835 (0.1255)		0.3148 (0.1521)		
39 Communications	309.7212 (57.1105)				0.5777 (0.1677)	−0.4744 (0.1616)	−0.0937 (0.0631)	0.0860 (0.0664)			1.0539 (0.2010)	−0.9139 (0.1745)
40 Business services	209.6513 (49.1545)	0.3108 (0.0718)			0.6781 (0.1759)					−0.1633 (0.0486)		
41 Miscell. services	−39.9043 (33.3057)	0.2123 (0.0790)			0.8264 (0.0970)	−0.3104 (0.1680)	−0.1408 (0.0747)					

See notes to table 6.1.

Table 6.3 Summary and diagnostic statistics for the restricted employment equations of table 6.2

Industry	$\bar{R}^2$	x_c^2	$\hat{\sigma}$	$x_{sc}^2(1)$	$x_{Fr}^2(1)$	$x_{\dot{r}}^2(2)$	$x_{\dot{r}}^2(1)$
1 Agriculture, etc.	0.9983	5.00 (5)	0.0136	0.08	5.96	0.02	0.06
2 Coal mining	0.9987	4.02 (4)	0.0155	0.00	0.25	1.18	0.32
3 Coke	0.9656	10.10 (5)	0.0551	0.00	13.82	0.50	2.96
4 Mineral oil and nat. gas	—	—	—	—	—	—	—
5 Petroleum products	0.8874	6.94 (6)	0.0663	0.00	1.89	1.93	0.33
6 Electricity, etc.	0.9909	7.59 (4)	0.0163	1.08	1.26	0.22	2.58
7 Public gas supply	0.9773	8.14 (6)	0.0290	4.60	1.11	4.12	5.42
8 Water supply	0.9520	10.06 (5)	0.0336	0.01	0.38	0.71	0.00
9 Minerals and ores nes	0.9760	3.84 (7)	0.0318	1.36	0.16	32.70	0.00
10 Iron and steel	0.9919	8.63 (6)	0.0291	0.20	4.59	2.08	0.77
11 Non-ferrous metals	0.9912	1.31 (2)	0.0202	4.25	2.19	2.75	0.05
12 Non-metallic min. pr.	0.9937	4.82 (5)	0.0174	1.82	4.70	2.09	4.48
13 Chemicals and mm fibres	0.9808	9.67 (7)	0.0151	4.76	3.53	1.65	1.29
14 Metal goods nes	0.9898	5.39 (5)	0.0174	0.21	5.96	1.69	4.74
15 Mech. engineering	0.9916	4.60 (3)	0.0141	0.17	0.21	0.02	1.09
16 Office machinery, etc.	0.9291	7.85 (5)	0.0280	0.38	1.10	0.76	4.48
17 Elect. engineering	0.9893	5.82 (4)	0.0103	1.79	0.01	0.41	1.12
18 Motor vehicles	0.9887	1.43 (4)	0.0176	4.16	0.88	1.55	1.58
19 Aerospace equipment	0.9847	7.20 (7)	0.0301	3.56	1.04	0.06	2.78
20 Ships and other vessels	0.9818	16.13 (8)	0.0323	0.45	0.61	0.40	4.46
21 Other vehicles	0.9972	2.85 (5)	0.0243	0.90	2.10	0.33	2.59
22 Instr. engineering	0.9759	2.44 (4)	0.0146	1.57	1.29	2.14	1.02
23 Manufactured food	0.9856	7.50 (5)	0.0154	0.43	0.48	6.76	2.46
24 Alcoholic drinks, etc.	0.9119	5.49 (6)	0.0288	0.10	1.43	0.71	3.57
25 Tobacco	0.9101	0.02 (2)	0.0430	4.95	16.07	0.09	0.04
26 Textiles	0.9985	5.09 (5)	0.0155	4.21	2.46	2.20	2.03
27 Clothing and footwear	0.9984	4.32 (8)	0.0110	0.36	1.92	0.62	0.03
28 Timber and furniture	0.9873	3.76 (6)	0.0133	0.08	3.73	0.91	0.85

		R^2	χ_r^2	$\chi_{SC}^2(1)$	$\hat\sigma$	$\chi_N^2(2)$	$\chi_{FF}^2(1)$	$\chi_H^2(1)$
29	Paper and board	0.9932	10.81 (6)	5.30	0.0186	0.14	1.73	6.16
30	Books, etc.	0.9341	9.52 (5)	1.76	0.0120	0.00	0.00	1.13
31	Rubber and plastic pr.	0.9834	2.51 (6)	0.14	0.0165	2.45	0.50	0.01
32	Other manufactures	0.9908	9.82 (6)	0.22	0.0144	0.37	1.11	0.02
33	Construction	0.9819	2.42 (3)	0.02	0.0137	0.10	0.73	0.27
34	Distribution, etc.	0.9603	4.63 (6)	0.32	0.0139	1.96	0.23	2.47
35	Hotels and catering	0.9169	4.17 (7)	0.58	0.0198	1.88	0.45	0.63
36	Rail transport	0.9975	9.84 (5)	0.03	0.0183	0.38	2.66	0.86
37	Other land transport	0.9766	4.12 (5)	0.13	0.0157	0.98	1.02	0.02
38	Sea, air and other	0.9278	2.87 (4)	2.23	0.0212	7.95	1.88	0.91
39	Communications	0.9388	7.59 (5)	0.53	0.0178	1.51	1.16	4.09
40	Business services	0.9940	9.26 (7)	0.98	0.0128	2.01	1.98	0.17
41	Miscell. services	0.9512	8.14 (8)	0.06	0.0222	0.47	0.39	1.91

Notes:

χ_r^2 is the chi-squared statistic for the test of r linear restrictions on the parameters of unrestricted employment equations (see table 6.1). The value of r is given in brackets after the statistic.

$\chi_{SC}^2(1)$ is the first order LM test of residual serial correlation.

$\chi_N^2(2)$ is a test of normality of the errors.

$\hat\sigma$ is equations' standard errors.

$\chi_{FF}^2(1)$ is Ramsey's RESET test of order 1.

$\chi_H^2(1)$ is a heteroscedasticity test of order 1.

$\bar R^2$ is the adjusted multiple correlation coefficient.

The underlying regressions and the test statistics reported in this table are computed on Microfit package. For details of relevant algorithms and references – see Pesaran and Pesaran (1987).

Table 6.4 Composite restricted industrial labour demand equations

	inpt/40	y_t	y_{t-1}	y_{t-2}	h_{t-1}	h_{t-2}	w_t	w_{t-1}	y_{ia}	y_{t-1ia}	d_t	d_{t-1}	T_t
1 Agriculture. etc.	5.9025 (57.5851)	0.4080 (0.1365)	0.3215 (0.1440)	-0.1981 (0.1169)	0.4782 (0.0669)		-0.5134 (0.0836)		-0.3886 (0.0480)				-1.3100 (0.1752)
2 Coal mining	-24.6379 (10.1993)	0.2845 (0.0338)	-0.4268 (0.0716)	0.2247 (0.0957)	1.3624 (0.1359)	-0.4332 (0.1680)	-0.2194 (0.0297)				-0.1226 (0.0326)		
3 Coke	-351.5712 (44.6561)		0.6330 (0.1471)				-0.3005 (0.0418)		1.0448 (0.1564)				
4 Mineral oil and nat. gas													
5 Petroleum products	-70.7959 (71.7711)	0.3640 (0.1324)			0.5185 (0.1348)		-0.3144 (0.0869)						-0.5087 (0.1297)
6 Electricity. etc.	42.7381 (26.8282)		0.5112 (0.1342)	-0.3648 (0.1475)	1.1202 (0.1862)	-0.4619 (0.1803)	-0.1490 (0.0746)				0.2793 (0.2408)	-0.3007 (0.1838)	
7 Public gas supply	-47.1096 (97.2188)		0.0611 (0.0659)		0.4191 (0.1524)		-0.1507 (0.0496)		0.5379 (0.1827)				-0.6014 (0.1995)
8 Water supply	-167.9418 (62.5607)	1.4846 (0.3476)			0.4752 (0.1039)		-0.4094 (0.0976)	0.1846 (0.1085)					
9 Minerals and ores nes	172.9158 (79.1246)	0.2655 (0.1265)			0.6931 (0.0790)		-0.1494 (0.0622)		-0.5337 (0.2560)			2.4681 (0.5508)	
10 Iron and steel	-349.9558 (58.8686)	0.1083 (0.0893)			0.4978 (0.0832)		-0.3873 (0.0777)		1.1803 (0.2928)				-0.9045 (0.2732)
11 Non-ferrous metals	-84.8257 (30.7245)	0.1817 (0.1286)	-0.3091 (0.1273)		1.2461 (0.1458)		-0.0756 (0.0481)	0.0756 (0.0481)	0.5854 (0.1789)				-0.5749 (0.1517)
12 Non-metallic min. pr.	-280.5702 (60.6439)	0.3101 (0.1511)			0.6919 (0.0877)		-0.2356 (0.1075)	-0.2214 (0.0959)	0.5170 (0.2901)				-0.3729 (0.2148)
13 Chemicals and mm fibres	-125.0557 (23.8339)				0.6205 (0.0693)		-0.2810 (0.0337)		0.6049 (0.0773)				
14 Metal goods nes	-32.2448 (25.5280)	0.4365 (0.0444)			0.5798 (0.0542)		-0.1671 (0.0817)						-0.1231 (0.0976)
15 Mech. engineering	-101.2152 (51.8451)	0.4909 (0.0750)	-0.3408 (0.1484)		0.5996 (0.2087)	-0.2925 (0.1792)	-0.1979 (0.1133)	-0.3348 (0.1163)		0.4802 (0.1746)			
16 Office machinery. etc.	-67.1178 (75.6691)				0.8571 (0.0721)		-0.2389 (0.1049)				1.0366 (0.5489)	-1.5206 (0.5314)	
17 Elect. engineering	106.1219 (25.5818)	0.3463 (0.0462)			0.3886 (0.0646)		-0.2592 (0.0771)	0.1351 (0.0637)	0.2548 (0.1399)	0.3684 (0.1099)	0.2694 (0.1979)	-0.9762 (0.2051)	
18 Motor vehicles	-74.0164 (48.8105)	0.5451 (0.0470)	-0.2618 (0.1197)		0.8395 (0.1614)	-0.1165 (0.0909)		-0.2102 (0.0666)	0.2625 (0.1099)		-0.2471 (0.0892)		
19 Aerospace equipment	200.3920 (53.1219)	0.0732 (0.0654)			0.7560 (0.1659)	-0.4659 (0.1440)		-0.1252 (0.0674)					-0.6788 (0.1586)
20 Ships and other vessels	-0.7667 (0.3086)	0.4809 (0.1171)	-0.4809 (0.1171)		1.4717 (0.1543)	-0.4717 (0.1543)			0.5103 (0.2000)	-0.5103 (0.2000)			

Industry	Constant												
21 Other vehicles	−165.4705 (58.7346)	0.3896 (0.0706)			0.9154 (0.0419)		−0.1680 (0.0552)	0.1064 (0.0564)	0.2078 (0.1235)		0.7687 (0.3109)	−0.7687 (0.3109)	
22 Instr. engineering	423.2630 (55.7285)		0.2115 (0.0825)	0.3539 (0.0987)	0.3177 (0.1267)	−0.2486 (0.1064)	−0.2377 (0.0581)	0.2377 (0.0581)			1.2396 (0.3043)	−2.6097 (0.3537)	−0.4510 (0.1973)
23 Manufactured food	−172.1572 (76.0519)	0.6697 (0.1734)			0.3177 (0.1742)		−0.1962 (0.0645)			0.1157 (0.1233)			−0.4844 (0.1411)
24 Alcoholic drinks, etc.	−15.1802 (73.4889)	0.2933 (0.1167)			0.7283 (0.1239)	0.2237 (0.1560)	−0.0945 (0.0919)	0.0591 (0.0882)					−0.3959 (0.1161)
25 Tobacco	−213.3698 (80.8449)	0.7424 (0.2840)			0.7367 (0.2225)	0.2633 (0.2225)							
26 Textiles	−69.3333 (39.2933)	0.3637 (0.0675)			0.5552 (0.0657)		−0.4337 (0.0753)					0.2960 (0.1265)	
27 Clothing and footwear	−68.9489 (11.9600)	0.4514 (0.0372)		−0.2759 (0.0871)	0.5364 (0.0411)		−0.3756 (0.0284)		0.0882 (0.1207)				
28 Timber and furniture	27.5732 (13.7004)	0.3925 (0.0352)			0.5144 (0.0572)		−0.2885 (0.0595)	0.1108 (0.0681)			−0.1174 (0.0282)		
29 Paper and board	−44.7394 (13.2869)	0.4680 (0.0652)	0.1585 (0.0925)		0.3644 (0.0842)		−0.2503 (0.0433)					−0.3259 (0.1040)	
30 Books, etc.	96.1742 (32.3071)	0.4094 (0.0946)	−0.2040 (0.0681)		1.3273 (0.1955)	−0.6121 (0.1602)	−0.0578 (0.0477)		−0.2125 (0.1434)				
31 Rubber and plastic pr.	−64.4432 (14.2846)	0.5398 (0.0588)	−0.1401 (0.0963)		0.6844 (0.0818)		−0.1820 (0.1007)					−0.3192 (0.1872)	
32 Other manufactures	60.3555 (20.0274)	0.2345 (0.0435)			0.6028 (0.0933)					−0.4274 (0.1287)		−0.3233 (0.0653)	
33 Construction	3.3516 (27.4087)	0.3475 (0.0858)	−0.3710 (0.1167)	0.1345 (0.0835)	0.9814 (0.0957)	−0.2355 (0.0955)	−0.3435 (0.0704)	0.3435 (0.0704)	0.4274 (0.1287)		−0.2830 (0.0705)		
34 Distribution, etc.	141.2744 (41.2202)		0.7842 (0.1615)	−0.2726 (0.1207)	0.6360 (0.0917)		−0.0409 (0.0356)		0.3916 (0.1500)	−0.5717 (0.1527)			
35 Hotels and catering	−58.7494 (44.4425)	0.3544 (0.1150)			0.7096 (0.1022)		−0.3876 (0.1191)	0.1959 (0.1094)					
36 Rail transport	−50.9886 (25.5141)	0.1307 (0.0894)	0.3372 (0.1055)		0.5187 (0.0978)		−0.2545 (0.0718)				0.8608 (0.2211)		
37 Other land transport	118.4359 (34.6439)		0.2123 (0.1302)	−0.2016 (0.1434)	1.0003 (0.1803)	−0.2638 (0.1884)					0.4509 (0.2304)		
38 Sea, air and other	67.2451 (92.1103)	0.1608 (0.1269)			1.2952 (0.1460)	−0.6002 (0.1460)	−0.2432 (0.1204)	0.1835 (0.1255)		0.3148 (0.1521)			
39 Communications	14.3221 (41.3966)	0.9014 (0.1808)	−0.3506 (0.1263)		0.8261 (0.1727)	−0.2785 (0.1579)	−0.1686 (0.0822)	0.1565 (0.0807)					−0.6566 (0.2354)
40 Business services	209.6513 (49.1545)	0.3108 (0.0718)	−0.4533 (0.1966)		0.6781 (0.1759)	−0.3104 (0.1680)				−0.1633 (0.0486)			
41 Miscell. services	−39.9043 (33.3057)	0.2123 (0.0790)			0.8264 (0.0970)		−0.1408 (0.0747)						

See notes to table 6.1.

Table 6.5 Summary and diagnostic statistics for the restricted employment equations of table 6.4

Industry	$\bar{R}^2$	x^2_j	$\hat{\sigma}$	$x^2_{Sc}(1)$	$x^2_{FF}(1)$	$x^2_N(2)$	$x^2_H(1)$
1 Agriculture, etc.	0.9983	5.21 (6)	0.0136	0.08	5.96	0.02	0.06
2 Coal mining	0.9987	6.84 (5)	0.0155	0.00	0.25	1.18	0.32
3 Coke (*)	0.9771	10.15 (8)	0.0449	0.24	0.67	0.27	1.87
4 Mineral oil and nat. gas	—	—	—	—	—	—	—
5 Petroleum products (*)	0.9178	13.40 (8)	0.0566	0.48	0.01	1.83	0.85
6 Electricity, etc.	0.9909	14.25 (5)	0.0163	1.08	1.26	0.22	2.58
7 Public gas supply (*)	0.9719	23.36 (7)	0.0322	1.29	0.00	4.86	1.42
8 Water supply	0.9520	10.18 (6)	0.0336	0.01	0.38	0.71	0.00
9 Minerals and ores nes	0.9760	3.90 (8)	0.0318	1.36	0.16	32.70	0.00
10 Iron and steel (*)	0.9933	12.88 (7)	0.0265	0.08	0.19	1.42	0.43
11 Non-ferrous metals (*)	0.9864	13.33 (5)	0.0250	0.01	3.47	0.20	1.89
12 Non-metallic min. pr. (*)	0.9935	12.21 (6)	0.0177	1.11	0.23	0.76	3.15
13 Chemicals and mm fibres (*)	0.9795	11.78 (9)	0.0156	3.51	1.80	0.96	1.14
14 Metal goods nes (*)	0.9877	12.31 (8)	0.0192	0.09	0.27	0.38	1.00
15 Mech. engineering	0.9916	4.63 (4)	0.0141	0.17	0.21	0.02	1.09
16 Office machinery, etc.	0.9291	9.49 (6)	0.0280	0.38	1.10	0.76	4.48
17 Elect. engineering	0.9893	11.58 (5)	0.0103	1.79	0.01	0.41	1.12
18 Motor vehicles	0.9887	4.82 (5)	0.0176	4.16	0.88	1.55	1.58
19 Aerospace equipment (*)	0.9878	6.31 (7)	0.0268	0.90	0.30	1.81	1.30
20 Ships and other vessels	0.9818	16.91 (9)	0.0323	0.45	0.61	0.40	4.46
21 Other vehicles	0.9972	12.07 (6)	0.0243	0.90	2.10	0.33	2.59
22 Instr. engineering	0.9759	2.46 (5)	0.0146	1.57	1.29	2.14	1.02
23 Manufactured food (*)	0.9837	13.89 (6)	0.0164	1.69	2.78	1.33	4.38
24 Alcoholic drinks, etc.	0.9232	15.42 (7)	0.0269	1.32	0.02	0.94	2.06
25 Tobacco (*)	0.8796	16.63 (9)	0.0497	0.25	8.22	0.65	7.62
26 Textiles	0.9985	5.59 (6)	0.0155	4.21	2.46	2.20	2.03
27 Clothing and footwear	0.9984	4.37 (9)	0.0110	0.36	1.92	0.62	0.03
28 Timber and furniture	0.9873	6.05 (7)	0.0133	0.08	3.73	0.91	0.85

29	Paper and board (*)	0.9927	12.00 (7)	0.0192	1.09	1.33	1.74	4.41
30	Books, etc.	0.9341	9.55 (6)	0.0120	1.76	0.00	0.00	1.13
31	Rubber and plastic pr. (*)	0.9818	8.01 (7)	0.0173	0.21	1.59	0.96	1.03
32	Other manufactures (*)	0.9917	13.49 (8)	0.0137	0.37	0.21	1.12	0.00
33	Construction	0.9819	2.58 (4)	0.0137	0.02	0.10	0.73	0.27
34	Distribution, etc.	0.9603	13.35 (7)	0.0139	0.32	1.96	0.23	2.47
35	Hotels and catering	0.9169	5.59 (8)	0.0198	0.58	1.88	0.45	0.63
36	Rail transport	0.9975	11.38 (6)	0.0183	0.03	0.38	2.66	0.86
37	Other land transport	0.9766	8.48 (6)	0.0157	0.13	0.98	1.02	0.02
38	Sea, air and other	0.9278	6.26 (5)	0.0212	2.23	7.95	1.88	0.91
39	Communications (*)	0.9351	8.03 (5)	0.0184	1.56	0.48	0.14	1.81
40	Business services	0.9940	9.33 (8)	0.0128	0.98	2.01	1.98	0.17
41	Miscell. services	0.9512	8.20 (9)	0.0222	0.06	0.47	0.39	1.91

See notes to table 6.3.

positive aggregate output influence. Only fifteen of the industries failed to demonstrate any technological change effects, although there are problem industries (10, 11, 26, 36, and 39) for which the technological change variables are (in sum) incorrectly signed. Other industries with *a priori* implausible parameter estimates include 23, 26, and 31, in which an unexpected positive second lagged dependent variable appears, and industry 25 which is unstable. Industry 20 also remains problematic: the differenced form reported in the PPK paper could not be improved upon, and this equation is retained here.

The histograms in figure 6.1–6.3 illustrate the long-run elasticities of employment with respect to industrial output, wages, and technological change as obtained from the results in table 6.2. Figure 6.1 shows the long-run output elasticities for thirty-eight industries, omitting industries 20 and 25; the two industries with incorrectly signed output effects show to the left of the vertical axis, while industry 21 demonstrates an implausibly high positive

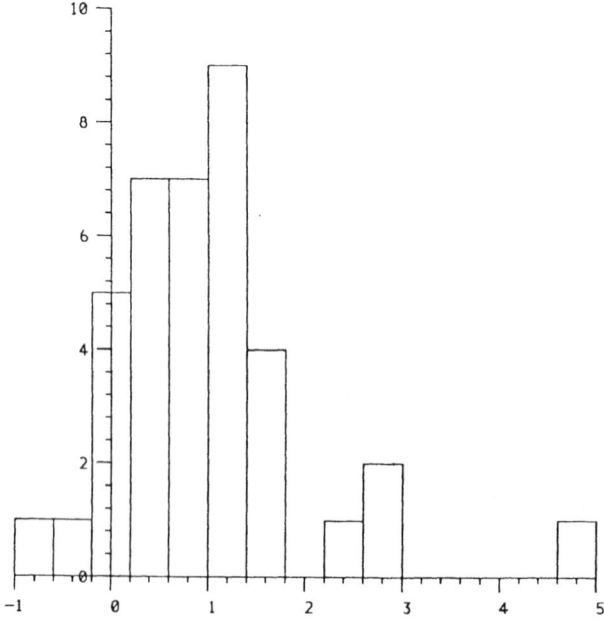

Figure 6.1 Long-run industry output elasticities from table 6.2

output elasticity (the equation for this industry has a coefficient on the lagged dependent variable in excess of 0.9). The output elasticities for the bulk of the industries, however, lie within the interval (0, 1.5) and the mean long-run output elasticity is 0.97. The histogram in figure 6.1 provides a clear illustration of the variability in the responsiveness of employment to output changes across industries, and this is confirmed by a standard deviation around the mean of 0.86. Similar observations can be made on the long-run real wage and technological change elasticities, which have means (standard deviations in brackets), −0.68 (0.66), and −0.41 (0.81) respectively.

The preferred equations set out in table 6.2 show the technological change variable d_t to be an adequate replacement for the time trend in some industries, but not all. Of the twenty-four industrial equations in which a significant time trend was found in PPK, fifteen are improved upon, in terms of the equation standard errors, by their equivalent estimate in table 6.2, while nine fit less

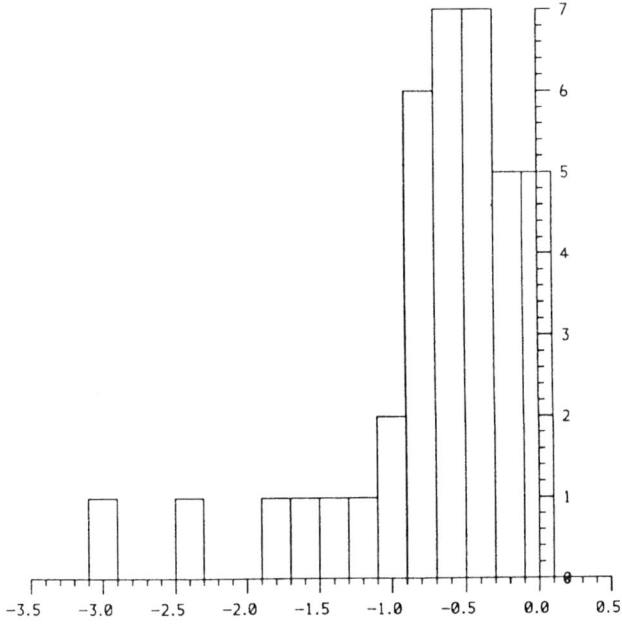

Figure 6.2 Long-run industry real wage elasticities from table 6.2

137

well in the absence of the time trend. Moreover, there are a further eleven equations which did not previously involve a time trend whose standard error is lower in table 6.2 than that in PPK, demonstrating the extra explanatory power of the additional lagged output and technological change variables. Since we prefer to replace a time trend with a variable with a more satisfactory theoretical basis, and given that the fit of this new set of equations is generally higher, these results, taken as a whole, can be seen as an improvement over those obtained previously.

Having made these points, however, closer comparison of the results in tables 6.2 and 6.3 with those in PPK reveals that in some cases the diagnostic test statistics on the new set of equations are less reasonable than those previously found, and in all sixteen industries have a preferable specification in the PPK paper. The superiority of the original equations in so many industries cannot of course be ignored, and for this reason we present a third set of industrial equations in tables 6.4 and 6.5 which are an amal-gamation of the results in table 6.2 and those in PPK. (The PPK

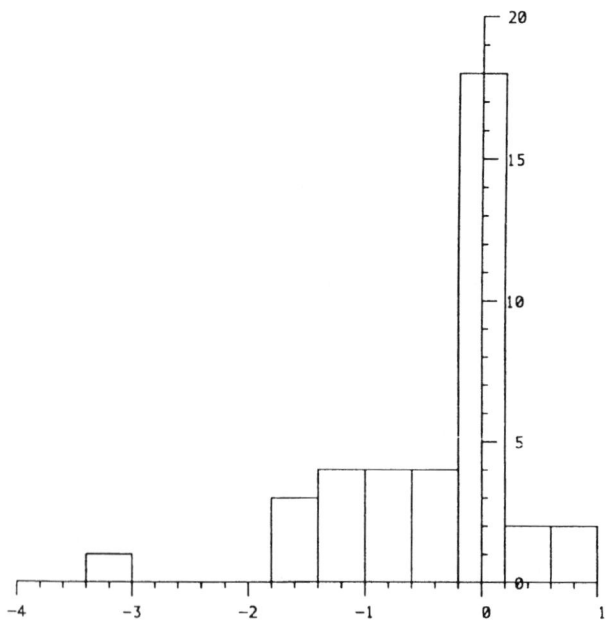

Figure 6.3 Long-run industry productivity elasticities from table 6.2

results are labelled *.) These results represent the most satisfactory set of equations that we have been able to obtain for explaining employment at the industrial level in the UK. As before, the long-run coefficients are represented diagrammatically in the histograms of figures 6.4–6.6. Estimated coefficients are once again largely of the expected sign, and of a reasonable magnitude. The mean and standard deviation (in brackets) of the plotted long-run elasticities are 0.86 (0.88), −0.54 (0.58), and −0.27 (0.72) for output, wages, and technological change respectively, confirming the considerable variability of long-run estimates across the industries and providing a reasonable *a priori* case for the use of disaggregated analysis.

6.4.4 Comparison with the aggregate relations

The following unrestricted and restricted aggregate employment equations, corresponding to the results discussed above, were also estimated:

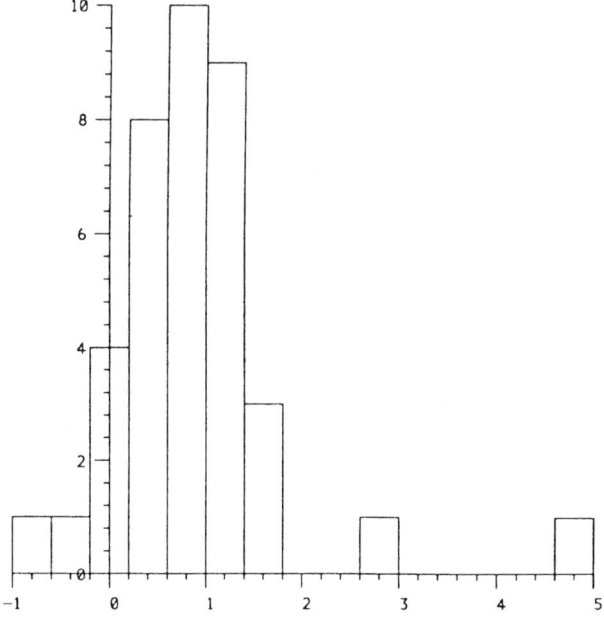

Figure 6.4 Long-run industry output elasticities from table 6.3

Disaggregation in econometric modelling

Unrestricted aggregate equation

$$h_{ta} = -137.45 + 0.49689 \ y_{ta} + 0.19565 \ y_{(t-1)a} + 0.11375 \ y_{(t-2)a}$$
$$(3.77) \ (6.39) \qquad\qquad (1.32) \qquad\qquad\qquad (1.03)$$

$$+ 0.33110 \ h_{(t-1)a} + 0.18986 \ h_{(t-2)a} - 0.34110 \ w_{ta}$$
$$(1.48) \qquad\qquad (1.17) \qquad\qquad (-5.13)$$

$$- 0.087043 \ w_{(t-1)a} - 0.046365 \ d_{ta}$$
$$(-1.00) \qquad\qquad (-0.13)$$

$$- 0.23405 \ d_{(t-1)a} \qquad\qquad\qquad\qquad\qquad (6.19)$$
$$(-0.82)$$

$\bar{R}^2 = 0.998, \quad \hat{\sigma} = 0.3316, \quad n = 29 \ (1956\text{--}1984)$

$\chi^2_{SC}(1) = 3.23, \quad \chi^2_{FF}(1) = 1.27, \quad \chi^2_N(2) = 0.67, \quad \chi^2_H(1) = 3.51$

The figures in brackets are t-ratios, $\hat{\sigma}$ is the standard error of the regression, $\bar{R}^2$ is the adjusted R^2, n is the number of observations.

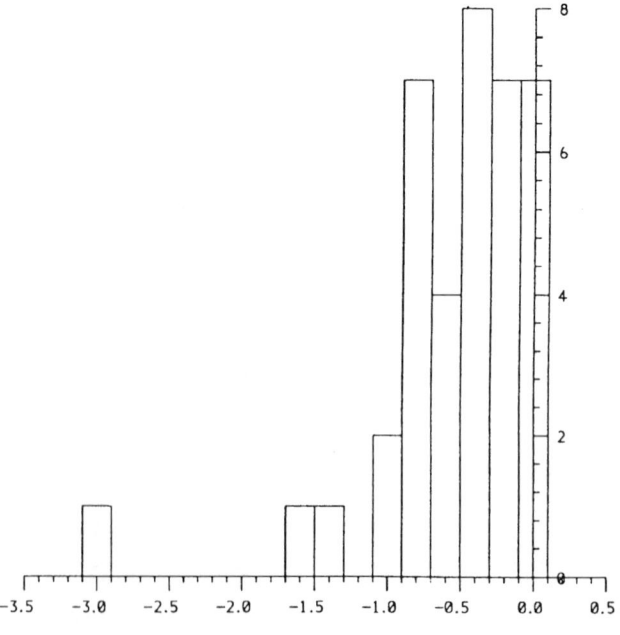

Figure 6.5 Long-run industry real wage elasticities from table 6.3

$\chi_{SC}^2(1)$, $\chi_{FF}^2(1)$, $\chi_N^2(2)$, $\chi_H^2(1)$ are diagnostic statistics distributed approximately as chi-squared variates (with degrees of freedom in parentheses), for tests of residual serial correlation, functional form misspecification, non-normal errors, and heteroscedasticity, respectively. (For more details about these test statistics and their computations see Pesaran and Pesaran, 1987.)

Restricted aggregate equation

$$h_{ta} = -99.28 + \underset{(11.06)}{0.49854}\ y_{ta} + \underset{(17.37)}{0.67897}\ h_{(t-1)a}$$
$$\underset{(-4.84)}{}$$

$$- \underset{(-7.53)}{0.31216}\ w_{ta} - \underset{(-2.33)}{0.12049}\ d_{(t-1)a}, \tag{6.20}$$

$$\bar{R}^2 = 0.997, \quad \hat{\sigma} = 0.3209, \quad n = 29\ (1956\text{--}1984)$$

$$\chi_{SC}^2(1) = 1.83, \quad \chi_{FF}^2(1) = 2.46, \quad \chi_N^2(2) = 1.68, \quad \chi_H^2(1) = 5.29$$

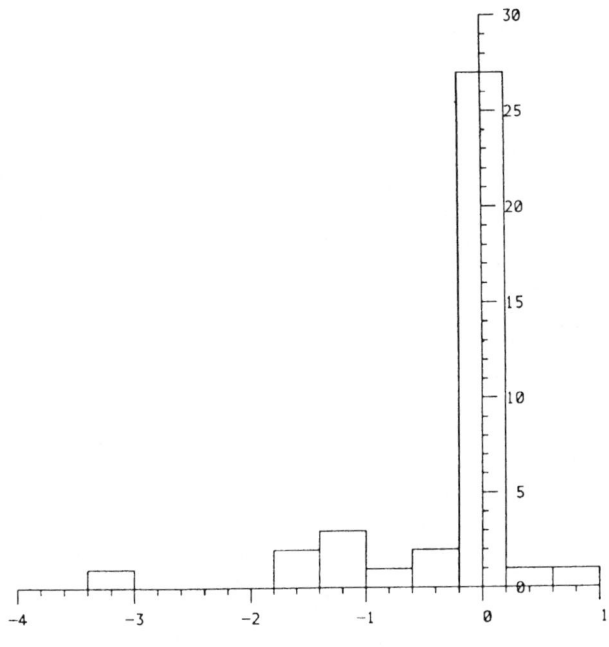

Figure 6.6 Long-run industry productivity elasticities from table 6.3

Disaggregation in econometric modelling

LM test on exclusion of $(y_{(t-1)a}, y_{(t-2)a}, h_{(t-2)a}, w_{(t-1)a}, d_{ta}) =$
4.47, cf $\chi^2(5)$
LM test on exclusion of $(y_{(t-1)a}, y_{(t-2)a}, h_{(t-2)a}, w_{(t-1)a}, d_{ta}, T_t) =$
5.90, cf $\chi^2(6)$

where h_{ta}, w_{ta}, and d_{ta} are the aggregate measures of employment, wages, and technological change derived from the industrial figures, and T_t is a linear time trend ($T_{1980} = 0$).

To check for the possible effect of the simultaneous determination of output, employment, and real wages on the OLS estimates, we also estimated the restricted aggregate equations using the instrumental variable method. With $z_t = \{1, h_{(t-1)a}, h_{(t-2)a}, y_{(t-1)a}, y_{(t-2)a}, w_{(t-1)a}, w_{(y-2)a}, d_{(t-1)a}\}$ as instruments, we obtained

$$h_{ta} = -86.86 + 0.4708\ y_{ta} + 0.7025\ h_{(t-1)a}$$
$$\quad\ (-3.36)\ \ (7.11) \qquad\quad (13.48)$$

$$\quad\ - 0.2783\ w_{ta} - 0.1365\ d_{(t-1)a}, \qquad\qquad (6.21)$$
$$\quad\ (-4.69) \qquad (-2.21)$$

$$\bar{R}^2 = 0.997, \quad \hat{\sigma} = 0.3258$$

Sargan's misspecification statistic $= 4.40$ cf $\chi^2(3)$,

$$\chi^2_{SC}(1) = 1.53, \quad \chi^2_{FF}(1) = 0.48, \quad \chi^2_N(2) = 3.83, \quad \chi^2_H(1) = 5.23$$

These clearly differ only marginally from the OLS results in (6.20).

The parameter estimates in (6.19) and (6.20) imply long-run elasticities with respect to aggregate output, real wages, and technological change of (1.68, −0.89, −0.59) for the unrestricted equation and (1.55, −0.97, −0.38) for the restricted equation.

6.4.5 Predictive performance and aggregation bias

Table 6.6 presents the prediction criteria developed in PPK for the aggregate equations (6.19) and (6.20) and the disaggregate equations of tables 6.1, 6.2, and 6.4. In each case the disaggregate model out performs the aggregate equation. The superiority (in terms of predictive performance) of the specifications in table 6.4 over those in table 6.2 can also be seen in the estimates presented in table 6.6. The computation of the statistic for the test of perfect aggregation also provides evidence in favour of the disaggregate model. In the case of the unrestricted version the value of the test statistic is 89.6 which is approximately distributed as $\chi^2(29)$. This strongly rejects the null hypothesis of perfect aggregation.

Bearing this finding in mind, we applied the tests of aggregation

Table 6.6 Relative predictive performance of the aggregate and the disaggregate employment functions*

	Unrestricted specifications	Restricted specifications	
	(Table 6.1)	(Table 6.2)	(Table 6.4)
Disaggregate criterion	0.1007	0.0856	0.0737
Aggregate criterion	0.1100[a]	0.1030[b]	0.1030[b]

Notes: *Results exclude industry 4 (Mineral oil and Natural gas).
[a]Corresponds to the unrestricted aggregate equation (6.19).
[b]Corresponds to the restricted aggregate equation (6.20).

bias discussed in section 6.3 to the aggregate and disaggregate employment equations. The results obtained are summarized in table 6.7. The first row of this table shows the statistics, q_1^*, for testing the hypothesis that the average of the long-run wage elasticities across industries is equal to -1. As discussed in the introduction to this chapter, much policy debate has centred around the extent to which aggregate employment in the UK is influenced by real wage levels. The unit long-run wage elasticity has emerged as the consensus view from this debate and it is for this reason that we use this *a priori* value in our test. The average of the estimated long-run wage elasticities obtained on the basis of the disaggregate results in the three tables 6.1, 6.2, and 6.4 is -0.66, -0.68, and -0.54 respectively, and these were each

Table 6.7 Tests of aggregation bias[†]

	Unrestricted specifications	Restricted specifications	
	(Table 6.1)[a]	(Table 6.2)[b]	(Table 6.4)[b]
$q_1^*(1)$ [wages]	0.63	5.13	17.20
$q_2^*(1)$ [wages]	0.32	2.46	5.18
$q_2^*(1)$ [output]	0.00	1.68	1.66
$q_2^*(1)$ [technology]	0.07	0.05	0.34

Notes: [†]Square brackets indicate variables over which restrictions are imposed; figures in round brackets show the number of restrictions imposed, s.
Test statistics are compared to $\chi^2(s)$. The q_1^* and q_2^* statistics are computed using the results (6.14) and (6.15), respectively.
[a]Results compared to unrestricted aggregate equation (6.19).
[b]Results compared to restricted aggregate equation (6.20).

compared to the consensus value of -1. As is clear, the hypothesized unit elasticity is accepted in the case of the unrestricted specifications, but when a more precisely determined set of results are considered, as in tables 6.2 and 6.4, the hypothesis is firmly rejected.

Since the q_1^* statistic does not take account of the sampling variation in the consensus estimate that it uses, a more appropriate test of aggregation bias is that based on the q_2^* statistic (see LPP and section 6.3). This test is based on a pseudo true aggregate elasticity obtained through estimation of the aggregate relation, and has the advantage that the same data and the same general specification are used in estimating the aggregate and the disaggregate elasticities. Row 2 of table 6.7 presents the results of this test for the specifications in tables 6.1, 6.2, and 6.4. The average wage elasticity across industries in table 6.1 is compared to -0.89 (the estimated long-run wage elasticity of equation (6.19)), while the averages from tables 6.2 and 6.4 are compared to -0.97 (obtained from the restricted aggregate equation (6.20)). Once again, the poorly determined set of equations in table 6.1 provide no evidence of aggregation bias. A similar conclusion is also obtained from the results of table 6.2. However, the hypothesis of no aggregation bias based on the more satisfactory estimates in table 6.4 is firmly rejected at the 5 per cent level, providing strong evidence in support of the claim that the aggregate relation overstates the responsiveness of employment to changes in wages. Similar tests on aggregation bias are reported in rows 3 and 4, for the long-run output and technological change elasticities in turn. Here, average output elasticities of 1.63, 1.23, and 1.24 are obtained from tables 6.1, 6.2, and 6.4 respectively, while the corresponding average estimates for the technological change elasticity were -0.46, -0.41, and -0.27. These estimates are compared to long-run output and technological change elasticities of 1.68 and -0.59 from the unrestricted equation (6.19), and of 1.55 and -0.38 from the restricted aggregate equation (6.20). In none of these tests is there any evidence of aggregation bias in the estimated coefficients.

Finally, to check the robustness of the above tests to the specification of the disaggregate model, we computed the Durbin-Hausman misspecification test statistic, q_3, as developed in LPP. For the set of unrestricted disaggregated results of table 6.1 and the unrestricted aggregate equation (6.19) we obtained a value of 48.56 which is distributed as a $\chi^2(7)$ since there are three regressors common to the aggregate and the disaggregate specifications (namely the intercept term, y_{ta} and $y_{(t-1)a}$). This result implies strong rejection of the orthogonality of the disaggregate residuals to the aggregate variables and sheds some doubt on the results of the aggregation bias tests. The misspecification of the disaggregate model might be due to the omission of industry-specific variables, measurement errors, functional form, or dynamic misspecification. It is therefore important that further research is carried out on the specification of the disaggregate employment equations and on the importance of aggregation bias in estimating long-run wage and output elasticities for the economy as a whole.

Concluding remarks

The application of the statistical methods recently developed by the authors to the study of employment equations in the UK provides some important insights for academics and policy makers alike. The estimated industrial employment equations show that there is a wide diversity in the responsiveness of labour demand to different influences across industries, illustrated most clearly by the histograms discussed in the previous section. In itself, this provides strong support for employing disaggregated analysis rather than aggregate analysis, since the latter cannot capture the structural detail that clearly exists.[14] The result of the test for perfect aggregation confirms that this detail is important even if we are interested only in the prediction of aggregate employment levels, discounting the possibility that errors in disaggregate relations might be offsetting ones. Further, the results of the aggregation bias tests show that the emphasis of policy makers on the importance of wage restraint in attempts to reduce unemployment may be misplaced. These tests confirm the view put forward in PPK that labour demand equations estimated at the aggregate level significantly overstate the extra employment that might be achieved through wage reductions, however these are achieved. In fact, a wage elasticity of around −0.6 is suggested by the disaggregate results, considerably less than the unit elasticity that has become the consensus view in the UK and which is supported by our own aggregate estimates.[15] The results do not, however, provide any evidence of aggregation bias in the long-run estimates of output and technological change elasticities. Taken together, therefore, these results provide an illustration of the gains to be made from disaggregate analysis, and of the dangers involved in aggregation.

Disaggregation in econometric modelling

Appendix 6A

With the exception of data on industrial investment, the data used in this study are the same as those employed in Pesaran *et al.* (1989), and are taken from the Cambridge Growth Project (CGP)

Table 6A.1 Classification of industry groups (in terms of the 1980 standard industrial classification)

Industry groups (CGP classification)	Division, class, or group
1 Agriculture, forestry, and farming	0
2 Coal mining	1113, 1114
3 Coke	1115, 1200
4 Mineral oil and natural gas	1300
5 Petroleum products	140
6 Electricity, etc.	1520, 1610, 1630
7 Public gas supply	1620
8 Water supply	1700
9 Minerals and ores nes	21, 23
10 Iron and steel	2210, 2220, 223
11 Non-ferrous metals	224
12 Non-metallic mineral products	24
13 Chemicals and man-made fibres	25, 26
14 Metal goods nes	31
15 Mechanical engineering	32
16 Office machinery, etc.	33
17 Electrical engineering	34
18 Motor vehicles	35
19 Aerospace equipment	3640
20 Ships and other vessels	3610
21 Other vehicles	3620, 363, 3650
22 Instrument engineering	37
23 Manufactured food	41, 4200, 421, 422, 4239
24 Alcoholic drinks, etc.	4240, 4261, 4270, 4283
25 Tobacco	4290
26 Textiles	43
27 Clothing and footwear	45
28 Timber and furniture	46
29 Paper and board	4710, 472
30 Books, etc.	475
31 Rubber and plastic products	48
32 Other manufactures	44, 49
33 Construction	5
34 Distribution, etc.	61, 62, 63, 64, 65, 67
35 Hotels and catering	66
36 Rail transport	71
37 Other land transport	72
38 Sea, air, and other	74, 75, 76, 77
39 Communications	79
40 Business services	81, 82, 83, 84, 85
41 Miscellaneous services	94, 98, 923, 95, 96, 97

Table 6A.2 *Blue Book* and Cambridge Growth Project industrial classifications

CGP classification		BB classification	
2	Coal	2	Coal and coke
3	Coke		
9	Minerals and ores nes	8	Metals
10	Iron and steel	9	Other minerals
11	Non-ferrous metals		
12	Non-metallic mineral products		
16	Office machinery	13	Electrical and instrument
17	Electrical engineering		engineering
22	Instrument engineering		
19	Aerospace equipment	15	Transport, other than motor
20	Ships		vehicles
21	Other vehicles		
24	Drink	17	Drink and tobacco
25	Tobacco		
29	Paper and board	21	Paper, printing, and publishing
30	Books		

Databank. For the sources of the data and the classifications of industry groups see the data appendix and table A in PPK. For convenience, table A is reproduced in this Appendix (table 6A.1).

Data on industrial investment in vehicles, in plant and machinery, and in buildings are available separately for the period 1954–84, from which total gross investment is constructed. There is not a one-to-one correspondence between the *Blue Book* (BB) industrial classifications for which the data are published and our own, however. Where the BB data are more disaggregated, this causes no problem, since we simply amalgamate the appropriate industries. There remain six areas in which the BB data are more aggregated than our own. These are listed in table 6A.2

In these cases, we have made the simplifying assumption that the investment reported by BB classification can be divided equally over the (more disaggregate) CGP industrial groups. This procedure is satisfactory if the CGP industry groups within the BB classifications show similar investment growths over the 1954–84 period. This is likely to be the case for the Coal and Coke Industries, but is less likely to hold in the case of the BB industry classifications 13 and 17.

147

Disaggregation in econometric modelling

Notes

1 This consensus estimate is also the same as the figure obtained by Beenstock and Warburton (1984) for their extended data set.

2 The econometric problems involved in the use of time trends in regression equations containing non-stationary variables are discussed, for example, by Mankiw and Shapiro (1985, 1986), and Durlauf and Phillips (1986).

3 The inclusion of first or higher order lags of h_t in the employment function can also be justified by appeal to aggregation over different types of labour or firms with different adjustment costs (Nickell, 1984).

4 To derive (7.2) in PPK from (6.5), let $r_y = r_w = 2$, and notice that when a simple linear trend is used as a proxy for a_t, then $a_t = a_{t-1} + b$, where b is a fixed constant, and

$$(\sum_{i=1}^{r_a-1} \gamma_{ia} L^{i-1}) a_t = (\sum_{i=1}^{r_a-1} \gamma_{ia}) a_t - b \sum_{i=2}^{r_a-1} (i-1) \gamma_{ia}$$

$$= \gamma_a a_t + \text{constant}$$

5 This is similar to the research strategy followed by Nickell (1984) and Burgess (1988).

6 Notice that the use of time trends in regression equations containing integrated stochastic processes is also subject to important econometric pitfalls and as argued in Mankiw and Shapiro (1985, 1986), and Durlauf and Phillips (1986) can lead to spurious inference.

7 See in particular Kaldor and Mirrlees (1962, pp. 176–7). Notice, however, that Kaldor's formulation abstracts from the effect of real wages on labour productivity, while ours does not.

8 For a review of more recent evidence see, for example Beggs (1984) and Baily and Chakrabarti (1985). Notice, however, that Beggs uses wage expenditures as a surrogate for investment data and his results may not be directly comparable to those obtained by Schmookler. On this see the comments by Schankerman (1984) on Beggs's paper.

9 See for example Theil (1954), Grunfeld and Griliches (1960), Boot and de Wit (1960), Zellner (1962), Gupta (1971), and Sasaki (1978).

10 From (5) note that $\boldsymbol{\beta}_i = (\beta_{i1}, \beta_{i2}, \ldots, \beta_{ik})' = (\text{intercept}, \psi_{i1}, \psi_{i2}, \gamma_{1y}, \gamma_{2y}, \ldots; \gamma_{1w}, \gamma_{2w}, \ldots; \gamma_{1a}, \gamma_{2a}, \ldots)$.

11 It is recognized that the application of the proposed Walt test may be problematic in finite samples when the restriction set is non-linear since the test is not invariant to the parameterization of the restrictions. See Gregory and Veall (1985) and LPP.

12 Notice that

$$d_{1954}(\lambda) = \lambda \sum_{i=0}^{\infty} (1 - \lambda)^i \log(GI_{1954-i})$$

and under $E[\log(GI_{1954})] = E[\log(GE_{1953})] = \ldots = \log(\bar{GI})$, we have

$$d_{01} = E[d_{1954}(\lambda)] = \log(\bar{GI})$$

13 For each industry the technological variable $d_i(\lambda)$, or d_i for short, is computed using (6.8), with the initial value given by (6.17) and the decay parameter, $\lambda = 0.10$.

14 Indeed, the relatively poor diagnostic statistics obtained in the case of some of the industrial equations indicate that there is likely to be scope for further structural detail in the form of industry-specific variables, and the use of different functional forms across industries.

15 Of course, estimated wage elasticities obtained in *unconditional* labour demand equations would be somewhat higher as reduced wage inflation helps encourage higher output levels.

Chapter seven

Optimal aggregation of linear net export systems

Edward E. Leamer

The number of distinct traded commodities is so great that it is impossible to discuss the determinants of trade coherently without some system of aggregation. Aggregation results of Fisher (1969) and Chipman (1976) are adapted here to aggregate a system of trade equations that explain the level of net exports of a set of fifty-six commodity groups. These commodity groups are combined if their net exports are similarly affected by measured factor supplies including land, labour and capital.

Aggregation is accomplished formally by acting as if the problem were to predict the disaggregated net export vector given the factor supplies. The penalty for prediction error is assumed to be quadratic. This prediction problem will rarely be faced in real settings. More often, the intent of aggregation is to facilitate understanding and communication. This is like the problem of constructing an optimal language: an optimal vocabulary trades off miscommunications from too many words against miscommunications from too few.

The prediction problem considered here is thus only a surrogate for the real problem of understanding and communication. What is really lost through aggregation are details of the determinants of trade, not prediction accuracy. What is gained is better understanding and easier communication of that which remains. No precise measures of these gains and losses seems possible, but I will argue that the prediction problem nonetheless yields results that at least partly solve the communication problem.

The fully disaggregated system that predicts the net exports of p commodities given k resource supplies has a total of $p \times k$ coefficients. The fully aggregated system has only $p + k$ coefficients, k to predict the aggregate given the k resource supplies and p to predict the components given the aggregate. This fully aggregated system can reproduce exactly the forecasts of the fully disaggregated system if the coefficient vectors for each of the commodities are proportional. Otherwise, there is a loss of information and an increase in expected loss from prediction error. This increased prediction error would have to be compared with the gains of simplification though these gains will usually be difficult to quantify.

The method of solving this aggregation problem is decision-theoretic in the sense that the coefficients of the linear system are treated like random variables drawn from the posterior distribution, given a data set. For this problem, certain and uncertain systems are mathematically equivalent since the solution depends on the posterior means of the coefficients and not on their variances. If the prior distribution for the parameters of the linear system is suitably diffuse, the increase in expected loss due to aggregation can be found by estimating two sets of equations, the first set predicting the aggregates given the explanatory variables, and the second set predicting the individual components given the aggregates but not the explanatory variables.

The problem of finding the optimal system with a given number of aggregates is analogous to the problem of finding the best regression equation with a given number of explanatory variables, in the sense that global optimization requires a complete enumeration. Since that enumeration can be quite expensive, an algorithm is used here that combines commodity classes and rearranges them to produce locally optimal aggregates. This algorithm uses sequences of observations of the complete system as inputs, and combines components of the system which have similar estimated coefficients.

The data set includes measurements of the resource endowments of fifty-eight countries which serve as explanatory variables for each of the fifty-six two-digit SITC (Standard Industrial Trade Classification) categories of net exports separately in 1958 and 1975. Commodity classes are therefore combined when they have similar sources of comparative advantage.

The one-digit SITC aggregation scheme with nine aggregates is compared with a locally optimal scheme also with nine aggregates. This locally optimal aggregation scheme is shown to be more accurate than the one-digit SITC scheme by a multiple of five or six. A system with only two aggregates does as well as the nine one-digit aggregates in 1958. Five aggregates are required to do as well as the one-digit scheme in 1975. The greatest problem with the one-digit SITC scheme is that SITC-04 (cereals) is combined with SITC-07 (coffee, tea, cocoa, spices, etc.), but the data suggest clearly that the sources of comparative advantage for these two classes are distinctly different categories of land, temperate in one

151

case and tropical in the other. Also, the 1958 data reveal that SITC-64 (paper and paperboard) and SITC-68 (non-ferrous metal manufactures) are better combined with SITC-24 (wood, lumber, and cork) and SITC-25 (pulp) than with SITC-67 (iron and steel) and SITC-65 (textile yarn, fabrics). One interpretation is that the raw material component of SITC-64 and SITC-68 is too great for them to be considered manufactured products. The one other result of this form is that the 1975 data strongly suggest that SITC-71 (machinery other than electric) and SITC-73 (transport equipment) ought not to be combined, apparently because of the relatively great effect of semi-skilled workers on SITC-73.

The plan of this paper is as follows. The basic aggregation results are reviewed in section 7.1 and specialized to partial aggregation in section 7.2. The computer algorithm is briefly described in section 7.3. The system of net export equations is reported in section 7.4 and concluding comments form section 7.5.

7.1 Full aggregation

The aggregation problem considered by Fisher (1969) is to form a forecast of a $p \times k$ vector y which is generated by the process

$$y = Bx + v \tag{7.1}$$

where B is a known $p \times k$ matrix, x is a $k \times 1$ random vector with known raw second moment $\mathrm{E}(xx') = M$, and v is a $p \times 1$ random vector distributed independently of x with mean $\mathrm{E}(v) = 0$. Though the system is written to allow all of the x variables to affect each of the y variables, exclusion restrictions would only amount to a special choice of B with some elements set to zero.

The penalty for an incorrect forecast is assumed to be quadratic

$$L = (y - \hat{y})'C(y - \hat{y})$$

where C is a given symmetric positive-definite matrix and $\hat{y}$ is a forecast of y. Under these assumptions the optimal forecast is linear in x:

$$\hat{y} = \hat{B}x$$

The matrix of coefficients $\hat{B}$ is not allowed to be equal to B because of certain aggregation restrictions. For example, $\hat{B}$ may be restricted to be a rank one matrix

$$\hat{B} = sb' \qquad (7.2)$$

where s and b are vectors, $b'x$ is the prediction of 'the' aggregate, and s_i is the share of component i in the sense that $s_i b'x$ is the prediction of the ith component.

It is convenient to suppress the matrix C in the quadratic loss function by setting $C = I$, which amounts only to premultiplying y and its prediction by a square root of C. Then the expected loss can be written as

$$\text{E}(L) = \text{tr}[(B - \hat{B})'(B - \hat{B})M] + \text{tr}\text{E}(vv') \qquad (7.3)$$

Fisher (1969, p. 167) demonstrates that minimization of (7.3) subject to the restriction (7.2) implies that b is the eigenvector of BMB' corresponding to the largest eigenvalue.

A problem with using an eigenvector b to form a model for an aggregate is that $b'x$ is not an optimal conditional prediction of any obvious aggregate quantity, and the interpretative simplicity of the resulting system can be rather badly damaged. Accordingly, $b'x$ is now restricted to be the optimal predictor of the aggregate $l'y$, where l is a $p \times 1$ vector of ones. It is straightforward to demonstrate that the optimal predictor of $l'y$ is $l'Bx$; thus we restrict b to

$$b = B'l \qquad (7.4)$$

Given this value of b, it is also straightforward to demonstrate, as in Chipman (1976, p. 692), that the optimal choice of the share vector s is

$$s = BMB'l/l'BMB'l \qquad (7.5)$$

and the increment to expected loss due to this choice of $\hat{B} = sb'$ is equal to

$$\Delta\text{E}(L) = \text{tr}(B - \hat{B})'(B - \hat{B})M$$

$$= \text{tr}\, V - l'V^2l/l'Vl \qquad (7.6)$$

where $V = BMB'$.

To decompose this increment to expected loss into contributions from each of the components of the aggregate we may write $\Delta\text{E}(L) = \text{tr}(V - Vll'V/l'Vl)$, and therefore associate with component i the loss penalty equal to the ith diagonal of

153

Disaggregation in econometric modelling

$V - V l l' V / l' V l$. This number does not indicate the amount by which expected loss would be reduced if this component were eliminated from the aggregate, since such an elimination would precipate a change in the predicting equations that would further reduce the loss of all the other components. An analogous problem besets attempts to measure the contribution of an individual variable in multiple regression.

Aggregation of uncertain systems

It is highly unlikely in practice that one would know the parameters of the system and the foregoing discussion has to be modified to deal with uncertainty. Most commonly, information comes in the form of previous observations of y and x. For this setting, Chipman (1976, 1977a, b) offers a classical treatment including tests of the hypothesis that the aggregation restrictions lower expected loss. The literature on the MIMIC models of Joreskog and Goldberger (1975) deals with the same proportionality constraints in multivariate systems and, in effect, provides classical tests of the aggregation restrictions. A Bayesian approach is used by Fisher (1969) and will also be used here. This approach requires only careful interpretation of the decomposition of y into Bx and v, i.e. Bx is the conditional mean of y given x and given any past observations of y and x. Consequently, B should be interpreted as the mean of the posterior distribution of the coefficients of the system. The error vector v then has two components: part of the error is due to the noise in the system and part is due to the fact that B is not exactly equal to the matrix of true coefficients of the system.

In order to select values for M and $E(vv')$ it is now assumed that a set of n previous observations of the vector (y_t, x_t), $t = 1, \ldots, n$ is drawn independently from a fixed multivariate normal distribution, and it is assumed that the prior distribution for the mean and covariance matrix of this distribution is suitably diffuse. Observations of y and x are collected into the $n \times p$ matrix Y and the $n \times k$ matrix X. The posterior mean of the matrix of coefficients of the system is then equal to the matrix of least-squares estimates

$$B = E(\beta | Y, X) = Y'X(X'X)^{-1}$$

where β is the $p \times k$ matrix of true coefficients. The error vector can then be written as $v = (\beta - B)x + \epsilon$, where ϵ is the $p \times 1$ system noise vector. Then the minimum expected loss conditional on Y and X is

$$\text{trE}(vv' \mid Y, X) = \text{trM}E((\beta - B)(\beta - B)' \mid Y, X) + \text{trE}(\epsilon\epsilon' \mid Y, X)$$

$$= \Sigma \, E[(\beta_i - B_i)'M(\beta_i - B_i) + \sigma_i^2 \mid Y, X] \quad (7.7)$$

$$= (\Sigma \, s_i^2)(1 + k/n)$$

where σ_i^2 is the variance of the residual in equation i, β_i is the ith row of the matrix of true coefficients β, index i selects one of the p equations and the following posterior moments are used

$$M = E(xx' \mid Y, X) = X'X/n$$

$$\text{Var}(\beta_i \mid Y, X) = s_i^2(X'X)^{-1}$$

$$E(\sigma_i^2 \mid Y, X) = s_i^2 = Y_i'(I - X(X'X)^{-1}X')Y_i/n$$

where Y_i is the ith column of Y. Note that these estimates of the second moments are not adjusted for degrees of freedom, which requires a special diffuse prior in the conjugate class. Normally, it is wise to adjust for degrees of freedom, but in this case some of the subsequent formulae are conveniently simple if no adjustment is made. Although none of the estimates of variance is corrected for degrees of freedom, the loss (7.7) does have the complexity penalty k/n indicating that uncertainty is an increasing function of the number of estimated parameters.

With B equal to the matrix of least-squares estimates and M equal to $X'X/n$, the matrix $V = BMB'$ becomes

$$V = Y'X(X'X)^{-1}X'Y/n. = B'X'XB/n$$

This allows us to interpret the increment to expected loss (7.6) as the difference between the sum of squared residuals when the data Y are regressed on the 'predicted' aggregate data and when they are regressed on X. The matrix of inner products of residuals formed by regressing the data on X is the $p \times p$ matrix

$$R = Y'(I - X(X'X)^{-1}X')Y = Y'Y - nV$$

If the aggregated data Yl are regressed on X, the predicted or systematic part of the aggregate is $a = X(X'X)^{-1}X'Yl$. The matrix of inner products of residuals formed by regressing Y on this systematic part of the aggregate is

$$R^* = Y'(I - a(a'a)^{-1}a')Y$$

155

Disaggregation in econometric modelling

$$= Y'Y - nVl(l'Vl)^{-1}Vl'$$

Then we can write the increase in expected loss as

$$\Delta E(L) = \text{tr}(R^* - R)/n$$

Furthermore, the minimum expected loss (7.7) can be written as $\text{tr}(R/n)(1 + k/n)$, and the percentage increase in expected loss due to aggregation is

$$\Delta E(L)/E(L) = \text{tr}(R^* - R)/\text{tr}(R)(1 + k/n) \tag{7.8}$$

Like an F-statistic, formula (7.8) indicates that aggregation is undesirable if the residuals increase substantially when the system is estimated with a form of two-stage least squares in which the first stage forms 'predicted' values of the aggregate by regression on the explanatory variables and the second stage regresses the components on these predicted values of the aggregates.

Treatment of the constant

The increment to expected loss (7.8) is zero if the system coefficient vectors are proportional across components of the aggregate; otherwise, formula (7.8) is a measure of the difference among the coefficient vectors including the constants. For many applications it may be more meaningful to ignore the constants. We can eliminate the constants from consideration by letting the prediction vector have its own set of constants $\hat{y} = \hat{a} + \hat{B}x$. It is straightforward to show that, for a given $\hat{B}$, the optimal choice of $\hat{a}$ is $\hat{a} = E(y - \hat{B}x) = (B - \hat{B})E(x)$. The optimal predictor becomes $\hat{y} = BE(x) + \hat{B}(x - E(x))$. With this value of $\hat{y}$, the expected loss (7.3) is modified only by replacing the raw moments $M = E(xx')$ by the centred moments $S = E(x - E(x))(x - E(x))'$. Since the constant term has a zero predictive variance, the corresponding row and column of S is zero, and the constant is dropped from consideration.

Clustering based on Y only

Many clustering algorithms are based only on data Y, and not on variables X that are intended to explain Y. These algorithms group components that are highly correlated with each other and with the associated aggregate. The methods that are discussed in this paper will do the same thing if the components are perfectly predicted by

156

the explanatory variables, that is if $Y = XB'$. This implies that the desirability of disaggregation may be measured by the increase in the residuals when the components are regressed on the aggregate, and no reference need be made to the X matrix. It is sufficient to find clusters which have components highly correlated with the corresponding aggregate.

7.2 Partial aggregation

The foregoing material deals with full aggregation with $\hat{B} = sl'B$ where $l'Bx$ is the optimal predictor of the aggregate $l'y$. To explore the consequences of partial aggregation, we proceed by applying this material to subsets of the elements of y. Premultiplying the system by $q \times p$ matrix A of zeros and ones, with $q < p$, reduces the number of equations from p to q. The matrix A of zeros and ones is an aggregation matrix if each column sum is equal to one, that is if $l'A = l'$, or equivalently if each column of A has one element equal to one and all the others equal to zero. The ith row of A, A_i, selects the components of the ith aggregate, and the condition $l'A = l'$ guarantees that each element of y is in one and only one aggregate. Application of the logic preceding equation (7.6) to each of the aggregates implies that the increment to expected prediction loss associated with the system with aggregation matrix A is

$$\Delta E(L) = \operatorname{tr} V - \sum_{i=1}^{q} A_i' VF_i VA_i / A_i' VA_i \tag{7.9}$$

where D_i is a diagonal matrix with A_i down the diagonal. The corresponding vector of shares for aggregate i is

$$s_i = D_i VA_i / A_i' VA_i \tag{7.10}$$

7.3 A computer algorithm

An ideal computer algorithm would minimize (7.9) by choice of aggregation matrices A_i for each value of q, the number of aggregates. But the number of $q \times p$ aggregation matrices for modestly large p is enormous, and calculation costs of a global minimization of (7.9) for most problems will accordingly be unacceptably high. What can be done at reasonable cost is to find locally optimal aggregates by transferring components between aggregates one at a time to reduce (7.9) until all possibilities of further reductions are exhausted, as is done by Hartigan's 'K-means algorithm' (1975, p. 84). The initial starting point that will be used for this local optimization algorithm is the set of q aggregates formed by coupling pairs of aggregates sequentially until only q remain. At each step, the pair of aggregates is coupled which causes the smallest increase in expected loss. Fisher's 'progressive merger procedure' (1969, p. 178) is similar.

A final defect of the solution just presented is that the share vectors (7.10) are not necessarily positive, although they do add to one. A negative share can be interpreted to mean that the component behaves the opposite of the aggregate, and allowing negative shares therefore destroys the interpretive clarity of an aggregate. Accordingly, the local optimization procedure described in the previous paragraph is altered to allow only positive shares, with components shifted among aggregates when a negative share occurs.

7.4 Aggregation of trade data

This section reports a locally optimal aggregation of a linear system of fifty-six equations that explain the level of net exports of the two-digit SITC commodity groups. The optimal system with nine aggregates is compared with the one-digit SITC system. The dependent variables are the net exports in thousands of dollars of these fifty-six commodities. Data were collected from fifty-eight countries (OECD plus selected developing countries) in 1958 and 1975. The system of trade equations explains net exports of each of the fifty-six commodity classes in terms of the following eleven resources:

Capital   = capital stock in million dollars, formed by accumulating and discounting investment flows over fifteen years

L_1 = thousands of professional/technical workers

L_2 = thousands of literate non-professional workers

L_3 = thousands of illiterate workers, assuming the worker literacy rate is the same as the population literacy rate

T_1 = thousands of hectares of land area, tropical-rainy climate

T_2 = thousands of hectares of land area, dry climate

T_3 = thousands of hectares of land area, humid meso-thermal climate

T_4 = thousands of hectares of land area, humid micro-thermal climate

Coal = value in thousands of dollars of production of primary solid fuel

Minerals = value in thousands of dollars of production of minerals

Oil = value in thousands of dollars of production of oil and gas

The theoretical foundation of this trade equation is the Heckscher–Ohlin–Samuelson trade model with Vanek's (1968) assumption of identical homothetic tastes. A list of assumptions including constant returns to scale and equal numbers of traded commodities and immobile factors can be shown to imply that net exports are a linear function of the resource endowments. Otherwise, the function is theoretically non-linear and the estimated equation should be thought to be a linear approximation, possibly a poor one. For a study of non-linearities as well as a full description of the sources of these data, see Leamer (1984).

The effects of aggregation on this system of equations are summarized in figure 7.1 in which the percentage increase in expected squared prediction error is expressed as a function of the number of aggregates. These percentages remain rather high in 1958 even when there are as many as eleven aggregates. With the 1975 data, very good loss control is achieved with eight or nine aggregates. The primary reason for this is that the deleterious effects of aggregation are swamped in 1975 by relatively noisy data which generate relatively large standard errors.

Also plotted in this figure is the loss control afforded by the one-digit SITC scheme with nine aggregates. The ineffectiveness of this scheme is very dramatically revealed by comparing these numbers with the loss control numbers implied by the locally optimal scheme with nine aggregates. Both for the 1958 data and for the 1975 data, the loss associated with the nine locally optimal aggregates is substantially below the loss for the one-digit SITC scheme. A system with only two aggregates does as well as the nine one-digit SITC groups in 1958. Five well-designed aggregates are required to do as well as the nine in 1975.

To help identify the sources of the problems with the SITC aggregation scheme, the shares and loss shares for the 1958 and 1975 data are reported in tables 7.1 and 7.2. The nine columns in each table refer to the one-digit SITC categories. For example, the column headed by the digit zero refers to SITC-0 which is composed of ten components (SITC-00, 01, 02, 03, 04, 05, 06, 07, 08, 09). The shares of these ten components reported in this first column are computed using formula (7.10). These shares indicate

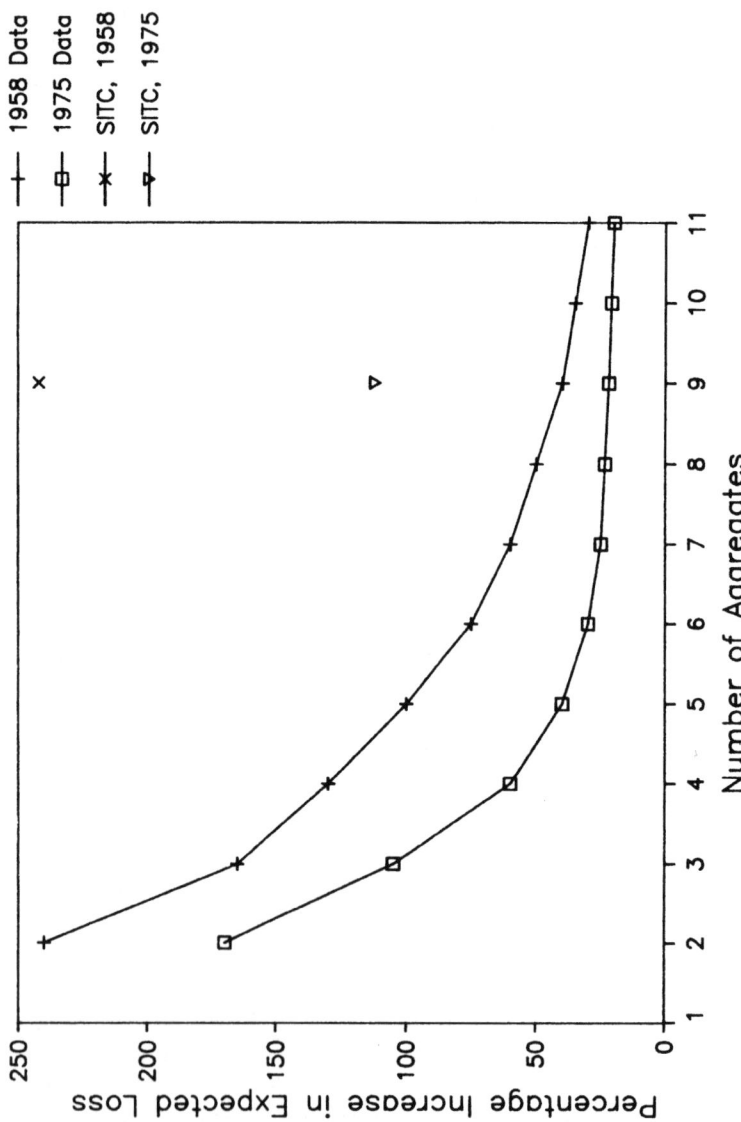

Figure 7.1 Expected prediction loss

Table 7.1 Share vectors and loss shares, SITC one-digit aggregation, 1958

SITC	0	1	2	3	4	5	6	7	8
Shares	0.04	0.18	0.04	−0.00	0.39	0.21	0.01	0.47	0.08
	0.18	0.82	0.07	1.00	0.64	−0.00	0.04	0.16	0.04
	0.08		0.09	0.00	−0.03	0.10	0.01	0.37	0.00
	0.04		0.15	−0.00		0.18	0.09		0.04
	0.10		0.10			0.06	0.35		0.00
	0.20		0.24			0.04	0.10		0.15
	0.07		0.04			0.02	0.30		0.69
	0.26		0.23			0.12	−0.05		
	0.03		0.03			0.27	0.15		
	−0.00								
Loss shares [a]	0.00	0.50	0.01	0.50	0.51	0.15	0.00	0.53	0.02
	0.02	0.50	0.04	0.50	0.38	0.00	0.01	0.02	0.01
	0.02		0.09	0.00	0.10	0.09	0.01	0.45	0.01
	0.02		0.06	0.00		0.07	0.27		0.37
	0.46		0.06			0.03	0.18		0.03
	0.05		0.58			0.24	0.02		0.05
	0.05		0.01			0.00	0.21		0.52
	0.40		0.15			0.30	0.22		
	0.00		0.01			0.10	0.09		
	0.00								
Loss shares [b]	0.50	0.01	0.13	0.08	0.00	0.00	0.22	0.04	0.01

Notes: [a] Shares of component in loss due to aggregate.
[b] Share of aggregate in total loss.

that in 1958 most of the variability of the SITC-0 aggregate was due to variability of SITC-01 (meat and meat preparations), SITC-05 (fruit, vegetables), and SITC-07 (coffee, tea, cocoa, spices, etc.). The loss shares reported in this column indicate the share of the loss due to each of the components, using the decomposition discussed following equation (7.6).[1] For SITC-0 in 1958, most of the loss was due to difficulties in forecasting SITC-04 (cereals) and SITC-07 (coffee, tea, cocoa, spices, etc.). The last row in each table contains the share of the total aggregation loss due to the indicated aggregate. These numbers indicate that a substantial portion of the aggregation inaccuracy is due to the incoherence of SITC-0. In 1958, 50 per cent of the total aggregation loss is attributable to SITC-0. In 1975, the figure is 37 per cent. Decomposition of these losses in these tables reveals that it is the fifth commodity – SITC-04 (cereals) – that is the main culprit, though in 1958 the eighth commodity – SITC-07 (coffee, tea, cocoa, spices, etc.) – is almost as great a problem. (Descriptions of the re-ordered SITC categories may be found in table 7.3.) It is not

Table 7.2 Share vectors and loss shares, SITC one-digit aggregation, 1975

SITC	0	1	2	3	4	5	6	7	8
Shares	0.01	0.97	0.03	0.01	0.34	0.28	−0.00	0.45	0.00
	0.09	0.03	0.18	0.94	0.63	−0.00	0.04	0.16	0.04
	0.03		0.01	0.05	0.03	0.08	−0.02	0.39	0.03
	0.01		0.18			0.11	0.02		0.35
	0.62		0.09			0.04	0.12		0.21
	0.14		0.11			0.10	0.04		0.03
	0.05		0.06			0.01	0.70		0.34
	−0.00		0.34			0.21	−0.04		
	0.06		0.02			0.16	0.13		
	0.01								
Loss shares [a]	0.00	0.50	0.00	0.48	0.48	0.20	0.00	0.58	0.00
	0.02	0.50	0.35	0.47	0.49	0.00	0.02	0.03	0.01
	0.01		0.01	0.04	0.03	0.08	0.01	0.39	0.00
	0.02		0.05	0.00		0.15	0.23		0.43
	0.74		0.16			0.04	0.12		0.07
	0.05		0.10			0.31	0.03		0.39
	0.08		0.01			0.00	0.14		0.09
	0.08		0.31			0.14	0.33		
	0.01		0.02			0.07	0.12		
	0.00								
Loss shares [b]	0.37	0.01	0.06	0.16	0.00	0.01	0.06	0.29	0.04

Notes: [a] Shares of component in loss due to aggregate.
[b] Share of aggregate in total loss.

Table 7.3 Composition of nine aggregates, 1958

Loss share	SITC	Description	Share	Loss share
Aggregate 1	11	Beverages	0.089	0.273
(0.10)	23	Crude rubber	0.185	0.383
	29	Crude animal, vegetable materials	0.050	0.047
	33	Petroleum, petroleum products	0.673	0.297
	52	Mineral tar, crude chemicals	0.002	0.001
Aggregate 2	00	Live animals	0.047	0.009
(0.20)	03	Fish, fish preparations	0.066	0.109
	24	Wood, lumber, cork	0.140	0.128
	25	Pulp, wastepaper	0.111	0.023
	27	Crude fertilizers, materials	0.038	0.022
	28	Metalliferous ores, scrap	0.226	0.197
	64	Paper, paperboard	0.191	0.370
	68	Non-ferrous metals	0.181	0.142

Aggregate 3	22	Oil-seeds, oil-nuts, oil kernels	0.191	0.500
(0.03)	26	Textile fibres	0.809	0.500
Aggregate 4	06	Sugar, sugar preparations, honey	0.227	0.515
(0.05)	07	Coffee, tea, cocoa, spices, etc.	0.766	0.482
	43	Animal, vegetable oils, fats, proc.	0.007	0.003
Aggregate 5	01	Meat, meat preparations	0.287	0.343
(0.16)	02	Dairy products, eggs	0.155	0.157
	05	Fruit, vegetables	0.361	0.352
	08	Feeding stuff for animals	0.056	0.012
	21	Hides, skins, furskins, undressed	0.061	0.026
	42	Fixed vegetable oils, fats	0.049	0.043
	63	Wood, cork manufactures	0.030	0.054
	85	Footwear	0.001	0.012
Aggregate 6	04	Cereals	0.781	0.549
(0.04)	12	Tobacco, tobacco manu.	0.169	0.431
	35	Electric energy	0.002	0.002
	41	Animal oils, fats	0.048	0.018
Aggregate 7	09	Miscellaneous food preparations	0.000	0.071
(0.05)	61	Leather, dressed furskins	0.015	0.019
	65	Textile yarn, fabrics, etc.	0.709	0.331
	66	Non-metallic mineral manufactures	0.152	0.430
	84	Clothing	0.124	0.149
Aggregate 8	54	Medicinal, pharmaceutical pro.	0.044	0.042
(0.19)	58	Plastic materials, cellulose, etc.	0.025	0.079
	62	Rubber manufactures nes	0.029	0.003
	67	Iron, steel	0.151	0.441
	69	Manufactures of metal	0.092	0.145
	72	Electrical machinery	0.196	0.098
	73	Transport equipment	0.463	0.192
Aggregate 9	32	Coal, coke, briquettes	0.096	0.393
(0.19)	34	Gas, natural and manufactures	0.001	0.010
	51	Chemical elements, compounds	0.052	0.026
	53	Dyeing, tanning, colouring mat.	0.025	0.009
	56	Fertilizers, manufactures	0.008	0.038
	57	Explosives, pyrotechnic products	0.005	0.001
	55	Essential oils, perfume materials	0.014	0.007
	59	Chemical materials, products nes	0.068	0.022
	71	Machinery, other than electric	0.568	0.176
	81	Sanitary, etc., fixtures, fittings	0.015	0.002
	82	Furniture	0.006	0.002
	83	Travel goods, handbags, etc.	0.000	0.001
	86	Prof., etc., instruments, etc.	0.024	0.037
	89	Misc. manuf. articles nes	0.120	0.276

Table 7.4 Composition of nine aggregates, 1975

Loss share	SITC	Description	Share	Loss share
Aggregate 1	03	Fish, fish prep.	0.04	0.50
(0.02)	29	Crude animal, veg. mat.	0.01	0.18
	33	Petroleum, petro. prod.	0.95	0.32
	52	Mineral tar, crude chemicals	0.00	0.01
Aggregate 2	25	Pulp, wastepaper	0.25	0.13
(0.09)	34	Gas, natural and manufactures	0.25	0.29
	35	Electric energy	0.01	0.00
	64	Paper, paperboard	0.21	0.29
	68	Non-ferrous metals	0.28	0.29
Aggregate 3	24	Wood, lumber, cork	0.32	0.50
(0.04)	28	Metaliferous ores, scrap	0.68	0.50
Aggregate 4	00	Live animals	0.01	0.01
(0.13)	08	Feeding stuff for animals	0.07	0.07
	12	Tobacco, tobacco manufactures	0.07	0.02
	21	Hides, skins, furskins	0.03	0.01
	22	Oil-seeds, nuts and kernels	0.26	0.24
	26	Textile fibres	0.14	0.16
	27	Crude fertilisers, materials	0.06	0.06
	32	Coal, cork, briquettes	0.35	0.42
	43	Animal, vegetable oils, fats, proc.	0.00	0.00
	81	Sanitary, etc., fixtures, fittings	0.00	0.01
Aggregate 5	01	Meat, meat preparation	0.11	0.10
(0.37)	05	Fruit, vegetables	0.13	0.35
	06	Sugar, sugar prep., honey	0.17	0.16
	07	Coffee, tea, cocoa, spices, etc.	0.18	0.14
	11	Beverages	0.04	0.08
	23	Crude rubber	0.02	0.01
	42	Fixed vegetable oils, fats	0.01	0.02
	63	Wood, cork manufactures	0.02	0.01
	82	Furniture	0.01	0.01
	83	Travel goods, handbags, etc.	0.01	0.00
	84	Clothing	0.20	0.10
	85	Footwear	0.09	0.05
Aggregate 6	04	Cereals	1.00	—
(0.0)				
Aggregate 7	02	Dairy products, etc.	0.01	0.16
(0.15)	56	Fertilizers, manufactured	0.03	0.22
	66	Non-metallic min. manuf.	0.05	0.09
	67	Iron and steel	0.79	0.25
	89	Misc. manuf. article nes	0.12	0.28

Aggregate 8	41	Animal oils, fats	0.00	0.03
(0.12)	62	Rubber manuf. nes	0.03	0.04
	65	Textile yarn, fabrics, etc.	0.07	0.27
	69	Manufacturers of metal	0.08	0.11
	72	Electrical machinery	0.24	0.29
	73	Transport equipment	0.58	0.26
Aggregate 9	09	Misc. food prep.	0.01	0.01
(0.08)	51	Chemical elements, compounds	0.07	0.22
	53	Dyeing, tanning, colouring mat.	0.02	0.06
	54	Medicinal, pharmaceutical	0.03	0.13
	55	Essential oils, perfume mat.	0.01	0.04
	57	Explosives, pyrotechnic prod.	0.00	0.00
	58	Plastic materials, cellulose, etc.	0.06	0.07
	59	Chemical materials, products nes	0.04	0.05
	61	Leather, dressed furskins	0.00	0.02
	71	Machinery, other than electric	0.69	0.17
	86	Prof., etc., instruments, etc.	0.07	0.24

surprising, then, to find cereals and coffee in separate aggregates in the locally optimal scheme to be discussed shortly. The reason that it is highly undesirable to aggregate together coffee and cereals is that comparative advantage in coffee, tea, etc. is strongly associated with abundance of Land 1 with a tropical rainy climate, whereas comparative advantage in cereals is strongly associated with abundance of Land 3 with a humid-mesothermal climate. By combining these two classes the information value of the climate classification is lost.

The other problem class in 1958 is SITC-6 with 22 per cent of the loss. Within that class the problem commodities are SITC-64 (paper, paperboard), SITC-65 (textile, yarn, fabrics, etc.), SITC-67 (iron and steel), and SITC-68 (non-ferrous metal manufactures). In the scheme subsequently discussed, paper and non-ferrous metal products are combined with SITC-24 (wood, lumber, and cork) and SITC-25 (pulp) since they all have comparative advantage associated with Land 4 on which the major soft-wood forests of the world are located. Textile yarn and iron/steel are each in different categories, perhaps because comparative advantage in the former was associated with capital and also labour in the two highest skill groups whereas the latter is associated only with labour in the highest skill group. The other major problem with the SITC scheme in 1975 is that SITC-71 (machinery, other than electrical) and SITC-73 (transport equipment) ought not to be combined, perhaps because Labour 2 has a relatively great effect on SITC-73.

The composition of the nine locally optimal aggregates is

165

indicated in tables 7.3 and 7.4. Included in these tables are the shares calculated by formula (7.10) and the losses calculated by formula (7.9). These losses have been normalized so that within an aggregate they add to one. The numbers in parentheses under each aggregate also indicate losses, but in this case add to one across aggregates. For ease of reading, the loss shares of the nine aggregates, the components with shares in excess of 0.10 and the corresponding shares are reported in table 7.5.

At a formal statistical level the aggregation schemes reported in tables 7.3 and 7.4 do significantly better than the one-digit SITC scheme. But my interest in forming the aggregates was not of course to predict the net exports of some hypothetical randomly selected country, but rather to collapse the fifty-six two-digit commodities into a manageable number which reveal, as clearly as possible, the salient aspects of international trade. I think this goal has been well achieved. The locally optimal aggregates can be thought of as being composed of commodities for which the sources of comparative advantage are similar. Using the 1958 data, there are two aggregates of raw materials, four of farm products and three of manufactured products. The raw materials are: (1) petroleum and (2) wood and ores. (I am omitting mention of the smaller components.) The farm products are: (3) textile fibres, (4) coffee and sugar, (5) fruit and meat, and (6) cereals. The manufactured aggregates, arranged in rough order of technological complexity are: (9) yarn, fabrics, and clothing, (8) transport equipment, electrical machinery, and iron and steel, and (9) chemicals and non-electrical machinery. Much of the aggregation loss is due to aggregate 8. If a system of ten aggregates is selected, the only major change that occurs is that aggregate 8 is split up, and SITC-66 (non-metallic mineral manufactures), SITC-67 (iron and steel) and SITC-69 (manufactures of metal) form a new class.

Table 7.5 suggests that the nine aggregates have not changed greatly over time. One large change is that in 1975 the 1958 aggregates 4 (coffee and sugar) and 5 (fruit and meat) are combined with clothing, footwear, and other labour-intensive manufactures to form aggregate 5. This is a reflection of the north to south movement of the location of production of these labour-intensive manufactures. But because this aggregate causes 37 per cent of the total loss in 1975, the aggregation of tropical agricultural products and labour-intensive manufactures is suspicious. However, 35 per cent of the loss caused by this aggregate is due to fruit and vegetables, and hardly any to manufactures. Moreover, if ten aggregates are used, this class still remains intact. The change that occurs is that SITC-67 (iron and steel) forms a class by itself,

Table 7.5 Major components of the nine aggregates (a) 1958, (b) 1975

Loss share	Major components (share)
(a)	
1 (0.10)	Petroleum (0.67), rubber (0.19)
2 (0.20)	Ores (0.23), paper (0.19), non-ferrous metals (0.18), wood (0.14), pulp (0.11)
3 (0.03)	Textile fibres (0.81), oil-seeds (0.19)
4 (0.05)	Coffee (0.77), sugar (0.23)
5 (0.16)	Fruit (0.36), meat (0.29), dairy (0.16)
6 (0.04)	Cereals (0.78), tobacco (0.17)
7 (0.05)	Textile yarn (0.71), min. manuf. (0.15), clothing (0.12)
8 (0.19)	Transport equip. (0.46), elect. mach. (0.20), iron and steel (0.15)
9 (0.19)	Machinery (0.57), misc. manuf. (0.12)
(b)	
1 (0.02)	Petroleum (0.95)
2 (0.09)	Non-ferrous metals (0.28), gas (0.25), pulp (0.25), paper (0.21)
3 (0.04)	Ores (0.68), wood (0.32)
4 (0.13)	Coal (0.35), oil-seeds (0.26), text, fibres (0.14)
5 (0.37)	Clothing (0.20), coffee (0.18), sugar (0.17), fruit (0.13), meat (0.11)
6 (0.00)	Cereals (1.0)
7 (0.15)	Iron and steel (0.79), misc. (0.12)
8 (0.12)	Transport equip. (0.58), elect. mach. (0.24)
9 (0.08)	Machinery (0.69)

leaving SITC-62 (rubber manufactures), SITC-65 (textile yarn, fabrics), SITC-66 (non-metallic mineral manufactures) and SITC-89 (miscellaneous manufacturing articles, nes) as an aggregate. A possible explanation for this result is that there exists another local optimum with the tropical agricultural products and the labour-intensive manufactures in different classes. But if the ten SITC one-digit aggregates are used as a starting point, the local optimization still creates this unusual class. The conclusion that seems warranted is that the 1975 data do not allow us to distinguish the sources of comparative advantage in tropical agricultural products and labour-intensive manufactures, even though the former are associated with abundance of tropical land and the latter with abundance of labour. This is an example in which prior information might alter substantially the estimates of the coefficients and lead to more appealing aggregates.

The least-squares estimates of the coefficients of the nine aggregates are reported in table 7.6. These coefficients in 1958 indicate that the sources of comparative advantage are roughly what you would expect. Comparative advantage in petroleum products is associated with oil availability. Capital, on the other hand, seems to create a demand for petroleum. The other raw material aggregate has relatively large coefficients on Land 4 and minerals. The four crops are associated respectively with Land 2, Land 1, Land 3, and Land 4. The first two aggregates (7 and 8) of manufactures have very large coefficients for the highest skilled labour variable. Finally, the last aggregate (machinery and chemicals) has a surprisingly large coefficient on the coal variable.

The 1975 coefficients have some substantial changes, the most interesting being the large negative coefficients for Labour 1 in each of the three aggregates of manufactures (7, 8, and 9). This suggests a dramatic change in the role of human capital as a source of comparative advantage in manufactures, a possibility which is further explored in Leamer (1984).

4.5 Concluding comments

The main purpose of this article is to demonstrate the usefulness of a formal treatment of aggregation in the context of a data analysis aimed at substantive issues. It has been demonstrated that a study of the sources of comparative advantage using one-digit SITC data has some severe shortcomings, the most prominent of which is that cereals and tropical agricultural products are inappropriately combined. It has also been shown that the 1975 data suggest aggregation of tropical agricultural products and labour-intensive manufactures. This kind of finding raises interesting questions as to why these products have similar sources of comparative advantage.

Finally, a number of problems with this analysis may be mentioned. With this kind of cross-section data set, the estimates can be very sensitive to outliers, and methods that reduce the weight of outliers might imply quite different aggregates. For that matter, the results presented here are only locally optimal, and other starting points could also imply quite different aggregates. A small amount of experimentation did not, however, yield drastically different aggregates. The loss function seems fairly flat in the sense that quite a bit of rearrangement is allowed without great increases in losses. In practice it would seem wise to take advantage of this by rearrangements that increase the interpretive clarity of the system.

Separate aggregation schemes were produced for 1958 and 1975. The differences are quite interesting, but in some settings it may be desirable to have one aggregation scheme for all years. This would require minor adjustments to the theory. Another interesting possibility would be to aggregate or to eliminate explanatory variables. For example, an interesting question is

Table 7.6 Coefficients of the nine aggregates (a) 1958 (b) 1975

	Cap	L_1	L_2	L_3	T_1	T_2	T_3	T_4	Coal	Min.	Oil
(a)											
1	-20.3	60	1.9	-0.7	-0.16	-0.17	-0.38	-0.52	-0.01	0.76	1.20
2	-1.1	-141	-0.8	3.4	0.01	0.08	-1.08	3.11	-0.50	0.95	-0.01
3	-3.5	-141	-9.2	4.1	0.18	1.02	0.84	-0.16	-0.01	0.17	0.51
4	-1.9	-216	4.8	4.0	1.14	-0.01	-0.30	-0.17	-0.15	0.03	-0.16
5	2.1	-38	5.4	-0.1	-0.20	0.20	2.81	-0.56	-0.85	0.18	0.22
6	7.3	-424	6.1	3.0	-0.12	-0.23	2.04	0.50	-0.22	0.22	0.20
7	3.1	236	13.6	-3.6	-0.23	0.05	-1.42	-0.43	-0.16	-0.34	-0.46
8	-2.2	940	-24.5	-12.9	-0.29	-0.30	-2.45	-1.23	0.93	-0.60	-0.47
9	2.8	-433	5.6	1.8	-0.13	-0.51	-1.99	-1.29	1.19	-0.63	0.54
(b)											
1	-19.9	179	-42	23.0	1.40	11.1	-7.7	5.70	-0.64	-1.03	0.44
2	-0.9	-151	-17	18.0	-1.20	-1.4	-2.8	4.70	-0.28	0.73	0.07
3	-6.6	771	-72	-6.1	0.91	-2.0	2.9	-0.53	0.02	0.10	0.03
4	-4.2	-194	-51	13.5	2.50	-2.2	5.5	-3.10	0.63	0.54	0.15
5	-6.1	233	14	3.0	0.12	-5.6	14.3	-11.50	-1.00	1.50	0.17
6	-2.1	518	-65	-10.2	-1.20	-4.1	11.9	-3.10	-0.03	0.90	0.15
7	17.7	-2315	106	55.2	-0.66	3.9	-12.0	1.10	-0.03	-0.55	-0.15
8	26.8	-2156	154	34.9	-0.02	4.2	-16.7	1.90	0.39	-1.60	-0.34
9	19.3	-1970	8	47.0	2.00	2.8	-22.8	4.20	2.20	-2.2	-0.30

whether the four categories of land are really necessary. Aggregation of the explanatory variables is theoretically straightforward, and is discussed in Fisher (1969). For a similar treatment of the omission of variables, see Lindley (1968).

Note

1   Incidentally, if the aggregate has only two components, then these loss shares are necessarily equal.

Chapter eight

The choice of aggregate production functions in Mexican industries

Thomas Sterner*

Introduction

This paper studies the relationship between elasticity estimates at different levels of aggregation. Elasticities for aggregated industries are compared to the average of the elasticities estimated from data at the individual industry level. The results show that it is not certain, even with simplifying assumptions about relative growth rates and other variables, that aggregate elasticities will coincide with or even be close to average ones.

Which level of aggregation to choose in econometric modelling is a crucial but difficult question. The assumption of a unique production function may be easier to defend at the level of individual industries but data for such industries, on the other hand, are often characterized by more uncertainty than aggregate data. Furthermore, the interpretation of elasticities at the aggregate and industry level is necessarily different since aggregate elasticities include substitution arising as a result of structural change.

The conditions for the existence of aggregate production functions are extremely restrictive (see, for example, Fisher, 1969 for a survey and references). Even for linear aggregation of linear models we find that consistency is an exceptional result and, in general, macro parameters depend not only on the corresponding micro parameters but on other parameters at the micro level as well (see, for instance, Theil 1954 and Lütjohann, 1974). For non-linear models the odds against perfect aggregation are generally worse (see Barker, 1970, 1974). However, even when paying lip service to 'the problem of aggregation' empirical economists often

* I wish to thank Terry Barker, Arie Kapteyn, Anders Klevmarken, Hashem Pesaran, and two anonymous referees for valuable comments on earlier versions of this paper.

feel that aggregation will presumably give reasonable approximations so long as elasticities are fairly similar and structural
change in output not too large (on the consumption side similar
assumptions are often made that income distribution does not
change 'too much').

Fisher, Solow, and Kearl (1977) remarked that aggregate estimates often do give reasonable results and, since it is not theoretically easy to say why, they explore the field by carrying out a
series of simulation experiments with constant elasticity of substitution functions.

The approach taken in this chapter is similar but, like Winters
(1980), we have chosen to use actual observed data rather than
purely simulated data. While simulations have the advantage of
allowing you to vary a number of crucial aspects systematically,
there is an obvious appeal in using actual data with all the inherent
problems of real-life statistics. Since we wanted to study aggregation under a wide variety of circumstances we needed data with
considerable variation in growth rates, factor prices, and elasticities
and have chosen Mexican industrial data.

8.1 Estimation methods and data used

To allow for the variability of performance of Mexican industries
we felt it necessary to work with a functional form that avoids
placing such strong restrictions on the elasticities to be estimated as
does the CES. There is a whole class of second-order Taylor
approximations to the cost function which could have been used
(e.g. the generalized Leontief, the generalized Cobb–Douglas, the
translog and the square-root quadratic). Several studies have
compared their properties with different types of data and, for
instance, Guilkey *et al.* (1983) conclude that the translog is fairly
dependable if reality is 'not too complex'. Not all studies agree, but
in our case we chose to work with the translog since it has the
advantage of being very frequently used (particularly on Third
World data). Spcification (8.1) below shows a translogarithmic
cost function with five inputs, capital K, labour L, intermediate
materials M, electricity E, and fuels F. Note that (8.1) allows for
non-neutral technical change and non-homotheticity.

$$\text{Ln } C = \alpha_0 + \alpha_y \ln Y + \alpha_t T + \sum_i \alpha_i \ln P_i + \frac{1}{2} \sum_i \sum_j \gamma_{ij} \ln P_i \ln P_j$$

$$+ \gamma_{ty} T \ln Y + \sum_i \gamma_{yi} \ln Y \ln P_i + \sum_i \gamma_{ti} T \ln P_i + \frac{1}{2} \gamma_{yy} (\ln Y)^2$$

$$+ \frac{1}{2} \gamma_{tt} T^2 \tag{8.1}$$

$i, j \in \{K, L, M, E, F\}.$

subject to the restrictions imposed by symmetry and linear homogeneity

$$\sum_i \alpha_i = 1, \quad \sum_i \gamma_{ij} = \sum_j \gamma_{ij} = 0, \quad \sum_i \gamma_{yi} = 0, \quad \sum_i \gamma_{ti} = 0, \quad \gamma_{ij} = \gamma_{ji} \tag{8.2}$$

Making the conventional assumptions and applying Shephard's Lemma allows us to derive the five cost-share equations (8.3)

$$S_i = \alpha_i + \sum_j \gamma_{ij} \ln P_j + \gamma_{yi} \ln Y + \gamma_{ti} T, \quad i = K, L, M, E, F \tag{8.3}$$

It should be observed that these cost shares sum identically to zero owing to restrictions (8.2) and therefore in estimation one of them has to be dropped to avoid over-identification. By imposing additional restrictions on the appropriate parameters, the functions can be constrained to impose Hicks's neutral technical change, homotheticity, homogeneity, constant returns, or even to a Cobb–Douglas specification. Sterner (1985), using the same data, found that these restrictions could generally be statistically rejected and we will therefore here use only the unrestricted model.

The study is based on yearly census data (1966–81) for Mexican manufacturing industry which exhibit many of the practical problems that occur in empirical work. Data availability restricted our estimations to eighteen four-digit industries representing around 70 per cent of the total covered by the census. Differences in growth rates and factor prices as between these industries are in some cases considerable, the most expansive industry growing almost three times as fast as the least expansive (Appendix 8A provides some information relating to factor price differences.)

Tables 8.1 and 8.2 show elasticities for the base year (1970) for all the eighteen four-digit industries mentioned along with estimates for some more aggregate (three-digit) industries. The latter have been made up by aggregating (adding) data for the corresponding four-digit industries. All estimates are full information

Disaggregation in econometric modelling

Table 8.1 Own-price elasticities

Industry	Elec.	Fuel	Mater.	Lab.	Cap.
3412	−0.36	−0.54	0.06	−0.19	0.32
Steel second.	(0.10)	(0.22)	(0.09)	(0.18)	(0.19)
3411	−0.45	0.27	−0.17	−0.93	0.10
Steel primary	(0.09)	(0.24)	(0.13)	(0.27)	(0.34)
3413	−0.29	−0.38	0.06	−0.07	0.23
Steel pipes	(0.26)	(0.21)	(0.10)	(0.17)	(0.24)
3421	−1.66	0.44	0.05	0.11	0.19
Copper	(0.37)	(1.15)	(0.03)	(0.15)	(0.22)
3423	0.04	0.09	−0.04	−0.67	−0.23
Aluminium	(0.16)	(0.18)	(0.08)	(0.18)	(0.29)
3811	−0.20	0.38	−0.11	−0.48	0.42
Automobiles	(0.31)	(0.34)	(0.07)	(0.21)	(0.84)
3011	−0.63	−0.42	−0.02	−0.35	−0.52
Car tyres	(0.19)	(0.35)	(0.15)	(0.12)	(0.61)
2711	−0.38	−1.57	−0.22	−0.39	−0.11
Paper & pulp	(0.10)	(0.29)	(0.09)	(0.05)	(0.15)
3341	−0.26	−0.15	−0.25	−0.59	−0.22
Cement	(0.12)	(0.19)	(0.10)	(0.15)	(0.12)
2051	−0.03	−2.66	−0.05	−0.68	−0.25
Flour	(0.35)	(0.51)	(0.01)	(0.07)	(0.11)
2132	−0.10	−1.17	−0.13	−0.20	−0.68
Beer	(0.05)	(0.61)	(0.15)	(0.16)	(0.19)
2093	−0.94	0.16	−0.02	−0.49	−0.24
Margarine	(0.19)	(0.60)	(0.03)	(0.13)	(0.21)
2098	−0.90	−0.73	−0.03	−0.66	−0.15
Fodder	(0.05)	(0.68)	(0.01)	(0.33)	(0.33)
2023	−2.41	0.18	−0.03	−0.32	−0.48
Milk	(0.40)	(0.92)	(0.05)	(0.11)	(0.17)
3321	−0.59	−1.53	−0.65	−0.40	−0.14
Plain glass	(0.26)	(0.31)	(0.68)	(0.09)	(0.38)
3323	−1.26	0.61	0.38	−0.64	−1.83
Glass fibre	(0.18)	(0.98)	(0.12)	(0.13)	(0.36)
3324	0.48	0.04	−0.37	−0.24	0.42
Glass bottles	(0.14)	(0.17)	(0.34)	(0.14)	(0.32)
2317	−0.17	−0.66	−0.05	−0.40	0.20
Fibres & text.	(0.14)	(0.31)	(0.05)	(0.16)	(0.28)
3-digit aggregate industries[a]					
332	0.48	−0.36	−0.39	−0.28	−0.07
Glass	(0.16)	(0.09)	(0.26)	(0.10)	(0.16)
341	−0.39	0.77	−0.08	−0.52	0.47
Steel	(0.06)	(0.14)	(0.09)	(0.12)	(0.24)
340	−0.37	0.35	−0.13	−0.44	0.44
Metals	(0.10)	(0.16)	(0.08)	(0.15)	(0.23)
200	−0.34	−0.36	−0.04	−0.31	−0.23
Foodstuffs	(0.13)	(0.23)	(0.02)	(0.10)	(0.10)

Notes: The elasticities shown refer to the base year 1970.

Approximate standard errors in parentheses. These have been calculated under the conventional assumption of non-stochastic cost-shares for simplicity. This might imply a slight underestimation of standard errors, in addition to the underestimation caused by the limited sample size. Moroney and Toevs (1977) do, however, find that the difference in estimated standard errors due to the assumption of non-stochastic cost shares is very small.

[a] 3-digit industries aggregated as follows:

332 = 3321 + 3323 + 3324   340 = 341 + 3421 + 3423
341 = 3411 + 3412 + 3413   200 − 2051 + 2132 + 2093 + 2098 + 2023

---

maximum likelihood estimated on time series for each industry separately. There are a number of unexpected signs and levels of significance are often low, but the reader should bear in mind that this type of problem is very common in empirical research, particularly with Third World data. One possible explanation is the lack of competition in many of the factor markets. (Details of the estimation procedures, variable definitions, statistics of fit, the tests carried out, etc. are available on request from the author.)

8.2 The effect of aggregation

In this paper we are above all interested in the relationship between elasticity estimates for aggregated and individual industries. One can easily see that the former do not always correspond very well to the average of the elasticities of the industries from which they are made up. Thus, for instance, the electricity elasticity of the glass industry 332 cannot be an average of the three constituent industries' (3321, 3 and 4) elasticities.

The method used is to compare aggregate elasticities systematically with the corresponding (weighted) average elasticities. The price elasticity of an individual industry estimated by (8.3) above is given by (8.4)

$$\varepsilon_{ij} = (\hat{\gamma}_{ij} + \hat{S}_i\hat{S}_j)/\hat{S}_i$$
$$\varepsilon_{ii} = (\hat{\gamma}_{ii} + \hat{S}_i^2 - \hat{S}_i)/\hat{S}_i$$
(8.4)

where the $\hat{S}$ are estimated cost-shares.

If we have R industries ($k = 1, \ldots, R$), the weighted average elasticities are given by (5)

$$\varepsilon_{ij}^w = \sum_k^R w_k \varepsilon_{ijk}$$
(8.5)

175

Disaggregation in econometric modelling

where the w_k are output weights.

By comparison, the aggregate elasticities ε_{ij}^a are given by reestimating system (8.3′) using average cost-shares and input-prices

$$S_i^a = \sum_k^R w_k S_{ik} = a_i + \sum_j \gamma_{ij} \ln(\sum_k^R w_k P_{jk})$$

$$+ \gamma_{yi} \ln(\sum_k^R Y_k) + \gamma_{ti} T \qquad (8.3')$$

The purpose of this chapter is to compare ε_{ij}^w and ε_{ij}^a with respect to situations in which there is a large or small difference in growth, price structure, and elasticities.

In fact there is, in general, no reason why average and aggregate elasticities should coincide. If, for instance, we are looking at an aggregate composed of a number of individual industries and one of these, the most labour intensive of all, happens to grow much more slowly than average, then this will tend to push down the labour coefficient for the entire aggregate. If wages are the factor which rises fastest in price then the model of analysis would tend to identify this as a negative price elasticity of labour in the aggregate industry. In such a case one would expect aggregate elasticities to be lower than the average of the individual industry elasticities.

If two industries grow at the same rate then there would seem to be less reason (at least as far as structural change is concerned) for aggregate and average elasticities to differ. There might, however, be other factors influencing the relationship between aggregate and average elasticities, such as differences in factor prices. We shall therefore look into the practical importance of these factors for aggregation results in our data.

In tables 8.1 and 8.2 the three-digit industries were aggregated according to type of product into what are conventionally considered as 'natural' branches. While this is common practice there is little analytical rationale for this approach, since the production processes involved have little in common (for instance as between primary steel processing, 3411, and the making of steel pipes, 3413). In some cases industries in completely different fields may have more in common (from the point of view of their production processes). However, when we carry the process of aggregation to higher levels, and ultimately to the industry total, we invariably end up adding together industries that are completely different in all respects.

To analyse how aggregate elasticity values compare to average ones, we need more cases than are provided by the natural three-digit industries. We have therefore aggregated all types of industry

Table 8.2 Elasticities of substitution

Industry	EF	EM	EL	EK	FM	FL	FK	LK
3412	0.70	−0.71	3.36	2.60	1.06	2.51	−4.02	0.27
	(5.98)	(0.63)	(1.65)	(2.36)	(0.54)	(1.92)	(2.43)	(0.91)
3411	3.95	0.51	2.51	−4.11	−0.42	−0.34	−1.82	1.20
	(0.93)	(0.26)	(1.59)	(1.42)	(0.36)	(1.25)	(1.59)	(1.98)
3413	−14.87	−0.01	−4.01	7.44	−0.77	0.48	5.67	−0.06
	(13.30)	(0.95)	(2.93)	(4.75)	(0.44)	(1.53)	(2.77)	(0.94)
3421	−94.04	0.06	12.60	21.10	0.31	23.66	−36.00	1.21
	(78.61)	(0.40)	(5.36)	(8.83)	(0.78)	(11.33)	(20.85)	(2.09)
3423	−0.31	0.01	2.39	−2.90	1.72	−0.14	−5.77	2.57
	(1.92)	(0.36)	(0.81)	(1.14)	(0.37)	(0.84)	(1.27)	(1.01)
3811	−143.89	−0.24	2.78	6.35	0.05	−1.75	8.86	−3.81
	(92.01)	(0.79)	(1.87)	(19.49)	(0.86)	(2.24)	(21.23)	(2.70)
3011	−38.57	0.63	0.83	2.88	−0.73	0.41	13.22	2.02
	(14.58)	(0.49)	(0.52)	(2.57)	(1.18)	(1.36)	(6.18)	(0.98)
2711	0.88	0.09	−0.30	1.73	2.06	1.89	0.49	−0.04
	(3.78)	(0.33)	(0.50)	(0.71)	(0.59)	(1.00)	(1.23)	(0.26)
3341	1.31	0.52	−0.22	0.20	1.19	−0.37	−0.29	1.37
	(0.86)	(0.55)	(0.52)	(0.51)	(0.65)	(0.71)	(0.50)	(0.32)
2051	−33.34	0.24	1.50	−4.70	3.07	6.23	0.34	3.78
	(25.65)	(0.51)	(3.22)	(4.95)	(0.78)	(5.67)	(12.59)	(0.82)
2132	−30.97	0.96	−0.21	0.69	1.28	1.67	4.82	1.04
	(5.36)	(0.22)	(0.27)	(0.54)	(0.88)	(1.29)	(2.89)	(0.46)
2093	4.13	0.28	2.30	19.39	−0.36	11.76	−19.74	2.75
	(33.23)	(0.54)	(5.58)	(9.69)	(0.69)	(9.26)	(17.61)	(3.71)
2098	148.35	−0.02	12.35	0.32	0.36	−11.63	4.48	5.00
	(31.02)	(0.24)	(5.69)	(9.46)	(0.84)	(23.87)	(51.64)	(10.34)
2023	76.87	0.50	−6.56	33.60	−1.02	19.03	−28.05	2.04
	(34.69)	(0.32)	(2.39)	(7.10)	(0.92)	(7.14)	(11.76)	(1.56)
3321	−11.25	4.50	−1.46	2.23	5.17	0.05	1.46	0.45
	(5.99)	(2.81)	(0.78)	(2.02)	(1.69)	(0.55)	(1.39)	(0.41)
3323	5.82	0.94	1.43	2.34	1.17	−2.94	−6.38	3.01
	(21.65)	(0.34)	(0.95)	(3.08)	(0.84)	(2.46)	(8.48)	(1.04)
3324	−2.17	−0.31	−0.42	−0.49	3.06	−0.24	−3.96	0.13
	(2.30)	(1.26)	(0.36)	(1.44)	(1.11)	(0.36)	(1.30)	(0.46)
2317	22.89	0.03	0.52	−1.20	0.01	4.55	−6.42	0.66
	(10.53)	(0.42)	(1.36)	(3.39)	(0.52)	(1.25)	(3.28)	(0.98)
3-digit aggregate industries								
332	−0.49	0.81	−0.70	−2.12	2.49	−0.14	−1.74	0.56
	(2.38)	(0.95)	(0.30)	(1.01)	(0.69)	(0.25)	(0.74)	(0.21)
341	8.73	−0.11	2.20	−2.33	−0.47	−1.17	−4.07	−0.69
	(1.84)	(0.41)	(0.98)	(1.61)	(0.54)	(1.03)	(1.78)	(0.91)
340	11.01	0.18	1.00	−3.07	−0.26	−0.33	−3.45	−1.75
	(2.78)	(0.50)	(1.29)	(2.08)	(0.57)	(1.46)	(2.21)	(1.04)
200	66.82	−0.11	−4.82	8.66	0.06	−0.55	−8.85	1.67
	(12.69)	(0.22)	(1.80)	(3.18)	(0.23)	(1.57)	(3.15)	(0.98)

See table 8.1 for footnotes.

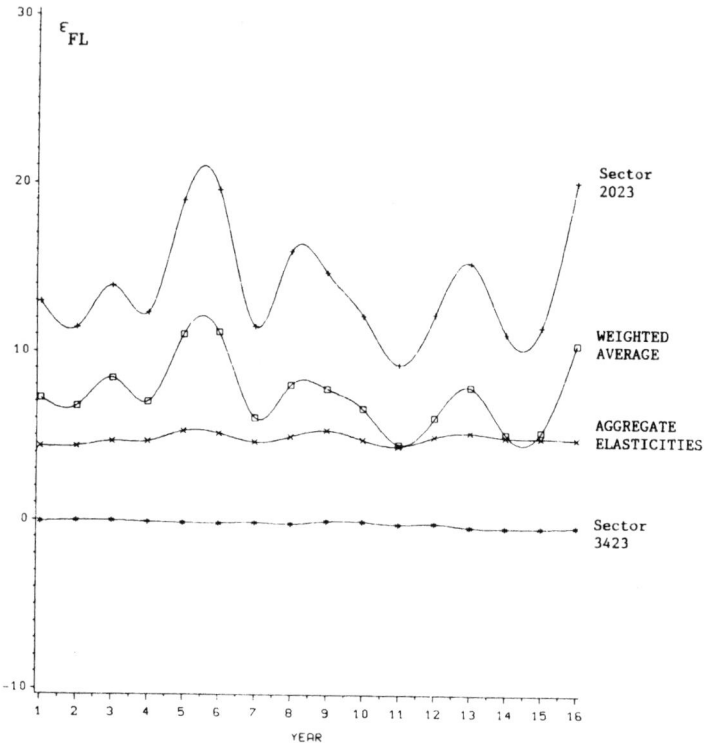

Figure 8.1 Elasticities (fuel/labour) in sectors 1,2 – average and aggregate

without taking into consideration whether they fit together naturally or not. To facilitate systematic comparison with individual elasticities, the industries are aggregated two by two and we have simply analysed all possible pairs of industries (a total of 153). The aggregation has been carried out by adding together the observed factor costs and output levels. Aggregate price indices were constructed as weighted averages of the respective price indices (using outputs as weights).

The flexibility of the translog means that a set of elasticities such as shown in tables 8.1 and 8.2 is estimated for each year. Naturally aggregate elasticities may diverge from average ones for all or some of the years covered. This is illustrated in figures 8.1–8.4 where a number of elasticities for the component industries are plotted along with the aggregate and average values. The first two

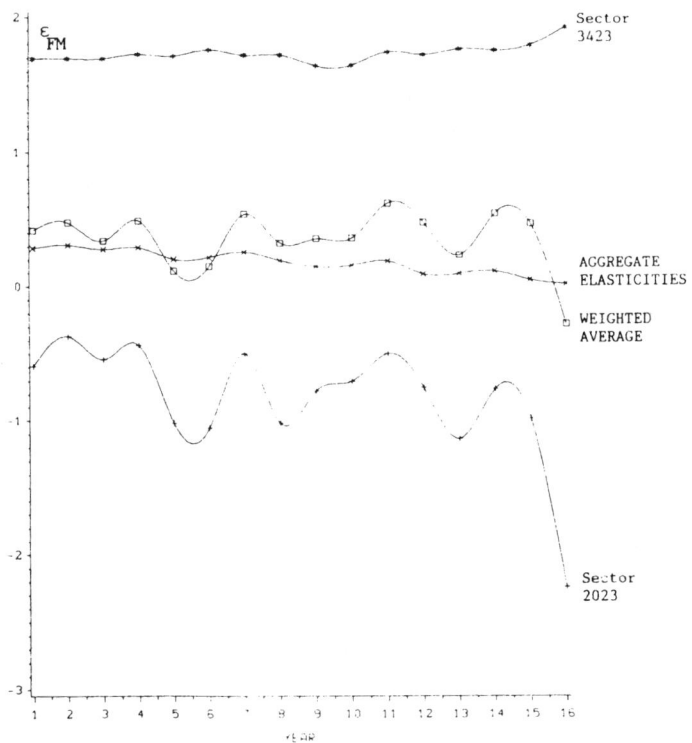

Figure 8.2 Elasticities (fuel/materials) in sectors 1,2 – average and aggregate

diagrams show what must be considered as quite close approximations. If these are typical we might assume that differences in input price structure and growth rates are not interfering too much and that the aggregation is surprisingly 'well behaved'. We might, however, find the opposite result dominating, e.g. figures 8.3 and 8.4 where the aggregate elasticity clearly has nothing whatsoever to do with the values estimated for the two industries individually. It is important to point out that the differences between these two sets of diagrams is in no way related to the precision of the estimates. Thus the statistical significance of the elasticities in figures 8.3 and 8.4 is not lower than for those in figures 8.1 and 8.2.

The purpose of carrying out such a large number of aggregations is to see if there is any tendency, in general or perhaps under certain specific conditions, for aggregate and average

179

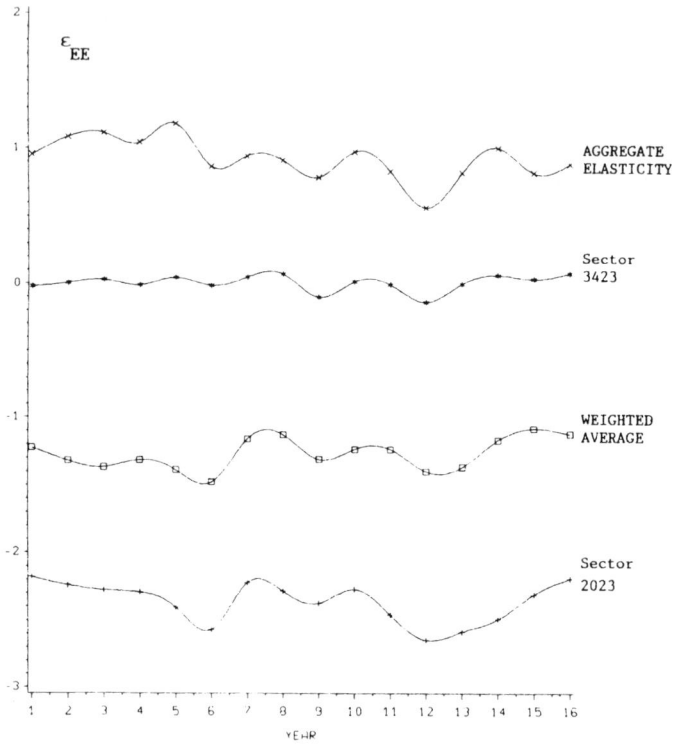

Figure 8.3 Elasticities (electricity) in sectors 1,2 – average and aggregate

elasticities to coincide. Such conditions might be, for instance, similar elasticity values, similar growth rates, or similar factor price structures.

To analyse our results we have therefore recorded for each aggregation, first, the average relative growth rates and relative input factor prices and, second, three indicators of how the average elasticity (weighted by output) compares to the aggregate for each year. The first of these (labelled 'close' in table 8.3) tells us the percentage of all elasticity observations for which the average is close to the aggregate value (defined as differing by less than one standard deviation). The second (labelled 'non-equal') gives the percentage of cases for which the hypothesis of equality can be statistically rejected at the 5 per cent confidence level. The third (labelled 'Out of range') shows the percentage for which the aggregate elasticity falls outside the range defined by the two

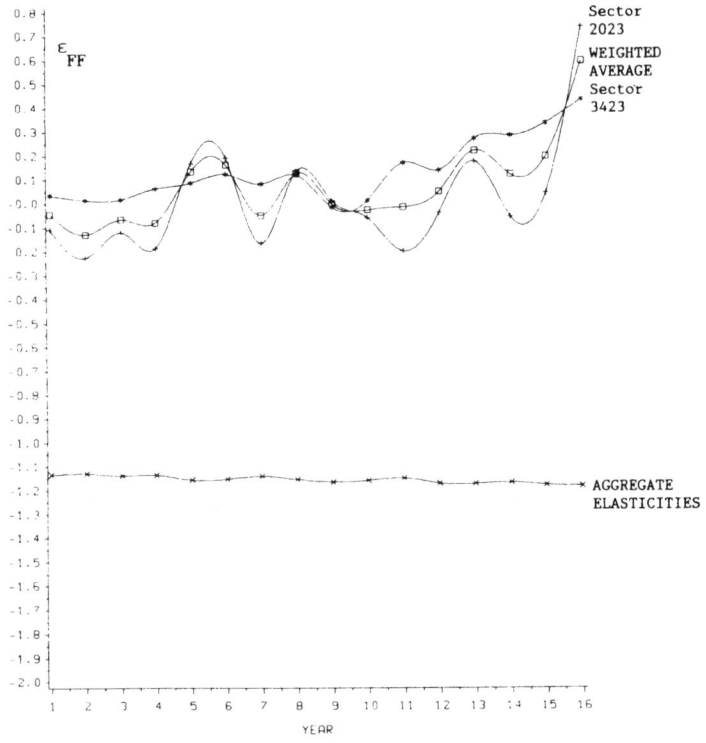

Figure 8.4 Elasticities (fuel, own-price) in sectors 1,2 – average and aggregate

industries' values. To illustrate the analysis, table 8.3 shows the results of aggregating one industry 3412 (secondary steel) with a number of other industries.

We can see that in some cases no aggregate elasticities are statistically different (at the 5 per cent level) from the average and most of them are 'close', while in other cases a significant number are 'non-equal'. The corresponding table for all the 153 aggregations carried out is not shown (but available on request). The results found were that average and aggregate elasticities were 'non-equal' in 17 per cent of all estimates and they were 'close' (in the rather generous sense defined above) in only 57 per cent. Forty per cent of the aggregate elasticities fell outside the range of the two component industries' elasticities.

181

Table 8.3 Results of aggregating secondary steel (industry 3412) with six other industries

	3411	3413	3421	3811	2711	3341
Differences in average growth[a] rate of:						
output	88.42	108.33	84.76	207.36	135.66	130.77
fuel prices	160.24	100.00	100.00	100.00	100.00	100.00
wages	94.35	84.45	91.83	101.03	116.59	115.23
mater. prices	77.86	88.61	148.40	111.52	90.45	127.98
elect. prices	113.31	75.40	112.58	67.68	85.46	49.09
Comparison of elasticities:						
Close values (%)	47.50	30.42	80.00	57.08	69.58	97.50
Non-equal values (%)	30.42	9.17	0.00	15.83	1.67	0.00
Out of range (%)	48.75	70.42	57.50	49.58	24.58	61.67

[a]Growth rates for industry *3412* are set to 100.0.

8.3 The size of cost shares

Table 8.4 shows that there is quite a variation in the way aggregate and average elasticities compare. The elasticities involving electricity and fuel are much more prone to inequality. This cannot be explained by their being 'less significant' than the other factors' elasticities. In fact among the ownprice elasticities the lowest t-values were generally to be found in the material and capital shares and not in the shares of electricity or fuels.

However, it may be possible that the small size of the two energy factors (as measured by their cost shares) offers part of the explanation: they exhibit greater random variation (for instance due to data errors) and the cost share does enter into the denominator of the equation for the elasticities. This would, however, only reduce the problem slightly since the divergence of aggregate and average elasticities also applies to a sizeable percentage of the factors with large cost shares.

A related question is whether our observed differences in elasticities at different levels are due to estimation problems. Thus, it might conceivably have been the case that errors at a disaggregated level cancel out so that statistics of fit were better at an aggregate level and estimators gave better approximations to true values than at the disaggregated level where there would be more disturbances. While it is true that statistics of fit such as the

R-square or Theils information inaccuracy did generally (though not always) improve somewhat with aggregation, we have been unable to find any relationship between how much these measures improved and the performance of our aggregate and average elasticities.

8.4 Differences in growth rates and input prices

Our main hypothesis in this chapter is that the differences between aggregate and average elasticities are due to structural change, i.e. different growth rates of the individual industries being aggregated. In this section we therefore carry out an analysis relating our two variables 'close' and 'non-equal' to the percentage difference in growth rates between the two constituent industries. We also want to include differences in their input factor prices, since this too could be a cause for differences in the elasticities estimated.

Table 8.5 shows regressions relating the percentage of elasticities that were 'close' and 'non-equal' to the percentage difference in growth rates between the two constituent industries and likewise to the percentage differences in each of the input factor prices. These percentages have been calculated symmetrically, i.e. always taking the larger as a percentage of the smaller. It should be observed that these dependent variables do not really qualify for this type of analysis and the regressions should merely be seen as a convenient way of summarizing results which are too long to be easily and systematically interpreted otherwise. The results should therefore be treated with due caution. They do, however, seem to show that the way aggregate elasticities compare to average elasticities is not explained by the

Table 8.4 Non-equality of average and aggregate elasticities

	Own price elasticities (%)		Elasticities of substitution (%)			
E	35	EF	43		
F	25	EM	9	FM	12
M	7	EL	20	FL	20
L	8	EK	27	FK	27
K	10				
		ML	8		
		MK	9	LK	12

Notes: E = electricity, F = fuels, M = intermediate materials, L = labour, K = capital.

regression variables included to describe how similar or dissimilar the industries are with respect to their growth rates and their factor input prices.[1]

In fact, several of the coefficients even have the 'wrong' sign and thus, for instance, the elasticities would be more likely to be equal or close to the average in the presence of rapid structural change (i.e. with different growth rates) than when the industries grow at the same pace. This is clearly contrary to what one would expect and we must conclude that structural change does not explain the differences in aggregate and average elasticities found in our material. We also inspected those industries that had similar prices and/or growth rates and found that, even for these, non-equality of the elasticities was quite common.

8.5 Some simulations

As a final way of seeing whether aggregate elasticities would be close to average ones in the absence of structural change and differences in input prices, a series of simulations was undertaken in which 'mock industries' were constructed. In each pair of industries the real input prices and output figures for the second industry were replaced by the corresponding figures from the first industry. The two were thus identical in size, growth rates, and factor prices. Only the observed cost shares were allowed to vary. The same number of runs was carried out and the result was that the number of cases for which equality could be rejected remained exactly 17 per cent. The number of elasticities that were 'close' increased marginally from 49 per cent to 60 per cent and a total of 27 per cent (compared to 49 per cent) of the aggregate elasticities fell outside the range of values defined by the two individual industries. Thus neither difference in input prices nor in growth rates appear to be important in this context since, even without any

Table 8.5 Regression equations with output and price differences

Dependent variable	Intercept	Differences in average growth rates					R^2
		output	wages	fuel	elec.	mater.	
Non-equality	17.91	−0.10	0.10	−0.00	0.01	−0.01	0.06
	(3.02)	(0.04)	(0.06)	(0.06)	(0.03)	(0.03)	
Close values	49.96	0.16	−0.07	0.11	0.02	0.03	0.08
	(4.19)	(0.05)	(0.08)	(0.09)	(0.05)	(0.04)	

Note: Standard errors in parentheses.

structural change at all in industry composition, and with identical prices, this type of aggregation bias persists.

The remaining case for which we might have hoped to find that aggregate and average elasticities would be close is that when elasticities themselves are similar. Unfortunately, with five cost shares there are fifteen elasticities and it is rather unlikely that all the elasticities for any pair of industries are really similar. However, we did study particularly those industries whose elasticities were at least as close as we could get (not separated by more than one standard deviation). Again we found that there was still a considerable number of non-equalities.

We also looked at those pairs of industries for which aggregation gave the 'best' results (i.e. coincided with average values) but again they were not generally characterized by any particular similarity between their elasticities. Nor did we observe any other systematic similarity that would have distinguished this group.

Conclusions

Our conclusions are thus rather negative: there is in general no reason to believe that aggregate elasticities relate systematically to the elasticities of the underlying industries and although they do so sometimes we have been unable to find any simple 'rule of thumb' to say why.[2] The absence of structural change and the equality of input prices do not reduce our aggregation bias. Nor does it appear to be enough to have similar elasticities. The only remaining possibility, which is of little practical interest, is when all of these conditions are fulfilled at the same time (i.e. the industries have very similar elasticities, growth rate, size, and factor prices). We know, however, from theory that not even in this rather hypothetical case could one be sure of getting aggregate elasticities close to average ones.

Appendix 8A

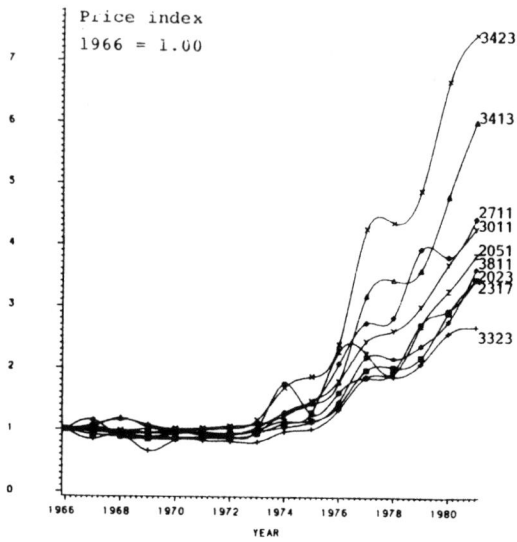

Figure 8A.1 Price indices for electricity – some individual industries

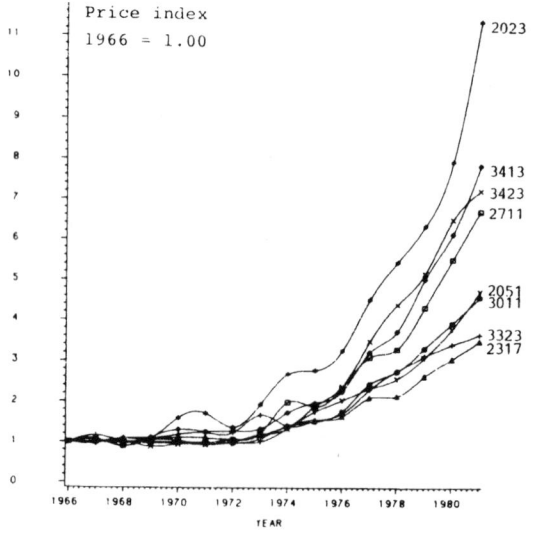

Figure 8A.2 Price indices for intermediate goods – some individual industries

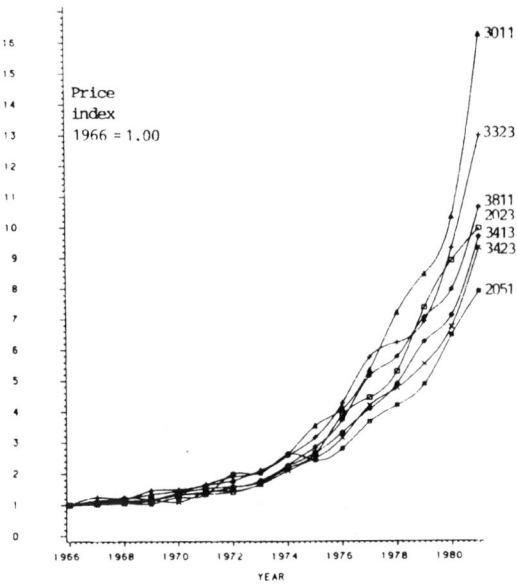

Figure 8A.3 Wage indices – some individual industries

Notes

1 The use of average growth rates and average relative factor prices over the whole period might have introduced some distortion; the ideal would have been to have the yearly figures for each individual industry, but this would hardly have been possible in our case.

2 The way in which aggregate elasticities deviate from average ones has not been discussed here. As already mentioned, one would expect that, if the expanding industry uses one particular factor intensively and that factor happens to be declining in price, then this would imply a greater (negative) elasticity for that factor in the aggregate than the average of the two industries. However, with five cost shares (as well as output and technical progress) the model is too complex for this kind of mechanism to be easily observed. We could find several instances in which this intuitive 'rule' applied but also cases in which it appeared not to do so.

Chapter nine

Disaggregation of the demand for hospital care

R.C.J.A. van Vliet and E.K.A. Van Doorslaer*

Introduction

In many fields of economics researchers have been forced to test their theoretical models of individual behaviour on aggregate data because of lack of individual data. However, the aggregation level of data can have a strong influence on the results of empirical econometric research. It is not surprising then that the theoretical problems associated with aggregation have received a great deal of attention among econometricians (see, e.g. Theil, 1954, Green, 1964, or Van Daal and Merkies, 1984).

In this chapter we confront some of the results of the theoretical literature on aggregation with the empirical consequences of aggregation in the context of the analysis of demand for hospital care. There has been an evolution in the estimation of hospital demand functions from macro to micro studies which has resulted in divergent findings. Most studies of aggregate demand at the regional level estimated extremely large effects of hospital bed supply whereas studies based on individual data typically found health status to have a dominant influence on hospital utilization. Very often, comparison of these studies is difficult because different data sources and model specifications have been used. In this chapter, we will estimate the *same* demand functions on both the macro and micro level using one data base in order to facilitate comparison.

* The authors would like to thank Jan van Dalen, José Geurts, Gerard van de Kuilen, and Brigitte Kerbusch for assistance, and the members of the research project 'Health insurance and medical consumption' and an anonymous referee for their comments on earlier drafts of this chapter. A longer version has appeared in *Applied Economics* (20, 7, 697–984, 1988).

The research reported here was supported in part by a grant from the Dutch health insurance company Zilveren Kruis which also provided the database used in this paper.

For this purpose, we use data on some 230,000 individuals who are insured with a private health insurance company in the Netherlands. The empirical analysis presented in section 9.3 is preceded by a discussion of the peculiarities of hospital demand functions (section 9.1) and by a theoretical examination of the consequences of aggregation (section 9.2).

9.1 The demand for hospital care

Demand functions for hospital care cannot be derived from a straightforward application of standard consumer theory in the same way as the demand for other goods and services. Feldstein (1977) has argued that inpatient treatment decisions can best be explained by viewing the patient-physician relationship as one of incomplete agency; i.e. treatment decisions reflect not only the patient's preferences and situation but also physician self-interest, peer pressure, and some medical ethical concern. Such 'partially benevolent' behaviour on the part of physicians generates a rather peculiar form of hospital care demand function: apart from relative prices, income, and 'taste' variables – i.e. the 'usual' demand variables – a vector of supply measures is added to reflect this direct influence of physician-agents on demand. The resulting empirical demand equation in a general implicit form then looks as follows (Pauly, 1980)

$$Q_D = D(P, X, Z)$$

where quantity demanded, Q_D, is measured by admissions and length of stay once admitted to the hospital, P is a vector of relevant user money and time prices, X includes other individual demand determinants such as income, health status, insurance coverage, and family size, and the Z vector represents a number of regional availability indicators of hospital beds and physicians.

Pauly (1980) has pointed out that the frequently estimated positive effect of the number of hospital beds or physicians per capita on the admission rate or length of hospital stay does not necessarily imply that suppliers create demand for their own services. Other explanations are: the existence of chronic excess demand, the response of patients to changes in the time or convenience cost of care, and the reaction of supply to high levels of demand in the past.

In this chapter, we do not want to settle the issue of whether or not demand creation is the theoretical explanation for observed availability effects. We want rather to illustrate the impact of

189

aggregation by analysing the same data set and the same equations at both the macro and micro level.

Most previous studies of demand for hospital care in the Netherlands have used aggregate regional data on utilization rates in the sixties or early seventies (see Van Doorslaer and van Vliet, 1986, for a survey). At that time, the Dutch government used a 90 per cent occupancy rate requirement to determine hospital tariffs. This requirement, which was abolished in the mid seventies, may have contributed to the extremely high bed elasticities which were estimated, *ceteris paribus*, in most of these studies: on average 0.6 for admission rates and 0.3 for mean length of hospital stay. Similar figures were found for the US and Britain (see, e.g. Cullis *et al.*, 1979, Van Doorslaer and van Vliet, 1986). In contrast, micro studies generally find that supply of hospital beds affects neither admission rates nor length of stay (e.g. Pauly, 1980, May, 1975).

Because our analysis is based on Dutch data it is useful to point out briefly a few characteristics of the Dutch health care system. Until 1986, about 70 per cent of the population was voluntarily or compulsory insured with the semi-public sick funds whereas most of the other 30 per cent bought private insurance coverage (in 1986, the voluntary sick fund insurance was abolished). The distinction between the two schemes is mainly based on income: the privately insured roughly constitute the upper three deciles of the income distribution. They can choose among a variety of insurance options including various degrees of cost-sharing with associated premium reductions, whereas the publicly insured have complete coverage for most types of medical service. General practitioners are paid on a capitation basis for public patients, and on a fee-for-service basis for private patients. Specialists are usually affiliated to one or more hospitals and remunerated by a fee-for-service, private fees being on average about twice as high as public fees. Since 1983, the output-based *per diem* financing of the hospitals has been supplemented by prospective reimbursement with fixed budgets per hospital.

Before we present the empirical results of our attempt to disaggregate the hospital demand functions, we shall first discuss some theoretical consequences of aggregation.

9.2 Aggregation of individual versus contextual variables

In the previous section, we pointed out that empirical demand functions for hospital care should contain, apart from the usual set of demand determining variables, a number of so-called availability indicators, such as regional bed and specialist density. These variables, which can only be defined on a regional level, are sometimes called 'contextual' (see, e.g. Langbein and Lichtman, 1978). The distinction between contextual and non-contextual (or individual) variables is important because the implications of aggregation are markedly different. We shall subsequently discuss the consequences of aggregation for the measures of association, aggregation, and specification bias, precision of estimates and consistency of regression results at both the micro and macro level.

9.2.1 Measures of association

Because contextual variables do not vary between individuals within the same region, the within-region variance is zero and the total variance is equal to the variance between the regions (when weighted with the size of the region). This implies that grouping individual observations to the regional level in question (e.g. by taking arithmetic means) does not change the variances of the contextual variables, while the covariances of these variables with other (non-contextual) variables are also not affected. Consequently, correlations between contextual and non-contextual variables increase when going from the micro to the macro level. This is not necessarily true for correlations among non-contextual variables which may increase, decrease, or remain invariant.

In general, it can be shown that grouping tends to inflate standardized measures of association for contextual variables (see also Cramer, 1964). Therefore, correlation coefficients, R^2's and beta-weights are unsuitable for cross-level comparisons. The elasticity figure, on the other hand, which is independent of both the unit of measurement and the level of aggregation, seems to be the most relevant statistic to use in cross-study comparisons when the aggregation levels of the data vary widely.

9.2.2 Aggregation and specification bias

The distinction between aggregation and specification bias in the context of linear regression analysis can be described as follows. Aggregation error exists if the expected value of a parameter estimator at an aggregate level ($\tilde{\beta}_x$) differs from the expected value of the corresponding parameter on the micro level (β_x), while no relevant explanatory variables are omitted; specification error arises when incorrect specification of the regression model leads to correlation between the independent variable and the error term (e.g. omitted variable bias). The consequences of the latter type of bias may differ greatly between individual and aggregate level: aggregation can both increase or decrease total specification bias depending on the relative change (due to grouping) of the correlation between the x-variable and the error term.

This means that, in the case of mis-specified models involving non-contextual explanatory variables, it is impossible to say *a priori* whether aggregation will result in a gain or loss. The danger of this type of bias is that on the basis of aggregate analysis erroneous inferences are made about individual behavioural relationships. This risk of 'ecological fallacy' can be avoided by refraining from cross-level inference and restricting conclusions to the macro relations only. However, if the explanatory variable in question is contextual, then its coefficient will be hardly affected by aggregation (van Vliet and Van Doorslaer, 1988).

9.2.3 Efficiency of estimators

Because grouping involves the loss of the information contained in the within-group variation of the observations, it is clear that we can expect some loss of efficiency in going from estimation on all individual observations to estimation based on group means, i.e. $\text{var}(\hat{\beta}_x) \leq \text{var}(\hat{\tilde{\beta}}_x)$ in a bivariate regression (see, e.g. Johnston, 1972, p. 231). The equality only holds when there is no within-group variation, i.e. when the explanatory variable is contextual.

If we have one contextual and one non-contextual explanatory variable, it can be shown that the relative efficiency loss for the former is smaller than for the latter variable. This result can be generalized to situations where we have several contextual variables and one individual variable.

9.2.4 Consistent aggregation

Estimating relations describing micro behaviour (like hospital care utilization) by means of aggregate data requires consistent aggregation (Van Daal and Merkies, 1984). This means that the macro relations have to be derived from the corresponding micro relations using the same aggregation formula (e.g. the arithmetic means in the preceding sections) for all variables in the equation. The problem is that, in most of the earlier studies of the demand for hospital care, log-linear equations have been estimated with regional arithmetic averages (e.g. Feldstein, 1977 and the Dutch studies alluded to in section 9.1). But the logarithm of an arithmetic average cannot be disaggregated to any meaningful micro equivalent. If the individual-level equation is assumed to be log-linear, then the aggregates have to be defined as *geometric* rather than arithmetic averages. Because the purpose of this paper is to explore the consequences of disaggregation while maximizing the comparability of our results to previous studies we will pursue both approaches in the empirical analysis which follows.[1]

9.3 Empirical analysis

In order to investigate empirically the consequences of aggregation in the context of the demand for hospital care, we have estimated a number of equations relating admission probability and length of hospital stay to various sets of explanatory variables. The estimations are performed on both the individual data and on an aggregate level.[2] A two-way stepwise procedure will enable us to discriminate between aggregation and specification effects (i.e. omitted variable bias). In this section, we first describe the estimation techniques and the data. Subsequently the estimation results are presented and discussed.

9.3.1 Model specification

We intend to investigate the following four relations on a micro as well as macro level:

$$DADM = f_1 (Z, X_1, X_2) \tag{9.1}$$

$$DADM = f_2 (Z, X_1, X_2, X_3, X_4) \tag{9.2}$$

$$LOS \quad = f_3 (Z, X_1, X_2) \tag{9.3}$$

$$LOS \quad = f_4 (Z, X_1, X_2, X_3, X_5), \tag{9.4}$$

where DADM (at the micro level) is a dummy variable indicating whether or not an individual was admitted to a short-stay hospital at least once in 1984; LOS denotes the length of stay in a short-term hospital once the individual had been hospitalized; the vector Z contains information on regional hospital capacity; X_1 and X_2 comprise variables commonly used in macro studies on hospital demand, whereas X_3–X_5 are in principle only available on individual levels (cf. table 9.1). Differences between the micro and macro results for these equations will provide indications as to the consequences of *aggregation bias*. The availability of variables X_3–X_5 in our data sets permits an investigation into the extent of *omitted variable bias*. This can be assessed by comparing the estimation results of equations (9.1) and (9.2), and those of equations (9.3) and (9.4).

In order to maximize comparability with previous studies on demand for hospital care we have used the following specifications for the estimation of equations (9.1)–(9.4):

1   The functions f_i are assumed to be linear in the coefficients.
2   Logarithmic transformations are used of those variables which on the micro level are more or less continuous (length of stay included).
3   In principle, arithmetic (instead of geometric) means are used on the macro level for the variables which are to be transformed, i.e. $\log(\bar{x})$ is used and not $\overline{\log(x)}$. We shall investigate the empirical consequences of this choice below.
4   For the estimation of the relations (9.1)–(9.4) on micro data the least squares method (LS) is used: OLS for (9.3) and (9.4), and WLS for (9.1) and (9.2). WLS is used in order to correct for the endogenous stratification procedure (see next section for details).
5   On the macro level the relations are estimated by means of WLS in order to adjust for the number of observations per region and to avoid heteroskedasticity.

9.3.2   Data

We have used data sets obtained from the Dutch private health insurance company Zilveren Kruis which were supplemented with data from other sources on regional characteristics such as supply of physicians and hospital beds. The basic data files include, for each of the 230,000 insured individuals, information on insurance coverage, age, sex, family size, place of residence, reimbursed medical expenses, and hospital admissions in 1983 and 1984. From these data files an admissions data set and a length of stay data set were constructed. The former was obtained by means of 'endogenous stratification' (Maddala, 1983), mainly for statistical reasons and in order to limit required computer resources. The estimation procedure was adjusted for this stratification (for details, see van Vliet and Van Doorslaer, 1988).

The information in these two data sets was aggregated to the so-called COROP-regions which provide a geographical division of the Netherlands into forty regions situated around primary and secondary regional centres. The number of observations per region varies approximately between twenty and 4,000 for both data sets.

Table 9.1 Description of the variables[a]

Variable	Description
Dependent variables	
DADM	dummy variable = 1 if at least one admission in 1984
LOS	length of hospital stay in days (in 1983 or 1984)
Explanatory variables: eqs (9.1) and (9.3)	
Hospital capacity (Z)	
BED	number of hospital beds in COROP-region per 10,000 population
SPEC	number of specialists in COROP-region per 10,000 population
Regional variables (X_1)	
DIST	distance from place of residence to nearest hospital (in km)
SF	% of inhabitants who are publicly insured (Holland divided in 24 regions)
GP	number of GPs per 1,000 population (Holland divided in 180 regions)
Expected consumption (X_2)	
EXDADM	expected admission probability based on age and sex
EXLOS	expected length of stay based on age and sex
Additional explanatory variables: eqs (9.2) and (9.4)	
Individual background characteristics (X_3)	
IGP	dummy variable = 1 if person has insurance coverage for costs of care provided by GPs
IDED	deductible amount for all medical expenses per family per year
IHCL	dummy variable = 1 if coverage for more luxury facilities in case of hospitalization
FSIZE	family size
Admission specific variables (X_4)	
MED83	amount of reimbursed health care expenditures in 1983
NADM83	number of hospital admissions in 1983
Length of stay specific variables (X_5)	
EXLOSD	expected length of stay based on the admission diagnosis
DMND	dummy variable = 1 if discharged on Monday
DFRST	dummy variable = 1 if admitted on Friday or Saturday
DSURG	dummy variable = 1 if surgically treated
DTWSP	dummy variable = 1 if treated by two specialists

Note: [a] The variables which are (more or less) continuous at the individual level have been logarithmically transformed, with the exception of EXDADM.

Disaggregation in econometric modelling

The explanatory variables to be used in the equations are grouped into six categories (see table 9.1).

The regional variables comprise: the distance to the nearest hospital (DIST) which is used as an indicator of time price, the percentage publicly insured in the region (SF) which affects the proportion of the supply capacity available to the privately insured, and the supply of general practitioners (GPs) which can be seen as a substitute for hospital care (cf. Feldstein, 1977).

The expected utilization based on age and sex is often used in macro studies in order to control for health-status differences between regions, the age–sex distribution per region being practically the only health-related indicator available at regional levels. The expected admission probability (EXADM) for each person is defined as the proportion of all insured in the same age–sex group who have been admitted to a hospital. The expected length of stay (EXLOS) is defined analogously.

The category of individual background characteristics comprises three insurance coverage variables (IGP, IDED, IHCL) and family size (FSIZE). Insurance coverage is, of course, important because it reduces out-of-pocket prices. In so far as home care can be a substitute for hospital care and family size is a proxy for home-care possibilities, family size can be expected to affect demand for hospital care negatively.

The admission specific variables are two indicators of medical consumption in the preceding year and thereby indicators of health status: total amount of reimbursed medical expenses (MED83) and number of hospital admissions (NADM83).

The length of stay specific variables are the expected length of stay on the basis of the admission diagnosis (EXLOSD) and four other variables related to hospital stay (DMND, DFRST, DSURG, DTWSP). The former variable is defined as the average length of stay in Holland for the diagnosis for which the patient is admitted to the hospital, thereby also distinguishing between the specialities of the attending specialists. This variable is supposed to measure case severity. The other variables are indicators of both health status and treatment policies of the hospital and the attending specialist. They have been shown to affect length of stay considerably (see, e.g. Cannoodt and Knickman, 1984).

From a demand point of view, the most important variable which seems to be missing in our data sets is (family) income (see section 9.1). This variable has, however, no particular relevance in the present analysis because, owing to the comprehensiveness of insurance coverage in Holland, the bill for hospital care faced by most consumers is virtually zero.

Table 9.2 Estimation results: admission probability[a]

	Eq. (9.1)				Eq. (9.2)			
	Micro		Macro		Micro		Macro	
BED	-0.001	(0.0040)	-0.005	(0.0076)	-0.008*	(0.0040)	-0.009	(0.0096)
SPEC	-0.002	(0.0024)	-0.003	(0.0051)	-0.002	(0.0024)	-0.007	(0.0055)
DIST	-0.000	(0.0007)	-0.002	(0.0041)	0.001*	(0.0007)	-0.003	(0.0056)
SF	-0.050*	(0.0112)	-0.063*	(0.0243)	-0.051*	(0.0111)	-0.061*	(0.0308)
GP	0.011*	(0.0042)	0.009	(0.0105)	0.013*	(0.0042)	0.018	(0.0167)
EXADM	0.977*	(0.0136)	1.054*	(0.1575)	0.768*	(0.0153)	0.946*	(0.2248)
IGP					0.006*	(0.0013)	0.014	(0.0174)
IDED					0.000	(0.0002)	0.004	(0.0062)
IHCL					0.003	(0.0017)	-0.003	(0.0431)
FSIZE					-0.004*	(0.0010)	0.002	(0.0175)
MED83					0.006*	(0.0002)	0.005	(0.0051)
NADM83					0.100*	(0.0030)	0.005	(0.0039)
INTERC	0.255*	(0.0553)	0.297*	(0.1152)	0.258*	(0.0548)	0.269	(0.1658)
$\bar{R}^2$	0.025		0.788		0.044		0.780	
F	889.5		25.1		811.4		12.5	

Notes: [a]Estimated standard errors are presented in parentheses.
In the last two lines the adjusted R^2-values and the F-values of the equations are reported.
The number of observations is 27,094 for the micro equations and forty for the macro equations.
See sub-section 9.3.1 for the statistical specification of the equations.
* indicates a coefficient which is significantly different from zero (two-tailed t-test, $p < 0.05$).

9.3.3 Estimation results

The estimation results of our analysis are reported in tables 9.2 and 9.3. The results with respect to the non-supply variables are, generally speaking, in line with theory and similar findings in the literature.[3] For example, it is found in many studies, the most authoritative being the Rand Health Insurance Experiment (Manning *et al.*, 1987, Newhouse *et al.*, 1981), that the extent of health insurance coverage is an important determinant of health care utilization. In accordance with those studies, we find in the micro version of equation (9.4) that people who are insured for the costs of services provided by the GP and those who enjoy more comprehensive coverage for hospital care, have a significantly higher probability of being admitted to a hospital. This effect may not be a pure price effect because it might capture some residual impact of self-selection of the insured in choosing the extent of coverage (see, e.g. Van de Ven and Van Praag, 1981).

As could be expected, EXADM and EXLOS have coefficients in equations (9.1) and (9.3) close to 1, which are, moreover, highly significant. In equations (9.2) and (9.4) these coefficients are reduced as a result of adding other health-related variables. The estimation results, furthermore, reemphasize the conclusion that health status is the primary determinant of hospital care utilization.

From tables 9.2 and 9.3 (partial) bed elasticities are calculated which are presented in table 9.4 together with the bivariate elasticities. The latter are quite high, which seems to be in accordance with the findings of the supply studies alluded to in section 9.1. Controlling for relevant explanatory variables, however, causes the bed elasticities with respect to admission probability to become negative in both the micro and macro versions of equations (9.1) and (9.3), which is in contrast to the results of all previous studies. In another study (Van Doorslaer and van Vliet, 1986) we argue that the most plausible explanation for this remarkable finding is that structural changes have taken place in the provision of hospital services in Holland since the mid seventies (see also section 9.1). An additional analysis revealed that the disappearance of a positive bed effect on admission probability and the reduced impact on length of stay was almost solely attributable to the inclusion of the expected utilization variables in equations (9.1) and (9.3). This result stresses the importance of controlling for health status. In the remainder of this section we shall look at some of the empirical results in more detail and link them with the theoretical implications of aggregation discussed in section 9.2.[4]

Table 9.3 Estimation results: length of stay[a]

	Eq. (9.3)				Eq. (9.4)			
	Micro		Macro		Micro		Macro	
BED	0.186*	(0.0366)	0.226*	(0.0785)	0.222*	(0.0324)	0.317*	(0.0863)
SPEC	0.026	(0.0219)	0.010	(0.0506)	0.025	(0.0194)	0.017	(0.0424)
DIST	0.001	(0.0061)	−0.041	(0.0305)	0.001	(0.0054)	−0.056	(0.0288)
SF	0.212*	(0.1026)	0.335	(0.2413)	0.265*	(0.0904)	0.257	(0.2264)
GP	0.021	(0.0392)	0.043	(0.1010)	0.042	(0.0348)	0.176	(0.1111)
EXLOS	1.041*	(0.0142)	0.972*	(0.1434)	0.541*	(0.0171)	0.319*	(0.2313)
IGP					−0.011	(0.0098)	0.094	(0.1228)
IDED					0.000	(0.0018)	0.021	(0.0449)
IHCL					−0.038*	(0.0113)	0.035	(0.1854)
FSIZE					−0.053*	(0.0092)	0.454*	(0.1458)
EXLOSD					0.661*	(0.0074)	1.255*	(0.2326)
DMND					0.147*	(0.0130)	1.392*	(0.6293)
DFRST					0.086*	(0.0117)	−0.287	(0.5824)
DSURG					0.083*	(0.0089)	−0.260	(0.3092)
DTWSP					0.184*	(0.0159)	0.441	(0.3396)
INTERC	−2.088*	(0.5101)	−2.118	(1.284)	−2.759*	(0.4512)	−4.152*	(1.785)
$\bar{R}^2$	0.163		0.813		0.354		0.908	
F	969.4		31.5		1088.2		28.6	

Notes: [a] The number of observations is 29,796 for the micro relations and 40 for the macro relations. See also the footnotes for table 9.2.

Disaggregation in econometric modelling

9.3.3.1 Measures of association

A commonly used measure for the association between two variables is the correlation coefficient. In our data sets the correlations of bed supply with admission probability and length of stay are 0.022 and 0.095 respectively for the micro data and 0.522 and 0.711 respectively for the macro data. This clearly illustrates the assertion in sub-section 9.2.1 that the correlation coefficient is affected by the level of aggregation. The corresponding bivariate elasticities are, in contrast, approximately equal, as can be seen from the first row of table 9.4. The bottom lines of tables 9.2 and 9.3 show that the fit of the equations is improved by factors ranging from 2.5 to 50 when macro instead of micro data are used. The R^2-values for the length of stay equations even reach levels that are rarely encountered in this kind of study. This is mainly due to the inclusion of two comprehensive health indicators, *viz.* EXLOS and EXLOSD. Although the coefficients of determination for the micro equations seem to be very low, the F-statistics indicate that they have in fact higher explanatory power than their macro equivalents.

9.3.3.2 Aggregation and specification bias

If we assume equations (9.2) and (9.4) to be correctly specified then the expected values of the parameter estimators based on the macro data would be equal to the corresponding estimators based on the micro data if we had used consistent aggregation, and there-

Table 9.4 Estimated bed supply elasticities[a]

	Admission probability		Length of stay	
	Micro	*Macro*	*Micro*	*Macro*
Bivariate elasticities	0.57***	0.62**	0.57***	0.57***
Eqs. (9.1), (9.3)	−0.014	−0.072	0.19***	0.23***
Eqs. (9.2), (9.4)	−0.14**	−0.14	0.22***	0.32***
Consistent aggregation	−	−0.26*	−	0.29***
Simultaneous model	−	−0.04	−	0.30***

Notes: [a]The elasticities in the upper half of the table are based on tables 9.2 and 9.3. Those in the lower half refer to equations with alternative specifications (see sub-section 9.3.3.4).
The elasticities with respect to admission probability are calculated at the mean.
[b]The asterisks denote the estimated significance level (using a two-tailed t-test) of the regression coefficients:
*　 : $0.05 < p \le 0.10$;
** : $0.01 < p \le 0.05$;
***:　 $p \le 0.01$.

200

fore the parameter estimates would not be different statistically. Close inspection of tables 9.2 and 9.3 reveals that for the co-efficients of the contextual and semi-contextual variables (i.e. hospital capacity (Z) and regional variables (X_1) respectively) this appears to hold in spite of the consistency problem. Thus, we do not detect any aggregation bias for these variables.[5] The same conclusion holds for equations (9.1) and (9.3).

Most of the parameter estimates for the variables X_2–X_5, which are in principle defined at the individual level, do not differ significantly between micro and macro data. This is, however, mainly due to the very large confidence intervals of these parameters on the macro level, resulting in very few statistically significant co-efficients. Exceptions to this general conclusion are the estimated effects of NADM83 in equation (9.2), EXLOSD in equation (9.4) and, most important, family size (FSIZE) in equation (9.4): on the micro level, FSIZE is estimated to have an interpretable, negative, and significant impact on length of stay, whereas on the macro level, we find a positive and significant coefficient. This provides an illustration of the possible danger of the ecological fallacy (see sub-section 9.2.2): on the basis of the macro result one might be inclined to conclude that family size affects length of stay positively, whereas in fact there is a negative association.

We now turn to omitted variable bias, which can be assessed by comparing the estimation results of equation (9.1) with those of (9.2) and equation (9.3) with (9.4). We expected especially the inclusion of extra health-related variables (vectors X_4 and X_5) to have mitigating consequences for the estimated supply effects. We observe, however, for the contextual and semi-contextual variables, that neither in the admission nor in the length of stay equations are the estimated parameters significantly different. This conclusion holds for the micro as well as the macro versions of the relations. The only substantial changes occur for the coefficients of the expected utilization variables, which is obviously a result of the strong correlations of these variables with X_4 and X_5. The effects of most of these variables are in themselves not of particular interest, although they increase the goodness of the fit, especially in the micro version of equation (9.4) as compared to equation (9.3).

9.3.3.3 Efficiency of estimates

We have already mentioned that grouping of the observations resulted in considerable losses in efficiency. This is primarily due to increased multi-collinearity among the independent variables (sub-section 9.2.3), which is indicated in our data sets by the increase of the average magnitude of correlations from approximately 0.1 for the micro data to 0.4 for the macro data. Tables 9.2 and 9.3 show that the estimated standard errors of the parameters of the contextual variables increase by approximately a factor of 2 when going from micro to macro data. This factor is approximately 2.5 for the semi-contextual variables and even larger than 10 for the non-contextual variables. So, in accordance with the theory discussed in sub-section 9.2.3, we conclude that grouping leads to considerable efficiency losses which are, moreover, much larger for the parameters of the non-contextual than for those of the contextual variables. The semi-contextual variables take an intermediate position.

9.3.3.4 Consistent aggregation and simultaneous models

In order to evaluate the empirical consequences of employing arithmetic rather than geometric means – the former being used in most macro studies and the latter being consistent aggregation (see sub-section 9.2.4) – we also estimated the macro versions of equations (9.2) and (9.4) on the basis of geometric means. The results with respect to the bed elasticities of this alternative specification are reported in the bottom half of table 9.4. They do not indicate major changes.

Finally, we also tried a simultaneous model with number of admissions affecting length of stay and vice versa. Such models are often used in macro studies. The bottom line of table 9.5 shows that this alternative specification hardly changes the supply elasticities. The same conclusion turned out to hold for the other parameters in both equations. In particular, the mutual effects of the endogenous variables also appeared to be far from significant. Our conclusion is therefore that estimating separate equations for the two hospital utilization variables yields equivalent results.

Conclusions and discussion

In this paper we have investigated, both theoretically and empirically, the consequences of disaggregating the often estimated demand function for hospital care, the latter being operationalized by admission probability and length of stay. This investigation was inspired by the observation that micro studies of hospital demand yield results that differ substantially from those obtained in macro studies. In particular, the strongly positive association between supply and utilization found in macro studies is not supported by the results of micro studies, which showed health status to be the predominant determinant of hospital utilization.

The most important consequences of disaggregation appeared to be as follows.

(a) *Aggregation and specification bias*, which appear to be inherent to all macro studies in which individual behaviour is estimated, had little consequence for the estimated hospital supply coefficients. However, the estimated coefficients in the macro relations of some non-contextual variables differed significantly from the corresponding coefficients estimated on micro data. This implies that one cannot obtain reliable estimates of the effects of non-contextual variables on the demand for hospital care on the basis of macro data. In such situations disaggregated data are indispensable.

(b) With respect to *omitted variable bias*, it was found that the inclusion in the equations of some additional explanatory variables, not usually available at regional levels, did not affect estimated supply elasticities in either the macro or in the micro equations. Together with the previous conclusion, this suggests that if it is one's objective to estimate the effects of hospital supply on individual utilization then it suffices to use macro data.

(c) The *efficiency* gain of disaggregation was very large for all explanatory variables in our empirical analysis, especially for the non-contextual.

(d) Two important differences in the *statistical specification* between micro and macro studies, *viz.* consistent versus inconsistent aggregation, and separate equations for admissions and length of stay versus a simultaneous model, did not appear to lead to diverging results.

Last but not least, an important finding of this study is that, in contrast to previous studies, the regional supply of hospital beds had no positive effect on admissions. This is probably due to major changes which have taken place in the provision of hospital care in Holland during the last ten years. The elasticity of bed supply with respect to length of hospital stay amounted to approximately 0.2–0.3, which is consistent with previous findings.

The above conclusions do not, of course, demonstrate that the results of previous macro studies concerned with the relation between hospital supply and utilization were not hampered by aggregation, specification and omitted variable bias or by specification peculiarities. We can only conclude that our results do not support the hypothesis that the contradictory findings of macro

Disaggregation in econometric modelling

and micro studies in the past are attributable to these sources of bias. It seems, therefore, that we should look for other explanations. One possibility seems to be the difference in data collection methods between macro and micro studies: macro data generally comprise the whole population whereas micro data is collected mostly by means of representative samples of the non-institutionalized population, with the additional danger of selectivity bias caused by the lower response rates of people in poor health or those who are hospitalized at the time of the interview. Our data base does not contain information on institutionalized people either, but since it is an administrative data base it has no selectivity problems. The former observation combined with the fact that our data base only refers to a sub-group of the Dutch privately insured, leads us to conclude that an analysis of recent data on all publicly as well as privately insured people is necessary to obtain a more conclusive test of the hypothesis that bed supply no longer affects admission rates in Holland.

Notes

1 Note that using arithmetic means implies that the expected values of the macro and micro level estimators $\hat{\beta}_x$ and $\hat{\beta}_x$ are not the same in general. Consequently, in such a case there is always the problem of aggregation bias, as defined in sub-section 9.2.2. However, what matters in the empirical practice is the extent to which estimated coefficients at both levels differ. Therefore, we shall interpret the notion of aggregation bias in the next section as the difference between estimated coefficients which may be due partly to taking averages (*pure* aggregation bias), and partly to the way in which the averages are calculated (*consistency* bias).

2 Before starting an analysis of hospital utilization, one should try to answer the following question. What is the appropriate level on which to perform the analysis? There are, in principle, four observation levels which can be considered in this case – the patient, the specialist, the hospital, and some geographical level – the choice depending on data availability and the study objective. Since it is virtually impossible to define unambiguously the service areas of specialists and hospitals and because the capacity effects thus cannot be estimated on these two levels, only the patient and the geographic level are considered in the present study.

3 Since we are mainly interested in the effects of supply on hospital utilization, we do not discuss the estimated effects of the other independent variables at length. For more thorough discussions the interested reader is referred to e.g. Andersen *et al.* (1975), Cannoodt and Knickman (1984), and Feldstein (1977).

4 Strictly speaking, the theoretical results of sub-sections 9.2.1 and 9.2.3

are not applicable to tables 9.2 and 9.3 because the macro equations in these tables refer to inconsistently aggregated data. However, the conclusions for the same equations aggregated consistently on the same data appeared to be similar.

5   The variance of the difference between the estimated parameters from the macro and micro data in cases of consistent aggregation can be shown to be equal to: $\text{var}(\hat{\beta}_x - \beta_x) = \text{var}(\hat{\beta}_x) - \text{var}(\beta_x)$. We have used this formula for testing the statistical significance of $\hat{\beta}_x - \beta_x$. The calculation of the variance in cases of inconsistent aggregation is quite complicated. Since inconsistent aggregation introduces an additional source of bias it is likely that the variance will be larger. Thus, we are using a conservative test of significance.

Chapter ten

Aggregation in discrete choice models: an illustration of non-linear aggregation

A. Colin Cameron*

Introduction

In this chapter aggregation is studied for the class of non-linear micro models most commonly employed by econometricians – discrete choice models, such as probit and logit models. Several previous studies on discrete choice models have considered issues of aggregation, but that work was done in isolation from the more general theory of non-linear aggregation.[1] This study is intended to illustrate the more general problem of aggregation of any non-linear micro model.

Typical applications of the binary choice model are to transportation mode choice (the dependent variable $y = 1$ if drive to work and $y = 0$ if travel by mass transit) and to labour force participation ($y = 1$ if work and $y = 0$ otherwise). Individual characteristics are treated as known non-stochastic quantities, or observations on stochastic quantities with analysis done conditional on their observed values.

Now suppose that individual characteristics are not observed, but prediction of aggregate behaviour is desired on the basis of aggregate data such as sample means. For example, a discrete choice model for transportation mode may be estimated using individual level data for a particular city. On the basis of these estimates policy makers may wish to predict transportation mode choice in other cities where only the averages of individual characteristics are known. More generally, given that the micro relation is a discrete choice model, what can be said about the implied macro behaviour?

* This paper is based on work supported by National Science Foundation Grant SES82–08180 at the Department of Economics, Stanford University. I am thankful for much helpful advice from Takeshi Amemiya, and for the comments of Jim Powell. This substantially revised version has benefited greatly from the comments of Hashem Pesaran and Larry Taylor.

Such aggregation questions are not easily answered for discrete choice models, because they are non-linear. To provide any answer, the parameters of the micro relation are assumed to be the same across all individuals. This assumption separates this work from many aggregation studies, such as Theil (1954) and Pesaran, Pierse, and Kumar (1989), where parameters vary across individuals but attention is restricted to the simpler linear model.

To fix ideas, consider the quadratic regression model: $E[Y_i | X_i]$ $= \beta_0 + \beta_1 X_i + \beta_2 X_i^2$, where Y_i and X_i are scalar random variables for the ith of N independent individuals, and β_0, β_1 and β_2 are parameters that do not vary across individuals. We wish to predict the population mean $E[Y]$, which is the expectation of the conditional mean $E[Y_i | X_i]$ with respect to the distribution of X_i. Thus $E[Y] = \beta_0 + \beta_1 E[X] + \beta_2 E[X^2]$.

We note two essential differences between aggregation for this model and aggregation for the linear regression model ($\beta_2 = 0$). First, $E[Y_i | X_i]$ evaluated at $X_i = E[X]$, the representative agent, does not equal the population mean $E[Y]$. The only exception is if there is no variation in the distribution of X, since only then does $(E[X])^2 = E[X^2]$. Second, evaluation of $E[Y]$ requires knowledge of more than just the mean of X. In this example, we need in addition either the second moment or the variance of X. Finally, note that, while this model is non-linear in X, it is linear in X and X^2. For more highly non-linear models, the evaluation of $E[Y]$ will clearly require specification of a distribution function for X.

More generally, we start with a given micro relation – a non-linear model with identical parameters across individuals – and attempt to find what sort of macro behaviour is implied. Aggregation is called complete if macro behaviour is associated with a unique micro relation, and vice versa. For non-linear models, this requires that restrictions be placed on the distribution of the micro explanatory variables. (For a linear model this would not be the case.) Kelejian (1980) and Stoker (1984) observed that these restrictions are analytically a special case of the definition of completeness of a class of densities. Therefore, a sufficient condition is that the distribution of explanatory variables be of exponential family form.

Of particular interest is the actual functional form of the implied macro relation. For a specified micro relation, here a discrete choice model, an exact form for the macro relation cannot be obtained unless the distribution of the explanatory variables is specified. (Again, this is not the case for linear models.) A particularly convenient result of McFadden and Reid (1975) is that the probit model with multivariate normal distributed explanatory

Disaggregation in econometric modelling

variables leads to a modified probit model for macro relation. Westin (1974) obtained a similar, though less tractable, result for the logit model.

Given an estimated micro relation, knowledge of the functional form of the implied macro relation, and aggregate moments of the explanatory variables, we are then able to predict aggregate behaviour. This topic has been pursued at some length in the engineering literature on transportation mode choice by Talvitie (1973), Watson and Westin (1975), Koppelman (1976a, 1976b), Koppelman and Ben-Akiva (1977), Reid (1978), in addition to Westin (1974) and McFadden and Reid (1975).

This chapter is organized as follows. Complete aggregation is discussed in section 10.1. Functional forms for the macro functions that arise from different distributional assumptions for the regressors in discrete choice micro models are studied in section 10.2. The prediction of macro behaviour from a micro model is the topic of section 10.3. Concluding remarks are made in section 10.4.

10.1 Complete aggregation

Stoker (1984) used the term complete aggregation structure to describe classes of micro functions and classes of densities of micro explanatory variables for which a particular macro relation is associated with a unique micro relation. The presentation here follows closely that of Stoker. The earlier similar work of Kelejian (1980) is discussed at the end of this section.

The micro relation or **micro function** for each individual is defined by

$$Y = K(X, \beta) \tag{10.1}$$

where Y is a scalar dependent variable, K is a scalar function, X is an M-dimensional column vector of explanatory variables, and β is a k-dimensional column vector of parameters.

In typical applications we have an underlying econometric model which includes regressors X, and additionally a disturbance whose mean conditional on X is assumed to be zero. Integrating out the disturbance term yields (10.1), where β may include unknown parameters of the distribution of the disturbances. For the linear regression model, the underlying regression model is $y = X\beta + \varepsilon$, $M = k$, and the micro function is $Y = X\beta$ (which does not include the unknown parameters of the distribution of the disturbance). For the discrete choice model, see subsection 10.2.1.

The parameters β are assumed to be the same across all individuals. This assumption separates this work from other aggregation studies, such as Theil (1954) and Pesaran, Pierse, and Kumar (1989), where parameters vary across individuals but attention is restricted to the simpler linear model. The explanatory variables may vary across individuals, being random variables from a common distribution with density $\pi(X|\theta)$, where θ is an L-dimensional column vector of parameters, $\theta \in \Theta$ the set of possible parameter values.

Integration over the range of the regressors yields the macro relation or **macro function**

$$E[Y] = \int K(X, \beta)\, \pi(X|\theta)\, dX \qquad (10.2)$$

$$\equiv \psi(\beta, \theta)$$

where it is assumed that this expectation exists and is finite.

Stoker defined aggregation to be **complete** if there is a one-to-one correspondence between the macro function $\psi(\beta, \theta)$ and the micro function $K(X, \beta)$, i.e. if and only if

$$\psi(\beta, \theta) \equiv \int K(X, \beta)\, \pi(X|\theta)\, dX = \int K(X, \beta')\, \pi(X|\theta)\, dX$$

$$\equiv \psi(\beta', \theta) \qquad (10.3)$$

for all $\theta \in \Theta$, implies

$$K(X, \beta) = K(X, \beta') \qquad (10.4)$$

Define $H(X) = K(X, \beta) - K(X, \beta')$. Then equivalently, aggregation is complete if and only if $\int H(X)\pi(X|\theta)\, dX = 0$ for all $\theta \in \Theta$, implies $H(X) = 0$. But this is just the definition of completeness for the family of densities $\pi(X|\theta)$, $\theta \in \Theta$.

This insight of Stoker (1984) and Kelejian (1980) is very useful, as complete families of distributions and their associated complete sufficient statistics play an important role in the theory of statistical inference.[2] In particular, the exponential family of distributions, which includes the multivariate normal distribution, is complete.

Aggregation is complete if the regressor variables are generated by a complete family of distributions, such as the exponential family. For linear micro functions, where $K(X, \beta) = X'\beta$, inspection of (10.3) and (10.4) reveals that this sufficient condition is much too strong – complete aggregation exists for any $\pi(X|\theta)$. But for non-linear micro functions, Stoker (1984) showed that $\pi(X|\theta)$ must be restricted for complete aggregation. This is a fundamental difference between aggregation of linear and non-linear micro functions.

Kelejian (1980) obtained similar results, using a slightly different specification for the macro function. The macro function defined by Stoker (1984) is the unconditional mean of Y (which depends on X only via θ, the parameters of the distribution generating X). Let Y_{it} and X_{it} be observations on Y and X for the ith of N individuals in the tth time period, assume Y_{it} and X_{it} are independent and identically distributed, and define $Y_t = \sum_{i=1}^{N} Y_{it}$ and $X_t = \sum_{i=1}^{N} X_{it}$. Kelejian (1980) instead defined the macro function to be the mean of Y_t conditional on X_t. Complete non-linear aggregation is then ensured if the distribution of X_{it} conditional on X_t is complete (Kelejian, 1980, pp. 143–8). Stoker's and Kelejian's results are essentially the same, since for $N \to \infty$ the conditional expectations approach is equivalent to the unconditional expectations approach (Kelejian, 1980, pp. 142–3).

10.2 Macro functions for discrete choice models

In this section we obtain the macro function when the micro function is a discrete choice model. Since the discrete choice model is non-linear, we need to choose a particular functional form for the distribution of X. From section 10.1, any member of a complete family of distributions will ensure complete aggregation. However, to obtain a tractable form for the macro function, we need to further restrict the choice of distribution of X.

The discrete choice model is defined in subsection 10.2.1. The specification of a particular distribution for X is a strong one, albeit one routinely made in some branches of statistics, such as multivariate analysis. The possibility of using weaker distributional assumptions, most notably a representative agent approximation to the macro function which requires knowledge of only the mean of X, is pursued in subsection 10.2.2. The usual candidate for the distribution of X is the multivariate normal distribution. In subsection 10.2.3 this is seen to lead to an especially tractable form for the macro function of the probit model. More generally, choosing a distribution that leads to a tractable form for the macro function is shown in subsection 10.2.4 to be similar to the choice of a natural conjugate prior density in Bayesian statistics. The robustness to departures from normality of the macro function for the probit model with X normally distributed is tested in subsection

10.2.5. The macro function when some or all explanatory variables are qualitative is considered in subsection 10.2.6.

10.2.1 General macro function

The (univariate binary) **discrete choice model** is defined by

$$p = \Pr(y = 1|X, \beta) = F(X'\beta) \tag{10.5}$$

where y takes the value of 1 if an event occurs and 0 if it does not occur, both X and β are k-dimensional column vectors and F is specified here to be any continuous cumulative distribution function. For the logit model, F is the c.d.f. of the logistic distribution, and for the probit model, F is the c.d.f. of the standard normal distribution.[3]

The specification (10.5) of the binary choice model can be derived by defining an index of the propensity of the event to happen

$$y^* = X'\beta - \varepsilon \tag{10.6}$$

where ε is an additive error term with distribution function F. When y^* crosses a certain threshold, the event of interest occurs and $y = 1$; otherwise $y = 0$. If the explanatory variables include a constant term, we can without loss of generality let the threshold be zero. For example, in a labour supply model we would say a person works if $y^* > 0$. Then

$$\Pr(y = 1|X, \beta) = \Pr(y^* > 0|X, \beta)$$

$$= \Pr(\varepsilon < X'\beta|X, \beta) \tag{10.7}$$

$$= F(X'\beta)$$

which is precisely (10.5). For further details, see Amemiya (1981).

The **micro function** for the **discrete choice model** is the expectation of the Bernoulli random variable y, conditional on X and β. This is simply $\Pr(y = 1|X, \beta)$, so that

$$Y = F(X'\beta) \tag{10.8}$$

i.e. $K(X, \beta)$ in (10.1) is $F(X'\beta)$ in this case.

Given a particular distribution for X, we can obtain the density function for $X'\beta$, say $g(X'\beta)$ where g is assumed to be continuous.

Disaggregation in econometric modelling

The **macro function** for the **discrete choice model** is therefore

$$E[Y] = \int F(X'\beta)g(X'\beta)\mathrm{d}X'\beta \tag{10.9}$$

i.e. $\psi(\beta, \theta)$ in (10.2) is given by the right-hand side of (10.9).

10.2.2 Representative agent and Taylor series approximations

Specification of the macro function requires the assumption of a particular distribution for individual characteristics (X). This is a strong assumption since rarely, if ever, will we know the true distribution. Before doing this, we may ask whether it is possible to obtain reasonable approximations to the macro function by making much weaker distributional assumptions.

The simplest approach is to estimate the macro function by the micro function for the mean individual, i.e. the individual with mean characteristics μ_X. Under this **representative agent** assumption, $E[Y]$ is estimated by

$$\tilde{Y} = F(\mu) \tag{10.10}$$

where $\mu = \mu'_X\beta$.

For non-linear models $\tilde{Y}$ will generally differ from $E[Y]$, i.e. the mean probability for the population will not equal the probability for the mean individual. By Jensen's inequality we have

$$E[Y] = E[F(X'\beta)] \gtrless F(E[X'\beta]) = F(\mu)$$

according to whether F is convex or concave on $(-\infty, \infty)$.

For discrete choice models when F is a distribution function, F will generally be convex for low values of $X'\beta$ (where low means negative and large in absolute value) and concave for high values (where high means positive and large). So the direction of the inequality will be ambiguous. However, for a high value of μ, high realizations of $X'\beta$ will be most common. Since these will fall along the concave portion of F we can expect $E[Y] < F(\mu)$ in this case. Similarly, for a low value of μ we expect $E[Y] > F(\mu)$. The following lemma gives sufficient conditions for putting a sign on the bias of $\tilde{Y}$.

Lemma

Let F be any c.d.f. symmetric about zero (i.e. $F(z) = 1 - F(-z)$) and concave for $z \geq 0$ (and hence convex for $z < 0$). Let Z have c.d.f. G such that $dG(z) \geq -dG(-z)$ and $\mu = E[Z] > 0$. Then

212

$$E[F(Z)] \geq F(E[Z])$$

A proof is given in the appendix to this chapter. The inequality is reversed when $E[Z] < 0$. The inequality of the lemma may be reversed if F is not symmetric. However, F is symmetric for all commonly used discrete choice models. When additionally G is symmetric about μ (i.e. $G(z) = 1 - G(-z + 2\mu)$), the condition on G can be rewritten as $dG(z) \geq dG(z + 2\mu)$, which is satisfied in both discrete and continuous cases if the density is unimodal.

The probit and logit models satisfy the conditions on F, and when X is symmetrically distributed with unimodal density the lemma implies

$$E[Y] < F(\mu), \quad \text{for } \mu > 0 \tag{10.11}$$

with the inequality reversed for $\mu < 0$. So if the event of interest occurs for more than half the population, the probability of occurrence for the average individual will exceed the average response for the population as a whole.

The motivation for the lemma and result (10.11) for discrete choice models is Jensen's inequality. Similar results may be possible for other micro functions. For example, if F is globally convex or globally concave, Jensen's inequality is directly applicable.

The representative agent estimate $\tilde{Y}$ in (10.10) can be obtained by taking a first-order Taylor series expansion of $Y = F(X'\beta)$ around μ, and then taking the expectation with respect to the distribution of X.[4] It might be expected that a second-order Taylor series expansion of $F(X'\beta)$ about μ would yield a better approximation, albeit at the expense of additionally requiring knowledge of the variance of X.

Talvitie (1973) proposed this method for the logit model, for which F is the logistic c.d.f. L, defined in (10.18). The approximation is

$$L(X'\beta) = L(\mu) + L(\mu)[1 - L(\mu)](X'\beta - \mu)$$

$$+ 0.5 \, L(\mu)[1 - L(\mu)][1 - 2L(\mu)](X'\beta - \mu)^2 + R_2 \tag{10.12}$$

where R_2 is a remainder term, and we have used $L(\mu) = [1 + \exp(-\mu)]^{-1}$ and $\dfrac{dL(\mu)}{d\mu} = L(\mu)[1 - L(\mu)]$. Taking expectations, and ignoring the remainder term, (10.12) yields

$$E[Y] = L(\mu) + \sigma^2 L(\mu)[1 - L(\mu)][\tfrac{1}{2} - L(\mu)] \qquad (10.13)$$

where $\sigma^2 \equiv \beta'\Sigma_x\beta$, and Σ_x is the variance–covariance matrix of X.

In Cameron (1985), it is shown that the remainder term R_2 may have expectation as large as

$$\max E[|R_2|] = \frac{1}{48} E[|X'\beta - \mu|^3] \qquad (10.14)$$

Similarly, the remainder term for a first-order Taylor series expansion, i.e. the representative agent approximation, may have expectation as large as $(\sqrt{3}/36)E(X'\beta - \mu)^2]$. So there is no guarantee that the Taylor series approximations may be good ones. The empirical performance of these approximations is discussed in subsections 10.2.3 and 10.3.2.

10.2.3 Macro function for X normally distributed

Assume that X has a multivariate normal distribution with mean μ_x and variance–covariance matrix Σ_x. Then $X'\beta \sim N(\mu \equiv \mu'_x\beta, \sigma^2 \equiv \beta'\Sigma_x\beta)$. Note that σ^2 denotes the variance of $X'\beta$, rather than the variance of ε in (10.6). Greater heterogeneity in the population leads to larger values of σ^2.

For the probit model, F is the standard normal c.d.f., denoted Φ, so

$$F(X'\beta) = \Phi(X'\beta) \equiv \int_{-\infty}^{X'\beta} (2\pi)^{-1/2} \exp\{-\tfrac{1}{2} z^2\} \, dz \qquad (10.15)$$

Using the convolution properties of the normal distribution, (10.9) becomes

$$E[Y] = \Phi[\mu(1 + \sigma^2)^{-1/2}] \qquad (10.16)$$

McFadden and Reid (1975) were the first to use this relationship in the context of aggregation of discrete choice models.

For this example, the macro function is no more complicated to evaluate than the micro function. This can be readily seen by the following alternative derivation of (10.16). The probit model assumes that ε in (10.6) has a standard normal distribution. When additionally $X'\beta$ is normally distributed with mean μ and variance σ^2, independently of ε, the index variable $y^* = X'\beta - \varepsilon$ is distributed as $N(\mu, 1 + \sigma^2)$. It then follows almost immediately that unconditionally

Aggregation in discrete choice models

Table 10.1 $E[\Phi(X'\beta)]$ for probit model when $X'\beta \sim N(\mu, \sigma^2)$

σ^2 μ	0.0	0.5	1.0	1.5	2.0
0.0	0.500	0.500	0.500	0.500	0.500
0.5	0.691	0.658	0.638	0.624	0.614
1.0	0.841	0.793	0.760	0.736	0.718
1.5	0.933	0.890	0.856	0.829	0.807
2.0	0.977	0.949	0.921	0.897	0.876

$$E[Y] = \Pr(y = 1) \tag{10.17}$$

$$= \Pr(y^* > 0)$$

$$= \Pr[(y^* - \mu)(1 + \sigma^2)^{-1/2} \geq -\mu(1 + \sigma^2)^{-1/2}]$$

$$= \Phi[\mu(1 + (1 + \sigma^2)^{-1/2}]$$

Table 10.1 gives $E[Y]$ for the probit model when X is normally distributed, for $\mu > 0$. These values are obtained directly from tables of the normal distribution. For $\mu < 0$, we use the relationship $\Phi(-z) = 1 - \Phi(z)$. In most applications we speculate that σ^2 for the probit model will be less than 1.0, since this value would correspond to an R^2 of approximately 0.5 in a regression of y^* (if this data existed) on X.[5]

Table 10.1 can be used to assess the reliability of the representative agent estimate $\tilde{Y} = \Phi(\mu)$, which corresponds to $\sigma^2 = 0$. For given $\mu > 0$, this overstates the value of the true macro function, as the lemma in subsection 10.2.2 proved more generally. For example, if $\sigma^2 = 0.5$ and $\mu = 1.0$, then the representative agent value of 0.841 considerably exceeds the true macro function value 0.793. Similarly, if $\sigma^2 = 1.0$ and $\mu = 0.5$, then the approximation of 0.691 also exceeds the true macro function value 0.638. Furthermore, the more heterogeneous is the population, i.e. the larger is σ^2, the greater the error in using $\tilde{Y}$.

For the logit model, we have

$$F(X'\beta) = L(X'\beta) \equiv \exp(X'\beta)[1 + \exp(X'\beta)]^{-1} \tag{10.18}$$

It is more convenient in this case to transform first to the unconditional density of Y. When $X'\beta$ has the continuous density function $g(X'\beta)$, the unconditional density of Y is

$$h(Y) = g(F^{-1}(Y)) \left| \frac{dF^{-1}(Y)}{dY} \right| \tag{10.19}$$

and the macro function is simply the unconditional mean

$$E[Y] = \int_0^1 Y h(Y) \, dY \tag{10.20}$$

For the logit model,

$$F^{-1}(Y) = \ln \frac{Y}{1-Y}, \qquad \frac{dF^{-1}(Y)}{dY} = \frac{1}{Y(1-Y)},$$

and when X is normally distributed,

$$g(X'\beta) = \frac{1}{\sqrt{2\pi\sigma^2}} \exp \left\{ -\frac{1}{2\sigma^2} (X'\beta - \mu)^2 \right\}.$$

Then (10.19) becomes

$$h(Y) = \frac{1}{\sqrt{2\pi\sigma^2}} \exp \left\{ -\frac{1}{2\sigma^2} [\ln \frac{Y}{1-Y} - \mu]^2 \right\} \frac{1}{Y(1-Y)} \tag{10.21}$$

This is the density function of the S_B distribution, which is discussed by Johnson (1949).

Recognizing this, Westin (1974), in some of the first published work on aggregate prediction from disaggregate binary choice models, considered the logit model with X normally distributed. However, the moments of the S_B distribution, including even the mean, are analytically intractable. So numerical integration techniques are needed to compute the moments of interest.

Such numerical integration yields a table corresponding to table 10.1 for the logit model, appropriately re-scaled.[6] This is reported in Cameron (1985). The logit and probit models give similar results, with the greatest difference being 0.010. This similarity is not surprising, since aside from the tails the standard normal and logistic c.d.f.s are almost identical.

Cameron (1985) found that differences between the representative agent estimate $\tilde{Y} = L(\mu)$ and the true value of the macro function when $X'\beta$ is normally distributed are similar to the differences for the probit model, presented earlier. Tables for the second-order Taylor series approximation (10.13), and a fourth-order Taylor series approximation, are also given in Cameron (1985). These generally do better than the representative agent estimate, except when μ (> 0) is small and σ^2 is large.

If one is prepared to assume X is normally distributed it seems sufficient to consider only the probit model. This is the most useful set of assumptions when dealing with aggregation of discrete choice models. The decision to use the probit rather than the logit model is of relatively small consequence. It is the assumption of normally distributed individual characteristics that needs to be given due consideration.

10.2.4 Alternative distributions for X

An interesting question is whether there are binary choice models and distributions of individual characteristics, other than the probit model with $X'\beta$ normal, that yield convenient analytical results.

From the derivation of (10.17) using the index variable approach, it is clear that for the probit model where ε is standard normally distributed, the natural convenient assumption for the distribution of X is the normal distribution, since then $X'\beta$ also has the normal distribution and the additive property of the normal distribution can be exploited. For the logit model, such a simple analytical result cannot be obtained. The logit model is obtained by assuming that ε is logistically distributed. If $X'\beta$ is normally distributed with mean μ and variance σ^2, independent of ε, the index variable y^* will be the sum of a normal variable and an (independent) logistic random variable. This combination does not lead to a simple distribution function for y^*. Furthermore, there appears to be no possible distributional assumption for $X'\beta$, apart from the degenerate distribution, that will yield a recognizable distribution for y^*. For example, assuming $X'\beta$ to be logistic is of no use, since the logistic distribution does not possess the additive property of the normal distribution.[7]

An alternative derivation of the binary choice model (10.15) is via the stochastic utility framework, see McFadden (1974). The unobserved index y^* is posited to be the difference between an

Table 10.2 $E[\Phi(X'\beta)]$ for probit model when $X'\beta \sim$ Student-$t(10)$

μ \ σ^2	0.0	0.5	1.0	1.5	2.0
0.0	0.500	0.503	0.504	0.504	0.504
0.5	0.691	0.664	0.645	0.632	0.622
1.0	0.841	0.799	0.769	0.747	0.730
1.5	0.933	0.894	0.864	0.839	0.819
2.0	0.977	0.951	0.927	0.905	0.887

Table 10.3 $E[\Phi(X'\beta)]$ for probit model when $X'\beta \sim$ Laplace

σ^2 μ	0.0	0.5	1.0	1.5	2.0
0.0	0.500	0.501	0.501	0.501	0.501
0.5	0.691	0.664	0.648	0.637	0.629
1.0	0.841	0.800	0.774	0.756	0.741
1.5	0.933	0.894	0.867	0.846	0.829
2.0	0.977	0.950	0.927	0.908	0.892

Table 10.4 $E[\Phi(X'\beta)]$ for probit model when $X'\beta \sim$ contaminated normal (0.1, 11)

σ^2 μ	0.0	0.5	1.0	1.5	2.0
0.0	0.500	0.501	0.501	0.502	0.502
0.5	0.691	0.662	0.643	0.629	0.619
1.0	0.841	0.797	0.766	0.744	0.726
1.5	0.933	0.894	0.862	0.836	0.815
2.0	0.977	0.951	0.926	0.903	0.883

agent's utility when the event of interest occurs and the utility when the event does not occur. Utility in each situation is a linear function of explanatory variables and an error term. The probit model is obtained by assuming the errors are normally distributed, while the logit model arises if the errors are independent type I extreme value distributed. Taking this approach leads to a similar conclusion to that using index models. For example, for the logit model we need a distribution for $X'\beta$ that is additive with the independent type I extreme value distribution. Analytically tractable results for the commonly used binary choice models can be obtained only for the probit model with individual characteristics normally distributed.[8]

For binary choice models other than the probit and logit, analytical results will generally be difficult to obtain. From the specified distribution function F of ε we can easily obtain the distribution function of y^* conditional on $X'\beta$, and the corresponding density function which we denote by $f(y^*|X'\beta)$. The problem is to find a functional form $g(X'\beta)$ for the density of $X'\beta$, such that for the specified conditional density $f(y^*|X'\beta)$, the resultant marginal density function

$$f(y^*) = \int f(y^*|X'\beta)g(X'\beta)dX'\beta \qquad (10.22)$$

is of a recognizable form.

This is very similar to the choice of a natural conjugate prior density in Bayesian statistics.[9] In the Bayesian framework, $g(X'\beta)$ is the prior density, ideally chosen to obtain a simple form for the posterior density $h(X'\beta \mid y^*) = f(y^* \mid X'\beta)g(X'\beta)/f(y^*)$. We wish to choose $g(X'\beta)$ to yield a simple form for $f(y^*)$. Clearly, results from Bayesian statistics can be applied here.[10]

For non-linear models other than discrete choice models, this Bayesian interpretation may also aid the choice of distribution.

10.2.5 Robustness of the normality assumption

For discrete choice models, the most tractable macro function is (10.16) for the probit model with X multivariate normally distributed. An interesting exercise is to check the robustness of (10.16) to departures of $X'\beta$ from normality.

Samples of size 10,000 were generated for various distributions of $X'\beta$ (with mean μ and variance σ^2) and the corresponding sample means of $\Phi(X'\beta)$ calculated. These are given in tables 10.2–10.4. Table 10.2 gives results for $X'\beta = \mu + \sqrt{0.8}\sigma Z$, where Z is Student-t distributed with 10 degrees of freedom. Table 10.3 gives results for $X'\beta = \mu + \sqrt{0.5}\sigma Z$, where Z is Laplace distributed with parameters 0 and 1 (i.e. mean 0 and variance 2). Table 10.4 gives results for $X'\beta = \mu + 0.9\sigma Z_1 + 0.1\sigma Z_2$, with $Z_1 \sim N(0, 0.5)$ and $Z_2 \sim N(0, 5.5)$, which is contaminated normal where 10 per cent of the sample has variance 11 times that of the remainder of the sample. In all three cases $E[\Phi(X'\beta)]$ increases as μ increases and decreases as σ^2 increases (for $\mu > 0$).

The values reported in table 10.1, which gives $E[\Phi(X'\beta)]$ assuming $X'\beta$ is normally distributed, are less than the corresponding values in tables 10.2–10.4. For example, suppose $\mu = 1.0$ and $\sigma^2 = 1.0$. Then $E[\Phi(X'\beta)]$ is 0.760 assuming a normal distribution for $X'\beta$, whereas $E[\Phi(X'\beta)]$ is 0.769 for $t(10)$, 0.774 for Laplace and 0.766 for the contaminated normal. The absolute differences between the values in tables 10.2–10.4 and table 10.1 increase as σ^2 increases, and increase only slightly, if at all, as μ increases. Departures from the normal distribution values are greatest for Laplace, followed by $t(10)$, contaminated normal and $t(20)$ (not reported here).

A crude measure of the relative differences between the values for the normal distribution and those for other distributions is the ratio of the effects of heterogeneity. We define the effect of heterogeneity when $X'\beta$ has c.d.f. G, mean μ and variance σ^2 to be

Disaggregation in econometric modelling

$$EH(G, \mu) = E[\Phi(X'\beta)|G, \mu, \sigma^2] - E[\Phi(X'\beta)|G, \mu, 0]$$

$$(10.23)$$

Then we consider

$$REH(G, \mu) = EH(N, \mu)/EH(G, \mu) \qquad (10.24)$$

where N is the c.d.f. of the normal distribution. The benchmark is REH = 1, since then $E[\Phi(X'\beta)]$ is the same regardless of whether the expectation is taken with respect to the possibly incorrect normal distribution for $X'\beta$, or with respect to the true distribution G.

In the example given above, i.e. $\mu = 1.0$ and $\sigma^2 = 1.0$, REH is 1.13 for $t(10)$, 1.21 for Laplace and 1.08 for contaminated normal. In virtually all cases $1.0 < REH < 1.25$, so assuming the normal distribution for $X'\beta$ when in fact its true distribution is one of the three considered here overstates the effect of heterogeneity, but by at most 25 per cent. This does not seem too bad, and outperforms the Taylor series approximations considered in subsection 10.2.2.

10.2.6 Segmentation with qualitative data

The simulation experiments compare results for the normal distribution to those for other continuous distributions. Clearly the normal distribution assumption is inappropriate for qualitative data.

For example, the explanatory variables may include sex and race dummies. Then we can segment the population by sex and race, determine the macro function $E[Y]$ conditional on each value of sex and race, and sum with weights equal to the fraction of the population in each sex–race group. This will place greater demands on data. For example, to use (10.16) we would need to know the mean and covariance matrix of the other explanatory variables, conditional on sex and race.

In the extreme case where all explanatory variables are qualitative, the macro function is easy to obtain, given knowledge of the proportions of the population in each of the segments formed by a unique value for the vector of qualitative variables. We need only evaluate the micro function (10.8) at each unique value of X, and form the weighted average with weights equal to the segment proportions.

Usually not all explanatory variables are qualitative. However, we may deliberately segment the population by converting continuous variables to qualitative variables, and evaluating (10.8) at the sample mean of X for each segment. It is clear from the results in this section, that this should be done within intervals of X for which the effect of heterogeneity, the variance of $X'\beta$, is as small as possible.

10.3 Macro prediction from micro models using macro data

The preceding section focused on obtaining a macro function for a given discrete choice model micro function. In this section these results are applied to a practical econometric problem.

The main context in which aggregation has been studied in the discrete choice model literature is that of wishing to predict aggregate behaviour, using an estimated discrete choice model as the basis for forecasts, but with access only to aggregate data on the regressor variables in the discrete choice model. This is presented in subsection 10.3.1. The estimation of the mean probability across the population of the event of interest is discussed in subsection 10.3.2. Since the mean probability equals the macro function, empirical studies that compute the mean probability are relevant to evaluating various approximations to the macro function. Estimation of the variance of the population average outcome is considered in subsection 10.3.3. The response of aggregate behaviour to changes in the distribution of the regressor variables is studied in subsection 10.3.4.

10.3.1 General framework

We wish to aggregate over individuals to predict population behaviour. The proportion of individuals with outcome $y = 1$ is a realization of the random variable

$$R = \frac{1}{N} \sum_{i=1}^{N} y_i \tag{10.25}$$

where y_i is the realization of the binary variable y for the ith of N independent individuals.

In most research on discrete choice models, individual characteristics are treated as known non-stochastic quantities, or observations on stochastic quantities with analysis done conditional on their observed values. For the binary choice model, the observed outcome variable for the ith individual is a realization of the random variable y_i which, conditional on $X_i = x_i$, is Bernoulli distributed with parameter $p_i = F(x_i'\beta)$. If individual characteristics are independent across individuals, then, conditional on x_1, ..., x_N, R is the average of N such independent but not identically distributed Bernoulli random variables. By the Liapounov central limit theorem, the asymptotic conditional distribution of R is given by

$$R \overset{a}{\sim} N\left(\frac{1}{N} \sum_{i=1}^{N} p_i, \ \frac{1}{N^2} \sum_{i=1}^{N} p_i(1 - p_i)\right) \tag{10.26}$$

where $p_i = F(x_i'\beta)$.[11]

Now suppose that individual characteristics $x_1, \ldots, x_N$ are not observed, but prediction of aggregate behaviour is desired on the basis of aggregate data such as $\bar{x}$. There are three reasons for this being of substantive interest.

First, this is exactly the aggregation problem that is the focus of this paper. Given that the micro function is a discrete choice model, what can be said about the implied macro behaviour?

Second, this problem arises in practice. For example, a discrete choice model for transportation mode may be estimated using individual level data for a particular city. On the basis of these estimates policy makers may wish to predict transportation mode choice in other cities where only the averages of individual characteristics are known.

Third, even when $x_1, \ldots, x_N$ are observed, conventional econometric practice is to make predictions (such as levels and derivatives) for the average individual ($x_i = \bar{x}$), rather than predicting for each individual and then averaging. For linear models the two approaches are coincident, but for non-linear models this is generally not the case.

When $x_1, \ldots, x_N$ are (unobserved) i.i.d. realizations of a random variable X with known distribution, the asymptotic distribution of R, conditional on $x_1, \ldots, x_N$ and β, can be approximated by

$$R \overset{a}{\sim} N(E[P], \frac{1}{N} E[P(1 - P)]) \tag{10.27}$$

where $P \equiv F(X'\beta)$, and the expectation is taken with respect to the distribution of P (or X).

10.3.2 *Estimating the mean probability*

The mean of R is $E[P]$, called the 'mean probability'. Since $E[P]$ is equivalent to $E[Y]$ in section 10.2, the estimation of the mean probability $E[P]$ has been already covered. Possible estimators can be obtained by assuming X is normally distributed, using the representative agent estimate, using a second-order Taylor series expansion, and sample segmentation.

A number of empirical studies compare the performance of these various estimators of the mean probability. A partial survey is given in Henscher and Johnson (1981). These studies use data where individual characteristics $x_1, \ldots, x_N$ are actually observed. Then the obvious estimator is the sample average of the individual predicted probabilities

$$\hat{p} = \frac{1}{N} \sum_{i=1}^{N} p_i = \frac{1}{N} \sum_{i=1}^{N} F(x_i'\boldsymbol{\beta}). \tag{10.28}$$

In general none of the methods that use only the sample average of $x_1, \ldots, x_N$ compares favourably with the estimate given in (10.28). The representative agent approximation is a poor one. Talvitie (1973) found that the second-order Taylor series approximation was no better.

The preferred estimates are generally ones that segment the population. A considerable literature addresses the question of how best to segment the population. For example, see Koppelman (1976b), Koppelman and Ben-Akiva (1977), and Reid (1978). From section 10.2, segmentation is better the more homogeneous the population within each segment. However, these empirical studies by their design have sufficient data to segment into reasonably homogeneous groups. In other empirical studies this may not be possible. Also, in other contexts we will actually desire an analytical function to use to approximate the macro function.

10.3.3 *Estimating variability in macro behaviour*

Virtually all studies consider only the estimation of $E[P]$, and ignore the variance of the population average probability R. The only exception is Watson and Westin (1975) who consider the logit model with X normally distributed, in which case $E[P(1 - P)]$ is an intractable moment of the S_B distribution.

For the probit-normal model, this moment is simpler. Cameron (1985) shows that, corresponding to (10.16), the estimate of the variance is

$$\frac{1}{N} \, \mathrm{E}[P(1-P)]$$

$$= \frac{1}{N} \, \Phi[\mu(1+\sigma^2)^{-1/2}]\{1 - \Phi[\mu(1+\sigma^2)^{-1/2}(1+2\sigma^2)^{-1/2}]\}$$

$$(10.29)$$

Note that this exceeds $1/N$ times the variance $\Phi(\mu)[1 - \Phi(\mu)]$ for the representative agent.

10.3.4 Changes in macro behaviour when population characteristics change

In section 10.2 and subsection 10.3.2, methods to estimate the mean probability were discussed. It is often useful to see how the mean probability changes when population characteristics change. Some of the estimation methods for $E[P]$ yield simple functional forms for the estimated changes in the moments of the population average probability when individual characteristics change.

Suppose that $X'\beta \sim N(\mu, \sigma^2)$, and consider the general binary choice model $P = F(X'\beta)$, where F is any continuous c.d.f. The density of P is given by

$$h(p) = \frac{1}{\sqrt{2\pi\sigma^2}} \exp\left\{-\frac{[F^{-1}(p) - \mu]^2}{2\sigma^2}\right\} \frac{\mathrm{d}F^{-1}(p)}{\mathrm{d}p} \qquad (10.30)$$

The change in the mean probability when the mean of $X'\beta$ changes by a small amount is given by the derivative

$$\frac{\mathrm{d}E[P]}{\mathrm{d}\mu} = \frac{\mathrm{d}}{\mathrm{d}\mu} \int_0^1 p \, \frac{1}{\sqrt{2\pi\sigma^2}} \exp\left\{-\frac{[F^{-1}(p) - \mu]^2}{2\sigma^2}\right\} \frac{\mathrm{d}F^{-1}(p)}{\mathrm{d}p} \, dp$$

$$(10.31)$$

$$= \int_0^1 p \, \frac{1}{\sqrt{2\pi\sigma^2}} \exp\left\{-\frac{[F^{-1}(p)^2 - \mu]}{2\sigma^2}\right\} \frac{[F^{-1}(p) - \mu]}{\sigma^2}$$

$$\times \frac{\mathrm{d}F^{-1}(p)}{\mathrm{d}p} \, dp$$

$$= \int_0^1 p \, \frac{\mathrm{d}}{\mathrm{d}p}\left(-\frac{1}{\sqrt{2\pi\sigma^2}} \exp\left\{-\frac{[F^{-1}(p) - \mu]^2}{2\sigma^2}\right\}\right) dp$$

$$= [0] + \int_0^1 \left(\frac{dF^{-1}(p)}{dp} \right)^{-1} \frac{1}{\sqrt{2\pi\sigma^2}} \exp\left\{ -\frac{[F^{-1}(p) - \mu]^2}{2\sigma^2} \right\}$$

$$\times \frac{dF^{-1}(p)}{dp} \, dp$$

$$= E\left[\left(\frac{dF^{-1}(p)}{dp} \right)^{-1} \right]$$

where the first term in the fourth line equals zero since F is a cumulative distribution function, so that $F(\infty) = 1$ implying $F^{-1}(1) = \infty$; the final equality follows directly from (10.30); and the operations of differentiation and integration can be interchanged if appropriate regularity conditions are satisfied. Differentiating the identity $F(F^{-1}(p)) = p$ w.r.t. p yields $f(F^{-1}(p)) \dfrac{dF^{-1}(p)}{dp}$ $= 1$, where f is the derivative of F, so that (10.31) can be rewritten as

$$\frac{dE[P]}{d\mu} = E_P[f(F^{-1}(P))] \tag{10.32}$$

Alternatively, note that $P = F(X'\beta)$ and $F^{-1}(P) = X'\beta$, so that (10.32) can be expressed in terms of the underlying distribution of $X'\beta$ as

$$\frac{dE[P]}{d\mu} = E_{X'\beta}\left[\frac{dF(X'\beta)}{dX'\beta} \right] \tag{10.33}$$

As expected, an increase in μ ($=\mu_x'\beta$) leads to an increase in the mean probability. Furthermore, the change in macro behaviour due to a change in the mean of the (normal) distribution of X equals the expectation of the change in micro behaviour due to a change in X.

Westin (1974) considered the special case of the logit model, where F is the logistic c.d.f. and (10.32) becomes

$$\frac{dE[P]}{d\mu} = E_P[P(1 - P)] \tag{10.34}$$

where P is S_B distributed. Since the first and second moments of the S_B distribution are analytically intractable, (10.34) needs to be computed by numerical methods. A similar stumbling block is reached if the expectation is taken with respect to $X'\beta$ using (10.33).

For the probit model it is more fruitful to use (10.33), which yields

$$\frac{dE[P]}{d\mu} = E_{X'\beta}[\phi(X'\beta)] \tag{10.35}$$

where ϕ is the standard normal density function. In this case we have

$$\frac{dE[P]}{d\mu} = (1 + \sigma^2)^{-1/2}\phi[\mu(1 + \sigma^2)^{-1/2}] \tag{10.36}$$

where ϕ is the density function of the standard normal distribution. This result was derived by Lancaster (1979). A typical application of this result is to consider an increase for all individuals of one unit in the value of the kth characteristic. From (10.36), the mean elasticity is

$$\frac{dE[P]}{d\mu_{xk}} \frac{\mu_{xk}}{E[P]}$$

$$= \beta_k(1 + \sigma^2)^{-1/2}\phi[\mu(1 + \sigma^2)^{-1/2}]\mu_{xk}\{\Phi[\mu(1 + \sigma^2)^{-1/2}]\}^{-1} \tag{10.37}$$

where μ_{xk} and β_k are the kth components of μ_x and β respectively.

Equations (10.32) and (10.33) can be generalized to other moments of P. Similar manipulations to those of (10.31) yield

$$\frac{dE[\Theta(P)]}{d\mu} = E_P\left[\frac{d\Theta(P)}{dP} f(F^{-1}(P))\right] \tag{10.38}$$

$$= E_{X'\beta}\left[\frac{d\Theta(F(X'\beta))}{dX'\beta}\right]$$

Sufficient conditions for (10.38) to hold are that $\Theta(0) = 0$ and $\Theta(1)$ is finite.

For the logit model, (10.38) will generally need to be computed numerically. For the probit model, the derivative of the variance of R is

$$\frac{d\text{Var}(R)}{d\mu} = \frac{1}{N} \frac{d\{E[P] - E[P]^2\}}{d\mu} \tag{10.39}$$

$$= \frac{1}{N} \left\{ \frac{dE[P]}{d\mu} - 2E[P] \frac{dE[P]}{d\mu} \right\}$$

$$= \frac{1}{N} (1 + \sigma^2)^{-1/2} \phi[\mu(1 + \sigma^2)^{-1/2}]$$

$$\times \{1 - 2\Phi[\mu(1 + \sigma^2)^{-1/2}]\}$$

using (10.16) and (10.36). Thus population variability in R increases as μ increases, for $\mu > 0$, and decreases as μ increases for $\mu < 0$.

The preceding derivatives consider changes in the moments of the mean probability due to changes in the mean of individual characteristics, holding constant the variance of individual characteristics. By similar derivation to that for (10.31)

$$\frac{dE[\Theta(P)]}{d\sigma^2} = \frac{1}{2\sigma^2} E_P\left[\frac{d\Theta(P)}{dP} f(F^{-1}(P))[F^{-1}(P) - \mu]] \right]$$

$$\tag{10.40}$$

$$= \frac{1}{2\sigma^2} E_{X'\beta}\left[\frac{d\Theta(F(X'\beta))}{dX'\beta} (X'\beta - \mu)] \right]$$

where sufficient conditions are again $\Theta(0) = 0$ and $\Theta(1)$ is finite.

For the mean probability of the probit model, (10.40) yields

$$\frac{dE[P]}{d\sigma^2} = \frac{1}{2\sigma^2} E_{X'\beta}[\phi(X'\beta - \mu)] \tag{10.41}$$

$$= -\frac{1}{2} \mu(1 + \sigma^2)^{-3/2} \phi[\mu(1 + \sigma^2)^{-1/2}]$$

Thus the mean probability decreases as heterogeneity increases, for $\mu > 0$, as table 10.1 indicated. Similarly, an expression for $d\text{Var}(R)/d\sigma^2$ can be obtained.

Other methods outlined in section 10.2 for estimating the mean probability can also be used to estimate changes in the mean probability when population characteristics change, in the obvious manner. Any weakness of the various methods in estimating the mean probability can be expected to carry through when using them to estimate changes in the mean probability. In addition, the calculus approach of this section is applicable only for small changes in population characteristics. Against these criticisms can be weighed the computational simplicity of some of the estimators given in this section.

Finally, we note that if we are only interested in estimating the change in the population mean of the dependent variable for a given change in the population means of the explanatory variables, Stoker (1980, 1986a) gives conditions under which an OLS or IV estimator using micro data is sufficient, i.e. even if the micro dependent variable is discrete, a micro discrete choice model need not be estimated. In particular, if X is normally distributed, then the OLS slope coefficients converge to the derivative of the macro function $E[Y]$ with respect to changes in μ_X.

10.4 Conclusions

For progress to be made in solving aggregation problems for discrete choice models, as with any other non-linear micro model, assumptions about the distribution of the explanatory variables need to be made. By far the most tractable results arise for the probit model with normally distributed explanatory variables. Indeed this case may be viewed as the prototypical example of tractable non-linear aggregation.

The restriction of the class of discrete choice models to probit models is not a great drawback, especially as we can transform logit parameter estimates to probit estimates with apparently little loss in accuracy.

The normality assumption is a strong one, though one made routinely in multivariate analysis. Simulation experiments suggest that this assumption does give reasonable results, and dominates the alternative of assuming the macro function to be the micro function of the respresentative agent.

The relevance of such assumptions and their associated data requirements will vary from problem to problem. To date most applications have been to transportation modal choice in the context of aggregate prediction from a micro model, using only aggregate data on characteristics. These empirical applications indicate that there is a substantial loss in accuracy if micro data are unavailable.

The converse problem is the interpretation of micro behaviour, given macro data. In particular, can we obtain estimates for the parameters of a micro function based on macro data and knowledge of the implied macro function? For space reasons this is only briefly mentioned here. The answer is yes, if estimates of $E[Y]$ and the parameters of the distribution generating regressor variables are available for a number of sub-groups of the population.

Consider the probit model with normally distributed regressors, for which the macro function is (10.16). Bouthelier and Daganzo (1979) and Hartman (1982) estimate the parameters β of the discrete choice model by maximum likelihood, using data on sample mean probability and means and variances of explanatory variables for a number of groups. Cameron (1985) instead proposed a modified non-linear minimum chi-square estimator which is asymptotically equivalent to maximum likelihood.[12] In the more general context of non-linear models with complete aggregation, Powell and Stoker (1985) proposed a related, though different, non-linear minimum chi-square estimator to estimate micro function parameters using macro data on both Y and X.

Appendix 10A: Proof of lemma

Denote $\mu \equiv E[Z]$ and recall $\mu > 0$. First consider the case $Z\varepsilon[0, \infty)$. The set $S = \{(Z, Y): Z\varepsilon[0, \infty), Y \leq F(Z)\}$ will be convex, since F is concave on $[0, \infty)$. The point $(\mu, F(\mu))$ lies on the boundary of this set, and hence there exists a supporting line $a + bZ$ at $(\mu, F(\mu))$ where

$$F(\mu) = a + b\mu \tag{A1}$$

$$F(Z) = a + bZ - \eta(Z) \tag{A2}$$

$$\eta(Z) \geq 0 \quad \forall \quad Z\varepsilon[0, \infty) \tag{A3}$$

$$a \geq \frac{1}{2}, \quad \text{since } \frac{1}{2} = F(0) = a + b.0 - \eta(0) \tag{A4}$$

By the symmetry of F, it can be similarly shown that for $Z\varepsilon(-\infty, 0)$ the supporting line at $(-\mu, F(-\mu))$ is $(1 - a) + bZ$ where

$$F(-\mu) = (1 - a) - b\mu \tag{A5}$$

$$F(Z) = (1 - a) + bZ + \eta(-Z) \tag{A6}$$

We have for Z with c.d.f. $G(z)$

$$E[F(Z)] = \int_{-\infty}^{\infty} F(z)\mathrm{d}\,G(z)$$

$$= \int_{-\infty}^{0-} F(z)\mathrm{d}\,G(z) + \int_{0}^{\infty} F(z)\mathrm{d}\,G(z)$$

$$= \int_{-\infty}^{0-} [(1-a) + bz + \eta(-z)]\mathrm{d}\,G(z)$$

$$+ \int_{0}^{\infty} [a + bz - \eta(z)]\mathrm{d}\,G(z)$$

$$= \{(1-a)\int_{-\infty}^{0-} \mathrm{d}\,G(z) + a\int_{0}^{\infty} \mathrm{d}\,G(z)\}$$

$$+ b\int_{-\infty}^{\infty} z\mathrm{d}\,G(z) + \{\int_{-\infty}^{0-} \eta(-z)\mathrm{d}\,G(z)$$

$$- \int_{0}^{\infty} \eta(z)\mathrm{d}\,G(z)\}$$

$$\leq a + b\mu + \{-\int_{0}^{\infty} \eta(z)\mathrm{d}\,G(-z) - \int_{0}^{\infty} \eta(z)\mathrm{d}\,G(z)\}$$

$$\leq a + b\mu$$

$$= F(\mu)$$

where (A4) implies the first inequality, and a sufficient though not necessary condition for the second inequality is that $\mathrm{d}\,G(z) \geq -\mathrm{d}\,G(-z), \forall z > 0$.

Notes

1   A notable exception is the work of Stoker, presented in section 10.1. He used the probit model with multivariate normally distributed regressors as a convenient example.
2   For example, see Rao (1973).
3   The linear probability model (LPM) does not fall into this class, since F is not a c.d.f. then. It is for exactly this reason – predicted probabilities may fall outside the (0, 1) interval – that its use is criticized. However, it should be noted that owing to its linearity many of the aggregation problems discussed here do not arise with the LPM.
4   This can be seen by similar methods to (10.12) and (10.13).
5   For the probit model with individual characteristics normally distributed, $y^* = X'\beta + \varepsilon \sim N(\mu'_x\beta, 1 + \beta'\Sigma_x\beta)$; $X \sim N(\mu_x, \Sigma_x)$; and cov $(y, X') = \beta'\Sigma_x$. This model can be obtained from (though does not necessarily imply) the multivariate normal model

$$\begin{bmatrix} Y^* \\ X \end{bmatrix} \sim N\left(\begin{bmatrix} u'_x\beta \\ \mu_x \end{bmatrix}, \begin{bmatrix} 1 + \beta'\Sigma_x\beta & \beta'\Sigma_x\beta \\ \Sigma'_x\beta & \beta'\Sigma_x\beta \end{bmatrix} \right)$$

The population coefficient of multiple correlation is therefore

$$Q^2 = \frac{\mathrm{cov}(y^*, X')(\mathrm{Var}(X))^{-1}\mathrm{cov}(y^*, X)}{\mathrm{Var}(y^*)} = \frac{\beta'\Sigma_x\beta}{1 + \beta'\Sigma_x\beta} = \frac{\sigma^2}{1 + \sigma^2}$$

Furthermore, $E[R^2] \simeq Q^2 + \dfrac{1}{N}(1 - Q^2)(K - 2Q^2)$, see, e.g. Theil

(1971, p. 191), so that for the probit model with X normal, $\sigma^2 = 1$

implies $E[R^2] \simeq 0.5\,(1 + \dfrac{K-1}{N})$.

6   See table 2.2 in Cameron (1985). Because the probit model is based on the standard normal distribution with standard deviation unity, whereas the logit model uses the logistic distribution with standard deviation $\pi(16\sqrt{3})^{-1}$, the parameters β in the two different models will be scaled differently; see Amemiya (1981, p. 1488). Amemiya actually suggested the multiple 1.6, but Cameron used 1.7, following Lancaster (1979) who used $15\pi(16\sqrt{3})^{-1} \simeq 1.70$ in a similar exercise. Then β for the logit model is 1.7 times β for the probit model, and the mean and variance of $X'\beta$ are re-scaled accordingly.

7   The properties of the logistic distribution are detailed in Johnson and Kotz (1970, ch. 22).

8   The stochastic utility approach is particularly useful for extending aggregation results for the binary probit-normal model to multi-choice models. For example, see Bouthelier and Daganzo (1979) and Hartman (1984). The resulting model is analytically similar to the random parameter probit model of Hausman and Wise (1978).

9   For example, conjugate priors can be found not only for the normal distribution, but also for other members of the exponential family of distributions. See Cox and Hinkley (1974, p. 370).

10 Bayesian results can also be applied directly to the random variable y which is Bernoulli distributed with parameter $P = F(X'\beta)$. If the prior distribution of P is the beta distribution with parameters a and b, then the posterior distribution of P given y is the beta distribution with parameters $(a + y)$ and $(b + 1 - y)$. It follows that the marginal distribution of y is the Bernoulli distribution with parameter $1/(a + b)$, which is the mean of the prior distribution. However, for this result to be of use we need to specify a and b. In the context of this paper the variation in P is due to the variation in individual characteristics, and obtaining estimates of a and b from the distribution of $F(X'\beta)$ will generally be analytically impossible. For this reason this approach is not taken here. (In a different context Heckman and Willis (1977) postulated that $a = \exp(X'\alpha)$ and $b = \exp(X'\beta)$, in which case $E[P] = L(X'(\alpha - \beta))$.)

11 Throughout section 10.3 we assume β is known. Virtually all studies of aggregate prediction in discrete choice models make this assumption. For brief discussions of aggregate prediction using an estimate $\hat{\beta}$, see Amemiya (1985, p. 286) and Lancaster (1979).

12 Suppose we have data for T groups, such as different regions or time periods, and for the tth group X_t is normally distributed with known

231

Disaggregation in econometric modelling

mean μ_{xt} and known covariance matrix Σ_{xt}. Then for the probit model, (10.16) implies

$$\Phi^{-1}(E[P_t]) = \mu'_{xt}\beta(1 + \beta'\Sigma_{xt}\beta)^{-1/2}$$

for $t = 1, \ldots, T$. Given an estimate $\bar{p}_t = \dfrac{1}{N_t}\sum_{i=1}^{N} y_{it}$, we rewrite this as

$$\Phi^{-1}(\bar{p}_t) = \mu'_{xt}\beta(1 + \beta'\Sigma_{xt}\beta)^{-1/2} + u_t$$

where u_t is an error with mean 0. An estimator for β, consistent as $N_t \to \infty$ for fixed T, is the non-linear weighted minimum chi-square (or non-linear weighted least squares) estimator which minimizes

$$\sum_{t=1}^{T} w_t\{\Phi^{-1}(\bar{p}_t) - \mu'_{xt}\beta(1 + \beta'\Sigma_{xt}\beta)^{-1/2}\}^2$$

This estimator was proposed by Cameron (1985), who also obtained the optimal choice of weights w_t. It is a variant of Berkson's minimum chi-squared estimator, which minimizes the above function with $\Sigma_{xt} = 0$, and corresponds to using the representative agent approximation $E[P_t] = \Phi(\mu_t)$. McFadden and Reid (1975) observed that Berkson's minimum chi-squared estimator is therefore inconsistent, unless $\Sigma_{xt} = 0$. They proposed a consistent estimator, which is less efficient than the above estimator with optimal weights.

Part II

Chapter eleven

Macroeconomic and microeconomic modelling: some issues

Chris Higson and Sean Holly

Introduction

One of the most active areas in economic modelling at present concerns the dialogue between macroeconomic and microeconomic modelling. The objective of this paper is to examine some of the issues that have arisen and to identify some of the difficulties.

Empirically based macroeconomic models date from the late 1930s and the pioneering work of Tinbergen. But it was not until sufficiently powerful computers became available in the 1950s that macroeconomic models became commonplace. Empirically based microeconomic models are, by contrast, of comparatively recent origin.

Models, in the sense of computer representations of some aspect of economic activity, can be categorized according to their scope, the type of data they use and the purposes they serve. The scope of a model can extend from individual households and firms, to individual products, industries, sectors, and regions, up to representations of individual countries and right up to the level of the world economy. The type of data can be company accounts, surveys of households, and panel data (both cross-section and time-series) as well as surveys of firms and industries and aggregated income and expenditure accounts at the national level. Models are also used for a variety of purposes. The most common is forecasting. They also provide a testbed for economic hypotheses, and a basis for the analysis of economic policy. This analysis can be descriptive, as when trying to trace through the effects of a policy change on some aspect of economic activity, and prescriptive, as with the use of models with policy optimization techniques.

Clearly there is a very wide range of models from which we can choose. We want to confine our attention to macroeconomic models of national economies, and to particular types of micro-economic model that use pooled or cross-section data on companies and on households. One of the features of these kinds of macroeconomic model is that they attempt to be *comprehensive* representations of an economy's behaviour with which forecasts of output, inflation, unemployment and the balance of payments can be made. A model which captures the main connections between instruments of fiscal and monetary policy and targets for output, inflation, and employment was until recently considered an adequate basis for demand management. The detailed microeconomic responses of households and firms to changes in policy instruments, though important for the overall effect, were not thought to require detailed understanding. The aggregate relationships in the macroeconomic model captured what mattered. Any variables appearing in the model but not actually explained by the model were regarded as strictly exogenous.

Most microeconomic models, by contrast, try to be *exhaustive* representations of particular forms of economic activity, without necessarily ensuring that all variables in the model not actually explained by the model are strictly exogenous.

Because of the costs of building and running macroeconomic models, comprehensiveness is bought at the expense of detail. But from a macroeconomic perspective this loss of detail only matters – so long as one is not actually interested in the effects of changing fiscal and monetary instruments at the level of households and firms – if there is aggregation bias. It is no coincidence that much of the interest in micro-to-macro modelling has arisen in areas where the underlying economic behaviour displays non-linearities, or discontinuities because of the effects of the personal tax and benefit system on households, and corporation taxes on companies.

In this chapter we shall concentrate on the issues raised by the use of microeconomic models of households and firms in conjunction with macroeconomic models. We shall not examine, in any great detail, the much more ambitious task implied by the micro-to-macro model of Eliasson (1984). This involves the complete replacement of traditional macro models with one built up from individual firms and households. We are not ruling out the possibility that models of this kind built up from firms, industries, and households will emerge in the UK. It remains true, nevertheless, that at the moment the best microeconomic models fall well short of this objective.

In the next section we consider the main features of some micro models of the tax and benefit system and micro models of the corporation tax system, confining our attention to the UK.

11.1 Microeconomic models of household and company taxes

We consider microeconomic models of the personal tax and benefit system first. One of the first computerized models of the tax and benefit system in the UK was developed at the Institute for Fiscal Studies in the early 1980s. At first, particular parts of the tax and benefit system were modelled for particular purposes (Dilnot and Morris, 1982, Morris and Dilnot, 1982). However, by 1984 the model covered the majority of the population and most aspects of the tax and benefit system (Dilnot, Kay, and Morris, 1984). In common with some later models of the tax and benefit system, the IFS model used data provided by the Family Expenditure Survey (FES). The FES is carried out on an annual basis by the Department of the Environment using approximately 7,000 households, drawn at random from the UK population (Kemsley, Redpath, and Holmes, 1980). The FES contains much which is not relevant to the tax and benefit system; indeed, its original purpose was nothing to do with the modelling of the personal tax system. However, since it contains detailed information on household income, and its source, it is possible from knowledge of other characteristics of the household to calculate the tax liabilities and entitlements to benefit of individuals and households. Given knowledge of the level and source of a household's income and of the various tax rates and allowances it is feasible to calculate 'precisely' the tax liability of that household. The same calculation can be carried out to determine entitlement to benefit. With 9,000 households it is then possible to examine the distributional effects of tax and benefit changes, to calculate marginal tax rates, and to explore the consequences of various reforms to the tax and benefit system.

To the extent that the sample of 9,000 households is representative of the population as a whole, it would be possible to estimate the total revenue which the government receives from direct taxation. However, there are a number of under-sampling and under-reporting errors in the FES sample. Certain types of income and expenditure – such as investment income, income from self-employment, and expenditure on tobacco and alcohol – are under-recorded. Also both the old and the very rich are under-sampled. Various procedures to minimize these problems have been proposed by Atkinson and Micklewright (1983), Atkinson (1983), and Atkinson, Gomulka, and Sutherland (1988), and implemented in another model of the tax and benefit system developed at the London School of Economics (Atkinson and Sutherland, 1988).

The use of a tax and benefit model to examine the gross revenue implications of series of tax changes is described in Atkinson and Sutherland (1988). The model they use is based on a slightly smaller sample of 5,824 tax units from the 1982/3 FES. To use the model for more recent years various updates are made. The changes in tax rates and allowances are straightforward. For different categories of income, grossing-up factors are derived from aggregate statistics or from the New Earnings Survey. Each class of income is then adjusted approximately to capture the change in income from the year in which the sample was collected to the year under examination. Atkinson and Sutherland examine the effects of the abolition of the married man's allowance and the doubling of child and single parent benefit. Using their model they are able to calculate both the precise effects (within the limits of the data) on a representative family, and the gross and net effects on exchequer revenue. The distributional effects can also be seen clearly.

We now turn to consider models of the corporation tax system. Taxation has a central role in modern theories of decision making by firms. For instance, in neoclassical theories of the firm, decisions about fixed capital or inventory accumulation depend, among other factors, upon the marginal cost of additional investment in fixed or working capital. This cost is a function of the various allowances that can be claimed against corporation tax, but the value of these tax allowances depends upon the firm's tax-paying position and this can have an important bearing upon the marginal user cost of capital and the marginal financial cost of holding inventories (see Edwards and Keen, 1985, Holly and Markose, 1986, Higson, 1987).

The need for reliable data on effective corporate tax rates as an input to empirical research on company behaviour has led to the development of models of company corporation tax payments. Modelling was needed for two reasons. The first is that asymmetries in the UK corporation tax system have generated significant differences between companies' effective tax rate. The second is that a company's effective tax rates are not fully disclosed in its accounts.

A pervasive phenomenon in the UK and elsewhere in the late 1970s and early 1980s was the accumulation of large stocks of tax losses by many firms, owing to low profitability and generous tax allowances on investment in plant and inventories, so that the effective tax rates faced by tax-exhausted companies were likely to be significantly different from those faced by companies without tax losses. There are few published measures of tax exhaustion. The *Corporation Tax Green Paper* (HMSO, 1982) produced some widely quoted aggregate data which showed that in 1982 the value of unused corporate tax allowances in the UK stood at £30bn and was growing at the rate of £5bn per year, so that in any year only half of companies were paying tax. However, at the macro level the modelling and even the measurement of tax exhaustion is not a straightforward matter. Two conditions are necessary for the existence of heterogeneous corporate tax rates. One is the existence of asymmetric tax rules whereby, while positive taxable earnings are taxed, if a company makes a loss for tax purposes either a refund of tax is available to the extent of profits in the previous period, or the tax loss can be carried forward against future profits. The Inland Revenue do not compensate companies for the cost of deferral. The second is the existence of market frictions and legal constraints preventing the transfer of tax liability between companies. Without barriers to tax arbitrage, we should expect corporate tax rates to equalize across companies. The difficulty arises because, though the corporation tax schedule is non-linear, market opportunities for arbitraging tax differences are strictly limited. Though there have been opportunities for mitigating tax asymmetry by trading losses in the market, notably through leasing, these opportunities appear to be limited (Cooper and Franks, 1983). An exception to this is that within a 50 per cent ownership group of companies there is free transfer of tax losses against contemporaneous profits between domestic companies. But the tax losses and profits of different (groups of) companies are not additive, suggesting that tax exhaustion is best modelled at the company level.

One way in which the aggregate extent of tax exhaustion can be estimated is by using models of companies in order to simulate on the basis of company accounts those companies which are tax exhausted. In the UK several company-level tax models have been reported. The best known of these is the corporation tax model which has been developed over several years at the IFS (see Mayer and Morris, 1982 and Devereux, 1986). A company-level tax model has also been developed at the LBS (see Higson, 1987), and models are reported by Inland Revenue (1982), Goudie (1984), and Levis and Morgan (1985). Models such as the IFS corporation tax model, or the LBS tax model have as their prime function the estimation of tax liabilities at the company level.

We shall describe in outline how a company's corporation tax liability is generated and thus the structure of models such as the LBS one. The main adjustments to convert accounting earnings to taxable profit have been for capital allowances and, until 1984, stock relief. Taxable profit is reduced by losses from other periods, or from other companies in a group or consortium. The balance of taxable profit after loss relief is apportioned to fiscal years and taxed at the appropriate corporation tax rate to give the UK corporation tax charge for the year. Part of this liability is treated as already discharged, by the net of Advanced Corporation Tax (ACT) collected on dividends paid to stock-holders, and borne by the company on dividends received; and by double-tax relief (DTR), which is the offsettable part of the overseas tax borne by the company on its overseas income. The balance is 'mainstream'. Hence in aggregate the UK tax liability of a company has been essentially a function of gross trading profit, fixed asset investment, stock building, net interest payments, and dividends. The LBS tax model essentially follows this structure. These tax-generating variables are taken from published accounts data for historic periods, or forecast into the future, and fed through the tax rules to generate capital allowances, stock relief, and losses carried forward and back. The resulting UK tax charge is reduced by ACT calculated on net dividends payments and any unrelieved ACT is also carried forward and back according to the tax rules.

Because tax losses have been endemic in the UK we need a history of tax payments for each company. Analysis is based on annual data from 1973 to 1986 for a sample of 656 companies which account for more than half the output of the UK industrial and commercial sector. Initially, we estimate effective tax rates annually for each company on the basis of the company's actual experience of tax resumption. These rates are of interest from a public policy standpoint in describing the *ex post* marginal burden of taxation. However, in terms of incentives, they are tax rates that would be used by firms with perfect foresight. Hence we also estimate the tax rates that might have been expected by firms on the assumption that earnings evolve stochastically and that future tax rules are unknown. The approach we use is to take the expectation of tax rates across the paths of taxable earnings generated from a random walk in operating earnings. The other tax generating variables are assumed to be functionally determined by earnings via a simple model of the firm, but both the earnings process and these functional relationships are exogenous with respect to the company's tax position. This methodology enables us to get point estimates of company tax positions in terms of both their expectation and their distribution.

11.2 Some drawbacks with the current generation of micro models

One of the most noticeable features of models of both the tax and benefit and corporation tax system is that they are almost entirely arithmetical or calibrated. No attempt is made to draw out the possible effects of changes in taxes on behaviour by households and firms. However, a number of efforts are in hand to enrich the behavioural content of the tax and benefit models. King (1988) discusses a number of behavioural changes, while considerable work is underway at the IFS to examine the effects of tax changes on work incentives and the supply of labour (Blundell *et al.*, 1987, Symons and Walker, 1986). This research shows how the behavioural content of microeconomic models of the tax and benefit system can be improved.

Difficulties arise, nevertheless, as the complexity and scope of this kind of model grow. In particular, at present only the impact effects on labour supply are considered. Ideally, a more dynamic analysis is required. In addition, there is a point after which it is important to endogenize wage and employment determination. Such a task is beyond the scope of data currently available for households. Thus there is much which the current generation of microeconomic models must take as given. Yet macroeconomic models are specifically designed to produce forecasts for wages, prices incomes, employment, etc. – though at an aggregate level – which the microeconomic modeller needs to drive the microeconomic model. In the next section we shall consider ways in which macroeconomic and microeconomic models could be used together.

As with the tax and benefit models, the current generation of company tax models are essentially 'calibrated'. The tax rules are programmed and company accounts data for the economic magnitudes that generate tax liability – profits, dividends, investment in stocks, and fixed capital, etc., – are input. Hence the economic behaviour proxied by the accounts data, in terms of the formal structure of the model at least, is independent of tax rules and tax rates. So although such a micro model is much richer than the macro model in terms of its level of operation, and its modelling of the tax laws, it is much poorer in terms of behavioural assumptions, either theoretical or econometric. Moreover, for future periods when accounting data are not available, company forecasts are based on data provided by forecasts from macro models. While at present company tax models have little behavioural content, this may be a transitional phase; indeed, a growing body of work is currently being undertaken into the effects of taxation on corporate stockbuilding, capital investment, and financial policy. However, we should not under-estimate the difficulties involved.

There is also a risk of survivorship bias. Because a prime function of company tax models is to generate estimates of companies' stocks of tax 'carry-forwards' for each period, mainstream 'tax losses', and unrelieved ACT, modelling is necessarily restricted to companies with a continuous record of accounting data on published data bases. From an average population of 2,500 companies per annum on Exstat, a requirement of survival over the period 1973–85 produced an initial sample of 910 firms. One particular group which is therefore excluded at present is the young, growing recently created sector.

Perhaps less obvious is the problem of relationships between companies in the data base. Accounting rules identify three classes of relationship between companies A and B depending on the degree of equity ownership: A can be an investment of B (< 20 per cent owned), and associate (20 per cent–50 per cent), or a subsidiary (> 50 per cent). Casual empiricism suggests that these rather crude accounting distinctions are increasingly unable to cope with the complex contractual and noncontractual relationships that exist between companies. We know that 'control' can exist without a formal, contractual nexus (see, for example, Nyman and Silbertson, 1978). A more recent development is the increasing use of complex contractual schemes, often marketed by financial institutions, which enable companies which believe that holding assets and liabilities off-balance-sheet is a thing of value, to enjoy many of the benefits of ownership of assets or subsidiaries without consolidating them.

In tax modelling we are forced to assume that the unit of analysis for tax purposes is the consolidated group for accounting, and data limitations force us to assume no consortium activity, and that all reported earnings and assets (UK and overseas) are subject to UK taxation. In the LBS tax model we attempt to reduce this problem by excluding companies with significant overseas activity. Tax models not based on accounts data (for example, models based on individual company tax assessments) may tend to make the other extreme assumption, of zero inter-company tax transfers. Goudie (1984) showed the discrepancy between aggregated micro forecasts and macro forecasts to be significant in forecasting company tax liabilities where there is widespread tax exhaustion. If UK and overseas asset structures and profitability were identical, then the problem caused by including overseas activities in a UK tax model would merely be one of scale. Predictions of the time of zero UK tax charge would not be affected, though estimates of the absolute size of, say, tax losses would be and, since imputation of ACT is not symmetrical between UK and overseas, the estimate of mainstream corporation tax would also be affected.

From our brief description of a few models of the tax and benefit system and of the corporation tax system it is clear why this is an attractive modelling approach, based on very rich data sources albeit with attendant problems. In the next section we consider some of the ways in which macroeconomic modelling, forecasting, and policy analysis could benefit from these microeconomic models.

11.3 Macro-model responses to micro models

In this section we consider a number of responses of macroeconomic modellers to recent work in microeconometric modelling. We do not consider how micro modellers might respond to macro modelling. We consider four main responses. The first two are relatively trivial and imply that macro modellers use some of the products of micro modelling to improve the specification of aggregate relationships. The third response involves operating micro and macro models in tandem, using some of the outputs of the macroeconomic model as inputs to the micro model and vice versa. The last response, and the most radical, would involve the replacement of most of the aggregate relationships in the macroeconomic models by a series of disaggregated models based on microeconomic data. We consider the prospect of this happening and some of the difficulties it would entail.

One of the problems we face when using large, traditional macroeconometric models, especially for policy simulation, is that they are often incapable of providing answers to a number of interesting questions involving structural, or supply-side changes. At their worst they are little better than semi-restricted vector autoregressive models which are quite useful for forecasting relatively slow-moving linear, dynamic processes, but very inadequate when forecasting economic magnitudes such as asset prices which by their nature can change very rapidly. They also perform particularly badly when there are significant non-linearities involving discontinuities. A particular illustration is provided by the direct and indirect tax system. We normally assume that the most important parts of macro econometric models are the behavioural equations, and it is these which attract the most scrutiny and criticism. Yet it is clear that using linear estimation techniques on

243

aggregate data to explain the relationship between personal income tax payments and incomes and tax rates is inadequate. Similar arguments can be applied to the indirect tax system. What has been the practice in the past, at least at the LBS, was to impose a relationship for personal taxes, and to use estimates of price and income elasticities and shares to estimate indirect tax payments of both duties and VAT.

This has proved to be a workable approximation, at least within the narrow confines of short-run forecasting. However, major structural reforms to the tax and benefit system could have a significant impact on both the level of revenues and household labour supply decisions. Yet the way in which our model is structured at present would make it very difficult to provide some overall estimates. One means by which much richer questions can be asked of a macro model is to carry out simulations of reforms using the LBS model in tandem with a micro model of the tax and benefit system. One initial obstacle to overcome arises from the static nature of the tax and benefit model. Macroeconomic models are almost invariably dynamic. If we wished to simulate the macroeconomic effects of a reform to the tax system, at the first stage we could calculate the effects on the micro model. After grossing up, this would then provide us with an initial estimate of the likely revenue implications of the tax reform. To extend the analysis into the future we should then need to use the macroeconomic model to forecast the increase in incomes and then feed this information back into the tax and benefit model in order to adjust each class of income, and then repeat the exercise. If within each time period – assumed to be a quarter – the revenue implications of the tax reform did not have immediate effects on income and expenditure, the interaction between the two models would be essentially recursive. Otherwise it might be necessary to iterate between the macro and the micro model until the difference between two successive passes was below some critical value.

It is easy to imagine that a similar procedure could be followed in order to link models of the corporation tax system to a macroeconomic model. In this case the initial aim would be to provide better estimates of the yield from corporation tax, given the asymmetries in the corporation tax system we discussed in the previous section. The macroeconomic model would provide estimates of profitability, and the microeconomic model would then compute the likely tax yield given information about the tax paying positions of individual companies.

This approach will only take us so far. To a large extent the macroeconomic model would still be doing most of the work by generating predictions for prices, investment, employment, wages, etc. However, it is reasonable to suppose that changes to personal and corporate taxes affect decisions by both households and firms and, while most macroeconomic models capture many of these effects at the aggregate level, it may be better to model them at the company and household level. In principle this would involve extending both the tax and benefit and the corporation tax models to predict labour supply and consumption at the household level, and investment at the company level. This would immediately strengthen the connections between the micro and the macro models.

However, as an interim measure there is an alternative and more modest way to allow for important household characteristics in determining labour supply. This is demonstrated by the way in which female participation is modelled at the moment in the LBS model. This has involved drawing on microeconometric studies to identify influences to use in macroeconomic relationships (Holly and Smith, 1987). Explanations of labour supply decisions are well documented in Killingsworth (1983) who discusses the recent theoretical and empirical literature. Much of the empirical work has been carried out on cross-section data sets like the General Household Survey, such as that by Layard, Barton, and Zabalza (1985). Holly and Smith (1987) adopted their analysis of an essentially static decision. Participation is determined by the probability of finding a job, the prospective real wage on accepting a job, and the level of the spouse's earned and unearned income. In that paper some rather simple results were presented for total female labour supply based on time-series data. The female population of working age, the relative level of female and male earnings, the average level of real earnings adjusted for the level of direct taxes, the rate of unemployment, and a time trend were included in a regression. The rate of unemployment is almost certainly a rather imperfect measure of the average probability of finding a job, and the time trend is a poor proxy for the omitted social and other factors which have caused female participation to increase over time. The results suggest, however, that participation can be explained quite well over the 1973–81 period and can be predicted accurately in the two years outside the sample.

This does not mean, however, that we have a relationship which will prove robust to major structural changes such as are envisaged to the tax and benefit system. The introduction of a transferable allowance or the abolition of the married man's allowance may have a major impact on the female labour supply decision. This is why the use of more developed micro models of household – and company – behaviour will help to gain a better understanding of the macroeconomic consequences of major tax reforms.

There has also been another form of response to micro modelling. Attempts have been made to use measures of otherwise unobservable factors in aggregated, time-series work. Corporate tax exhaustion provides one example of the way in which macro modellers can make use of the results of microeconometric modelling. It is now common practice to derive macroeconomic relationships from the maximizing behaviour of firms and households. For example, in neoclassical theories of the firm decisions about fixed capital or inventory accumulation depend, among other factors, upon the marginal cost of additional investment in fixed or working capital. This cost is a function of the various allowances that can be claimed against corporation tax, but the value of these tax allowances depends upon whether the firm is tax exhausted or not and can have an important bearing upon the marginal user cost of capital, and the marginal financial cost of holding inventories (see Edwards and Keen, 1985, Holly and Longbottom, 1985, Holly and Markose, 1986).

With this approach the degree of tax exhaustion is being treated as (weakly) exogenous to the behaviour of the firm, though clearly it is not. Strictly speaking, in the presence of non-zero net investment in fixed capital the marginal decision to invest in fixed capital may not be separable from the marginal decision to accumulate inventories. If a firm is on the borderline between being able and not being able to claim allowances, the decision to invest may use up available taxable profits and alter the marginal cost of inventories, or for that matter, the marginal cost of subsequent investment projects (subsequent in the sense of time rather than the next project with the highest net return).

It should also prove possible to use micro models of households in order to derive measures of income distribution or measures of true marginal tax rates to use in aggregate relationships.

The last possibility we want to consider is that the current generation of macroeconomic models will be superseded by large-scale microeconometric models. We think that this is unlikely. It is not obvious that the widespread use of cross-section or pooled samples will yield sufficient benefits to outweigh the costs of having a much larger model. In addition, cross-section data are expensive to collect and are rarely timely, so there would be difficulties when forecasting. In addition, trying to use household and company data to explain all the economic decisions of households and firms, and to draw all of this together in order to predict economy-wide movements in wages, employment, prices, and international trade, as well as financial decisions, is a daunting task.

At the conceptual level, there are meaningful macroeconomic magnitudes, such as the price level and the exchange rate, which are not amenable to microeconomic analysis. It is true also that in the physical sciences there are perfectly adequate models of the behaviour of gases and fluids which do not rely on explanations of the behaviour of individual atoms or molecules. In this sense macroeconomic reasoning as a way of characterizing the behaviour of economic systems has still got a lot of life in it, and macroeconomic models as embodiments of this type of reasoning are unlikely to succumb to microeconomic models, though there would be considerable benefits to both parties.

Chapter twelve

MICROFKA: integrating a micro labour-supply model and a macro model of the Dutch economy

Peter ten Hacken and Arie Kapteyn

Introduction

It has been known for a long time that consistent aggregation of microeconomic relationships is only possible under restrictive conditions. Some classic and some newer references in this respect are Theil (1954), Muellbauer (1975), Barnett (1979). Yet, applied macroeconomics is mainly still proceeding under the representative agent assumption. Even when consistent aggregation is possible, for instance when relationships are linear, estimation of these relationships for macro and for micro data tends to yield quite different results. A standard example is a simple Keynesian consumption function, which typically exhibits a far larger marginal propensity to consume in macro time-series data than in micro cross-section data. Various explanations have been advanced for this phenomenon, including the relative income and the permanent income hypothesis (Duesenberry, 1967, Friedman, 1957). Pakes (1983) analyses in more general terms the differences between micro and macro relations that arise as a result of explanatory variables that exhibit a group structure. An example of such a situation is provided by the micro model used in this paper: preferences of agents are allowed to depend on the behaviour of others in their social reference group. For individual agents the behaviour of others is exogenous, but at a macro level one observes the behaviour of agents jointly and reference group behaviour is no longer exogenous. Thus macro behaviour differs from micro behaviour (see section 12.1 for a more detailed exposition).

If one wants to have well-behaved macro relations, the obvious way to proceed is to start from a well-behaved micro model and to aggregate the micro relations. Generally, aggregation will have to be done numerically, because micro relations will in general not satisfy restrictive conditions for aggregation. This is particularly

248

true when micro models are rich in institutional detail, as in the case of labour-supply models that take into account effects of taxation and social security on individual behaviour (cf. Hausman, 1985, Moffit, 1986).

In this paper we aim at a well-behaved macro labour-supply function, which is obtained by numerical aggregation of micro household labour-supply relations. The micro relations stem from a model which explains, for each household, the hours worked of all household members by wages, demographic factors, and the social security and fiscal system. As mentioned, the model incorporates habit formation and interdependence of preferences.

The macro labour-supply relation basically is a micro labour-supply simulation model, in which the effects of changes in exogenous variables on micro behaviour are traced out and then added up. This simulation model replaces the macro labour-supply relation in a recent model of the Dutch economy. The macro model is called FK85. The integrated micro-macro model is called MICROFKA. The micro model is fully integrated into the macro model in that the macro part generates changes in the explanatory variables of the micro model, whereas the resulting changes in aggregate labour supply feed back into the macro model.

The paper is organized as follows. In section 12.1 the micro model is described briefly, section 12.2 gives some details of the macro model, and in section 12.3 the combined micro/macro model is described. In section 12.4 we present some simulations with the combined model to see how well the combined model tracks developments in the 1980s. Section 12.5 presents some policy simulations, and we conclude with an evaluation in section 12.6.

12.1 The micro model of labour supply

The model of labour supply developed by Kapteyn and Woittiez (1988) starts from the Hausman and Ruud (1984) specification of the joint labour-supply decision of male and female partners in a household:

$$\tilde{h}_M = \delta_M + \gamma_M w_M + \alpha w_F + \beta_M \mu^*$$
$$\tilde{h}_F = \delta_F + \gamma_F w_F + \alpha w_M + \beta_F \mu^* \tag{12.1}$$

$$\mu^* = \mu + \theta + \delta_M w_M + \delta_F w_F + \frac{1}{2}(\gamma_M w_M^2 + \gamma_F w_F^2) + \alpha w_M w_F$$

Disaggregation in econometric modelling

where:

$\tilde{h}_M$: number of hours per week the male partner prefers to work,

$\tilde{h}_F$: number of hours per week the female partner prefers to work,

μ : non-labour income per week,

w_M: after tax wage rate per hour for the male,

w_F : after tax wage rate per hour for the female,

Greek symbols, except μ, are parameters.

This model is extended by making the translation parameters, δ_M and δ_F, dependent upon:

(1) the number of hours worked by this individual one year ago (habit formation);

(2) the mean number of hours worked by other individuals in the same 'social group' (preference interdependence). A social group is simply defined as the set of individuals who share sex, age, and education characteristics. In the sample we distinguish four education levels and four age brackets; thus there are thirty-two different social groups;

(3) the log of household size. The means of the logs of household sizes in social groups are also used as explanatory variables.

For each household and for both δ_M and δ_F, four social groups are relevant: the individual's own social group (i.e. all other individuals who share the same characteristics), his or her partner's social group, the social group that only differs from the individual's own social group with respect to sex, and, finally, the social group that only differs from the partner's social group with respect to sex. The exact specifications for δ_M and δ_F are given in appendix 12A.

In itself the specification of the household labour-supply model is not very different from specifications found elsewhere in the literature, except for the introduction of preference interdependence. The introduction of the social groups is a rather primitive way of attempting to allow for Veblen and band-wagon effects. Since the social groups are partly defined in terms of age, one can also ascribe part of their influence on preference parameters as cohort effects. Although cohort effects is a more familiar term in economics than reference-group effects, their interpretation is similar. In any case, for empirical analysis, the exact interpretation of the social group influences is not very important.

250

The system of labour-supply equations (12.1) is consistent with utility maximization under a linear full-income constraint. The dependent variable is *preferred hours*, that is the number of hours each individual says he or she wants to work given their current wage rate. This information is elicited directly by means of a survey question. Since the question invites the respondent to state a preferred number of hours given the current after tax wage rate, the respondent is actually given a linear budget constraint. An exception is formed by respondents who are unemployed and receive unemployment (or welfare) benefits. They are being asked whether they are looking for a job. The answer is assumed to be the result of explicit utility comparison between not working while receiving a benefit and working an optimal number of hours while not receiving a benefit. In this situation, someone who is looking for a job is assumed to have a positive number of preferred hours, whilst someone who is not looking for a job is assumed to have a number of preferred hours equal to zero. In estimation, preferred hours are deemed to be the appropriate dependent variable, because this variable is not constrained by institutional constraints or demand-side factors.

For single people a completely analogous model has been specified for males and females separately. The parameters of the model are estimated for a 1985 labour-market survey (the so-called OSA-survey), which covers 850 families and 341 single people. For each respondent in the survey, all explanatory variables as well as the number of preferred hours and the number of hours actually worked are known. Various versions of the model have been estimated. For MICROFKA we use the most elaborate version of the model.

The estimated model shows:

small male wage effects on preferred hours,
sizeable female wage effects,
modest effects of unemployment benefits on the willingness to work,
a strong negative effect of household size on the preferred number of hours of the female in a household,
strong habit formation, especially for females,
modest, but statistically significant, preference interdependence.

(For further details the reader is referred to Kapteyn and Woittiez, 1986. Appendix 12A presents the full micro model.)

12.2 The macro model FK85

FK85 is a quarterly macro model of the Dutch economy. The model has been developed by the Netherlands Central Planning Bureau in 1985 and it is being used by the Netherlands government for short and medium term forecasting (CPB 1985).

The model consists of about 1,000 difference equations of which, approximately 200 are behavioural equations, divided into a 'real' part and a 'monetary' part. The 'real' part contains separate blocks for:

> consumption,
> investments,
> stocks,
> depreciation,
> import,
> export,
> production capacity,
> labour market,
> prices,
> taxes,
> social security.

For MICROFKA the labour market is most important, because here the original aggregate labour-supply equation is replaced by the micro simulation model. In FK85 employment is sub-divided in employment of firms, government, medical services, and other services. Only employment of firms is endogenous; for the other sectors, employment is equal to the demand for labour which is exogenous.

Aggregate labour supply, S, is explained by an exogenous demographic trend, S_t, combined with a discouraged worker effect, proxied by the discrepancy between S_t and demand by firms, government, and services.

$$\Delta S = \Delta S_t + 0.1 g_{10}(\Delta DF + \Delta EG + \Delta EM + \Delta EO - \Delta S_t)_{-1} \quad (12.2)$$

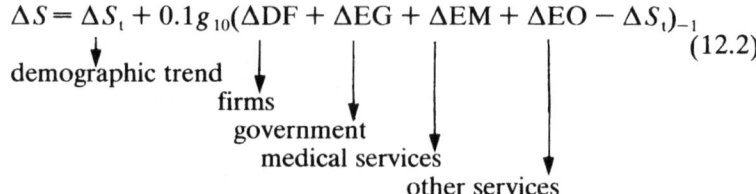

demographic trend
firms
government
medical services
other services

g_{10} is a lag function,

$$S = S_{-1} + \Delta S \qquad (12.3)$$

Labour supply remaining for firms, SF, becomes

$$SF = S - EG - EM - EO \qquad (12.4)$$

The demand for labour by firms, DF, is determined endogenously by the capacity utilization rate. Unemployment results from excess supply, $SF - DF$, and the unemployment function of Kooiman and Kloek (1979)

$$\Delta U = \Phi(\frac{SF - DF}{SF} / U_f \sqrt{2\pi})_{-1} \Delta \frac{SF - DF}{SF} \qquad (12.5)$$

where:

U = unemployment as a fraction of SF,
Φ = cumulative normal distribution function,
U_f = friction unemployment as fraction of SF (unemployment which still exists although demand is equal to supply).

Figure 12.1 summarizes the structure of the macro model of supply and demand so far. The left hand side shows total labour supply, of which a part, SF, remains for firms. Demand for labour by firms is determined elsewhere in the model. Between the blocks excess supply, $SF - DF$, determines a point on the graph of the unemployment function (12.5). The unemployment function is increasing in excess supply but less than proportionally, since a higher level of labour supply makes it easier to fill vacancies and this in itself tends to reduce unemployment. Unemployment becomes equal to $U \times SF$, whereas the remaining part of SF is the employment of firms, represented by the lower part of the right hand block. As an example, assume that for demographic reasons SF increases, then this will translate partly into an increase of unemployment and partly into an increase of employment, other things being equal.

12.3 MICROFKA

The macro labour-supply equation described in the previous section can hardly be seen as a description of behaviour of individuals. In particular, the fact that wages do not appear to play a role is somewhat remarkable. At the same time, the household

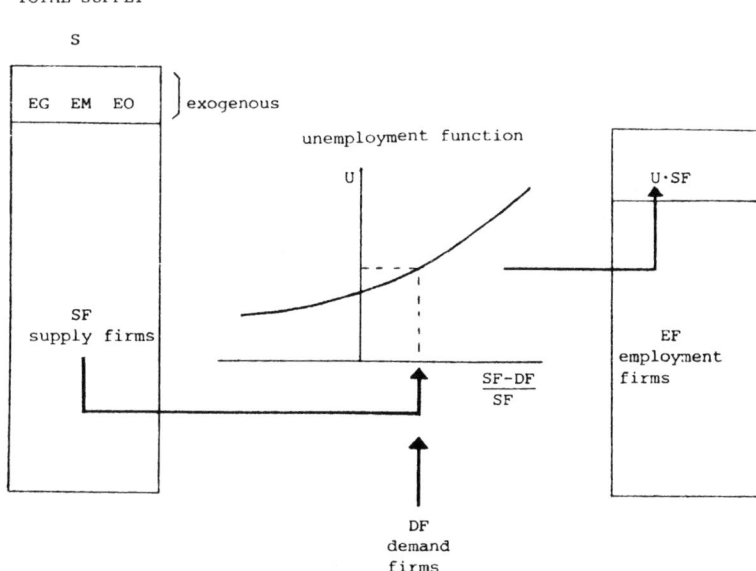

Figure 12.1 The macro model of labour supply and demand

labour-supply model introduced in section 12.1 does not allow for exact aggregation, for various reasons. In the first place, if the system (12.1) held in its simple form for all households then the aggregate labour-supply equation would contain not only average wages, but also second-order population moments of the wage distribution in society. In the second place, the dependent variables in the micro model are truncated at zero which makes perfect aggregation illusionary (cf. Blundell, 1988). Third, the decision to participate or not for the unemployed requires explicit utility comparison at the micro level, which again is impossible to model in terms of aggregates.

To overcome the aggregation problem, we adopt the following approach. For a sample of households we compute labour supply for each household using the micro model explained in section 12.1 and given the values of explanatory variables. Total labour supply in the sample is the sum of hours supplied by all households together and the aggregate labour supply in the population is derived by properly 'inflating' the sample total. The resulting level of aggregate labour supply is used in the macro model instead of

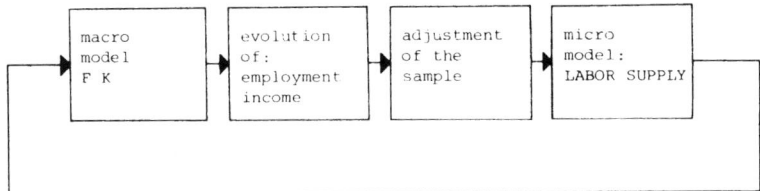

Figure 12.2 The simulation procedure

the original aggregate labour-supply equation. One may note that the new calculation of aggregate labour supply makes labour supply dependent on many more variables than before.

The next step is to solve the macro model for all other endogenous variables, given the total labour supply computed on the basis of the micro-simulation model. The computed values of the endogenous variables in the macro model are used in the next quarter to update the variables appearing as explanatory variables in the micro model. For example, if according to the macro model real wages increase by 1 per cent from one quarter to the next, then all wages in the sample are increased by 1 per cent. Similarly, if the macro model indicates a change in employment then in the sample we adjust employment by either laying off people or by assigning them a job, whichever is appropriate. In this way we may hope to keep the sample representative of the population in each period of the simulation.

Once the sample characteristics have been adjusted on the basis of the macro model's predictions we can again compute aggregate labour supply and feed this into the macro model, etc. The procedure is summarized in figure 12.2. Our procedure of using both a micro model and a macro model to simulate the economy is quite straightforward and can be used for any other micro relation which does not satisfy exact aggregation.

Let us now describe in more detail the operation of the combined micro-macro model. The simulation with MICROFKA starts with the OSA sample in the second quarter of 1981. Recall that the OSA data have been used for the estimation of the micro model. The only problem from the viewpoint of simulating the past is that the sample was drawn in 1985. Hence the sample has been reweighted in such a way that it can be considered to be representative of the population in 1981. Through 1985 the following procedure is followed for each quarter:

1   With the income and benefit growth rates, computed by FK85 in the previous quarter, for each household, incomes, wages, and benefits are adjusted proportionally.

2   When employment, computed by FK85 in the previous quarter, implies a reduction of employment in the sample, a number of employed people are laid off, i.e. their actual number of hours worked becomes zero. If FK85 implies a growth in employment, a number of unemployed people get a job. Their actual number of hours worked is then set equal to their preferred number of hours. Both people who get laid off and people who find a job are chosen randomly.

3   For each person who is unemployed, preferred hours are computed using the micro model. The utility level of working the preferred number of hours is compared with utility at zero hours and receiving a benefit. The benefit level is either the actual benefit observed in the sample, or, if being laid off during the simulation period, 80 per cent of previous wage income, taking into account a minimal social security level for total household income. The number of hours that yields the highest utility is defined as being the preferred number of hours.

4   The macro labour supply in years is computed using sample means. For each sub-sample (families, single men, single women) the mean labour supply is computed in hours per week. For employed people this is the number of hours per week actually worked and for unemployed people it is the preferred number of hours per week. Sample means are multiplied by population numbers and divided by 40 (a full-time job is assumed to amount to forty hours a week) to yield macro labour supply in years. Owing to the composition of the sample, labour supply thus defined only covers, people between twenty and sixty-five. The labour supply of people under twenty and over sixty-five is taken as exogenous and obtained from official statistics

$$S = \frac{1}{40} \, \mathrm{AF} \, \frac{1}{850} \, (\sum_{k=1}^{850} (h_{\mathrm{M}k} + h_{\mathrm{F}k}) + \sum_{\{k:\mathrm{M \, unemployed}\}} \tilde{h}_{\mathrm{M}k}$$

$$+ \sum_{\{k:\mathrm{F \, unemployed}\}} \tilde{h}_{\mathrm{F}k})$$

$$+ \frac{1}{40} \text{ ASM } \frac{1}{143} \left(\sum_{k=1}^{143} h_{Mk} + \sum_{\{k:\text{M unemployed}\}} \tilde{h}_{Mk} \right)$$

$$+ \frac{1}{40} \text{ ASM } \frac{1}{198} \left(\sum_{k=1}^{198} h_{Fk} + \sum_{\{k:\text{F unemployed}\}} \tilde{h}_{Fk} \right)$$

$$+ \text{ A65}$$

$$+ \text{ A20}$$

$$+ \text{ Au20}$$

where:

			age
AF	:	number of families in the Netherlands, male	< 65
ASM	:	number of single men in the Netherlands	20 < < 65
ASF	:	number of single women in the Netherlands	20 < < 65
A65	:	working population	> 65
A20	:	employed single persons	< 20
Au20	:	unemployed single persons	< 20
850	:	number of families in the sample, with male	< 65
143	:	number of single men in the sample	20 < < 65
198	:	number of single women in the sample	20 < < 65
k	:	household index	
h_{Mk}	:	number of hours per week actually worked, male	
h_{Fk}	:	number of hours per week actually worked, female	
$\tilde{h}_{Mk}$	:	preferred number of hours per week, male	
$\tilde{h}_{Fk}$	:	preferred number of hours per week, female	

Labour supply is determined by exogenous population growth (the A-variables) and endogenous mean hours per week in the sample.

5 The aggregate labour supply thus computed replaces the labour supply predicted by the original equation in FK85. Given aggregate labour supply, FK85 simulates the economy for one quarter. Next, the outcomes of the simulation of the economy for this quarter are used to update the exogenous variables for the micro model and the simulation starts again at point 1.

We notice that the simulation according to 1, through 5 involves a number of assumptions. The most important ones are:

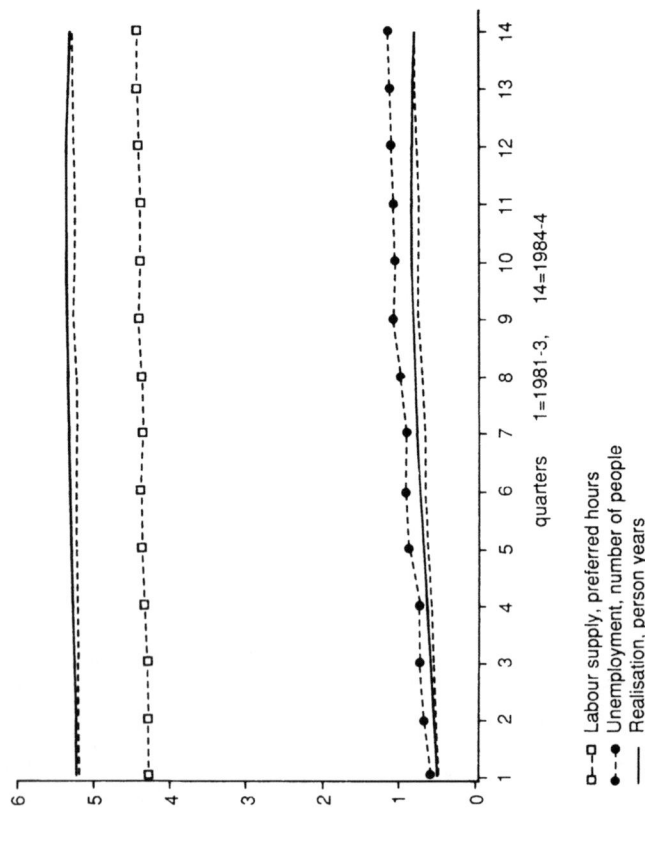

x mill.

quarters   1=1981-3,   14=1984-4

□--□ Labour supply, preferred hours
●--● Unemployment, number of people
●   Realisation, person years
---- Simulation with MICROFKA, person years

Figure 12.3 MICROFKA – labour supply and unemployment

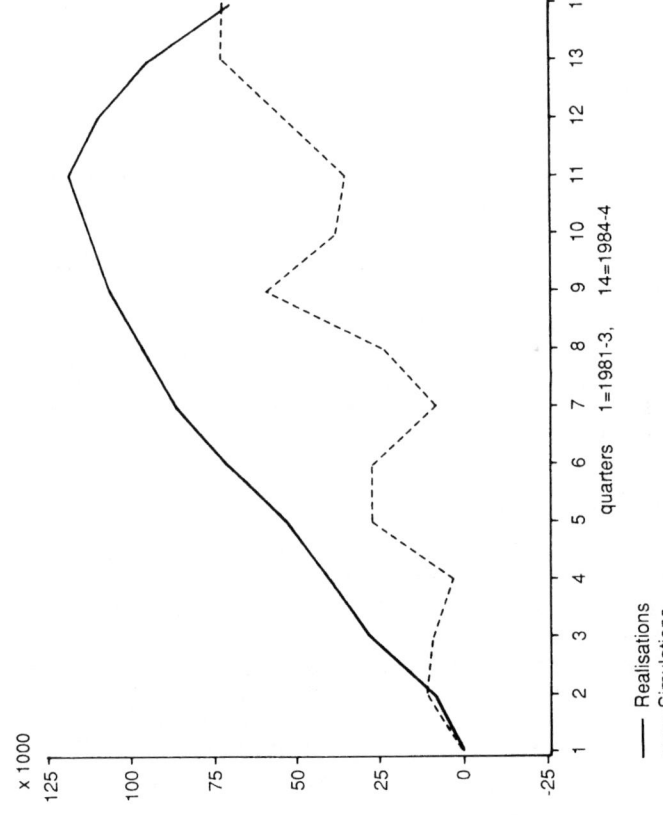

Figure 12.4 Labour supply (cumulative changes)

The relationships describing household labour supply are time invariant, i.e. the parameters of the micro model are constant over time. A person's preferred hours change only when an explanatory variable changes (wage rate, benefit, lagged hours, social group means). A person's actual hours change only in the case of losing or finding a job;
unearned incomes and wage rates of all households change proportionally;
when employment changes, for each person the probability of losing a job, or finding one, is the same.

Given the model it is clear that variations in macro labour supply can be caused by:

a change in employment: people in the sample can find or lose a job and so change hours from zero or their actual worked hours to their preferred hours;
demographic growth, incorporated by the exogenous A-variables;
a change in the explanatory variables of micro labour supply. Compared with the original equation for labour supply (12.2), in MICROFKA labour supply is explicitly dependent on wages, benefits, social group means, and demographics. These variables are of special interest in simulations of policy changes.

12.4 Simulation results

Fourteen quarters, 1981–3 through 1984, are simulated with MICROFKA. Table 12.1 shows some annual averages. Besides actual and simulated values for labour supply, employment, and unemployment, preferred labour supply is calculated on the basis of total number of preferred hours in the sample. We also present the number of unemployed calculated on the basis of the sample.

The simulated values are below the actual values although the relative differences are small. Since not all unemployed people want to work full time, the number of unemployed persons exceed the unemployment in person-years. According to the model, employed people on average would prefer to work less than they actually do since the aggregate preferred number of hours is about 20 per cent below labour supply as defined in the previous section. The graphs in figure 12.3 show labour supply and unemployment for each quarter. The scale of figure 12.3 makes it difficult to get a good feeling for the differences between actual and simulated labour supply. Figure 12.4 presents the differences between realiz-

Table 12.1 MICROFKA, labour market (x mill.)

	1981 $2e\frac{1}{2}$	1982	1983	1984
Labour supply				
actual number of person years	5.235	5.297	5.338	5.295
simulated number of person years	5.200	5.217	5.226	5.259
aggregate number of preferred hours	4.276	4.362	4.378	4.424
Employment				
actual number of person years	4.691	4.570	4.506	4.500
simulated number of person years	4.685	4.565	4.492	4.474
Unemployment				
actual number of person years	0.544	0.727	0.832	0.794
simulated number of person years	0.515	0.652	0.734	0.785
simulated number of persons	0.676	0.899	1.031	1.140

ations in a different way. The graphs in figure 12.4 represent cumulative changes occurring since 1981–3. Obviously, simulated labour supply shows more variation than the realized values do. According to the realizations, labour supply grows in the first eleven quarters; after that it decreases. In the fourteenth quarter, labour supply exceeds the level of 1981–3 by 69,000 person years. The simulated labour supply follows a path which fluctuates between quarters and adds 72,000 person years.

It should be noted here that the realizations are in fact rather shaky. Aggregate labour supply is measured by the sum of employment and unemployment. Employment in industry is measured twice a year by means of a large-scale survey. Unemployment is measured by the number of people who are registered at a labour exchange and who claim to be looking for a job of at least twenty hours a week. These people are then all assumed to be looking for a full-time job. Being registered at a labour exchange is a condition for being eligible for unemployment benefits. For people who are not eligible for unemployment benefits (like married females entering the labour market) there is no compelling reason to register at a labour exchange. For this reason official unemployment may be an under-estimate of the true unemployment rate. On the other hand the administration of the labour exchanges is notorious for its poor quality. Recent research suggests that at least 30 per cent of those who are registered as job seeking either have a job or are not available for paid work (they may have dropped out, be disabled or be in full-time education).

In figures 12.5 and 12.6 we present the simulated time paths for males and females separately. Here, also, the graphs show

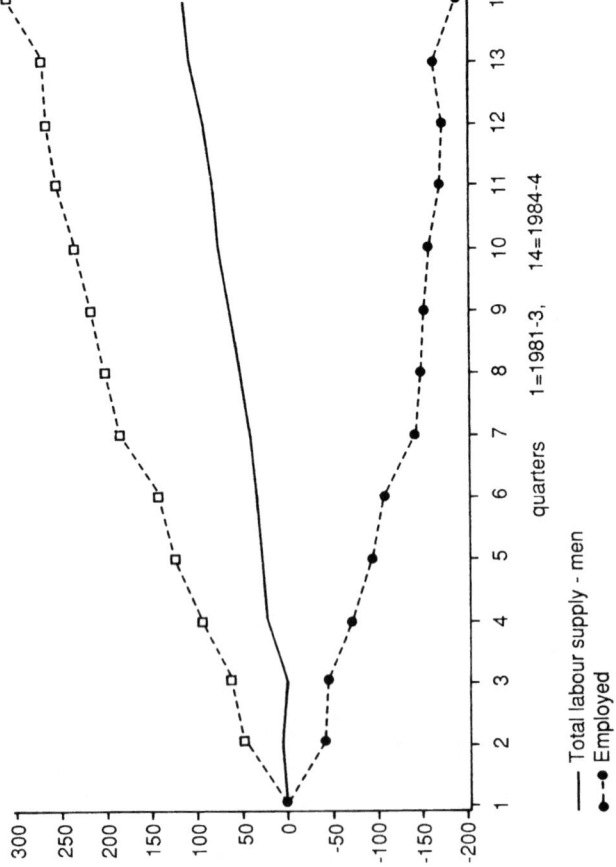

Figure 12.5 Labour supply – men (cumulative changes × 1,000)

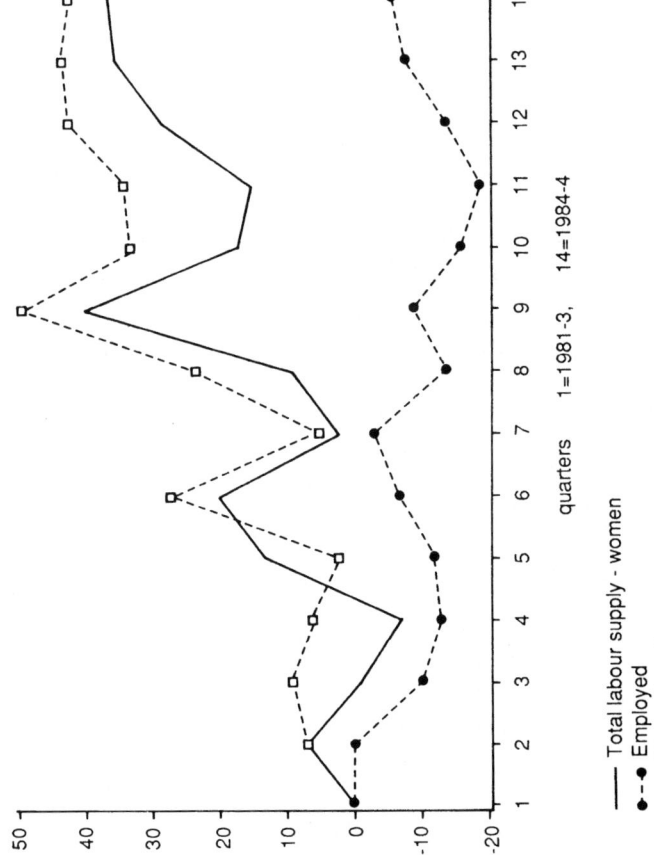

Figure 12.6 Labour supply – women (cumulative changes × 1,000)

Table 12.2 MICROFKA, mean hours per week by education level

education level	hours actually worked		preferred hours, unempl.	
	start	end	start	end
Men				
1	41.10	41.10	36.40	34.90
2	40.70	40.30	33.20	34.30
3	41.80	41.60	36.70	36.00
4	42.70	42.70	35.30	35.70
Women				
1	24.10	23.90	14.20	17.90
2	27.90	28.90	19.80	20.50
3	31.80	31.50	21.70	22.30
4	31.60	32.00	27.60	29.30

cumulative changes relative to the initial value. For men, labour supply follows an almost straight line resulting from a slowly increasing unemployment and a slowly decreasing employment. For women, labour supply fluctuates during the simulation period. The fluctuations are mainly caused by unemployed women whose preferred number of hours tend to vary quite considerably. Since the number of unemployed females in the sample is small, the observed fluctuations may be due to changes in the behaviour of only a few women.

In table 12.2 the changes in number of hours actually worked by employed and the preferred number of hours for unemployed people are presented for each education level, for men and women separately. Behaviour across the four education levels does not vary dramatically. The aggregate labour supply of men is mainly a function of population growth and macro employment while, for women, wages and reference group effects in the micro model play an important role as well.

Further macro results are shown in table 12.3. For some prices and quantities year-to-year changes are given in percentages. Shares and labour variables are given in percentage points and millions of person years respectively. To save space annual numbers are presented rather than quarterly figures.

The lower half of table 12.3 shows the same numbers calculated with FK85. The differences between the two simulations show up mainly for the labour market variables. Apparently a change in labour supply does not affect the rest of the model in the case of excess labour supply (which was the predominant situation during the first half of the 1980s). In FK85 the aggregate discouraged worker effect combined with population growth results in an

Table 12.3 MICROFKA and FK85

		1981 $2e\frac{1}{2}$	1982	1983	1984
Prices					
wages in private firms	%	2.6	6.2	3.5	0.7
consumption	%	4.2	3.9	2.8	1.9
exports (exclusive of energy)	%	2.8	0.6	3.2	3.7
labour costs	%	−8.1	4.8	1.6	−0.9
Quantities					
consumption	%	−0.2	−0.4	−0.2	0.9
investment by private firms	%	−4.2	−1.0	1.8	7.1
exports (exclusive of energy)	%	1.7	−2.9	10.3	10.8
imports	%	−0.0	2.5	5.8	6.3
net national income, NNI	%	4.1	−3.5	2.5	3.1
gross value added	%	0.8	−3.1	2.9	2.8
labour productivity	%	2.6	0.0	4.8	3.1
Shares					
capacity utilization rate		91.5	90.2	91.4	92.4
balance of payments % NNI		5.9	1.7	3.0	4.9
government deficit % NNI		−8.4	−9.8	−10.5	−10.2
taxes % NNI		28.4	29.3	27.0	25.8
total payroll taxes % NNI		20.2	22.3	24.4	23.0
Labour market					
supply	D	5.20	5.22	5.23	5.26
employment	D	4.68	4.57	4.49	4.47
unemployment	D	0.52	0.65	0.73	0.79
FK 85					
Prices					
wages in private firms	%	2.5	5.7	3.1	0.4
consumption	%	4.2	3.8	2.6	1.8
exports (exclusive of energy)	%	2.8	0.6	3.1	3.6
labour costs	%	−8.2	4.5	1.4	−1.0
Quantities					
consumption	%	−0.0	−0.2	−0.2	0.4
investment by private firms	%	−4.1	−0.8	1.4	6.6
exports (exclusive of energy)	%	1.7	−2.9	10.4	10.9
imports	%	0.1	2.7	5.7	6.1
net national income, NNI	%	4.1	−3.5	2.4	2.9
gross value added	%	0.8	−3.0	2.9	2.7
labour productivity	%	2.6	0.1	4.6	2.8
Shares					
capacity utilization rate		92.1	90.6	91.0	91.9
balance of payments % NNI		4.2	2.9	2.9	4.1
government deficit % NNI		−8.7	−9.6	−10.3	−9.6
taxes % NNI		29.0	28.5	27.8	27.4
total payroll taxes % NNI		20.6	22.0	24.6	23.5
Labour market					
supply	D	5.23	5.27	5.32	5.32
employment	D	4.70	4.61	4.52	4.49
unemployment	D	0.53	0.66	0.80	0.83

Notes: % = year-to-year changes in percentages.
  D = absolute values in millions of person years.

increase in labour supply by 99,000 person years. MICROFKA generates an increase of only 72,000.

These 72,000 are the result of the following factors:

a decrease in employment, by about 210,000 person years. In the sample a corresponding group is laid off. For these people labour supply is now defined as preferred hours instead of number of hours actually worked;

population growth (exogenous);

changes in the preferred hours of unemployed people resulting from changes of income and reference-group effects (as more people become unemployed, the mean number of hours in one's reference group decreases, and through preference inter-dependence this tends to lower the number of hours one wants to work).

The actual increase according to FK-data was 69,000 for those years.

12.5 Policy with MICROFKA

As part of the process of economic policy making, FK85 is commonly used to forecast effects of alternative government policies. Here we consider two examples of policies that might be pursued, and we analyse their effects by means of both FK85 and MICROFKA. In keeping with the customary approach to policy analysis of the Netherlands Central Planning Bureau, effects of policies are presented in the form of cumulative deviations from a reference path. The reference path describes the evolution of the economy under a regime of no policy change as presented in section 12.4.

First, suppose that either by collective bargaining between employers and labour unions or through direct government measures the autonomous change of wages is 2 per cent lower than would have occurred without these events. In table 12.4 the results of this autonomous decrease in wages are shown according to both FK85 and MICROFKA. Since it turns out that the labour market is the only part of both models where differences occur we only present the outcomes of both models with respect to labour-market variables.

For both models employment rises, relative to the reference path, as a result of decreasing labour costs. Since in FK85 labour supply is almost exogenous (except for a discouraged-worker effect) the increase in employment by 19,300 person years leads to an almost equal reduction in unemployment, by 18,000. In

Table 12.4 Wage changes using MICROFKA and FK85

		1981 $2e\frac{1}{2}$	1982	1983	1984
MICROFKA wages: −2%					
Labour market					
supply	D	−3.8	9.4	8.2	13.3
employment	D	2.2	4.5	9.4	20.2
unemployment	D	−6.0	4.9	−1.2	−6.9
FK 85 wages: −2%					
Labour market					
supply	D	−0.0	0.4	0.5	1.3
employment	D	2.4	4.6	8.8	19.3
unemployment	D	−2.4	−4.2	−8.3	−18.0

Note: D = difference with the reference path, 1,000 person years.

Table 12.5 Benefit changes using MICROFKA and FK85

		1981 $2e\frac{1}{2}$	1982	1983	1984
MICROFKA benefits: −10%					
Labour market					
supply	D	4.5	9.7	11.6	23.8
employment	D	0.0	−1.4	−2.3	−1.6
unemployment	D	4.5	11.1	13.9	25.4
FK 85 benefits −10%					
Labour market					
supply	D	−0.0	−0.1	−0.3	−0.4
employment	D	−0.2	−2.2	−4.1	−3.8
unemployment	D	0.2	2.1	3.7	3.4

Note: D = difference with the reference path, 1,000 person years.

MICROFKA employment is 20,200 better than in the reference path, but now the effect on unemployment is substantially more modest. However, this is mainly a matter of differences in the definition of unemployment.

In the reference simulation about 210,000 people are being laid off during the 1981–4 period. Whenever someone is being laid off, MICROFKA defines labour supply for this person as the preferred number of hours (which is often lower than the previous actual number of hours, especially for those who have been unemployed for a substantial period of time), whereas FK85 assumes that everyone who is unemployed is looking for a full-time job. Thus the FK85 definition of unemployment tends to be higher than that for MICROFKA. Accordingly, a reduction in unemployment due to a larger number of people employed tends to be lower in MICROFKA than in FK85.

As a second policy, consider the case where all unemployment benefits and welfare benefits (but not old age and disability benefits) are lowered by 10 per cent in the first quarter of the simulation. Now FK85 generates a decrease of the government budget deficit because payments of benefits decrease. Since the fall in disposable income of benefit recipients has a negative effect on private consumption (by half a percentage point) there is a slight fall in economic activity. In table 12.5 employment falls by 3,800 person years. Unemployment increases by almost the same amount.

The labour-market effects shown by MICROFKA are quite a bit different. The decrease in benefits leads to an increase in labour supply, mainly by unemployed people, by 23,800 person years. Obviously, the lower benefits make it preferable for more people to work than to receive a benefit and not work. The contrast between the outcomes of both models points to the fundamentally different theoretical basis of both models. In FK85, there is simply no role for incentive effects of the unemployment insurance system. It is only income effects of changes in the system that play a role, through their influence on consumption. MICROFKA, on the other hand, is fully neoclassical as far as labour supply is concerned.

12.6 Concluding remarks

This paper presents a first attempt to integrate a micro labour supply model and a full-blown macro model of the Dutch economy. So far, the results have to be taken only as an illustration of the potential of an integrated micro-macro model. There are various problems with the current version:

a rather small sample,
rather primitive dynamics in the micro model,
only limited institutional detail,
a short simulation period.

At this moment we are re-estimating the micro model for a much larger panel of households. The panel is bi-annual with surveys in April and October of each year, starting in April 1984.

This will give us a chance to improve the dynamics of the model and to base simulations on a much larger micro data set. Also, recently computer programs have been completed that describe the Dutch tax and social security system for each year since 1983. These programs will also be incorporated into the model so that a larger range of policies can be analysed.

Appendix 12A

$$h_{Mk} = \delta_{Mk} + \gamma_M w_{Mk} + \alpha w_{Fk} + \beta_M \mu_k^*,$$

$$k = 1, \ldots, N$$

$$\tilde{h}_{Fk} = \delta_{Fk} + \gamma_F w_{Fk} + \alpha w_{Mk} + \beta_F \mu_k^*,$$

$$\mu_k^* = \mu_k + \theta + \delta_{Mk} w_{Mk} + \delta_{Fk} w_{Fk} + \frac{1}{2}(\gamma_M w_{Mk}^2 + \gamma_F w_{Fk}^2)$$

$$+ \alpha w_{Mk} w_{Fk}$$

where $\tilde{h}_{Mk}$ = number of hours the male partner in household k would like to work per week,

$\tilde{h}_{Fk}$ = number of hours the female partner in household k would like to work per week,

w_{Mk} and w_{Fk} = after tax marginal wage rates of male and female, respectively,

μ_k = (weekly) non-labour income of household k,

N = total number of households,

$\theta, \gamma_M, \gamma_F, \alpha, \beta_M, \beta_F$ are parameters.

$$\delta_{Mk} = \delta_{M0} + \pi_M fs_k + \eta_{MM}[\zeta_M(h_{Mk}(-1) - \pi_M fs_k)$$

$$+ (1 - \zeta_M)\{\kappa_M(\tilde{h}_M(-1) - \pi_M \tilde{f}\tilde{s})$$

$$+ (1 - \kappa_M)(\lambda_{MM}(\tilde{h}_{MMk}(-1) - \pi_M \tilde{f}\tilde{s}_{Mk})$$

$$+ (1 - \lambda_{MM})(\tilde{h}_{FMk}(-1) - \pi_M \tilde{f}\tilde{s}_{Fk}))\}]$$

$$+ \eta_{MF}[\kappa_F(\tilde{h}_F(-1) - \pi_F \tilde{f}\tilde{s})$$

$$+ (1 - \kappa_F)(\lambda_{MF}(\tilde{h}_{MFk}(-1) - \pi_F \tilde{f}\tilde{s}_{Mk})$$

$$+ (1 - \lambda_{MF})(\tilde{h}_{FFk}(-1) - \pi_F \tilde{f}\tilde{s}_{Fk}))] + \eta_{MM}(1 - \zeta_M)v_{MMk}$$

$$+ \eta_{MF}v_{MFk}$$

$$\delta_{Fk} = \delta_{F0} + \pi_F fs_k + \eta_{FF}[\zeta_F(h_{Fk}(-1) - \pi_F fs_k)$$

$$+ (1 - \zeta_F)\{\kappa_F(\bar{h}_F(-1) - \pi_F \bar{\bar{fs}})$$

$$+ (1 - \kappa_F)(\lambda_{FF}(\bar{h}_{FFk}(-1) - \pi_F \bar{fs}_{Fk})$$

$$+ (1 - \lambda_{FF})(h_{MFk}(-1) - \pi_F \bar{fs}_{Mk}))\}] + \eta_{FM}[\kappa_M(\bar{h}_M(-1)$$

$$- \pi_M \bar{\bar{fs}}) + (1 - \kappa_M)(\lambda_{FM}(\bar{h}_{FMK}(-1) - \pi_M \bar{fs}_{Fk}(-1))$$

$$+ (1 - \lambda_{FM})(\bar{h}_{MMk}(-1) - \pi_M \bar{fs}_{Mk}))] + \eta_{FF}(1 - \zeta_F)v_{FFk}$$

$$+ \eta_{FM}v_{FMk}$$

where fs_k = logarithm of the size of household k,

$\bar{fs}_{Mk}$ = mean of the logarithm of the size of the households in the social group of the male in family k,

$\bar{fs}_{Fk}$ = mean of the logarithm of the size of the households in the social group of the female in family k,

$\bar{\bar{fs}}$ = mean of the logarithm of the size of the households in society as a whole,

π_M, π_F = are parameters,

$\bar{h}_{MMk}$ = mean hours worked per week by other men in the same social group as the male in family k,

$\bar{h}_{FFk}$ = mean hours worked per week by other women in the same social group as the female in family k,

$\bar{h}_{MFk}$ = mean hours worked per week by women in the same social group as the male in family k,

$\bar{h}_{FMk}$ = mean hours worked per week by men in the same social group as the female in family k,

$\bar{h}_M$ = the mean of the number of hours worked by all men in society,

$\bar{h}_F$ = the mean of the number of hours worked by all women in society,

$v_{MMk}, v_{FFk}, v_{MFk}, v_{FMk}$ = error terms that are uncorrelated with $\bar{h}_{MMk}, \bar{h}_{FFk}, \bar{h}_{MFk}$ and $\bar{h}_{FMk}$ and have zero-mean,

$\kappa_M, \kappa_F, \lambda_{MM}, \lambda_{FF}, \lambda_{MF}, \lambda_{FM}$ are parameters.

270

Chapter thirteen

Macro to micro linkage: some experiments with the UK commodity flow accounts

Terry Barker*

Introduction

The problem of linkage between aggregate macroeconomic models and models of different sectors of the economy is a serious one which until this book has hardly been addressed in the literature. Nevertheless, it has been a fairly common practice to use a macro model to provide estimates and forecasts of national economic aggregates, then to divide these up by one means or another to give disaggregated results. An example in the UK is the Department of Trade and Industry's Disaggregated Industrial System, which relies on the Treasury Model to provide the necessary aggregates. Yet little is known of the implications of such linkage for simulation or forecasting and little has been done on the comparison of different methods of linkage on forecasting performance. This chapter is intended to contribute some evidence on these implications and methods.

More work has been done on a similar problem, linkage between national macro models (Ball (ed.), 1973, Lambelet, 1985). This involves ensuring that, in a linked set of models covering the world economy, total exports equal total imports. However, the adding-up constraints are different, and there may be other differences in treatment required because disaggregation is by country rather than by industry or functional category.

The chapter is concerned first with setting out the basic methodological issues involved in linkage between macro variables and their components in macroeconometric models (section 13.1), then addressing a particular econometric question of how disaggregated variables can be related to their aggregate counterparts in macro-to-micro linkage (section 13.2). The relationships are

* The financial support provided by the UK Economic and Social Research Council's Macroeconomic Modelling Consortium and Cambridge Econometrics (1985) Ltd is gratefully acknowledged. The author is also grateful for the comments on the paper given by the participants to the conference.

271

illustrated by an application to the quarterly data of the UK Central Statistical Office's Commodity Flow Accounts (CFAs) of December 1986 in section 13.3.

13.1 Disaggregation in macroeconometric models

There are two approaches to disaggregation in macro models, as discussed by Almon (1986) in the more limited context of assessing industrial impacts of policy: the 'two-model' approach involves a macro model which is linked to a micro model or an industrial model, with or without repeated solutions of the two models to ensure consistency; the 'integrated model' approach incorporates all the relationships of interest in one model.

The two-model approach estimates a conventional macro model with a set of aggregate relationships for consumers' expenditures, investment, and other macro variables, disaggregating only when it is regarded as essential or useful. The disaggregation is not necessarily consistent in that the grouping chosen for one variable need not match that in other related variables. For example, it is usual to disaggregate exports into manufactures and other goods, but to disaggregate investment differently. This means that the implicit commodity demands are not necessarily the same as the implicit commodity supplies for the different groups of commodities distinguished in different parts of the model. The solution of the macro model might then be linked to a set of industrial outputs, the usual extra disaggregation which is required, by means of a simple input-output model, although other techniques could be used.

This approach is adopted by those who have a macro model already and wish to use it to give disaggregated results, or by those who for institutional reasons wish to keep disaggregated forecasts consistent with a fixed set of macro forecasts. The method was developed by Preston (1975) with the Wharton model and has reached perhaps its most sophisticated version in industrial linkage in the DRI model of the US economy (Eckstein, 1983). Chapter 12 above by ten Hacken and Kapteyn gives a description of the approach as used in linking a micro model with a macro model with repeated solutions of both models.

In the DRI model the industrial sub-model contains a large number of production, employment, and investment equations that relate these variables to a set of 'generated' industrial outputs obtained by applying classification converters to final demand variables to obtain a final demand vector in the industrial classification. This vector is then multiplied by $(I - A)^{-1}$ where A is the input-output matrix to obtain the generated industrial outputs which are in turn related to actual output. The macro model is not re-solved using the results of the industrial sub-model.

The second approach is to estimate the model at the full level of disaggregation desired, and then to sum the components to obtain total investment, imports, exports, gross domestic product, and other macro variables. There are no independent macro equations for these variables. (Consumers' expenditure is an exception because there are theoretical reasons, and the budget constraint, making the estimation of an aggregate equation desirable rather than estimation of a set of individual expenditure equations. Disaggregation by type of household is another matter.)

This second approach is an option for industrial linkage although it would seem unnecessary in the case of many micro models, such as the Dutch labour-supply model, in which the micro model is disaggregating only one or two equations of the macro model, in that repeated solutions of the two models (as described in chapter 12) will achieve much the same results.

The integrated modelling approach was adopted by the Cambridge Growth Project for the UK economy (Barker and Peterson, 1987) and by a number of other groups for other economies, for example the Norwegian model MODAG (Bergan, Cappelen, Longva, and Stolen, 1986) or the INFORUM models (Almon, 1986, Nyhus, 1986). This approach, in principle at least, ensures consistency and coherence between the disaggregated simulations and projections and the aggregated ones. In the first two-model approach it is always necessary to have a residual sector showing the difference between the sum of the components and the total from the macro model. The question then arises whether the total should be adjusted or replaced and the macro model resolved, or whether the components should be scaled to add to the macro total.

scores on internal consistency, so that simulated changes at the micro level will also show as changes in macro variables. In the two-model approach, without repeated solutions to achieve consistency, the macro solution is unaffected. A related advantage in the integrated approach is that a coherent explanation can be given for the feed-back between micro variables and macro variables, a feature wholly lacking if the macro results are fixed.

The two-model approach scores on ease of implementation but by far its most attractive feature is the fact that the same structure can be adopted in order to provide disaggregated projections from a number of macro models of an economy, assuming a common set of aggregate macro variables. It is aspects of this feature which are the subject matter of the rest of this chapter.

13.2 Macro-to-micro linkage

Assuming that the two-model approach to disaggregation, without feed-back, is being followed, the question to be addressed is: how should disaggregated variables be related to their aggregate counterparts and how should the adding-up restriction be imposed, if at all? The problem in forecasting is that the only information which is usually available is the forecasts of the macro model and the past values of the disaggregated variables. (Any further link with other variables disaggregated in a similar fashion is a second-order question, ignored in the analysis below.) This rules out theoretically appealing systems of consistent disaggregation such as the linear expenditure system or the Rotterdam system for consumers' expenditures, because prices are not available.

Some of the possible methods of disaggregation, given these limitations, are:

1   use of simple ratios calculated from the most recent input-output table or other data source;
2   estimation of single equation econometric relationships with or without adding up imposed on the results;
3   estimation of a system of relationships with adding-up imposed in the estimation.

13.3 Some experiments with the UK commodity flow accounts (CFAs)

The data

The CFAs are a set of quarterly, constant (1980) priced, accounts for the UK economy 1979Q1 to 1986Q2 disaggregated by forty-nine sectors ('commodities'), mostly corresponding to principal products of industries in the 1980 Standard Industrial Classification. The supplies are divided into home output and imports and the demands into consumer, government, fixed investment, stockbuilding and industrial domestic demand, and export demand. Supplies and demands are not balanced (one purpose of constructing the accounts has been to identify the sources of the residual error in the National Accounts) and the accounts also show the demand-less-supply discrepancy for each sector. The quarterly data are seasonally adjusted. The set of accounts used here was published in December 1986 and is consistent with the 1986 edition of UK CSO *National Income and Expenditure* (the

Blue Book). A description of the derivation and uses of the CFAs has been published in *Economic Trends* (Astin, 1985).

It is clear that the data on the domestic components of demand are partly constructed by means of a deterministic procedure involving the use of fixed converters derived from input-output tables with vectors of final demand and industrial output. In these cases the estimated forecasting systems are partly representing official procedures and the results need interpretation as such. However, the data on output and foreign trade seems to have been collected by grouping of direct observations.

For the purposes of the macro-to-micro experiments, the data for the last six quarters (1985Q1 to 1986Q2) has been omitted from the sample period in the regressions and used as in the tests of the forecasting ability of different methods, although this is not strictly necessary for the tests.

Macro-to-micro systems

Four systems for generating disaggregated data for final-demand vectors, imports, and output have been tested. (Note that the generation of final-demand vectors is a critical link in the derivation of industrial output forecasts from macro models.) A further system, utilizing the input-output table and generating 'calculated' domestic outputs, which are then regressed on actual output, is planned but not yet implemented. The systems are:

1   extrapolated growth (EG). The average growth rates of the last four periods of the sample are extrapolated to provide forecasts. Adding up is not guaranteed;
2   fixed ratios (FR). The ratios of each component to the total are held at their average value for the forecast period. Adding up is guaranteed;
3   unrestricted single equation regressions (UR). Regressions (described below) are estimated on the sample data and fully dynamic forecasts made over the forecast period. Adding up is not guaranteed;
4   restricted single equation regressions (RR). The regressions are restricted so that less significant parameters are zero. Adding up is not guaranteed.

Criteria for evaluating the systems

The test undertaken to evaluate the systems is the calculation of root-mean-squared-errors (RMSE) for quarterly forecasts outside the period of estimation. Many further tests can be envisaged of forecasting ability, structural stability, and medium-term forecasting performance, but the RMSE test serves well for comparative summaries.

The single-equation regressions

The single-equation method for projecting each component of supply and demand starts with the estimation by OLS of the equation:

$$Y = B1 + B2*AGY$$
$$+ B3*AGY(-1)$$
$$+ B4*AGY(-4)$$
$$+ B5*Y(-1)$$
$$+ B6*Y(-4)$$
$$+ B7*TIME \tag{13.1}$$

where Y is the series of quarterly observations on the CFA component (1979 Q1 to 1985 Q1),
AGY is the series of the corresponding component for the whole economy,
TIME is a time trend (1980 Q1 = 0),
and (-1) indicates a lag of one quarter.

The estimating equation is not log-linear because it is used for stockbuilding and discrepancies, both of which are often negative. The linear form also means that the expected values of the components will automatically add up to the whole-economy totals. (This is a property of OLS with linear systems, although it only holds if all the independent variables appear in all the component equations. If some independent variables are omitted because the equation is badly behaved, or if estimated parameters are restricted, then such adding up is not guaranteed.)

The restricted versions of equation (13.1) are found after a procedure which starts with the OLS estimates, then progressively restricts to zero the least significant estimates for $B2$ to $B7$ until the absolute values of all the t-ratios are greater than one, and that for the time trend is greater than two.

The equations as specified were modified for the effects of the miners' strike of 1984–5 by introducing dummy variables for 1984

Q1 to Q4 into the equations for coal, coke, and petroleum products.

Results and conclusions

The main results are presented as sets of tables showing RMSE for the four systems of forecasting. Tables 13.1 to 13.4 summarize the results for each system; appendix tables 13A.1 to 13A.9 give the observed values over the forecast period and the forecasts at the level of each component of supply and demand, together with RMSE for individual commodities.

The results can be described in two sets of conclusions, the first being those expected from the data, statistical theory, and previous work and the second being less expected and more challenging.

Expected results:

1   The errors increase the further into the future the projections are made. There are occasional instances where this does not occur, but generally the errors are about twice as high in the sixth quarter, compared to the first. In the case of the extrapolated growth model, the errors for imports rise catastrophically; but this is due to explosive growth of forecast gas imports, which in practice would be removed from the forecast. (It is worth noting that, if any of the systems were to be used, several of such outlying forecasts would be removed.)

2   The restrictions to significant coefficients improve the RMSE for five out of the eleven categories shown, although even here the improvement is not substantial. However, the scale of the improvement in these instances is enough to justify restricting the equations so that the coefficients are significant.

3   Comparing forecasts of different components of domestic demand, those for government, industrial, and consumer demand are more accurate, in relation to their absolute magnitudes, than those for fixed investment or stockbuilding. This only reflects the greater variance in the data on investment. The low errors for industrial demand may be a result of the method used.

Less expected results:

1   The fixed ratio system substantially out-performs the others for forecasts of exports and imports. This result is all the

Table 13.1 Extrapolated growth model (EG)—RMSE of quarterly forecasts, £(1980)million

	Output	Import	Supply	Cons. exp.	Gov.	GDF CF	Stk. bldg	Export	Ind. dem.	Demand	D-S
1985 Q1	40.2	33.7	63.6	15.5	8.3	20.3	27.8	18.5	11.2	60.2	62.0
Q2	64.6	46.4	94.2	16.2	10.5	22.0	24.2	22.5	16.4	72.4	74.2
Q3	75.3	70.8	114.2	20.1	8.7	18.9	17.1	42.3	17.5	88.0	63.0
Q4	91.7	157.2	132.2	28.5	10.2	24.3	27.5	37.9	21.9	97.0	92.4
1986 Q1	119.0	569.2	181.4	31.8	10.4	20.5	22.8	59.5	29.3	134.0	98.2
Q2	107.3	2583.0	174.8	35.2	13.4	32.8	30.7	66.1	25.5	136.8	89.5
ALL 6 QUARTERS	83.0	576.7	126.7	24.5	10.3	23.1	25.0	41.1	20.3	98.1	79.9

Source: UK CSO CFAs, Dec. 1986.

Table 13.2 Fixed-ratio model (FR)—RMSE of quarterly forecasts, £(1980)million

	Output	Import	Supply	Cons. exp.	Gov.	GDF CF	Stk. bldg	Export	Ind. dem.	Demand	D-S
1985 Q1	47.4	30.6	74.2	15.8	7.3	28.8	36.9	18.8	11.3	69.8	162.0
Q2	71.0	23.7	89.1	15.6	8.2	12.2	312.3	18.3	18.2	65.4	108.0
Q3	80.7	23.9	95.3	17.5	7.7	16.6	58.9	28.6	16.7	68.7	76.6
Q4	85.5	27.6	98.4	28.0	9.9	18.9	94.9	22.9	19.4	86.4	155.7
1986 Q1	115.7	33.3	137.7	31.9	9.5	15.2	394.4	31.4	21.0	75.5	134.2
Q2	99.3	36.3	123.9	31.8	11.4	17.7	83.5	41.3	19.8	87.4	102.8
ALL 6 QUARTERS	83.2	29.2	103.1	23.4	9.0	18.2	163.5	26.9	17.7	75.5	123.2

Source: UK CSO CFAs, Dec. 1986.

Table 13.3 Single–equation unrestricted model (UR)—RMSE of quarterly forecasts, £(1980)million

	Output	Import	Supply	Cons exp.	Gov.	GDF CF	Stk. bldg	Export	Ind. dem.	Demand	D-S
1985 Q1	58.4	38.4	78.5	14.3	5.7	24.8	21.0	33.1	9.0	69.0	78.5
Q2	56.1	36.9	78.3	15.4	8.8	15.7	24.2	34.0	14.9	67.4	73.5
Q3	72.7	39.7	99.4	16.9	5.9	16.6	23.9	48.6	17.5	103.3	70.5
Q4	88.8	47.7	111.1	24.1	9.0	16.5	32.4	53.7	18.4	129.2	92.5
1986 Q1	120.9	55.8	157.9	40.8	8.0	17.2	24.6	62.6	26.4	143.2	101.5
Q2	101.1	71.3	156.1	45.0	11.5	17.3	30.2	79.1	21.4	179.9	109.2
ALL 6 QUARTERS	83.0	48.3	113.6	26.1	8.1	18.0	26.0	51.8	17.9	115.3	87.6

Source: UK CSO CFAs, Dec. 1986.

Table 13.4 Single–equation restricted model (RR)—RMSE of quarterly forecasts £(1980)million

	Output	Import	Supply	Cons exp.	Gov.	GDF CF	Stk. bldg	Export	Ind. dem.	Demand	D-S
1985 Q1	52.9	36.0	79.7	17.0	6.2	25.6	22.9	31.4	10.1	66.7	73.3
Q2	57.0	35.1	76.4	17.0	7.4	14.0	25.9	36.0	16.3	66.2	73.9
Q3	70.8	39.7	97.1	18.2	5.9	16.7	24.9	47.8	18.6	98.2	75.2
Q4	84.1	49.1	111.0	24.9	8.8	15.9	31.7	48.2	20.9	120.0	87.8
1986 Q1	119.2	57.9	149.5	43.6	8.7	17.1	24.5	59.4	27.6	135.8	87.4
Q2	100.5	76.8	156.3	45.6	11.2	18.5	31.7	78.9	25.4	176.7	102.2
ALL 6 QUARTERS	80.7	49.1	111.7	27.7	8.2	18.0	26.9	50.3	19.8	110.6	83.3

Source: UK CSO CFAs, Dec. 1986.

more striking because these data are more firmly based than the data for domestic demand components. The improvements are across the board, and appear for nearly all the components.

2 The most simple model of extrapolated growth does best on the one-quarter-ahead forecasts for most of the series considered. This points to the scale of the improvements which may be possible with the introduction of more sophisticated error-correction mechanisms in the estimated equations or the use of Box-Jenkins methods, although the data series are very short.

3 The effects of movements in the macro variables on their components, with the exception of those in total exports and imports, appear to be small and poorly determined. It may be that developments at the industrial level may be more important than those at the macro level.

4 Three of the systems each gave substantially different forecasts for many of the same variables. This indicates that there may be considerable room for mixing the different methods, choosing those appropriate to each component of demand or commodity group, so as to improve the overall forecast.

Appendix 13A

Table 13A.1 Observed totals for UK commodity flow accounts

		1984		1985				1986	
		Q3	Q4	Q1	Q2	Q3	Q4	Q1	Q2
COMMODITY SUPPLY									
Domestic supply	(£m80)	111268	112598	113891	114323	114361	115741	115835	116895
Import supply	(£m80)	17282	18123	17686	17501	17496	18008	17706	18154
Total supply	(£m80)	128550	130721	131577	131824	131857	133749	133541	135049
COMMODITY DEMAND									
Industrial demand	(£m80)	49756	50272	50915	51034	50788	51436	51153	51902
Consumer demand	(£m80)	36538	37068	37448	37597	38295	38621	38977	39610
Gov't demand	(£m80)	12793	12753	12712	12790	12711	12780	12768	12780
Investment demand	(£m80)	11544	11550	12123	11172	11571	11462	11803	11485
Stockbuilding	(£m80)	−157	334	29	393	62	120	489	−96
Domestic demand	(£m80)	110474	111977	113227	112986	113427	114419	115190	115681
Export demand	(£m80)	17297	18158	18189	18514	17986	18448	18026	18630
Total demand	(£m80)	127771	130135	131416	131500	131413	132867	133216	134311
Residual error	(£m80)	−779	−586	−161	−324	−444	−882	−325	−738
CHANGE IN SUPPLY		(% change on corresponding quarter of previous year)							
Domestic supply	(%pa)	3.1	3.0	3.7	3.6	2.8	2.8	1.7	2.2
Import supply	(%pa)	9.3	10.9	9.4	3.0	1.2	−0.6	0.1	3.7
Total supply	(%pa)	3.9	4.1	4.4	3.6	2.6	2.3	1.5	2.4

CHANGE IN DEMAND

Industrial demand	(%pa)	3.2	2.9	3.9	3.6	2.1	2.3	0.5	1.7
Consumer demand	(%pa)	0.8	2.1	3.2	2.2	4.8	4.2	4.1	5.4
Gov't demand	(%pa)	1.6	0.2	0.8	0.4	-0.6	0.2	0.4	-0.1
Investment demand	(%pa)	11.7	5.9	10.1	-1.9	0.2	-0.8	-2.6	2.8
Domestic demand	(%pa)	2.6	2.9	3.8	2.9	2.7	2.2	1.7	2.4
Export demand	(%pa)	7.1	9.3	7.8	10.2	4.0	1.6	-0.9	0.6
Total demand	(%pa)	3.2	3.7	4.4	3.9	2.9	2.1	1.4	2.1

Source: UK CSO CFAs, Dec. 1986.

Table 13A.2 Extrapolated growth model (EG)–short-term forecasts for whole economy by aggregating components

		1984		1985				1986	
		Q3	Q4	Q1	Q2	Q3	Q4	Q1	Q2
COMMODITY SUPPLY									
Domestic supply	(£m80)	111312	112394	113402	114321	115264	116230	117219	118231
Import supply	(£m80)	17040	18019	18421	18963	20125	24360	44160	143180
Total supply	(£m80)	128351	130412	131823	133284	135389	140590	161379	261412
COMMODITY DEMAND									
Industrial demand	(£m80)	49775	50181	50520	50863	51208	51557	51910	52265
Consumer demand	(£m80)	36543	37269	37429	37590	37753	37917	38081	38248
Gov't demand	(£m80)	12795	12751	12771	12792	12813	12834	12856	12878
Investment demand	(£m80)	11502	11569	11784	12006	12235	12471	12715	12967
Stockbuilding	(£m80)	−122	446	−13	−13	−13	−13	−13	−13
Domestic demand	(£m80)	110492	112214	112491	113238	113996	114766	115549	116345
Export demand	(£m80)	17118	18016	18286	18567	18857	19158	19470	19794
Total demand	(£m80)	127609	130230	130778	131805	132853	133924	135019	136139
Residual error	(£m80)	−742	−182	−1046	−1479	−2536	−6666	−26360	−125273
CHANGE IN SUPPLY		(% change on corresponding quarter of previous year)							
Domestic supply	(%pa)	3.0	2.8	3.0	3.7	3.6	3.4	3.4	3.4
Import supply	(%pa)	7.7	11.5	11.5	12.5	18.1	35.2	139.7	655.1
Total supply	(%pa)	3.6	3.9	4.1	4.9	5.5	7.8	22.4	96.1

CHANGE IN DEMAND

Industrial demand	(%pa)	3.2	2.6	2.8	3.3	2.9	2.7	2.8	2.8
Consumer demand	(%pa)	0.5	2.6	2.9	2.4	3.3	1.7	1.7	1.8
Gov't demand	(%pa)	1.5	0.4	1.3	0.5	0.1	0.7	0.7	0.7
Investment demand	(%pa)	11.6	6.6	6.6	5.6	6.4	7.8	7.9	8.0
Domestic demand	(%pa)	2.4	3.0	3.1	3.2	3.2	2.3	2.7	2.7
Export demand	(%pa)	5.6	10.0	7.5	10.7	10.2	6.3	6.5	6.6
Total demand	(%pa)	2.8	3.9	3.7	4.2	4.1	2.8	3.2	3.3

Source: UK CSO CFAs, Dec. 1986.

Table 13A.3 Extrapolated growth model (EG)–RMSE of commodity forecasts, £(1980)million

	Output	Import	Supply	Cons exp.	Gov.	GDF CF	Stk. bldg	Export	Ind. dem.	Demand	D-S
1 Agriculture, etc.	198.5	29.7	219.4	17.3	2.0	0.6	34.7	48.3	38.5	101.7	38.2
2 Coal mining	657.7	106.0	650.9	24.3	0.7	0.0	97.4	21.9	91.0	255.9	242.3
3 Coke	29.6	70.6	13.1	6.1	0.2	0.0	0.0	14.6	11.2	38.9	12.3
4 Min. oil and nat. gas	219.7	85.8	223.5	0.0	0.0	0.0	57.2	169.8	49.6	176.1	52.5
5 Petroleum products	79.2	551.3	567.5	19.1	8.0	0.0	67.3	55.9	32.1	81.5	321.5
6 Electricity, etc.	104.7	15.7	98.8	51.8	5.6	0.0	0.0	24.6	26.7	94.7	45.3
7 Public gas supply	69.9	25412.7	59.8	63.9	2.7	0.0	0.0	1.5	3.9	66.3	19.2
8 Water supply	5.1	0.0	5.1	0.4	1.3	0.0	0.0	0.0	2.4	1.2	5.2
9 Minerals and ores nes	8.2	60.7	66.1	0.0	0.8	0.0	11.5	63.9	11.6	58.5	39.9
10 Iron and steel	75.6	12.7	81.4	0.0	0.0	0.5	27.2	36.6	31.4	61.6	35.8
11 Non-ferrous metals	70.8	41.2	112.5	0.0	0.0	0.0	70.7	39.9	51.8	167.5	43.2
12 Non-metallic min.pr	19.5	13.7	35.6	1.3	1.7	1.7	6.5	15.7	17.2	24.1	60.9
13 Chemicals, mm fibres	187.9	37.7	254.6	6.0	13.3	1.7	31.7	108.2	86.2	197.2	38.6
14 Metal goods nes	109.3	25.8	145.4	2.9	4.2	14.2	9.4	21.8	23.4	44.4	148.0
15 Mech. engineering	169.0	41.2	216.7	3.5	11.6	104.9	66.7	29.9	69.7	110.3	159.0
16 Office machinery	343.8	410.1	750.6	1.8	1.7	33.4	34.5	344.9	21.7	565.6	64.0
17 Elect. engineering	220.3	75.1	291.2	44.1	56.9	38.0	79.8	68.0	52.9	325.0	154.8
18 Motor vehicles	105.9	84.3	195.6	119.9	12.0	42.4	52.6	38.5	13.3	218.8	113.8
19 Aerospace equipment	43.4	134.1	107.2	0.0	122.7	199.3	66.6	24.0	1.9	200.9	62.5
20 Ships, etc.	13.1	152.0	99.0	1.7	6.2	137.7	52.8	43.2	3.0	130.9	58.8
21 Other vehicles	8.1	5.3	10.1	1.7	0.0	5.4	8.8	9.4	11.2	11.0	13.3
22 Instr. engineering	20.1	46.2	65.6	7.4	6.5	21.5	8.5	28.1	1.2	26.8	20.0
23 Manufactured food	31.7	38.9	33.7	89.4	8.6	0.0	105.5	22.8	29.0	207.9	194.2
24 Alcoholic drinks	14.4	14.7	17.0	16.8	0.0	0.0	16.6	12.6	1.9	38.1	17.8
25 Tobacco	37.6	30.4	53.1	21.0	0.0	0.0	9.3	6.9	0.2	48.6	19.3

26 Textiles	28.4	26.3	10.4	2.2	0.5	1.0	17.6	29.3	6.7	16.9	24.3
27 Clothing and footwear	13.9	33.7	25.3	8.2	2.5	0.0	32.3	9.7	3.1	71.7	36.3
28 Timber and furniture	11.7	27.7	38.4	7.6	2.7	6.0	19.7	6.9	7.6	16.3	113.7
29 Paper and board	24.9	49.4	72.0	0.5	2.8	1.6	7.5	26.1	26.0	51.2	39.5
30 Books, etc.	14.5	20.2	33.3	3.0	3.5	0.0	8.5	9.0	8.9	24.3	22.5
31 Rubber, plastic prd	29.7	18.2	16.7	1.0	1.7	1.2	10.7	14.3	9.2	33.2	29.7
32 Other manufactures	54.5	106.6	159.7	45.9	1.5	0.2	52.7	77.4	0.6	128.0	49.8
33 Construction	150.0	0.4	150.3	29.6	35.8	368.2	65.3	0.2	70.5	124.9	223.8
34 Distribution, etc.	215.3	8.0	207.1	89.5	10.5	24.6	0.0	58.3	24.2	82.8	78.3
35 Hotels and catering	51.5	17.1	39.1	35.4	7.1	0.0	0.0	19.7	2.1	31.8	30.7
36 Rail transport	62.5	1.8	60.8	4.9	1.3	0.0	0.0	0.9	15.4	19.9	22.2
37 Other land trans.	24.5	1.7	23.5	12.5	1.3	2.9	0.0	0.6	9.9	21.6	65.8
38 Sea, air and other	133.7	91.5	225.0	19.4	1.8	2.1	0.0	56.9	35.5	88.9	61.2
39 Communications	25.1	9.7	35.4	18.0	7.1	33.4	0.0	28.1	3.8	53.5	28.1
40 Business services	91.2	52.9	153.9	13.4	1.8	0.8	0.0	157.1	28.6	147.5	434.5
41 Misc. services	13.3	5.9	16.3	16.4	51.6	28.2	0.0	17.5	7.2	45.9	17.7
42 PAD	20.4	0.0	20.4	0.0	21.1	0.0	0.0	0.0	0.0	21.1	20.3
43 NHS and public ed.	7.6	0.0	7.6	0.0	25.4	0.0	0.0	0.0	0.0	25.4	25.0
44 Own. of dwellings	24.3	0.0	24.3	16.4	0.0	0.0	0.0	0.0	0.0	16.4	28.7
45 Tourist exp.	0.0	55.7	55.7	178.2	0.0	0.0	0.0	66.1	0.0	115.3	35.0
46 Sales by F. B.	0.0	0.0	0.0	10.8	30.4	2.4	0.0	13.6	1.9	45.1	18.8
47 Net indirect tax	46.8	0.0	46.8	37.9	4.9	23.4	0.0	0.0	50.1	46.8	0.0
48 Unallocated	180.7	1.5	179.2	0.0	0.0	0.0	1.7	1.4	0.0	2.3	177.1
49 Nat. A/c – CFA	0.0	236.0	236.0	151.5	21.2	36.0	94.2	170.7	0.0	321.7	351.1
All commodities	83.0	576.7	126.7	24.5	10.3	23.1	25.0	41.1	20.3	98.1	79.9

Source: UK CSO CFAs, Dec. 1986.

Table 13A.4 Fixed-ratio model (FR)– short-term forecasts for whole economy by aggregating components (1 to 48)

		1984		1985				1986	
		Q3	Q4	Q1	Q2	Q3	Q4	Q1	Q2
COMMODITY SUPPLY									
Domestic supply	(£m80)	111312	112394	113901	114333	114371	115751	115845	116905
Import supply	(£m80)	17040	18019	17652	17467	17462	17973	17672	18119
Total supply	(£m80)	128351	130412	131552	131800	131833	133724	133517	135024
COMMODITY DEMAND									
Industrial demand	(£m80)	49775	50181	50918	51037	50791	51439	51156	51905
Consumer demand	(£m80)	36543	37269	37507	37656	38355	38682	39038	39673
Gov't demand	(£m80)	12795	12751	12710	12788	12709	12778	12766	12778
Investment demand	(£m80)	11502	11569	12124	11173	11572	11463	11804	11486
Stockbuilding	(£m80)	-122	446	30	401	63	122	499	-98
Domestic demand	(£m80)	110492	112214	113289	113055	113491	114484	115263	115744
Export demand	(£m80)	17118	18016	18131	18455	17928	18389	17968	18570
Total demand	(£m80)	127609	130230	131419	131510	131419	132873	133231	134315
Residual error	(£m80)	-742	-182	-133	-290	-414	-851	-285	-709
CHANGE IN SUPPLY		(% change on corresponding quarter of previous year)							
Domestic supply	(%pa)	3.0	2.8	3.5	3.7	2.7	3.0	1.7	2.2
Import supply	(%pa)	7.7	11.5	6.9	3.7	2.5	-0.3	0.1	3.7
Total supply	(%pa)	3.6	3.9	3.9	3.7	2.7	2.5	1.5	2.4

CHANGE IN DEMAND

Industrial demand	(%pa)	3.2	2.6	3.6	3.7	2.0	2.5	0.5	1.7
Consumer demand	(%pa)	0.5	2.6	3.1	2.6	5.0	3.8	4.1	5.4
Gov't demand	(%pa)	1.5	0.4	0.8	0.5	-0.7	0.2	0.4	-0.1
Investment demand	(%pa)	11.6	6.6	9.7	-1.7	0.6	-0.9	-2.6	2.8
Domestic demand	(%pa)	2.4	3.0	3.8	3.0	2.7	2.0	1.7	2.4
Export demand	(%pa)	5.6	10.0	6.6	10.1	4.7	2.1	-0.9	0.6
Total demand	(%pa)	2.8	3.9	4.2	4.0	3.0	2.0	1.4	2.1

Source: UK CSO CFAs, Dec. 1986.

Table 13A.5 Fixed-ratio model (FR)–RMSE of commodity forecasts, £(1980)million

	Ouput	Import	Supply	Cons. exp.	Gov.	GDF CF	Stk. bldg	Export	Ind. dem.	Demand	D-S
1 Agriculture, etc.	186.0	25.9	185.6	20.5	1.9	2.0	359.3	22.6	116.1	184.2	32.3
2 Coal mining	394.5	12.8	385.2	13.7	0.8	0.0	1837.2	11.9	47.9	170.6	294.9
3 Coke	13.7	8.5	8.5	3.4	0.2	0.0	0.1	7.9	5.9	16.1	33.4
4 Min. oil and nat. gas	59.8	61.0	90.2	0.0	0.0	0.0	392.8	94.3	36.1	105.9	52.9
5 Petroleum products	86.5	174.6	252.2	6.9	8.7	0.0	693.9	51.8	11.9	76.7	347.8
6 Electricity, etc.	70.9	30.5	101.7	18.4	6.8	0.0	0.1	30.4	13.8	58.3	62.3
7 Public gas supply	54.2	4.6	50.1	28.5	2.8	0.0	0.1	1.0	1.2	32.7	33.2
8 Water supply	7.9	0.0	7.8	3.1	1.4	0.0	0.1	0.0	0.5	2.3	5.1
9 Minerals and ores nes	3.3	44.9	42.1	0.0	0.7	0.0	8.4	34.3	9.1	34.2	36.8
10 Iron and steel	57.4	13.7	49.2	0.0	0.0	0.6	168.5	20.1	25.3	50.7	52.2
11 Non-ferrous metals	38.6	28.5	47.9	0.0	0.0	0.0	113.2	70.4	32.6	80.7	95.8
12 Non-metallic min.pr	63.8	3.5	70.5	2.7	2.0	3.6	59.3	3.8	15.1	17.9	67.6
13 Chemicals, mm fibres	84.8	48.6	102.6	12.2	14.5	4.1	235.4	25.6	30.8	62.3	68.5
14 Metal goods nes	122.5	4.3	131.2	6.3	4.2	23.2	22.4	13.4	16.3	27.2	165.6
15 Mech. engineering	91.1	41.4	177.0	3.4	11.7	34.7	83.1	41.6	35.1	67.6	207.7
16 Office machinery	113.3	87.9	145.6	3.1	2.0	41.8	429.7	84.1	12.3	88.2	217.5
17 Elect. engineering	121.2	33.3	116.3	53.3	12.6	58.3	849.1	23.2	31.5	76.1	207.3
18 Motor vehicles	98.3	56.8	107.6	42.2	4.8	88.4	173.1	19.1	11.1	137.9	218.0
19 Aerospace equipment	68.2	71.8	88.1	0.0	66.3	104.3	533.5	52.6	6.3	77.8	65.9
20 Ships, etc.	43.7	38.9	82.4	0.6	4.5	38.6	55.0	48.4	9.2	137.9	55.9
21 Other vehicles	16.5	6.5	23.0	4.4	0.0	2.9	24.3	10.5	4.2	12.8	12.8
22 Instr. engineering	25.9	62.3	88.0	4.8	6.8	20.2	24.6	50.2	1.6	87.6	35.6
23 Manufactured food	221.9	36.4	238.1	103.1	9.2	0.0	69.7	24.8	69.9	61.2	203.0
24 Alcoholic drinks	20.9	4.0	19.2	24.8	0.2	0.0	140.4	11.9	1.6	23.2	20.5
25 Tobacco	48.1	11.0	42.7	25.2	0.0	0.0	106.8	12.4	0.6	40.8	22.5

26 Textiles	14.5	12.8	20.8	8.6	0.7	0.5	56.1	10.6	9.3	31.4	63.4
27 Clothing and footwear	16.3	20.3	13.7	26.7	2.8	0.0	848.4	7.6	4.4	30.8	131.5
28 Timber and furniture	82.4	21.0	103.8	6.3	2.6	24.0	83.9	7.0	19.7	11.1	127.4
29 Paper and board	47.0	9.6	51.9	3.4	2.7	3.6	28.9	7.0	18.2	20.4	75.0
30 Books, etc.	23.0	6.4	24.2	19.1	3.7	0.0	134.1	7.4	26.4	12.4	45.3
31 Rubber, plastic prd	15.0	26.0	30.0	1.2	1.4	2.5	41.5	5.5	6.0	12.7	53.6
32 Other manufactures	40.7	76.6	117.3	17.4	1.7	0.2	192.7	41.2	5.9	81.6	64.0
33 Construction	130.3	0.1	128.8	15.9	30.7	247.7	128.4	0.1	31.7	285.3	515.7
34 Distribution, etc.	88.6	3.9	87.7	66.6	11.2	32.0	0.1	11.9	13.1	112.4	77.1
35 Hotels and catering	25.4	12.7	19.0	38.0	8.6	0.0	0.1	13.6	1.5	22.2	132.9
36 Rail transport	23.5	3.4	26.6	7.7	1.6	0.0	0.1	0.8	6.7	5.4	25.8
37 Other land trans.	61.3	4.1	65.0	5.3	1.6	2.8	0.1	0.6	8.2	14.9	196.4
38 Sea, air and other	59.3	34.2	91.2	13.6	2.3	3.7	0.1	57.7	10.2	82.0	148.3
39 Communications	89.0	9.0	98.4	19.8	7.8	29.8	0.1	18.8	46.7	114.5	27.4
40 Business services	576.4	10.6	582.3	39.4	2.0	0.8	0.1	113.2	54.0	223.0	1037.6
41 Misc. services	55.6	1.2	57.1	48.1	57.9	28.6	0.1	12.6	13.5	69.9	42.1
42 PAD	122.8	0.0	122.1	0.0	31.1	0.0	0.1	0.0	0.0	144.9	19.2
43 NHS and public ed.	157.2	0.0	156.4	0.0	25.2	0.0	0.1	0.0	0.0	161.8	24.5
44 Own. of dwellings	104.8	0.0	104.1	108.8	0.0	0.0	0.1	0.0	0.0	75.3	27.5
45 Tourist exp.	0.0	31.3	32.3	98.6	0.0	0.0	0.1	53.7	0.0	60.0	37.0
46 Sales by F. B.	0.0	0.0	0.0	11.3	34.3	44.5	0.1	9.6	1.5	17.6	25.8
47 Net indirect tax	51.1	0.0	49.6	59.4	28.0	13.8	0.1	0.0	44.9	56.6	0.0
48 Unallocated	181.8	1.6	180.2	0.0	0.0	0.0	20.2	1.1	0.0	2.3	174.2
49 Nat. A/c – CFA	0.0	236.2	236.3	151.5	21.2	36.0	94.3	170.6	0.0	321.8	350.6
All commodities	83.2	29.2	103.1	23.4	9.0	18.2	163.5	26.9	17.7	75.5	123.2

Source: UK CSO CFAs, Dec. 1986.

Table 13A.6 Single-equation unrestricted model (UR)— short-term forecasts for whole economy by aggregating components

		1984		1985				1986	
		Q3	Q4	Q1	Q2	Q3	Q4	Q1	Q2
COMMODITY SUPPLY									
Domestic supply	(£m80)	111312	112394	114762	115184	115444	117055	117455	118545
Import supply	(£m80)	17040	18019	17106	17023	17063	17287	17130	17567
Total supply	(£m80)	128351	130412	131868	132207	132507	134343	134585	136113
COMMODITY DEMAND									
Industrial demand	(£m80)	49775	50181	50781	50992	50749	51409	51201	51877
Consumer demand	(£m80)	36543	37269	37547	37829	38544	39051	39297	40054
Gov't demand	(£m80)	12795	12751	12702	12770	12713	12791	12812	12792
Investment demand	(£m80)	11502	11569	12108	11310	11533	11459	11737	11440
Stockbuilding	(£m80)	−122	446	70	494	131	139	642	−70
Domestic demand	(£m80)	110492	112214	113207	113395	113669	114850	115689	116092
Export demand	(£m80)	17118	18016	18124	18471	18126	18449	18246	18761
Total demand	(£m80)	127609	130230	131331	131866	131795	133299	133935	134853
Residual error	(£m80)	−742	−182	−537	−341	−712	−1044	−650	−1260
CHANGE IN SUPPLY		(% change on corresponding quarter of previous year)							
Domestic supply	(%pa)	3.0	2.8	4.3	4.5	3.7	4.1	2.3	2.9
Import supply	(%pa)	7.7	11.5	3.6	1.0	0.1	−4.1	0.1	3.2
Total supply	(%pa)	3.6	3.9	4.2	4.0	3.2	3.0	2.1	3.0

CHANGE IN DEMAND

Industrial demand	(%pa)	3.2	2.6	3.4	3.6	2.0	2.4	0.8	1.7
Consumer demand	(%pa)	0.5	2.6	3.2	3.0	5.5	4.8	4.7	5.9
Gov't demand	(%pa)	1.5	0.4	0.7	0.3	-0.6	0.3	0.9	0.2
Investment demand	(%pa)	11.6	6.6	9.5	-0.5	0.3	-0.9	-3.1	1.1
Domestic demand	(%pa)	2.4	3.0	3.8	3.4	2.9	2.3	2.2	2.4
Export demand	(%pa)	5.6	10.0	6.6	10.2	5.9	2.4	0.7	1.6
Total demand	(%pa)	2.8	3.9	4.1	4.3	3.3	2.4	2.0	2.3

Source: UK CSO CFAs, Dec. 1986.

Table 13A.7 Single-equation unrestricted model (UR)–RMSE of commodity forecasts, £(1980)million

	Output	Import	Supply	Cons exp.	Gov.	GDF CF	Stk bldg	Export	Ind. dem.	Demand	D-S
1 Agriculture, etc.	72.1	67.9	49.2	12.0	1.2	1.1	47.1	27.3	61.6	124.7	39.4
2 Coal mining	141.7	21.3	182.5	7.7	0.3	0.0	28.2	14.3	49.9	56.1	142.0
3 Coke	8.4	14.2	9.9	1.9	0.1	0.0	0.0	9.6	6.2	17.8	47.2
4 Min. oil and nat. gas	227.7	153.3	161.0	0.0	0.0	0.0	53.8	176.9	56.6	255.5	116.1
5 Petroleum products	188.6	163.4	140.2	17.0	3.3	0.0	58.7	113.9	60.2	102.4	182.0
6 Electricity, etc.	124.1	37.1	152.4	46.0	4.2	0.0	0.0	29.4	16.1	99.4	55.8
7 Public gas supply	74.3	48.1	68.0	52.6	1.4	0.0	0.0	4.7	1.6	53.7	21.4
8 Water supply	2.5	0.0	1.9	0.5	1.0	0.0	0.0	0.0	0.7	0.6	8.0
9 Minerals and ores nes	7.1	50.3	39.9	0.0	0.7	0.0	10.6	69.1	9.7	45.0	35.8
10 Iron and steel	98.3	31.2	116.8	0.0	0.0	0.6	36.0	44.6	40.3	75.9	63.3
11 Non-ferrous metals	22.9	46.9	87.4	0.0	0.0	0.0	97.3	41.5	23.9	101.2	58.0
12 Non-metallic min.pr	93.0	12.8	98.1	1.4	1.4	1.7	7.0	28.7	36.1	44.5	63.2
13 Chemicals, mm fibres	198.3	35.9	294.6	11.3	8.6	1.4	28.9	31.0	66.5	126.9	80.4
14 Metal goods nes	140.8	6.0	141.5	2.3	2.4	10.4	20.0	13.4	14.2	23.6	94.6
15 Mech. engineering	252.0	89.8	411.4	3.4	17.3	71.8	74.1	306.2	69.3	282.8	109.4
16 Office machinery	134.1	340.1	503.4	1.4	1.4	22.1	70.1	409.1	11.9	1604.1	239.9
17 Elect. engineering	287.8	48.7	315.0	33.6	19.5	55.2	95.7	25.9	26.0	112.2	211.4
18 Motor vehicles	38.4	152.7	138.4	77.7	5.7	139.8	114.6	102.2	8.5	201.5	101.7
19 Aerospace equipment	173.8	65.3	185.1	0.0	73.7	123.8	96.2	53.9	19.0	135.8	69.4
20 Ships, etc.	17.7	46.2	45.2	1.1	17.3	37.4	59.9	44.1	4.4	120.7	59.9
21 Other vehicles	8.5	4.3	9.5	2.4	0.0	7.6	10.3	8.4	5.6	12.2	14.0
22 Instr. engineering	35.8	60.5	72.3	5.3	3.9	6.2	11.2	54.1	1.2	47.0	15.4
23 Manufactured food	126.0	64.9	68.5	30.6	5.6	0.0	74.2	21.2	44.2	47.6	162.9
24 Alcoholic drinks	15.9	6.6	12.8	36.4	0.1	0.0	18.8	6.1	1.9	22.2	34.2
25 Tobacco	34.5	18.8	31.9	19.0	0.0	0.0	10.2	9.8	0.6	32.7	24.2

26 Textiles	22.4	6.7	17.7	11.1	0.4	0.5	9.0	16.8	9.8	27.9	16.9
27 Clothing and footwear	11.0	25.8	22.2	32.2	1.5	0.0	24.1	6.2	3.8	27.7	23.5
28 Timber and furniture	85.8	90.5	242.5	3.4	1.6	7.6	20.4	9.8	7.0	51.9	115.6
29 Paper and board	25.9	11.4	26.3	0.9	1.5	1.2	8.0	24.5	6.6	11.0	24.5
30 Books, etc.	38.0	9.8	39.4	2.8	2.1	0.0	9.1	3.7	4.6	13.7	52.6
31 Rubber, plastic prd	46.7	49.4	22.7	0.6	0.7	1.2	9.9	7.0	5.0	13.4	12.2
32 Other manufactures	14.9	35.0	40.9	40.4	1.2	0.6	60.3	65.3	1.1	72.0	44.4
33 Construction	393.5	0.5	302.1	13.8	38.0	159.9	52.5	0.4	17.7	475.6	267.7
34 Distribution, etc.	135.7	8.6	117.9	57.0	6.6	30.6	0.0	20.5	16.5	93.4	151.9
35 Hotels and catering	69.2	16.0	82.8	112.7	5.2	0.0	0.0	19.2	2.2	42.1	96.1
36 Rail transport	25.7	2.7	23.6	11.8	1.0	0.0	0.0	0.9	14.3	9.0	18.8
37 Other land trans.	42.6	2.8	41.3	8.6	1.2	2.0	0.0	1.2	11.7	21.7	52.7
38 Sea, air and other	61.7	20.6	73.7	15.7	1.1	3.2	0.0	164.1	19.8	233.4	183.0
39 Communications	53.0	3.6	67.5	46.4	4.7	33.4	0.0	30.0	11.6	87.5	54.3
40 Business services	36.9	77.4	245.5	49.5	1.2	0.5	0.0	125.6	25.7	196.3	214.4
41 Misc. services	36.3	8.6	15.9	60.6	34.4	17.8	0.0	14.0	6.4	31.5	104.1
42 PAD	15.9	0.0	21.9	0.0	42.2	0.0	0.0	0.0	0.0	21.7	13.9
43 NHS and public ed.	29.1	0.0	29.9	0.0	31.7	0.0	0.0	0.0	0.0	28.5	33.6
44 Own. of dwellings	10.7	0.0	10.1	23.7	0.0	0.0	0.0	0.0	0.0	17.5	49.1
45 Tourist exp.	0.0	54.1	57.6	159.9	0.0	0.0	0.0	80.3	0.0	60.5	45.4
46 Sales by F. B.	0.0	0.0	0.0	29.0	20.7	106.0	0.0	20.0	0.9	33.0	21.0
47 Net indirect tax	32.7	0.0	59.6	107.8	13.6	10.0	0.0	0.0	77.6	47.3	0.0
48 Unallocated	354.6	2.4	337.5	0.0	0.0	0.0	2.4	2.0	0.0	8.3	298.2
49 Nat. A/c – CFA	0.0	355.3	328.8	126.6	18.9	28.9	57.5	283.2	0.0	280.7	349.1
All commodities	83.0	48.3	113.6	26.1	8.1	18.0	26.0	51.8	17.9	115.3	87.6

Source: UK CSO CFAs, Dec. 1986.

Table 13A.8 Single-equation restricted model (RR)— short-term forecasts for whole economy by aggregating components

		1984		1985				1986	
		Q3	Q4	Q1	Q2	Q3	Q4	Q1	Q2
COMMODITY SUPPLY									
Domestic supply	(£m80)	111312	112394	114537	115021	115251	116865	117203	118443
Import supply	(£m80)	17040	18019	17192	17100	17156	17378	17381	17993
Total supply	(£m80)	128351	130412	131729	132121	132407	134243	134584	136436
COMMODITY DEMAND									
Industrial demand	(£m80)	49775	50181	50737	50968	50720	51322	51153	51778
Consumer demand	(£m80)	36543	37269	37604	37871	38616	39099	39436	40126
Gov't demand	(£m80)	12795	12751	12670	12807	12702	12807	12762	12792
Investment demand	(£m80)	11502	11569	12178	11297	11576	11458	11739	11431
Stockbuilding	(£m80)	-122	446	-50	484	82	27	531	-146
Domestic demand	(£m80)	110492	112214	113140	113427	113697	114713	115622	115981
Export demand	(£m80)	17118	18016	17967	18281	17945	18210	17917	18387
Total demand	(£m80)	127609	130230	131107	131708	131642	132923	133539	134367
Residual error	(£m80)	-742	-182	-622	-414	-765	-1320	-1046	-2068
CHANGE IN SUPPLY			(% change on corresponding quarter of previous year)						
Domestic supply	(%pa)	3.0	2.8	4.1	4.3	3.5	4.0	2.3	3.0
Import supply	(%pa)	7.7	11.5	4.1	1.5	0.7	-3.6	1.1	5.2
Total supply	(%pa)	3.6	3.9	4.1	3.9	3.2	2.9	2.2	3.3

CHANGE IN DEMAND

Industrial demand	(%pa)	3.2	2.6	3.3	3.5	1.9	2.3	0.8	1.6
Consumer demand	(%pa)	0.5	2.6	3.4	3.1	5.7	4.9	4.9	6.0
Gov't demand	(%pa)	1.5	0.4	0.5	0.6	-0.7	0.4	0.7	-0.1
Investment demand	(%pa)	11.6	6.6	10.2	-0.6	0.6	-1.0	-3.6	1.2
Domestic demand	(%pa)	2.4	3.0	3.7	3.4	2.9	2.2	2.2	2.3
Export demand	(%pa)	5.6	10.0	5.6	9.0	4.8	1.1	-0.3	0.6
Total demand	(%pa)	2.8	3.9	4.0	4.1	3.2	2.1	1.9	2.0

Source: UK CSO CFAs, Dec. 1986.

Table 13A.9 Single-equation restricted model (RR)–RMSE of commodity forecasts, £(1980)million

	Output	Import	Supply	Cons exp.	Gov.	GDF CF	Stk. bldg	Export	Ind. dem.	Demand	D-S
1 Agriculture, etc.	72.1	68.9	49.2	11.8	2.3	0.8	46.4	20.1	69.0	131.6	56.0
2 Coal mining	132.5	22.3	114.0	6.9	0.5	0.0	33.7	7.8	54.8	52.3	94.8
3 Coke	8.4	14.8	8.1	1.7	0.1	0.0	0.0	5.2	6.8	15.9	41.7
4 Min. oil and nat. gas	235.9	142.4	176.4	0.0	0.0	0.0	62.4	149.3	45.8	253.0	127.4
5 Petroleum products	142.3	150.6	135.9	27.6	13.2	0.0	67.6	137.0	60.0	88.6	170.8
6 Electricity, etc.	111.8	26.1	136.4	48.6	3.7	0.0	0.0	27.6	16.1	96.7	61.6
7 Public gas supply	82.8	153.5	79.7	53.3	1.5	0.0	0.0	5.4	1.7	53.7	24.1
8 Water supply	1.9	0.0	2.0	0.8	0.9	0.0	0.0	0.0	0.7	0.8	11.2
9 Minerals and ores nes	3.8	50.4	49.4	0.0	0.8	0.0	10.4	66.7	10.2	40.7	37.9
10 Iron and steel	94.6	25.2	71.0	0.0	0.0	0.7	34.8	30.0	47.1	44.6	61.2
11 Non-ferrous metals	22.9	66.1	85.5	0.0	0.0	0.0	99.7	48.9	23.9	101.4	53.6
12 Non-metallic min.pr	97.4	7.2	100.4	1.2	1.1	2.0	8.2	27.3	44.2	41.4	63.6
13 Chemicals, mm fibres	178.9	34.4	282.6	9.6	7.5	1.2	30.8	34.7	63.3	127.0	90.0
14 Metal goods nes	134.8	5.5	141.0	1.5	2.2	11.3	19.9	13.2	10.1	20.5	107.1
15 Mech. engineering	240.8	67.3	421.3	2.5	16.0	76.0	74.8	306.2	72.2	285.7	102.7
16 Office machinery	113.8	336.6	464.1	2.7	1.1	16.7	68.2	439.7	17.5	1494.6	263.2
17 Elect. engineering	291.9	53.8	312.8	20.7	22.6	55.5	94.0	41.6	25.8	116.5	124.3
18 Motor vehicles	39.4	106.5	159.2	136.5	6.9	89.6	112.6	93.2	8.6	211.9	84.3
19 Aerospace equipment	172.0	62.6	190.3	0.0	64.0	118.7	95.0	42.5	19.7	120.7	63.5
20 Ships, etc.	16.8	43.8	41.7	1.0	17.1	33.1	56.1	31.8	5.5	144.3	55.1
21 Other vehicles	7.2	4.2	9.6	2.1	0.0	8.3	9.6	8.6	6.5	11.9	18.2
22 Instr. engineering	37.0	78.3	73.2	5.1	4.8	6.6	15.5	50.3	1.4	111.6	18.0
23 Manufactured food	109.0	58.9	40.8	32.5	4.8	0.0	97.1	26.7	47.2	126.0	153.3
24 Alcoholic drinks	15.8	6.6	12.5	37.1	0.1	0.0	21.9	3.3	1.8	24.3	34.7
25 Tobacco	34.7	15.7	37.0	18.8	0.0	0.0	10.7	10.0	0.6	35.3	21.3

26 Textiles	22.0	10.5	40.0	11.4	0.4	0.6	7.4	18.2	9.6	29.2	30.6
27 Clothing and footwear	10.4	21.7	26.8	30.4	1.4	0.0	15.4	6.6	3.4	27.9	25.8
28 Timber and furniture	99.2	98.4	237.4	3.9	1.4	10.0	19.5	9.7	30.9	56.4	77.1
29 Paper and board	28.6	11.4	25.7	1.1	1.4	1.4	7.8	25.5	8.0	11.8	28.1
30 Books, etc.	55.2	10.1	60.9	2.6	2.7	0.0	10.7	4.6	9.4	13.7	58.8
31 Rubber, plastic prd	56.4	65.8	28.6	0.5	0.9	1.2	9.1	7.0	4.5	13.4	9.2
32 Other manufactures	12.8	34.8	40.9	38.1	0.8	0.6	65.3	61.7	0.9	74.8	42.8
33 Construction	366.1	0.4	300.4	14.2	38.3	194.0	59.7	0.2	20.7	183.1	288.0
34 Distribution, etc.	138.1	6.5	98.5	97.0	5.8	33.1	0.0	19.5	14.7	92.6	155.4
35 Hotels and catering	75.0	15.8	78.4	116.5	4.6	0.0	0.0	19.4	2.2	48.3	28.7
36 Rail transport	23.1	3.5	16.6	10.3	0.7	0.0	0.0	0.6	13.3	9.7	22.6
37 Other land trans.	40.9	3.4	39.5	4.5	0.9	3.0	0.0	1.3	5.8	17.2	52.4
38 Sea, air and other	61.7	16.8	85.5	19.1	1.1	2.4	0.0	132.3	20.3	233.4	177.1
39 Communications	52.1	4.5	75.1	44.1	4.1	25.7	0.0	29.9	32.6	101.7	62.5
40 Business services	26.3	87.5	206.3	49.4	1.0	1.1	0.0	144.2	32.1	195.3	205.5
41 Misc. services	25.6	9.7	21.4	60.4	30.0	38.0	0.0	16.0	8.0	28.7	103.3
42 PAD	10.0	0.0	20.0	0.0	35.2	0.0	0.0	0.0	0.0	21.8	10.8
43 NHS and public ed.	31.1	0.0	34.7	0.0	33.0	0.0	0.0	0.0	0.0	29.6	34.6
44 Own. of dwellings	10.7	0.0	10.0	3.5	0.0	0.0	0.0	0.0	0.0	13.2	45.1
45 Tourist exp.	0.0	50.5	54.6	157.2	0.0	0.0	0.0	72.0	0.0	65.4	45.6
46 Sales by F. B.	0.0	0.0	0.0	28.5	17.9	107.4	0.0	12.5	1.0	41.1	19.4
47 Net indirect tax	47.2	0.0	72.3	100.7	22.3	8.0	0.0	0.0	93.0	39.7	0.0
48 Unallocated	364.6	1.2	369.6	0.0	0.0	0.0	2.0	1.6	0.0	8.8	323.3
49 Nat. A/c – CFA	0.0	353.0	334.3	142.2	17.7	33.7	53.3	253.7	0.0	311.1	295.4
All commodities	80.7	49.1	111.7	27.7	8.2	18.0	26.9	50.3	19.8	110.6	83.3

Source: UK CSO CFAs, Dec. 1986.

Chapter fourteen

What determines the bank borrowing and liquid lending of UK companies? Explanations based on aggregated and disaggregated data*

Christopher Green, Gopa Chowdhury, and David Miles

Introduction

Company bank borrowing is important for both microeconomic and macroeconomic reasons. At the microeconomic level, bank borrowing is a major component of company debt. Therefore, a fully satisfactory explanation of the capital structure of UK companies must include an analysis of their bank borrowing. At the macroeconomic level, it is widely believed that aggregate bank borrowing is a principal driving variable of the broad monetary aggregates, especially sterling M3. On this view, control of bank borrowing in general, or borrowing by companies in particular, is likely to be a prerequisite for control over the broad monetary aggregates.

It seems clear that a complete account of the determinants of aggregate company bank borrowing must rest both on macro-economic or economy-wide factors, and on microeconomic or company-specific factors. Despite this, the empirical basis for understanding the behaviour of aggregate company bank borrowing in the UK has rested largely on a series of aggregate time-series studies (see Green, 1984 for a survey of this literature). In contrast, the present authors have recently reported on the results of a large-scale study which used company accounts data to model the determinants of a range of company short-term financial decisions, including among others the flow of short-term bank

* This is a shortened version of a paper with the same title issued as FIM working paper no 4, UWIST, March 1988. The opinions expressed in this paper are those of the authors and not necessarily those of the Bank of England. We thank Mark Goode for valuable research assistance on this paper. Mark Goode's time was funded by the Jane Hodge Foundation.

borrowing (see Chowdhury, Green, and Miles, 1986, hereafter: CGM). In this chapter our principal goal is to assess and compare the results of research into company bank borrowing using aggregated and disaggregated data. However, we do not concentrate exclusively on bank borrowing but aim to set it in the more general context of overall company financial decisions. This leads us to examine in particular the relationship between company sector bank borrowing and its lending in the form of liquid financial assets.

The chapter is organized as follows. Section 14.1 sketches out the main features of aggregate company financing over the last twenty years as shown by Central Statistical Office (CSO) data, and considers the problems involved in interpreting these data. In section 14.2 we turn to the disaggregated data which were used in our earlier paper. We give an account of the aggregate flows implied by these disaggregated data, and provide some descriptive measures of the nature and extent of differences in financial structure within the company sector. In section 14.3 we compare the results of the main aggregate time-series studies of bank borrowing with those of our disaggregated study. In this comparison we focus in particular on the impact of interest rates, as these are the key variables through which the authorities can, in practice, seek to control aggregate borrowing. In section 14.4 we utilize the disaggregated results to provide a simple accounting of the relative magnitudes of company-specific and economy-wide effects in determining both aggregate bank borrowing and liquid lending. Finally section 14.5 contains some concluding remarks.

14.1 The interpretation of aggregate company borrowing and lending

The central fact concerning UK company finance over the last two decades is usually thought to be the long-term switch by the company sector from borrowing in the capital markets to a greater reliance on borrowing from banks. See for example, Bain (1986). The rapid expansion in bank borrowing in the early seventies can be seen in panel 1.1 of table 14.1. However, when viewed in relation to company profits (table 14.1, panel 1.2) this looks to be a distinctly temporary affair. During the most recent decade, bank borrowing relative to corporate profits has only been a few percentage points higher than in the second half of the 1960s. The company sector's use of the capital markets is reflected in the data on 'other borrowing'. But the picture is not one of a smooth transition from the capital market to bank finance. Measured in

Table 14.1 Industrial and commercial companies–net borrowing requirement and its financing,[a] 1966–85

	(1) Bank borrowing	(2) Liquid lending	(3) Net bank borrowing (1)+(2)	(4) Other borrowing	(5) Other financial lending	(6) Net borrowing requirements (3)+(4)+(5)	(7) Gross trading profits[b]
1.1 In millions of pounds at current prices							
1966–70	2,879	–664	2,215	4,406	–185	6,436	26,231
1971–75	13,111	–7,242	5,869	7,511	–279	13,101	39,878
1976–80	17,874	–11,349	6,525	11,774	–570	16,915	101,157
1981–85	28,489	–20,834	7,655	15,536	–6,967	16,224	213,491
1.2 As percentage of gross trading profits							
1966–70	11.0	–2.5	8.5	16.8	–0.7	24.5	
1971–75	32.9	–18.2	14.7	18.8	–0.7	32.9	
1976–80	17.7	–11.2	6.5	11.6	–0.6	16.7	
1981–85	13.3	–9.7	3.6	7.2	–3.3	7.6	
1.3 As percentage of net borrowing requirement							
1966–70	44.7	–10.4	34.3	68.5	–2.9		
1971–75	100.0	–55.3	44.7	57.3	–2.1		
1976–80	105.6	–66.5	39.1	69.6	–3.4		
1981–85	168.4	–123.2	45.2	91.8	–41.2		

Source: Economic Trends Supplement 1987.

Notes: [a]— = acquisitions of assets (outflows of funds); + = acquisitions of liabilities (inflows of funds).
[b]Net of stock appreciation.

relation to company profits, the decline in the use of the capital markets dates from the late seventies and not, as is sometimes claimed, from the early seventies. The picture is further complicated when company sector transactions in liquid assets ('liquid lending') are taken into account. The early seventies saw a surge in liquid lending of a magnitude comparable to that in bank borrowing. Since then, the pace of liquid lending has slackened, but it still remains much higher than in the sixties. In contrast, *net* liquid bank borrowing (that is: bank borrowing net of liquid lending) as a proportion of profits has fallen in comparison both with the early seventies and with the late sixties. Moreover, the ratio of *net* liquid borrowing to borrowing from the capital markets has, apart from the early seventies, remained remarkably stable.

The short-term relationship between bank borrowing and liquid lending can be described simply by means of moving regressions. The quarterly flow of real bank borrowing was regressed on the flow of real liquid lending using a window of sixteen quarters. The first and last observations were moved forward one quarter at a time over the period 1963:1–1985:2. A similar exercise was performed, regressing real net liquid borrowing on the change in real GDP. The results of these exercises which are intended only to describe the data are shown in figure 14.1. Apart from reaffirming the fact that the early seventies were different from the rest of the period, the regressions suggest a surprising stability (though not a high significance) in the relationships between bank borrowing, liquid lending, and the change in real output. The estimated slope coefficients show that, in the short run, increased bank borrowing is associated with reduced liquid lending.[1] This suggests that it is the net liquidity position which is important for companies in the short run. Moreover, net liquid borrowing is mostly negatively related to the change in GDP, suggesting a counter-cyclical pattern to net borrowing.

Aggregative time-series studies are potentially non-informative about the underlying causes of these movements in bank borrowing and liquid lending. Implicitly, any aggregative study must rely on the 'representative firm' argument. In this framework, aggregate data are the outcome of the optimizing decisions of a large number of firms which differ from the representative firm only in respect of a random error. In the present problem however, the data are not consistent with relevant theories. Miller and Sprenkle (1980) have studied the precautionary demand for money by firms where borrowing is possible. However, in their model, it is only the net position of the firm *vis-à-vis* the bank which is of importance. Their analysis cannot explain why the same company

303

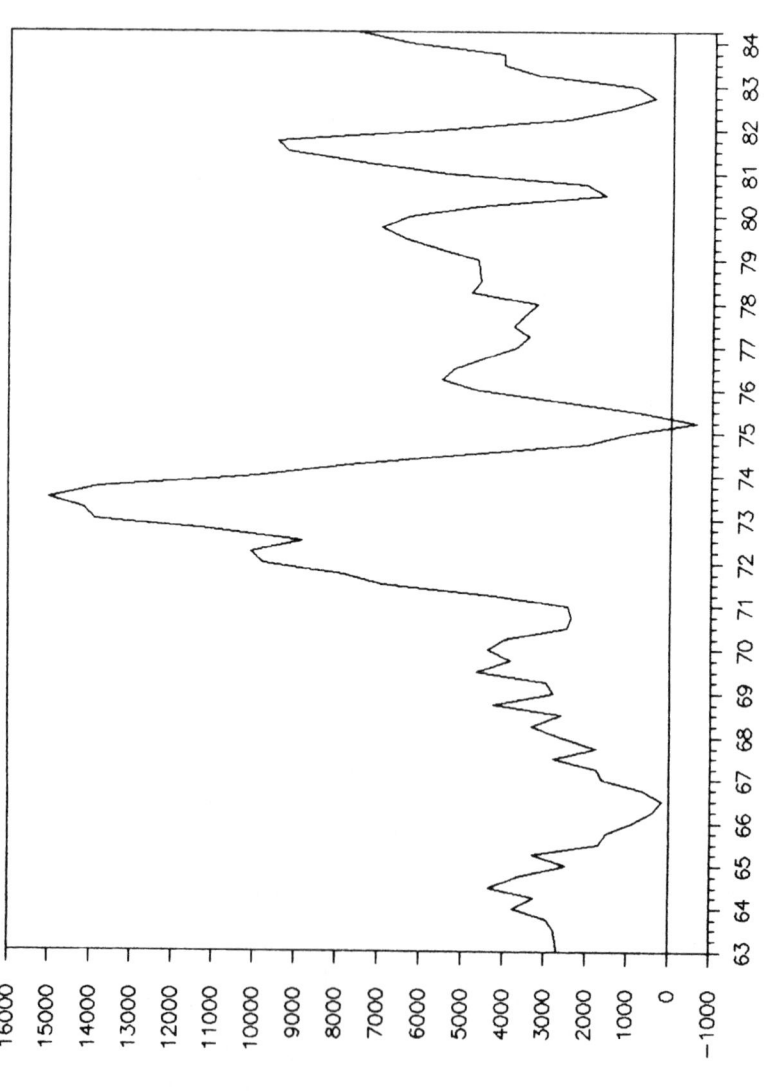

Figure 14.1 Bank borrowing, 1963:4–1985:1 (in real terms at annual rates)

may borrow from banks and acquire liquid assets simultaneously. Likewise, mainstream corporate finance theory implies that companies borrow to increase their investments in risky assets, not safe ones. In certain respects the problem is akin to the dividend puzzle: why do firms simultaneously borrow and pay dividends? Here, the question is: why should a firm borrow from banks and simultaneously increase its holdings of capital-certain assets mainly in the form of deposits with banks?

The liquid lending puzzle (as we can call it) differs from the dividend puzzle in one important respect. Much less is known about how far it is the same firms which are doing the bank borrowing and liquid lending, or whether it is different firms: one group primarily borrowers, the other primarily lenders. This suggests that there are two possible classes of explanation of the puzzle. The first would be aggregative in nature and would postulate that firms behave in essentially the same way. An explanation along these lines is proposed by Oulton (1981). In his view, liquid asset holdings can be explained as a response to bankruptcy risks. The sale of fixed assets and (less obviously) borrowing are typically costly ways to raise cash. Thus firms hold liquid assets to reduce the risks that they will have to hold a 'fire sale' of assets in the event of a succession of unfavourable profit outcomes.

The second class of explanation would be more disaggregative in nature and would hypothesize that the economy could be divided into two broad groups of firms: one primarily borrowing from banks and the other primarily acquiring liquid assets. The membership of these groups of firms would not necessarily be the same from period to period. Such a two-sector account of the liquid lending puzzle could in turn be explained in two possible ways. The first possibility is that firms have identical preferences but face different financial constraints. On this view, it is the different constraints which lead some firms primarily to borrow and others primarily to lend. The second possibility is that firms' preferences differ, for example, because of the different nature of their business. On this view, one type of firm always acts differently from the other. A particular example of this situation would arise if there were economies of scale, so that large firms acted differently from small ones.

There are several reasons to think that a two-sector model of firm behaviour might be a plausible candidate for explaining company sector bank borrowing and liquid lending in the UK. The structure of industry has been radically altered in the last fifteen years by the growth of companies associated with North Sea Oil exploitation and in the face of shrinking markets and declining profits. Meanwhile, profitability in other less 'traditional' activities has held up rather better than in manufacturing. This suggests at least two candidates for a two-sector model of company borrowing and lending, i.e.: oil and non-oil, and traditional manufacturing and non-manufacturing. Sample survey data on the liquidity ratios of large companies published by the CSO since 1983 suggest that companies in the manufacturing, oil, and non-oil non-manufacturing sectors do indeed have significantly and persistently different liquidity ratios.

A rather different factor suggesting the need for a more disaggregated approach to company borrowing and lending is the maturity structure of bank borrowings. An unknown proportion of the expansion in bank borrowing since 1970 has been in the form of longer-term debt with a maturity of up to ten years. Such debt is a relatively good substitute for corporate bonds, new issues of which have all but disappeared from the UK since 1970 (see Bank of England, 1981). It would be consistent with the Miller-Sprenkle argument if those companies acquiring liquid assets were largely companies which were borrowing long term from banks, while companies who were borrowing short term were generally not acquiring liquid assets. In other words, in assessing the liquid lending puzzle it seems important to distinguish between long-term and short-term bank borrowing – a distinction which can be investigated more readily with disaggregated than with aggregated data.

14.2 Aggregate characteristics of disaggregated data

We turn next to the disaggregated data used in our earlier study (CGM, 1986). These data consist of the published annual accounts of a sample of 694 medium and large quoted non-financial companies each of which reported in every year from 1971 through 1983. The sample companies represent about 35 per cent of all UK industrial and commercial companies by pre-tax profits. The data are those collected by DATASTREAM; the sources and structure of these data are described fully in our earlier paper. The size of this sample compares favourably with that used by the CSO, which consists of about 750 companies, accounting for about one half of total company profits. There are, of course, some conceptual differences between ordinary company accounts and data reported to the CSO. However, Edwards, Kay, and Mayer (1987) have argued that the accounting data of firms are mostly quite satisfactory for economic analysis, and we did not attempt a tortuous process of adjustment.

One problem involved in aggregating company accounts data

Table 14.2 DATASTREAM sample–net borrowing requirement and its financing[a] (annual averages)

	(1) Bank borrowing due within one year	(2) Liquid lending	(3) Net bank borrowing (1)+(2)	(4) Long-term debt	(5) Equity issues	(6) Net trade credit given	(7) Net borrowing requirement (3)+(4)+(5)+(6)	(8) Total company income[b]
1.1 In millions of pounds at current prices								
1969–70	−31	−17	−48	436	285	270	145	3,452
1971–75	282	−512	−230	865	357	339	1,331	6,695
1976–80	411	−458	−117	884	556	403	1,797	13,194
1981–83	440	−1,724	−1,284	1,341	1,052	461	1,570	19,187
1.2 As a percentage of total company income								
1969–70	−0.9	−0.5	−1.4	12.6	8.3	7.8	27.4	
1971–75	4.2	−7.6	−3.4	12.9	5.3	5.1	19.9	
1976–80	3.1	−3.5	−0.4	6.7	4.2	3.1	13.6	
1981–83	2.3	−9.0	−6.7	7.0	5.5	2.4	8.2	

Source: DATASTREAM

Notes: "−" = acquisitions of assets (outflows of funds); + = acquisitions of liabilities (inflows of funds).
[b]Inclusive of stock appreciation and non-trading income.

has to do with the fact that companies report at different times of the year. However, according to the CSO (1985), the weighted average accounting period of companies in its sample from Inland Revenue sources ends at about the beginning of December. This argues for the use of data directly in the national accounts without any timing adjustments. Consequently, our aggregate data, though not precisely aligned, are nevertheless constructed on a similar basis to those of the CSO. In utilizing the data to model economic behaviour, we aligned external data (interest rates and the like) to company report years on a quarterly basis. For example, companies which report in the second quarter were assumed to be influenced by movements in market interest rates up to the end of the first quarter. This means that disaggregated company accounts data enjoy an important advantage over aggregate data. In principle, the timing of the impact of explanatory variables can be more precisely estimated with the disaggregate data than it can with the aggregate data.

The aggregate sources and uses statement of our DATA-STREAM sample is contained in table 14.2. There are some differences of definition between these data and the aggregate data.[2] The main difference is that bank borrowing under one year (including overdrafts) is shown here as a separate variable. Liquid lending covers broadly the same sub-categories of assets as its CSO counterpart. Companies are not required to report total bank borrowing separately. Therefore our data on company loan capital include, indistinguishably, long-term borrowing from banks as well as corporate bonds and other borrowings with a maturity over one year. Table 14.2 gives a broadly similar picture of aggregate company finances as does table 14.1, although, in the DATA-STREAM figures, there does not appear to be a perceptible surge in bank borrowing in the early seventies. This may be due, in part, to an increase in bank borrowing with a maturity of over one year relative to borrowing from the capital market during this period. These data appear separately in table 14.1 but are included indistinguishably under 'long-term debt' in table 14.2.

We can take a first look at differences in company short-term financial behaviour by examining the distribution of their liquidity ratios narrowly defined as the ratio of the stock of bank borrowing due within one year (B) to the stock of cash, deposits, and similar claims (L). Figure 14.2 provides year-by-year frequency distributions of this narrow liquidity ratio.[3] In this chart, each segment of a vertical bar shows the number of companies with a liquidity ratio falling into that particular class. If the company sector could be divided into two groups we would expect such frequency

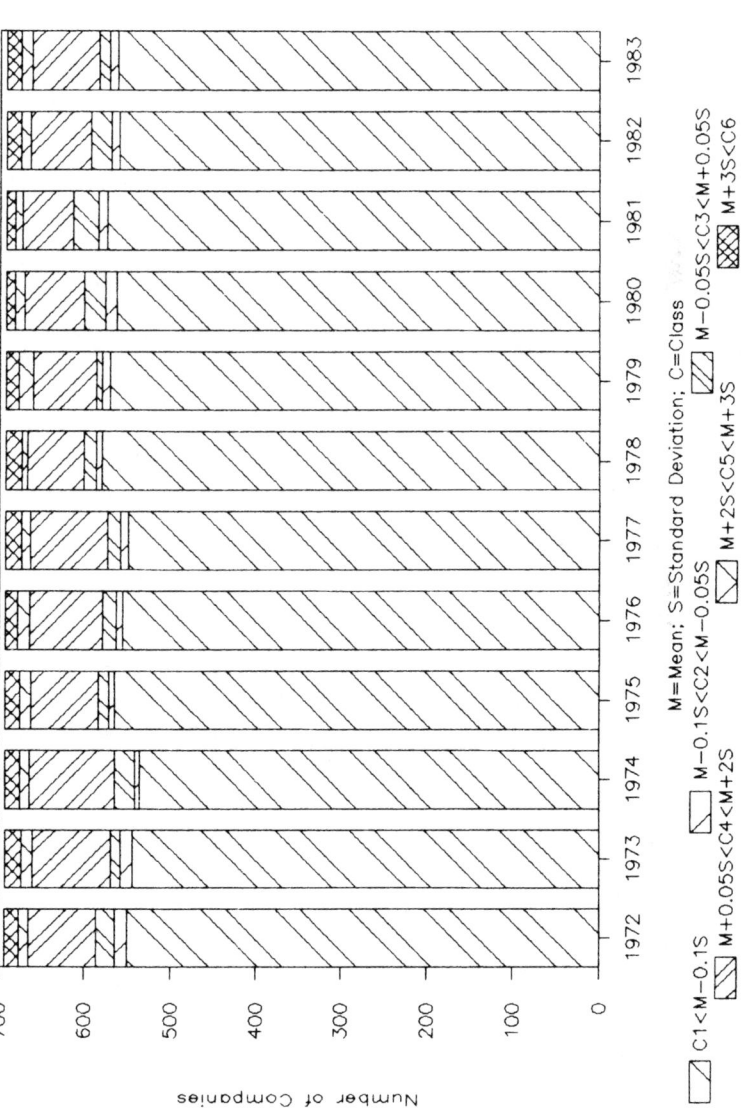

Figure 14.2 Frequency distributions – narrow liquidity ratios (B/L)

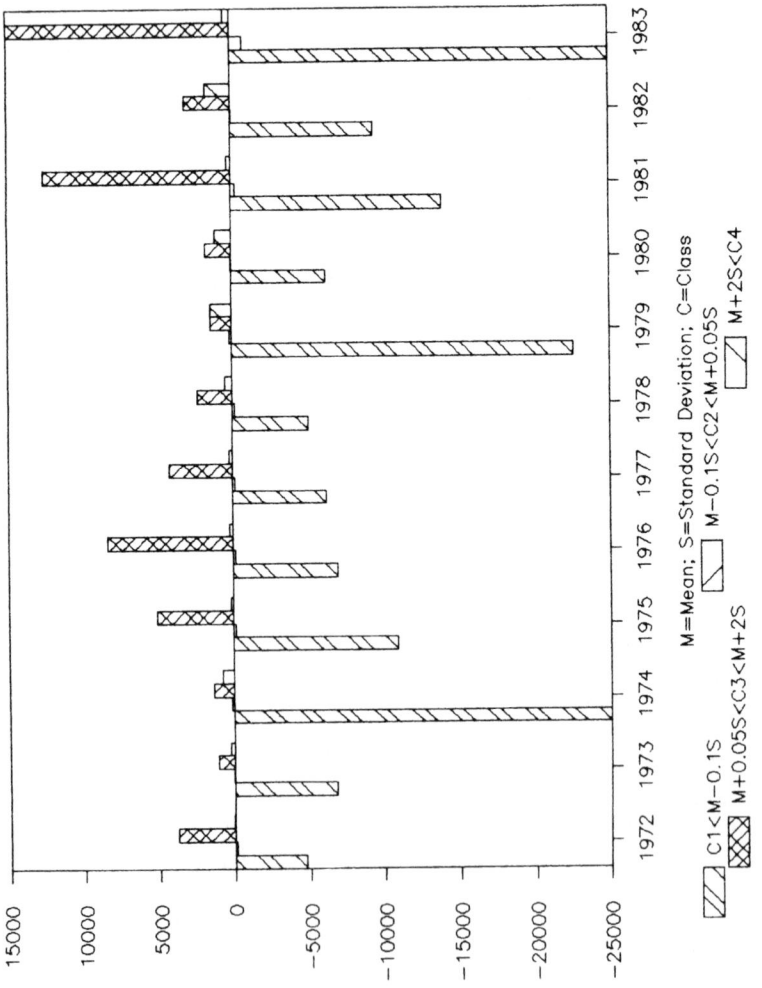

Figure 14.3 Frequency distributions – net borrowing (FB–FL) by value

Table 14.3 Representative interest rate semi-elasticities–aggregate time-series studies

| | | Own rate $RBL + x\%$ | | Cross rates | | | |
| | | | | RLA | | REU | |
		Impact	Long-run	Impact	Long-run	Impact	Long-run
1 Bank borrowing							
SPENCER-MOWL 1987	(1967–77)	-0.0015	-0.0140	—	—	—	—
MAYES-SAVAGE 1980	(1963–77)	-0.0019	na	0.0019*	na	—	—
MOORE-THREADGOLD 1985	(1965–81)	-0.0009	na	—	—	—	—
CUTHBERTSON-HMT 1982	(1965–80)	-0.0020	-0.0272	—	—	0.0010	0.0212
CUTHBERTSON-I 1985	(1965–80)	-0.0100	-0.0767	0.0110	0.0434	0.0000	0.0133
CUTHBERTSON-II 1985	(1965–80)	-0.0970	-0.2915	0.1000	0.2555	0.0050	0.0338
2 Liquid lending		*RLA*		*RG5*		*REU*	
JACKSON-TMD 1984	(1972–82)	0.0182	0.2248	-0.0127	0.0085	-0.0030	-0.0100

Notes: *Imposed equal and opposite to the coefficient on RBL + x%.

CUTHBERTSON-HMT: Re-estimate of the equation in the Treasury Model.
CUTHBERTSON-I: Cuthbertson's 'basic' equation.
CUTHBERTSON-II: Equation in which the cumulative borrowing requirement replaces the income variable (GDP).
JACKSON-TMD: Equation for time deposits including deposits with building societies, local authorities and OFIs.

All studies utilize quarterly data.

RBL + x%   Base Rate + "x"% (usually 1%).
RLA   Local Authority 3-month rate.
REU   Eurodollar 3-month rate.
RG5   Five-year government bond yield.

distributions to be strongly bimodal, each mode representing a different sub-sector. Although the distributions of the narrow liquidity ratio are, indeed, bimodal, it is difficult to know how much importance to attach to the smaller mode. The distributions are dominated by the vast majority of companies (over 500) which fall into the class of companies having liquidity ratios which are less than 0.1 standard deviation below the mean.[4] Moreover, the clearest feature of these frequency distributions is their relative stability from year to year, indicating that company liquidity positions mostly change rather slowly over time relative to the average. Figure 14.3 shows frequency distributions for the flow of net liquid borrowing (bank borrowing net of liquid asset accumulation) with the frequency in each class now represented by the aggregate value of net company borrowing or lending in this class rather than by the number of companies.[5] This presentation gives more weight to larger companies (measured by net liquid borrowings) and therefore gives a somewhat sharper picture of the importance of the two-sector hypothesis as an explanation of aggregate company liquid borrowing and lending. In figure 14.3, a bimodal pattern of net liquid borrowing is a good deal more marked, with two significantly different groups of companies evident in almost all years of the sample.[6]

14.3 Comparisons between aggregative and disaggregated results

Apart from Jackson (1984) who studied the allocation of company sector gross liquid assets among their components, the aggregative time-series studies summarized here are all confined solely to company bank borrowing. Table 14.3 gives representative data on interest rate semi-elasticities from these studies. Each semi-elasticity gives the proportionate response of bank borrowing to a 100 basis point increase in the corresponding interest rate. The first four studies suggest that the impact effect of a change in the own rate of interest (base rate) is relatively small. Unfortunately, it is difficult to have much confidence in these figures. In general, these semi-elasticities actually measure the effect of a change in base rate relative to other interest rates, and it is difficult for the authorities to alter interest-rate differentials in this way. In the long run, it is possible that a rise in the general level of interest rates will curb bank borrowing to a more meaningful extent, but this cannot be ascertained from many of these studies. An equally serious difficulty is evident when account is taken of Cuthbertson's two final sets of estimates which use a rather longer list of explanatory variables than the first four studies. The effect of the additional variables is to increase the own and cross interest semi-elasticities by factors of up to 10. Such large discrepancies do not give much confidence that we have arrived at a satisfactory 'best estimate' of the interest elasticity of bank borrowing. One point of interest, however, is that the latter estimates are closer in order of magnitude to those found by Jackson for companies' liquid asset holdings. Even less can be said in general terms about the impact of scale variables such as output, as the definitions of these variables vary more widely from study to study than do the definitions of the interest-rate variables. Estimated output elasticities vary within a range of 0.1 to 0.5 in the short run and 0.5 to 1.0 in the long run. The corporate borrowing requirement has recently been thought to be of importance in determining bank borrowing. Only Cuthbertson tests this explicitly and he does find it to be significant. In our own disaggregated study, the corporate borrowing requirement and its components do form an important determinant of bank borrowing.

Table 14.4 Interest rate semi-elasticities in quick finance equations

	Bank borrowing	Liquid assets	Trade credit given	Trade credit received
1 Short-run semi-elasticities				
Inter-bank rate	0.308	−0.163	−0.090	−0.053
CD rate	0.315	0.137	0.095	0.048
Covered Euro $ rate	−0.002	0.003	0.001	0.002
LCB base rate	−0.007	0.027	−0.001	0.009
Simultaneous rise in all rates	0.002	0.004	−0.005	0.006
2 Long-run semi-elasticities: four-equation model				
Inter-bank rate	−2.306	0.909	0.128	1.073
CD rate	2.377	−1.016	−0.095	−1.094
Covered Euro $ rate	0.009	−0.002	−0.005	−0.008
LCB base rate	0.012	0.049	−0.034	−0.022
Simultaneous rise in all rates	0.050	−0.060	−0.006	−0.051
3 Long-run semi-elasticities: three-equation model [a]				
Inter-bank rate	−0.007	−0.718	0.225	
CD rate	0.165	0.573	−0.134	
Covered Euro $ rate	−0.021	0.017	−0.011	
LCB base rate	−0.151	0.144	−0.089	
Simultaneous rise in all rates	−0.014	0.016	−0.009	

[a] Net trade credit given semi-elasticities are calculated using the outstanding stock of gross trade credit given.

Overall, these studies contribute rather little towards understanding the interactions between bank borrowing and liquid lending. On the one hand, it appears that a particular and sustained pattern of interest-rate relativities would be required to support a long-term expansion in both bank borrowing and liquid lending. On the other hand, although the influence of activity variables could explain this trend, their influence is generally inconsistent with the counter-cyclical pattern of net borrowing.

The methodology of our own disaggregated study is different from that of the aggregated studies, and full details are contained in our earlier paper. In brief, our model sought to explain the allocation of companies' short-term (or 'quick') finance among four components: short-term bank borrowing, liquid lending, trade credit given, and trade credit received. We therefore modelled gross borrowing and lending simultaneously. We interpret total quick finance to be the residual or 'buffer' financing in the company accounts. Firms are assumed to have no control over total quick finance in the short run as it is the outcome of longer-term decisions on investments, sales, long-term finance, and the like. Firms can, however, control the composition of quick finance, and it is this composition that we seek to explain. This set-up is sufficiently flexible to allow for both a long-term expansion in bank borrowing and liquid lending, and for cyclical movements in net borrowing. Some of the explanatory variables in our work parallel those in aggregated studies, especially interest rates and credit control variables. However, in contrast to aggregate studies, we were able to study the influence of a wide range of company-specific variables. These included a detailed breakdown of the cash flows which make up the corporate borrowing requirement (we call these 'mainstream' cash flows); sales and cost of sales; and individual company stock adjustment effects modelled by the lagged stocks of quick finance and of equity and loan capital. We also included tax variables which are thought to influence corporate financial decisions and which may therefore affect the allocation of quick finance. Finally we included measures of economies of scale and the internal organization of the firm (such as vertical integration) which may affect company behaviour in a non-linear way and which could not be included at all in aggregate studies.

Interest semi-elasticities from the CGM paper are shown in table 14.4. The semi-elasticities are calculated to give the effect of a change in interest rates sustained over one quarter. This provides approximate comparability with aggregate studies using quarterly data. The short-run semi-elasticity of bank borrowing with respect to base rate is about the same order of magnitude as in the main group of aggregative studies. The same is true for the effect of the Eurodollar rate. On the other hand, we find that the CD rate and the interbank rate (which do not appear at all in the aggregative studies) have a very much larger impact on borrowing and lending. The impact of the interbank rate on bank borrowing is nearly 50 times that of the base rate, and it implies that a 100 basis points increase in the interbank rate reduces bank borrowing over one quarter by a staggering 31 per cent. These estimates correspond to a 100 basis point change in the interest rate *differential*. It is clear that the effect of a rise in the general level of interest rates is much smaller, since the CD and interbank rates are essentially offsetting in all the quick finance equations. The semi-elasticity of bank borrowing associated with a rise in all interest rates is 0.002. Moreover, we found that the sum of the interest rate coefficients in the bank borrowing equation was not significantly different from zero. This restriction was not found to hold in the other quick finance equations. An additional feature of our results, which cannot easily be investigated using aggregate data, concerns the impact of interest rates on trade credit. Our results imply that a rise in the general level of interest rates induces companies in our sample to increase their *net* trade credit received by a small but significant amount. It implies that these companies can squeeze other (mostly smaller) companies into lending more to them when interest rates rise. This is consistent with survey evidence and the comments of smaller companies reported by the Wilson Committee (1980).

To calculate the long-run effects of interest-rate changes, we consider, for illustrative purposes, a stock equilibrium in which all net cash flows are zero. Stocks of quick finance are then determined by factors such as interest rates and tax rates, as well as by the size of the firm. To determine the stability of this long run we first investigated the eigenvalues of the matrix of lagged stocks. All were positive and real but that associated with the trade-credit received equation exceeded unity, indicating instability. There were other problems with the separate trade-credit received and given equations which led us to consider a condensed three-equation system in which we explain bank borrowing, liquid assets, and *net* trade-credit given (trade-credit received less trade-credit given). The eigenvalues of this system were both positive, real, and less than unity.[7] We have therefore computed two sets of long-run interest rates semi-elasticities, one associated with gross trade-credit equations and the other with a net trade-credit equation. In the four-equation model, the long-run coefficients replicate some properties of the short-run coefficients, although the signs of the main effects in the liquid assets equation are perverse. However, these results are more optimistic about the impact of a change in the general *level* of interest rates on bank borrowing in the long run. Turning to the (possibly) more plausible three-equation model, we observe a very interesting phenomenon in the bank borrowing equation. The largest differential effects now involve the CD rate and base rate. This suggests that the interbank rate affects lending in the short run and base rate determines it in the longer run. There are no longer any perverse signs in the interest rate responses. The effect of higher interest rates in increasing net trade credit received as well as liquid assets carries over from the short run to the long run. Perhaps most important, these results suggest that the impact of a rise in the general level of interest rates on bank borrowing is relatively small, with a 100 basis point increase reducing the stock of bank debt by less than 2 per cent in the long run.

Our comments on the influence of other variables on quick finance flows can be brief. The largest single set of influences on bank borrowing and liquid lending proved to be the mainstream cash flows of a company, although these flows differed in their effects from item to item. Statistically, these flows were far more important than the bulk of the other variables in the regressions, although, as we shall see, the quantitative magnitude of their effect in aggregate is smaller than that of certain other variables. Nevertheless, these results are consistent with the idea that quick finance flows act, to some extent, as a buffer to other activities in the short run. In so far as different cash flows have different effects on bank borrowing and liquid lending, these results also imply that aggregate studies which rely on the use of a single activity variable as regressor (such as output or the corporate borrowing requirement) are likely to produce seriously misleading estimates. The preponderance of different activities appears to have differing effects on company borrowing and lending.

14.4 The implications of disaggregated results for aggregate borrowing and lending

We turn next to the implications of the CGM study for aggregate borrowing and lending. Our major interest is in exploring the extent to which the evolution of these aggregates can be explained by our disaggregated model, and how far differences in behaviour among individual companies contribute to such an explanation. Unfortunately, mere inspection of estimated coefficients and significance tests will not provide an estimate of the importance of inter-firm differences in explaining aggregate bank borrowing and liquid lending. The regression coefficients in the model measure the marginal effects of variables associated with individual companies, whereas, in aggregate, intra-marginal effects may be more important. We have therefore utilized a simple descriptive simulation approach which can be summarized as follows.

The linear regression model for disaggregated company sector data can be written

$$Y_{nt} = \beta_{on} + \sum_{i=1}^{I} \beta_i X_{int} + U_{nt} \tag{14.1}$$

where Y_{nt} is the endogenous variable

X_{int} ($i = 1, \ldots, I$) are the explanatory variables

β_i ($i = 1, \ldots, I$) are slope coefficients

β_{on} ($n = 1, \ldots, N$) are firm-specific constants

     $n = 1, \ldots, N$ Companies

     $t = 1, \ldots, T$ time periods

$\hat{Y}_{nt}, \hat{\beta}_i$ are the fitted values of Y_{nt}, β_i

If we consider (14.1) to be the standard regression model, each of the terms

$$Z_{int} \equiv \hat{\beta}_i (X_{int} - \bar{X}_i), \; i = 1, \ldots, I; \; \bar{X}_i = \frac{1}{nt} \sum_n \sum_t X_{int} \tag{14.2}$$

can be interpreted as showing the contributions of the nt^{th} observation of the ith explanatory variable to the fitted value of the nt^{th} observation of the endogenous variable $\hat{Y}_{nt}$. A company-cum-time-series plot of these data would provide a decomposition of the fitted values in terms of the explanatory variables.

Consider now the cross-company aggregates

$$Z_{it}^* \equiv \hat{\beta}_i \sum_n (X_{int} - \bar{X}_i)$$

These are the aggregate time-series analogues of the individual company decompositions (Z_{int}) but they are constructed using the disaggregated data and regression coefficients. The regression

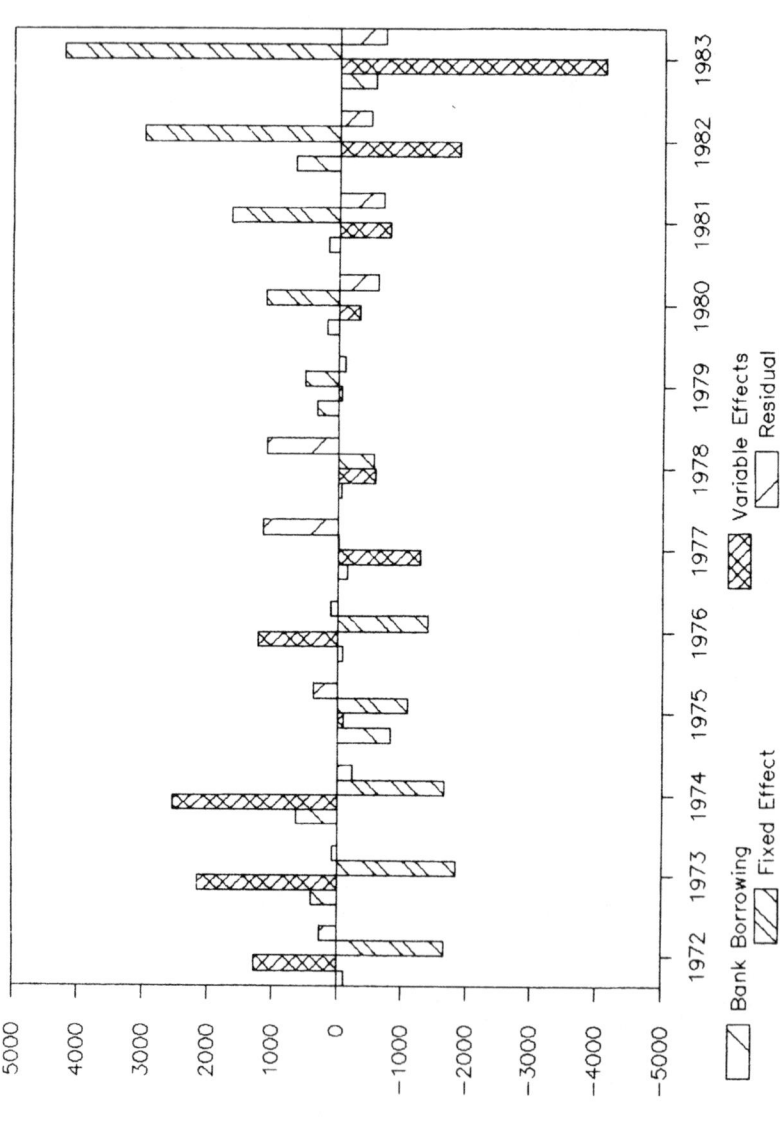

Figure 14.4 Aggregate bank borrowing – variable and fixed effects

residuals can similarly be summed across companies and the aggregate values of the endogenous variable can be decomposed into the fitted values and residuals.

For compactness, we show here the results of two such decompositional exercises. Figure 14.4 shows, year by year: aggregate bank borrowing, the total contribution of all the explanatory variables calculated as $\sum_i Z_{it}^*$, the contribution of the fixed effect, and the aggregate residual. The fixed effect is a proxy for effects specific to each company which are not measured directly by the explanatory variables and in models of this kind, it is normally constant over time for each company. However, in our regression, all company-specific stocks and cash flows were divided by a measure of company size as a correction for heteroscedasticity. Thus, the contribution of the fixed effect to the value of cash flows varies from period to period and so provides a measure of the importance of systematic size-related differences in company behaviour. It is evident from figure 14.4 that, in terms of fit, disaggregated equations do not perform as well in explaining the aggregates as do equations which are estimated directly using the aggregates. This of course is to be expected. More striking, however, is that the fixed effect and the total of the variable effects each sum to a magnitude which is a multiple of fitted bank borrowing. The fixed and variable effects are, however, generally of opposite sign. The fitted values of the flow of bank borrowing are thus seen to be the outcome of an interaction between two much larger but opposing forces.

In the second such exercise (figure 14.5) we have concentrated on the variable effects and have segregated the explanatory variables into five groups shown in table 14.5 (note the difference in scale between figures 14.4 and 14.5). Each bar in figure 14.5 thus shows $\sum_{i=j(1)}^{j(k)} Z_{it}^*$ where $j(1), \ldots, j(k)$ corresponds in each case to the list of k explanatory variables in group j ($j = 1, \ldots, 5$). The groupings of exogenous variables are largely self-explanatory, aiming as they do to discriminate between macroeconomic and policy influences, microeconomic influences such as cash flows which aggregate easily, and non-linear effects which do not aggregate easily. Figure 14.5 shows the total impact of interest rates to be mostly quite modest, although the impact of individual interest rates (i.e. differentials) is much larger. Moreover, interest rate effects increased bank borrowing relative to the mean during

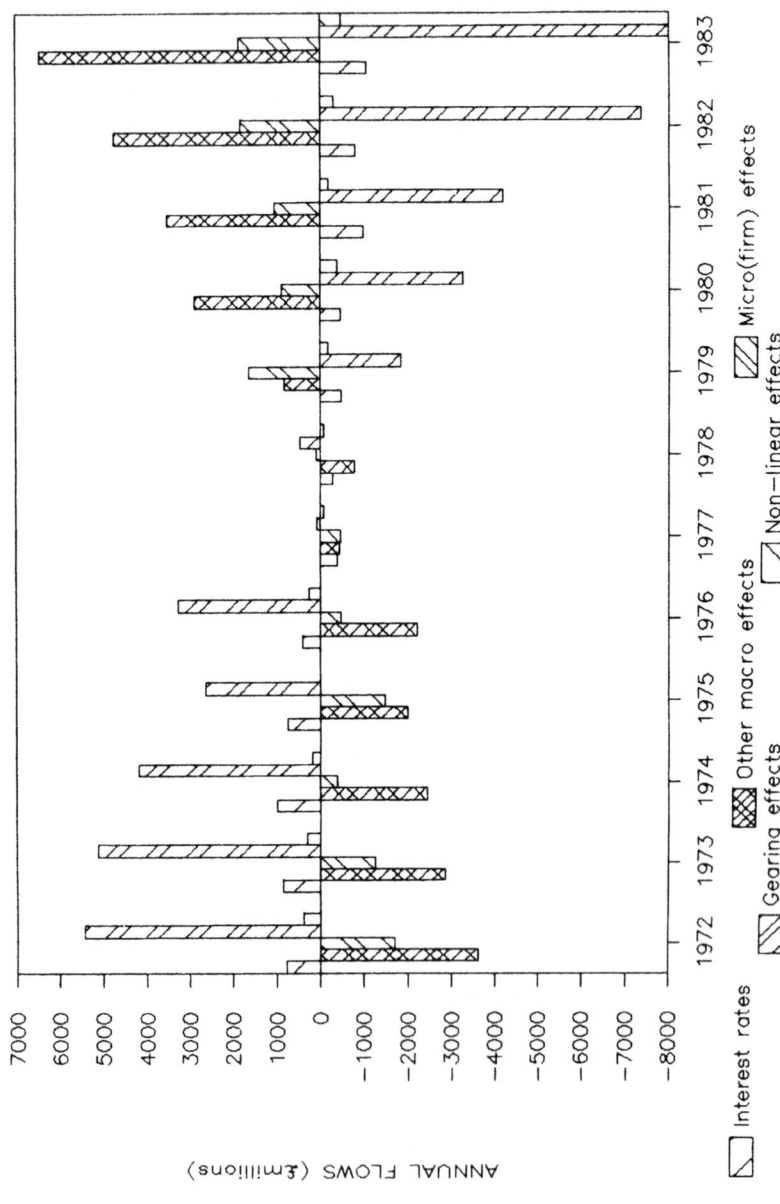

Figure 14.5 Aggregate bank borrowing – contribution of major variables

Table 14.5 Grouping of explanatory variables

1	**Interest rates**	
	Interbank rate	Covered Eurodollar rate
	CD rate	Base rate
2	**Other macroeconomic effects**	
	Debt/equity tax discrimination	Corset dummy (period of operation)
	Debt/retentions tax discrimination	Corset dummy (period when effective)
	Retentions/equity tax discrimination	Exchange control dummy
	Unemployment rate	
3	**Microeconomic (firm) effects**	
	Fixed investment	Sale of fixed assets
	Stocks	Net miscellaneous sources
	Dividends	Profits
	Taxes	Sales
	Capital issues	Cost of sales
	Loan capital	
4	**Lagged stocks (gearing effects)**	
	Trade credit received	Liquid assets
	Trade credit given	Loan capital
	Bank borrowing	Equity and preference
5	**Non-linear effects**	
	Rate of return on capital	Company sales/total sales
	Profits/sales	

the early 1970s, while reducing it later. However, the dominant feature is again the existence of two large and offsetting effects associated with macroeconomic variables other than interest rates, and lagged stocks of assets and liabilities. It should be noted, however, that other macroeconomic variables consist mainly of tax variables, whose effects are powerful in size, but whose statistical significance was mostly marginal. Nevertheless, it seems clear that such effects are important and require further investigation. The lagged stocks reflect stock adjustment activity by firms and the magnitude of these effects is further evidence of the importance that firms do attach to the structure of their balance sheets. Non-linear effects are relatively unimportant. However, it must be emphasized that size-related firm-specific effects are contained in the fixed effect and this clearly is of considerable importance. The decompositions of aggregate liquid lending (not shown) do not consist of such large offsetting forces. The fixed and variable effects are mostly offsetting but the latter are more closely related to actual liquid lending flows. Among the variable effects, lagged stocks continue to be important but so too are other micro-economic effects (primarily firms' cash flows). Non-linear effects not related to firm size are no more important for liquid lending than for bank borrowing.

These decompositions suggest that bank borrowing is distinctive in being the outcome of a number of very large but conflicting pressures. They therefore provide evidence in support of the view that bank borrowing acts as the principal 'buffer stock' in company accounts. As regards the liquid lending puzzle, all but one group of variables reflect in aggregate the parameters of the disaggregated regression results. These results strongly imply that bank borrowing and liquid lending are substitutes with respect to virtually all the explanatory variables in the model: shocks which increase borrowing reduce lending, and vice versa. This explains the cyclical pattern but not the long-term trend in borrowing and lending. The only group of explanatory variables which have qualitatively the same marginal effect on aggregate borrowing and lending are the microeconomic (firm) effects, mainly company cash flows. Among these, profits were the main source of increased aggregate lending, and fixed investment the main source of increased aggregate borrowing.

14.5 Summing-up

It seems clear that company bank borrowing cannot easily be viewed in isolation from liquid lending. Over the last two decades, bank borrowing and liquid lending have both expanded rapidly. However, bank borrowing net of liquid lending has a cyclical pattern and tends to vary inversely with the growth in output in the economy as a whole. In our analysis of differences in company behaviour we found a number of factors which could help explain either the long-term trend in bank borrowing and liquid lending, or the cyclical behaviour of net borrowing. We cannot, however, claim to have uncovered a complete picture of these factors, because different variables were found to be important in different ways. It seems clear that there are significant differences in the way 'large' and 'small' companies make financing decisions, although larger companies borrow and lend more than smaller companies partly just because they are larger. Nevertheless, differences in marginal responses between large and small companies do imply that there are economies of scale in short-term financing decisions. This suggests that the next step in this line of research should be a more thorough theoretical and empirical examination of the factors which characterize inter-firm differences.

From a theoretical point of view, our results are more consistent with a 'buffer stock' view of the role of bank borrowing than of liquid lending. Even when aggregate bank borrowing is 'small', the forces operating on it are 'large'. As far as monetary policy is concerned we are generally more pessimistic about the impact of a change in interest rates on bank borrowing than are the major aggregate studies. Our results suggest that even the long-run effect of a change in the level of interest rates is relatively small. Moreover, we show fairly conclusively that manipulating interest-rate differentials does not offer much promise, as the responses here are so large as to give rise to potentially disruptive flows of funds. Given our framework, some of these results are perhaps not surprising. We have taken as given a number of variables which in the longer run are likely themselves to be responsive to interest-rate changes, notably mainstream cash flows. In this respect our equations are more like structural equations, whereas the aggregate time-series studies are more like reduced forms. However, the results are significant because they imply that bank lending is not easily controlled over any time period by interest rate changes, unless those interest rate changes also affect real company activity. Our results suggest that the 'transmission mechanism' may be from interest rates to real activity and thence to bank borrowing but it is not from interest rates direct to bank borrowing – in any run, be it short, medium, or long.

Notes

1   The sign conventions used in the regressions are the same as in table 14.1.
2   The DATASTREAM sample is not complete in 1969–70. Incomplete data for these years are given in table 14.5 so as to achieve as long a run of data as possible. Subsequent analyses of the DATASTREAM data are confined to the period 1972–83, post-CCC.
3   It is customary to define a liquidity ratio as the ratio of assets to liabilities. However, at least some of our companies had no bank borrowings outstanding in all years of our sample. As all companies had some liquid assets outstanding throughout, it proved easier to calculate liquidity ratios in inverse form as the ratio of liabilities to assets. We also examined a broader liquidity ratio, defined essentially as the inverse of the liquidity ratio for large companies published in CSO, *Financial Statistics*. This provided a broadly similar picture to that of the narrow liquidity ratio.
4   The distribution of companies by size is severely skewed and it proved infeasible to choose a reasonably compact number of classes of equal size within which to represent the frequencies. The actual classes (of unequal size) for all our frequency distributions are six in number ($C1, \ldots, C6$) defined by:

$$
\begin{array}{lcl}
 & & C1 < (M - 0.1\,S) \\
(M - 0.1\,S) & < & C2 < (M - 0.05\,S) \\
(M - 0.05\,S) & < & C3 < (M + 0.05\,S) \\
(M + 0.05\,S) & < & C4 < (M + 2\,S) \\
(M + 2\,S) & < & C5 < (M + 3\,S) \\
(M + 3\,S) & < & C6
\end{array}
$$

where M is the mean and S the standard deviation of the distribution. These class sizes were chosen by computer after some experimentation with frequency distributions for a variety of measures of liquidity and borrowings. Our aim was to generate distributions which described different features of the data in a broadly comparable way.

5   In other words the frequencies are shown as (number of companies in the class $\times$ average net borrowings or lendings of those companies).

6   Since the means of the two groups concerned are always more than two standard deviations apart, their difference is statistically significant. Economic significance for aggregate borrowing and lending lies in the size of the two groups as well as in the difference between their mean values.

7   Because of the constraint that the separate components of quick finance must sum to the exogenously given total, any one of the quick finance equations can always be calculated identically from the other three (or two). Hence there is always one less eigenvalue than the number of equations in the model.

Chapter fifteen

Some threshold problems in modelling the company sector

G. Meeks*

There are two standard arguments for disaggregated modelling of the company sector. The first is that the modeller – perhaps shareholder, takeover bidder, or union negotiator – is primarily concerned with the performance and prospects of an individual company (see Goudie and Meeks, 1981, 1982). The second applies to the modeller who is primarily concerned with the sector aggregate: the diversity of company behaviour may be so great that disaggregated modelling is the most efficient way to capture sector behaviour.[1] In this paper a third argument is presented: even if the modeller is interested only in the sector and not in the individual agent, and even if all companies are identical in their response to given market stimuli, nevertheless threshold effects in companies' responses may still make disaggregation the most efficient route to aggregate conclusions.

The general form of the argument is that, say, a million pound fall in profits may lead to substantial changes in other variables for company A but no change for company B if the two companies lie on different sides of certain statutorily or institutionally determined thresholds. Estimates of the aggregate effect on the sector of a fall in profits will depend upon the distribution of companies around the respective threshold. The argument is illustrated with three thresholds faced by British companies in the postwar period: one arising from taxation rules, another from dividend control legislation, and a third from the credit-rating procedures of financial institutions.

Consider first a simplified calculation of the company sector's taxable income, where the taxable income (Y^t) of individual company i is:

---

* This paper is a by-product of a research project financed by the Leverhulme Trust, whose help is gratefully acknowledged.

$$Y_i^t = Y_i^b - A_i \tag{15.1}$$

where Y_i^b is company i's income before deducting tax allowances and A_i is company i's tax allowances. A disaggregated model which computed variables company by company would then give a taxable income for the company sector

$$Y_c^t = \sum_i Y_i^t = \sum_i (Y_i^b - A_i) \tag{15.2}$$

Computing variables at the sector level, using only sector aggregates would instead give the sector's taxable income as

$$Y_a^t = \sum_i Y_i^b - \sum_i A_i \tag{15.3}$$

However, since tax rules apply a threshold or constraint ($Y_i^b - A_i \geqslant 0$, i.e. tax cannot be negative), the two models will only give the same value for sectoral taxable income on the condition

$$Y_a^t = Y_c^t \quad \text{if} \quad Y_i^b > A_i \text{ for all } i \tag{15.4}$$

However, often in recent years in Britain, $Y_i^b < A_i$ for many companies (i.e. there has been widespread 'tax exhaustion'); in these circumstances, Y_a^t, the value of taxable income obtained from an aggregate model, may significantly understate the true value, Y_c^t, obtained from a disaggregated model: T_a, taxation's share of Y_a^t, as estimated by an aggregate model, will fall below T_c, the figure estimated by the tax authorities with a micro model.

We have estimated the quantitative importance of this threshold problem using a disaggregated model of corporate taxation and compared its predictions with those for a counterpart model based

Table 15.1 Taxation estimates from a disaggregated model of the UK company sector as a percentage of corresponding estimates from an aggregate model (T_c^t / T_a^t)

1976	103	1983	114
1977	103	1984	109
1978	108	1985	111
1979	102	1986	112
1980	111	1987	114
1981	108	1988	112
1982	114		

Source: Own calculations using a macro-micro model as detailed in Goudie and Meeks (1984).

on aggregate data. The tax model and the company sector model in which it is embedded are too complex to report in any detail here – they are summarized in Goudie (1984) and Goudie and Meeks (1984) – but table 15.1 gives the upshot, the value of T_c/T_a generated by the two models. According to these estimates, incorporating micro information on which companies have reached the crucial thresholds produces taxation figures as much as 14 per cent higher than those of the macro model.

The second area where micro data on threshold effects can inform macro modelling is dividend payments. The conventional model in the literature has desired dividends, D_d, adjusting over time so as to achieve a target payout ratio, and responding also to any tax penalties imposed upon dividend distributions (see Lintner, 1956, Feldstein, 1967, 1970, King, 1971, Hansen, 1987). However, in the UK at various stages in the sixties and seventies, a maximum dividend, D_m, has been set for each company by the government as part of its counter-inflationary restraints on incomes.

Hansen and Goudie (1988) estimate that in periods of dividend control up to 50 per cent of large UK companies have been paying roughly D_m, the maximum permitted. Whether they would have chosen to pay more in the absence of the legislation (i.e. $D_d >$ D_m) is a more difficult question requiring estimates of D_d. Hansen and Goudie attempt a microeconometric answer, estimating for each company in their sample a dividend model incorporating dummy variables designed to capture the effects of dividend controls. They conclude that in the seventies at least a quarter of their sample paid smaller dividends than they would have chosen in the absence of controls (the coefficient on the respective dummy variables was significantly negative on the usual statistical tests for 26 per cent of the companies; it was negative, but not always significantly so, for 72 per cent of the sample).

For some companies, then, which were already at the threshold, profit growth would not elicit extra dividend payments; for others, who were well below the threshold, normal behaviour would be unconstrained; while for a third group, who were a little way below the threshold, controls would dampen the normal dividend response to profits. The value of incorporating micro information on these thresholds will of course be evident not just in constructing aggregate estimates for a period in which controls were in force but also in estimating a forecasting model for subsequent years based on observations during the controls.

The third example of a threshold problem is company failure. The standard instrument for forecasting company failure has been multiple discriminant analysis: this has been widely used in the finance literature and by practitioners in finance to combine different dimensions of a firm's financial health (see Beaver, 1966, Altman, 1968, Taffler, 1982, Goudie, 1987). The resulting single Z score for the company at issue (Z_i) is then compared with a critical Z score (Z_c) which, observation of past failures suggests, has commonly spelled the death of companies. For the academic, $Z_i < Z_c$ has proved a relatively successful predictor of failure; this success may well have been reinforced by the fact that, for the credit analyst, $Z_i < Z_c$ has become a signal to withhold or withdraw credit, action which could itself often precipitate failure.

We have incorporated a discriminant model of failure in the disaggregated model of the UK company sector mentioned earlier in the discussion of thresholds in the tax system. The resulting set of models enables us to identify which companies would be forced below the Z_c threshold by given macroeconomic developments. Furthermore, a simulation exercise we have carried out with the models illustrates one way that threshold effects can combine with the diverse economic circumstances of individual firms to yield unexpected results. We simulated the effect on the death rate among the top 100 UK companies of applying successive depreciations or appreciations of the exchange rate. The results are reported in full in Goudie and Meeks (1987). Two examples illustrate the theme of this paper. First, the relationship between exchange and failure rates turned out in the illustrative runs to be strikingly non-linear: as might be expected, depreciation reduced the death rate, but, more surprisingly, rarely did a 10 per cent depreciation save more companies than one of 5 per cent and yet a 20 per cent depreciation sometimes saved more than twice as many as one of 10 per cent. Then, second, the changes were asymmetric: in one year, seven companies were saved by a 20 per cent depreciation but only two extra fatalities were induced by a 20 per cent increase in the exchange rate.

The conclusion from these examples can be expressed using the hypothetical case of a £1 million fall in company sector profits which was mentioned in the introduction. First, how would it affect taxation flows from the corporate to the government sector? That would depend on which companies reported $Y_i^b < A_i$; in the limiting case there could be no reduction in taxation payments. Second, how would the profit fall affect dividend flows from the corporate to the personal sector? That would depend on which companies were in the position $D_d > D_m$; in the limiting case there could be no reduction in dividends. Third, how would this fall affect the corporate death rate (and consequently economic capacity)? That would depend which companies it drove into the potentially fatal zone, $Z_i < Z_c$: if many companies lay initially just above Z_c, the mortality rate could be seriously affected.

Estimates from our own disaggregated modelling of the company sector illustrate the quantitative importance of these threshold effects. They help to buttress a case for disaggregation which could hold even if the modeller had no interest in results for individual companies and even if companies did not differ greatly in their objectives.

Note

1   Hansen (1987) argues this in the case of dividend behaviour.

Bibliography

Aigner, D.J. and Goldfeld, S.M. (1974) 'Estimation and prediction from aggregate data when aggregates are measured more accurately than their components', *Econometrica*, 42: 113–34.

Allen, R.G.D. (1963) *Mathematical economics*, 2nd edn., London: Macmillan.

Almon, C. (1986) 'The industrial impact of macroeconomic policies in the INFORUM model', paper presented to the 8th International Conference on Input-Output Modelling, Sapporo, Japan.

Alphen, H.J. van and Merkies, A.H.Q.M. (1976) 'Distributed lags in construction: an empirical study', *International Economic Review*, 17: 411–30.

Altman, E.I. (1968) 'Financial ratios, discriminant analysis and the prediction of corporate bankruptcy', *Journal of Finance*, 589–609.

Amemiya, T. (1981) 'Qualitative response models: a survey', *Journal of Economic Literature*, 19: 1483–537.

—— (1985) *Advanced econometrics*, Cambridge, Mass.: Harvard University Press.

Andersen, R., Kravitz, J., and Anderson, O.W. (eds) (1975) *Equity in health services: empirical analysis in social policy*, Cambridge, Mass.: Ballinger Publishing Company.

Arndt, S.W. (ed.) (1982) *Political economy of Austria*, American Enterprise Institute for Public Policy Research, Washington and London.

Arrow, K.J. (1962) 'The economic implications of learning by doing', *Review of Economic Studies*, 29: 155–73.

Astin, J. (1985) 'Commodity flow accounts for the United Kingdom', *Economic Trends*, May.

Atkinson, A.B. (1983) 'Adjustments to the family expenditure survey data', ESRC Programme on Taxation, Incentives and the Distribution of Income, Research Note 7, mimeo, London School of Economics.

Atkinson, A.B. and Micklewright, J. (1983) 'On the reliability of income data in the Family Expenditure Survey 1970–1977', *Journal of the Royal Statistical Society, Series A*, 146: 33–61.

Atkinson, A.B. and Sutherland, H. (1988) 'Taxation of husband and wife in the UK and changes in the tax-benefit system', in Atkinson, A.B. and

Sutherland, H. (eds), 'Tax-benefit models', ST/ICERD Occasional Paper No.10, London School of Economics.

Atkinson, A.B., Gomulka, J. and Sutherland, H. (1988) 'Grossing-up FES data for tax-benefit models', ESRC Programme on Taxation Incentives and the Distribution of Income, Discussion Paper No. TIDI/105.

Baily, M.N. and Chakrabarti, A.K. (1985) 'Innovation and productivity in US industry', *Brookings Papers on Economic Activity*, 2: 609–32.

Bain, A.D. (1986) 'The change and innovation in the mix of financial instruments: the UK experience', in Fair, D.E. (ed.), *Shifting frontiers in financial markets*, Dordrecht: Martinus Nijhoff.

Ball, R.J. (ed.) (1973) *The International Linkage of National Economic Models*, Amsterdam: North Holland.

Ball, R.J. and St Cyr, E.B.A. (1966) 'Short term employment functions in British manufacturing industry', *Review of Economic Studies*, 33: 179–207.

Bank of England (1981) 'The UK corporate bond market', *Quarterly Bulletin*, March: 54–8.

Barker, T.S. (1970) 'Aggregation error and estimates of the UK import demand function', in Hilton, K. and Heathfield, D.F. (eds), *The econometric study of the United Kingdom*, London: Macmillan.

Barker, T.S. (1974) 'The major determinants of Britain's visible imports, 1949–1966', unpublished Ph.D. thesis, Cambridge University.

Barker, T.S. and Peterson, A.W.A.P. (1987) *The Cambridge Multisectoral Dynamic Model of the British Economy*, Cambridge: Cambridge University Press.

Barnett, W.A. (1979) 'Theoretical foundations for the Rotterdam model', *Review of Economic Studies*, 46: 109–30.

Beaver, W.H. (1966) 'Financial ratios as predictors of failure', in *Empirical Research in Accounting: Selected Studies, 1966*, Institute of Professional Accounting, London (January 1967).

Beenstock, M., and Warburton, P. (1984) 'An econometric model of the UK labour market', mimeo, City University Business School.

Beggs, J.J. (1984) 'Long-run trends in patenting', in Griliches, Z. (ed.) *R&D, patents and productivity*, Chicago: University of Chicago Press.

Bergan, R., Cappelen, A., Longva, S., and Stolen, N.M. (1986) 'MODAG A – a medium term annual macroeconomic model of the Norwegian economy', discussion paper of the Central Bureau of Statistics, Oslo, Norway.

Blackorby, C., Primont, D., and Russell, R. (1978) *Duality, separability and functional structure: theory and applications*, Amsterdam: North Holland.

Blanchard, O.J. (1987) 'Aggregate and individual price adjustment', *Brookings Papers on Economic Activity*, 1: 57–122.

Blundell, R. (1986) 'Econometric approaches to the specification of life cycle labour supply and commodity demand behaviour', *Econometric Reviews*, 5(1): 89–146.

(1988) 'Consumer behaviour: theory and empirical evidence, a survey', *Economic Journal*, 98: 16–65.

Blundell, R., Ham, J., and Meghir, C. (1987) 'Unemployment and female labour supply', *Economic Journal*, 97, Conference Papers Supplement: 44–64.

Boot, J.C.G. and de Wit, G.M. (1960) 'Investment demand: an empirical contribution to the aggregation problem', *International Economic Review*, 1: 3–30.

Borooah, V.K. (1979) 'Starts and completions of private dwellings: four models of distributed lag behaviour', *Journal of Economic Studies*, 6: 204–15.

Bouthelier, F. and Daganzo, C.F. (1979) 'Aggregation with multinomial probit and estimation of disaggregate models with aggregate data: a new methodological approach', *Transportation Research*, 13B: 133–46.

Box, G.E.P. and Jenkins, G.M. (1970) *Time Series Analysis, Forecasting and Control*, San Francisco: Holden-Day.

Brechling, F. (1965) 'Relationship between output and employment in British manufacturing industries', *Review of Economic Studies*, 32: 187–216.

Budd, A., Dicks, G., Holly, S., Keating, G., and Robinson, W. (1984) 'The London Business School econometric model of the UK', *Economic Modelling*, 1(4): 355–420.

Burgess, S.M. (1988) 'Employment adjustment in UK manufacturing', *Economic Journal*, 98: 81–103.

Cameron, A.C. (1985) 'Estimation and prediction in discrete choice models using aggregate data', Stanford University, Economic Workshop Technical Paper No. 2.

Cannoodt, L.J. and Knickman, J.R. (1984) 'The effects of hospital characteristics and organizational factors on pre- and post-operative lengths of hospital stay', *Health Services Research*, 19–5: 561–85.

Central Statistical Office (1985) *United Kingdom National Accounts: Sources and Methods*, 3rd Edition, London: HMSO.

— (1986) *Financial Statistics*, London: HMSO.

Chipman, J.S. (1976) 'Estimation and aggregation in econometrics: an application of the theory of gneralized inverses', in Zahair Mashed, M. (ed.) *Generalized inverses and applications*, New York: Academic Press.

Chipman, J.S. (1977a) 'Statistical problems arising in the theory of aggregation', in Krishnaiah, P.R. (ed.), *Proceedings of the symposium on applications of statistics*, Amsterdam: North Holland Publishing Co.

Chipman, J.S. (1977b) 'Towards the construction of an optimal aggregative model of international trade: West Germany, 1963–1975', *Annals of Economic and Social Measurement*, 6: 535–54.

Chowdhury, G., Green, C.J., and Miles, D.K. (1986) 'An empirical model of company short-term financial decisions: evidence from company accounts data', Bank of England Discussion Paper, 26.

Cooper, I.A. and Franks, J.R. (1983) 'Interaction of investment and financing decisions when the firm has unused tax credits', *Journal of Finance*, May.

Cox, D.R. and Hinkley, D.V. (1974) *Theoretical statistics*, London: Chapman and Hall.

Bibliography

Cramer, J.S. (1964) 'Efficient grouping, regression and correlation in Engel curve analysis', *Journal of the American Statistical Association*, 59: 223–50.

Cullis, J.G., Foster, D.F., and Frost, C.E.B. (1979) 'The demand for inpatient treatment: some recent evidence', *Applied Economics*, 12: 43–60.

Cuthbertson, K. (1985) 'Sterling bank lending to UK industrial and commercial companies', *Bulletin of the Oxford University Institute of Economics and Statistics*, 47(2): 91–118.

Daal, J. van and Merkies, A.H.Q.M. (1984) *Aggregation in economic research*, Dordrecht: Reidel.

Darroch, J., Jirina, M., and McDonald, J. (1986) 'The sum of finite moving average processes', *Journal of Time Series Analysis*, 7: 21–5.

Deutsch, E. (1988) *Faktornachfrage auf Strukturierten Arbeitsmärkten; Theorie und Empirie am Beispiel Österreichs*, Frankfurt: Athenäum.

Devereux, M.P. (1986) 'The IFS model of UK corporation tax', IFS Working Paper No. 984, Institute of Fiscal Studies, London.

Dilnot, A.W. and Morris, C.N. (1982) 'The impact of the budget on household living standards', House of Commons Library Background Paper, March.

Dilnot, A.W., Kay, J.A., and Morris, C.N. (1984) *The reform of social security*, Oxford University Press.

Duesenberry, J.S. (1967) *Income, saving and the theory of consumer behaviour*, Cambridge, Mass.: Harvard University Press.

Durbin, J. (1954) 'Errors in variables', *Review of International Statistical Institute*, 22: 23–32.

Durlauf, S.N. and Phillips, P.C.B. (1986) 'Trends versus random walks in time series analysis', mimeo, New Haven, Conn.: Yale University.

Eckstein, O. (1983) *The DRI model of the US economy*, New York: McGraw-Hill Book Company.

Edwards, J. and Keen, J.S.S. (1985) 'Taxes, investment and Q', *Review of Economic Studies*, 52: 665–79.

Edwards, J., Kay, J., and Mayer, C. (1987) *The economic analysis of accounting profitability*, Oxford University Press.

Eliasson, G. (1984) *The firm and financial markets in Swedish micro-to-macro model (MOSES) – theory, model and verification*, Industrial Institute for Economic and Social Research, Stockholm.

Engle, R.F. and Granger, C.W.J. (1987) 'Co-integration and error correction: representation, estimation and testing', *Econometrica*, 55: 251–76.

Engle, R.F., Hendry, D.F., and Richard, J.F. (1983) 'Exogeneity', *Econometrica*, 51: 277–304.

Erber, G. (1986) 'A dynamic multisectoral model of production, investment and prices based on flexible cost functions', *Vierteljahrshefte zur Wirtschaftsforschung*, 3: 108–9.

Feldstein, M.S. (1967) 'The effectiveness of the British differential profits tax', *Economic Journal*, 77: 947–53.

——— (1970) 'Corporate taxation and dividend behaviour', *Review of Economic Studies*, 37: 57–72.

(1977) 'Quality change and the demand for hospital care', *Econometrica*, 45–7: 1681–1702.

Fisher, F.M. (1969) 'The existence of aggregate production functions', *Econometrica*, 37: 553–77.

Fisher, F.M., Solow, R.M., and Kearl, J.M. (1977) 'Aggregate production functions: some CES experiments', *Review of Economic Studies*, 44(2): 137.

Fisher, W.D. (1962) 'Optimal aggregation in multi-equation prediction models', *Econometrica*, 30: 744–69.

(1969) *Clustering and aggregation in economics.* Baltimore: Johns Hopkins University Press.

(1979) 'A note on aggregation and disaggregation', *Econometrica*, 47: 739–46.

Fomby, T., Hill, R.C., and Johnson, S. (1984) *Advanced econometric methods*, New York: Springer-Verlag.

Forni, M. (1987) *Aggregazione, Dinamica ed Esogeneità*, Department of Political Economy, University of Modena.

Friedman, M. (1957) *A theory of the consumption function*, Princeton: Princeton University Press.

Fuchs, V. (1978) 'The supply of surgeons and the demand for surgical operations', *Journal of Human Resources, Supplement* 13: 35–56.

Fuchs, V. and Kramer, M. (1973) *Determinants of expenditures for physician's services in the United States 1948–1968*, New York, NBER/HEW.

Gaag, J. van der, Rutten, F.F.H. and Praag, B.M.S. van (1976) 'Determinants of hospital utilization in the Netherlands', *Health Services Research*, 10–3: 264–77.

Godley, W.A.H., and Shepherd, J.R. (1964) 'Long-term growth and short-term policy', *National Institute Economic Review*, 29: 26–38.

Gonzalo, J. (1988) 'Cointegration and aggregation', working paper, Economics Department, University of California, San Diego.

Gorman, W.M. (1959) 'Separating utility and aggregation', *Econometrica*, 27: 469–81.

Gorman, W. (1968) 'The structure of utility functions', *Review of Economic Studies*, 35: 369–90.

Goudie, A.W. (1984) 'Tax exhaustion: estimates from a disaggregated model of corporate tax liabilities', *Applied Economics*, 16(2): 205–24.

(1987) 'Forecasting corporate failure: the use of disciminant analysis within a disaggregated model of the corporate sector', *Journal of the Royal Statistical Society*, Series A, 150: 69–81.

Goudie, A.W. and Meeks, G. (1981) 'Medium-term projections of individual companies' financial flows', *Accounting and Business Research*, 11: 291–302.

(1982) 'The effects of macroeconomic developments on individual companies' flows of funds', *Omega*, 10: 361–71.

(1984) 'Individual agents in a macroeconomic model', *Journal of Policy Modelling*, 6(3): 289–309.

(1987) 'Export and die: the exchange rate and company failure in a macro-micro model', DAE Working Paper No. 885, University of Cambridge.

Granger, C.W.J. (1980a) 'Testing for causation: a personal viewpoint', *Journal of Economic Dynamics and Control*, 2: 329–52.

(1980b) 'Long-memory relationships and the aggregation of dynamic models', *Journal of Econometrics*, 14: 227–38.

(1987) 'Implications of aggregation with common factors', *Economic Theory*, 3: 208–22.

Granger, C.W.J. and Hatanaka, M. (1964) *Spectral analysis of economic time series*, Princeton: Princeton University Press.

Granger, C.W.J. and Morris, M.J. (1976) Time series modelling and interpretation, *Journal of Royal Statistical Society, A*, 139: 246–57.

Green, C.J. (1984) 'The demand and supply of bank credit in the United Kingdom: a survey', mimeo.

Green, H.A.J. (1964) *Aggregation in economic analysis*, Princeton: Princeton University Press.

Gregory, A.W. and Veall, M.R. (1985) 'Formulating Walt tests of non linear restrictions', *Econometrica*, 53: 1465–8.

Grunfeld, Y. and Griliches, Z. (1960) 'Is aggregation necessarily bad?' *Review of Economics and Statistics*, 42: 1–13.

Guilkey, D.K., Lovell, C.A.K., and Sickles, R.C. (1983) 'A comparison of the performance of three flexible functional forms', *International Economic Review*, 591–616.

Gupta, K.L. (1971) 'Aggregation bias in linear economic models', *International Economic Review*, 12: 293–305.

Hannan, E.J. (1970) *Multiple time series*, New York: Wiley.

Hansen, S.L. (1987) 'An empirical investigation of dividend decisions in the UK', unpublished Ph.D.thesis, University of Cambridge.

Hansen, S.L. and Goudie, A.W. (1988) 'The effects of dividend controls on company behaviour', *Applied Economics*, 20: 143–64.

Hartigan, J. (1975) *Clustering algorithms*, New York: John Wiley.

Hartman, R.S. (1982) 'A note on the use of aggregate data in individual choice models', *Journal of Econometrics*, 18: 313–35.

Hausman, J.A. (1978) 'Specification tests in econometrics', *Econometrica*, 45: 1251–71.

Hausman, J. (1985) 'The econometrics of nonlinear budget sets', *Econometrica*, 53: 1255–82.

Hausman, J. and Ruud, P. (1984) 'Family labor supply with taxes', *American Economic Review*, 74: 242–48.

Hausman, J.A., and Wise, D.A. (1978) 'A conditional probit model for qualitative choice: discrete decisions recognizing interdependence and heterogeneous preferences', *Econometrica*, 46: 403–26.

Heckman, J.J. and Willis, R.J. (1977) 'A beta-logistic model for the analysis of sequential labor force participation by married women', *Journal of Political Economy*, 85: 27–58.

Hendry, D.F., Pagan, A.R., and Sargan, J.D. (1984) 'Dynamic specification', in *Handbook of Econometrics*, 2, Amsterdam: Van Nostrand.

Henscher, J.A. and Johnson, L.W. (1981) *Applied discrete choice modelling*, London: Croom Helm.

HMSO (1982) Corporation Tax Green Paper, Cmnd 8456, London: HMSO.

Disaggregation in econometric modelling

HM Treasury (1985) *The relationship between employment and wages,* review by Treasury Officials.

Higson, C. (1987) 'Modelling the UK corporation tax system', unpublished Working Paper, LBS, London.

Holly, S. and Longbottom, A. (1985) 'A "Q model" of industrial and commercial fixed investment', Centre for Economic Forecasting Discussion Paper No. 141, London Business School.

Holly, S. and Markose, S. (1986) 'Disaggregated inventories in manufacturing', CEF Discussion Paper No. 25-86, London Business School.

Holly, S. and Smith, P. (1987) 'A two-sector analysis of the UK labour market', *Oxford Bulletin of Economics and Statistics,* 49: 79-102.

Hooijmans, E.M. and Rutten, F.F.H. (1984) 'The impact of supply on the use of hospital facilities. Differences between high and low income groups in the Netherlands', *Acta Hospitalia,* 2: 14-48.

Hooijmans, E.M. and van de Ven, W.P.M.M. (1982) 'Implementing a health status index in a structural health care model', in van der Gaag, J., Neeman, W.B., and Tsukahara, T. (eds), *Economics of Health Care,* New York: Praeger.

Ilmakunnas, P. (1986) 'Aggregation of micro forecasts', in Kähkönen, J. and Ylä-Liedenpohja, J. (eds), A tribute to Arvi Leponiemi on his 60th birthday, *Acta Academiae Oeconomicae Helsingiensis,* Series A(48): 37-47.

Ilmakunnas, P. and Lassila, J. (1988) *Talonrakennustoiminnan ennustemalli,* (A Forecasting Model for Building Constructions), Series C45, Research Institute for the Finnish Economy.

Inland Revenue (1982) 'The computer simulation model for forecasting and costing corporation tax in the United Kingdom', mimeo, Inland Revenue.

Jackson, P.D. (1984) 'Financial asset portfolio allocation by industrial and commercial companies', Bank of England Discussion Paper No. 8 (Technical Series).

Jeffreys, H. (1937) *Scientific Inference* (reissued with addenda), Cambridge University Press.

(1948) *Theory of Probability* (second edition), Oxford University Press.

(1961) *Theory of Probability* (third edition), Oxford University Press.

Jeffreys, H. and Wrinch, D. (1921) 'On certain fundamental principles of scientific inquiry', *Philosophical Magazine,* 42: 369-90.

Johnson, N.L. (1949) Systems of frequency curves generated by methods of translation, *Biometrica,* 36: 149-76.

Johnson, N.L. and Kotz, S. (1970) *Continuous univariate distributions: vol. 2,* Boston: Houghton Mifflin.

Johnston, J. (1972) *Econometric Methods,* New York: McGraw-Hill.

Joreskog, K. and Goldberger, A. (1975) 'Estimation of a model with multiple indicators and multiple causes of a single latent variable', *Journal of the American Statistical Association,* 70: 631-9.

Jorgenson, D.W., Lau, L.J. and Stoker, T.M. (1982) 'The transcendental logarithmic model of aggregate consumer behaviour', in Basman, R.

and Rhodes, G. (eds), *Advances in Econometrics*, Greenwich, Conn.: JAI Press.

Kaldor, N. (1957) 'A model of economic growth', *Economic Journal*, 67: 591–624.

—— (1961) 'Capital accumulation and economic growth', in Lutz, F.A. and Hague, D.C. (eds), *The theory of capital*, London: Macmillan.

Kaldor, N. and Mirrlees, J.A. (1962) 'A new model of economic growth', *Review of Economic Studies*, 29: 174–92.

Kapteyn, A. and Woittiez, I. (1986) 'Preference interdependence and habit formation in family labor supply', working paper, Tilburg University.

Keating, G. (1985) 'The financial sector of the LBS model', in Currie, D. (ed.), *Advances in monetary economics*, London: Croom Helm.

Kelejian, H.H. (1980) 'Aggregation and disaggregation of nonlinear equations', in Kmenta, J. and Ramsey, J.B. (eds), *Evaluation of econometric models*, New York: Academic Press.

Kemsley, W.F.F., Redpath, R.U., and Holmes, M. (1980) *Family Expenditure Survey handbook*, London: HMSO.

Kennan, J. (1979) 'The estimation of partial adjustment models with rational expectations', *Econometrica*, 47: 1441–55.

Killingsworth, D. (1985) *Labour supply*, Cambridge University Press.

King, M. (1971) 'Corporate taxation and dividend behaviour: a comment', *Review of Economic Studies*, 38: 377–80.

King, M. (1988) Tax policy and family welfare, in Atkinson, A.B., and Sutherland, H. (eds), *Tax-benefit models*, ST/ICERD Occasional Paper No. 10, London School of Economics.

Kohn, R. (1982) 'When is an aggregate of a time series efficiency forecast by its past?', *Journal of Econometrics*, 18: 337–49.

Kooiman, P. and Kloek, T. (1979) 'Aggregation of micro markets in disequilibrium', working paper, Erasmus University, Rotterdam.

Koppelman, F.S. (1976a) 'Methodology for analyzing errors in prediction with disaggregate choice models', *Transportation Research Record*, 592: 17–23.

—— (1976b) 'Guidelines for aggregate travel prediction using disaggregate choice models', *Transportation Research Record*, 610: 19–24.

Koppelman, F.S. and Ben-Akiva, M.F. (1977) 'Aggregate forecasting with disaggregate travel demand models using normally available data', in Visset, E.J. (ed.), *Transport decisions in an age of uncertainty*, The Hague: Martinus Nijhoff.

Lambelet, J.C. (1985) 'Should systems like LINK be used for long-range forecasts and simulations?', *Economic Modelling*, 2(2): 83–92.

Lancaster, T. (1979) 'Prediction from binary choice models: a note', *Journal of Econometrics*, 10: 387–9.

Langbein, L.I. and Lichtman, A.J. *Ecological inference*, Series on Quantitative Applications in the Social Sciences, No. 07–11, Sage University Press, Beverly Hills.

Lau, L.J. (1980) 'Existence conditions for aggregate demand functions', Technical Report No. 248, Institute for Mathematical Studies in the

Social Sciences, Stanford University, Stanford, California.

(1982) 'A note on the fundamental theory of exact aggregation', *Economics Letters*, 9: 119–26.

Layard, R., and Nickell, S. (1985) 'The causes of British unemployment', *National Institute Economic Review*, 111: 62–85.

(1986) 'Unemployment in Britain', *Economica*, 53: S121–69.

Layard, R., Barton, M., and Zabalza, A. (1985) 'Married women's participation and hours', *Economica*, special issue.

Leamer, E.E. (1978) *Specification searches*, New York: John Wiley.

(1984) *Sources of international comparative advantage: theory and evidence*, Cambridge, Mass.: MIT Press.

Lee, K.C., Pesaran, M.H., and Pierse, R.G. (1990) 'Testing for aggregation bias in linear models', *Economic Journal*, forthcoming.

Leontief, W.W. (1947) 'Introduction to a theory of the internal structure of functional relationships', *Econometrica*, 15: 361–73.

Levis, M. and Morgan, E.J. (1985) 'The 1984 Budget: Effects of corporate tax and investment', University of Bath Discussion Paper No. 67.

Lindley, D.V. (1968) 'The choice of variables in multiple regression', *Journal of the Royal Statistical Society*, Series B, 31: 31–66.

Lintner, J.K. (1956) 'Distribution of incomes of corporation among dividends, retained earnings and taxes', *Proceedings of the American Economic Association, American Economic Review*, 27, 2: 97–118.

Lippi, M. (1987a) 'The coefficients of the Wold representation of rational spectrum stochastic vectors as functions of the spectral density coefficients', Department of Political Economy, University of Modena.

(1987b) 'A note on aggregation of log-linear error-correction models', working paper, Department of Political Economy, University of Modena.

(1988a) 'On the dynamic shape of error correction models', *Journal of Economic Dynamics and Control*, 12: 561–85.

(1988b) 'On the dynamics of aggregate macroequations: from simple microbehaviour to complex macroequations', in Dosi, G., Freeman, C., Nelson, R., Silverberg, G., and Soete, L. (eds), *Technical change and economic theory*, London: Frances Pinter.

Liu, L.-M. and Hanssens, D.M. (1982) 'Indentification of multiple-input transfer function models', *Communications in Statistics*, A 11: 297–314.

Liu, L.-M., Hudak, G.B., *et al.* (1983) *The SCA system for univariate-multivariate time series and general statistical analysis*, Scientific Computing Associates, DeKalb, Illinois.

Lovell, C.A.K. (1973) 'A note on aggregation bias and loss', *Journal of Econometrics*, 1: 301–11.

Lütjohann, H. (1974) *Linear aggregation in linear regression*, Stockholm: Sundt offset.

Lütkepohl, H. (1984a) 'Linear transformations of vector ARMA processes', *Journal of Econometrics*, 26: 283–93.

(1984b) 'Forecasting contemporaneously aggregated vector ARMA processes', *Journal of Business and Economic Statistics*, 2: 201–14.

(1985) 'Comparison of predictors for temporarily and contemporaneously aggregated multivariate time series', working paper, Department of Economics, University of California, San Diego.

(1987) *Forecasting aggregated vector ARMA processes*, Berlin: Springer.

McFadden, D. (1974) 'Conditional logit analysis of qualitative choice behaviour', in Zarembka, P. (ed.), *Frontiers in econometrics*, New York: Academic Press.

McFadden, D. and Reid, F. (1975) 'Aggregate travel demand forecasting from disaggregate demand models', *Transportation Research Record*, 534: 24–37.

Maddala, G.S. *Limited-dependent and qualitative variables in econometrics*, Cambridge University Press.

Malinvaud, E. (1956) 'L'aggrégation dans les modèles économiques', *Cahiers du Seminaire d'Econometrie*, 4: 69–146.

Mankiw, N.G. and Shapiro, M.D. (1985) 'Trends, random walks, and tests of the permanent income hypothesis', *Journal of Monetary Economics*, 16: 165–74.

(1986) 'Do we reject too often? Small sample properties of tests of rational expectations models', *Economics Letters*, 20: 139–45.

Manning, W.G., Newhouse, J.P., Duan, N., Keeler, E.B., Leibowits, A., and Marquis, M.S. (1987) 'Health insurance and the demand for medical care: evidence from a randomized experiment', *American Economic Review*, 77(3): 251–77.

May, J.J. (1975) 'Utilization of health services and the availability of resources', in Anderson, R., Kravitz, J., and Anderson, O.W. (eds) *Equity in health services: empirical analysis in social policy*, Cambridge, Mass.: Ballinger Publishing Company.

Mayer, C. and Morris, C.N. (1982) 'A disaggregated model of UK corporation tax', IFS Working Paper No. 33, Institute of Fiscal Studies, London.

Merkies, H.Q.M. and Bikker, J.A. (1981) 'Aggregation of lag patterns with an application in the construction industry', *European Economic Review*, 15: 385–405.

Miller, M.H. and Sprenkle, C.H. (1980) 'The precautionary demand for narrow and broad money', *Economica*, 47: 407–21.

Moffitt, R. (1986) 'The econometrics of piecewise-linear budget constraints', *Journal of Business and Economic Statistics*, 4: 317–28.

Moore, B.J. and Threadgold, A.R. (1985) 'Corporate bank borrowing in the UK 1965–1981', *Economica*, 52: 65–78.

Moroney, J.R. and Toevs, A. (1977) 'Factor costs and factor use: an analysis of labor, capital and natural resource inputs? *Southern Economic Journal*, October: 222–39.

Morris, C.N. and Dilnot, A.W. (1982) 'The tax system and distribution 1979–82', in Kay, J.A. (ed.), *The 1982 Budget*, Oxford: Basil Blackwell.

Muellbauer, J. (1975) 'Aggregation, income distribution and consumer demand', *Review of Economic Studies*, 42: 525–43.

(1976) 'Community preferences and the representative consumer', *Econometrica*, 44: 979–99.

Nerlove, M. (1972) 'On lags in economic behaviour', *Econometrica*, 40: 221–51.

Nerlove, M., Grether, P.M., and Carvalho, J.L. (1979) *Analysis of economic time-series*, Orlando, Fla.: Academic Press.

Netherlands Bureau of Statistics (1983) *Sociale Maandstatistiek.*

Netherlands Central Planning Bureau (1985) *Freia-Kompas '85*, monograph no.28, Netherlands Central Planning Bureau.

Newhouse, J.P., Manning, W.G., Morris, C., Orr, L., Duan, N., Keeler, E., Leibowitz, A., Marquis, K., Marquis, M.S., Phelps, C., and Brook, R. (1981) 'Some interim results from a controlled trial of cost sharing in health insurance', *The New England Journal of Medicine*, 305: 1501–7.

Nickell, S. (1984) 'An investigation of the determinants of manufacturing employment in the United Kingdom', *Review of Economic Studies*, 51: 529–57.

Nyhus, D. (1986) 'The INFORUM-ERI international system of macro-economic input-output models', paper presented to the 8th International Conference on Input-Output Modelling, Sapporo, Japan.

Nyman, S. and Silberston, A. (1978) 'The ownership and control of industry', *Oxford Economic Papers*, 30: 74–101.

Oulton, N. (1981) 'Liquidity, fixed investment and the firm: a dynamic stochastic approach', mimeo.

Pakes, A. (1983) 'On group effects and errors in variables in aggregation', *Review of Economics and Statistics*, 65: 168–73.

Pauly, M.V. (1980) *Doctors and their workshops: economic models of physician behaviour*, University of Chicago Press, Chicago.

Peiris, M.S. (1987) 'On the study of some functions of multi-variate ARMA processes', unpublished working paper, Monash University.

Pesaran, M.H. (1973) 'The small sample problem of truncation remainders in the estimation of distributed lag models with autocorrelated errors', *International Economic Review*, 14: 120–31.

(1988) 'Costly adjustment under rational expectations: a generalization', UCLA Working Paper No. 480.

Pesaran, M.H. and Pesaran, B. (1987) *Microfit: an interactive econometric software package*, Oxford University Press.

Pesaran, M.H. and Smith, R.J. (1986) 'A unified approach to estimation and orthogonality tests in linear single equation econometric models', unpublished ms., Cambridge University.

Pesaran, M.H., Pierse, R.G., and Kumar, M.S. (1986) 'On the problem of aggregation in econometrics', Discussion Papers on Structural Analysis of Economic Systems, No. 1, University of Cambridge.

(1989) 'Econometric analysis of aggregation in the context of linear prediction models', *Econometrica*, 57: 861–88.

Peston, M.H. (1959) 'A view of the aggregation problem', *Review of Economic Studies*, 27: 58–64.

Popper, K. (1959) *The logic of scientific discovery*, London: Hutchinson.

Poterba, J.M. (1983) 'Divided taxes and corporate financial policy', unpublished Ph.D. thesis, Oxford University.

Powell, J.L. and Stoker, T.M. (1985) 'The estimation of complete aggregation structures', *Journal of Econometrics*, 30: 317–44.

Preston, R.S. (1975) 'The Wharton long-term model: input-output within the context of a macro forecasting model', *International Economic Review*, 16: 3–16.

Rao, C.R. (1973) *Linear statistical inference and its applications*, 2nd edn, New York: John Wiley.

Reid, F.A. (1978) 'Minimizing error in aggregate predictions from disaggregate models', *Transportation Research Record*, 673: 59–65.

Rozanov, Y. (1967) *Stationary random processes*, San Francisco: Holden Day.

Rutten, F.F.H. (1978) 'The use of health care facilities in the Netherlands: an econometric analysis', doctoral dissertation, Centre for Research in Public Economics, Leyden University.

Ruud, P.A. (1984) 'Tests of specification in econometrics', *Econometric Review*, 3: 211–42

Sargent, T.J. (1978) 'Estimation of dynamic labor demand schedules under rational expectations', *Journal of Political Economy*, 86: 1009–44.

Sasaki, K. (1978) 'An empirical analysis of linear aggregation problems. The case of investment behavior in Japanese firms', *Journal of Econometrics*, 7: 313–31.

Schankerman, M. (1984) 'Comment' on Beggs' paper, in Griliches, Z. (ed.), *R&D, patents, and productivity*, Chicago: University of Chicago Press.

Schmookler, T. (1966) *Invention and Economic Growth*, Cambridge, Mass.: Harvard University Press.

Sims, C.A. (1970) 'Discrete approximations to continuous distributed lags in econometrics', *Econometrica*, 38: 545–64.

—— (1972) 'Money income and causality', *American Economic Review*, 62: 540–52.

—— (1974) 'Distributed lags', in Intriligator, M. and Kendrick, D. (eds), *Frontiers in quantitative economics*, Amsterdam: North Holland.

Smyth, D. (1984) 'Short-term employment functions when the speed of the adjustment depends on the unemployment rate', *Review of Economics and Statistics*, 63: 138–42.

Sonnenschein, H. (1972) 'Market excess demand functions', *Econometrica*, 40: 549–63.

Steele, R. and Gray, A.M. (1982) 'Statistical cost analysis: the hospital case', *Applied Economics*, 14: 491–502.

Sterner, T. (1985) 'Energy use in Mexican Industry', unpublished Ph.D. thesis, University of Gothenburg, Sweden.

Stoker, T.M. (1982) 'The use of cross-section data to characterize macro functions', *Journal of the American Statistical Association*, 77: 369–80.

Stoker, T.M. (1984) 'Completeness, distribution restrictions, and the form of aggregate functions', *Econometrica*, 52: 887–907.

(1986a) 'Aggregation, efficiency and cross-section regression', *Econometrica*, 54: 171–88.

(1986b) 'Simple tests of distributional effects on macroeconomic equations', *Journal of Political Economy*, 94: 763–93.

Symonds, E. and Walker, I. (1986) 'Reform of personal taxation: a brief analysis', *Fiscal Studies*, May: 34–48.

Symons, J.S.V. (1985) 'Relative prices and the demand for labour in British manufacturing', *Economica*, 52: 37–49.

Taffler, R.J. (1982) 'Forecasting company failure in the UK using discriminant analysis and financial ratio data', *Journal of the Royal Statistical Society*, Series A, 145: 342–58.

Tahvanainen, M. and Lindqvist, M. (1983) *Volume Index of Building Construction 1980=100*, Studies No. 88, Central Statistical Office of Finland, Helsinki.

Talvitie, A. (1973) 'Aggregate travel demand analysis with disaggregate demand models', *Proceedings: transportation research forum*, 14: 583–603.

Theil, H. (1954) *Linear aggregation of economic relations*, Amsterdam: North-Holland.

(1971) *Principles of econometrics*, New York: Wiley.

Tiao, G. and Wei, W. (1976) 'Effects of temporal aggregation on the dynamic relationships of two time-series variables', *Biometrika*, 63: 513–23.

Trivedi, P.K. (1985) 'Distributed lags, aggregation and compounding: some econometric implications', *Review of Economic Studies*, 52: 19–35.

Van Doorslaer, E.K.A. and van Vliet, R.C.J.A. (1986) 'A built bed is a filled bed? An empirical reexamination', paper presented at the First International Congress on Regional Variations in Provision, Utilization and Outcomes of Health Care, Copenhagen.

Vanek, J. (1968) 'The factor proportions theory: the N-factor case', *Kyklos*, 21: 749–56.

Ven, W.P.M.M. van de and Praag, B.M.S. van (1981) 'The demand for deductibles in private health insurance. A probit-model with sample selection', *Journal of Econometrics*, 17: 229–52.

Vliet, R.C.J.A. van and Van Doorslaer, E.K.A. (1988)) 'Disaggregation of the demand for hospital care', *Applied Economics*, 20(7): 969–84.

Watson, P.L. and Westin, R.B. (1975) 'Transferability of disaggregate mode choice models', *Regional Science and Urban Economics*, 5: 227–49.

Weiss, A. (1984) 'Systematic sampling and temporal aggregation in time series models', *Journal of Econometrics*, 26: 271–81.

Westin, R.B. (1974) 'Predictions from binary choice models', *Journal of Econometrics*, 2: 1–16.

White, H. (1984) *Asymptotic theory for econometricians*, London: Academic Press.

Wilson Committee (Committee to Review the Functioning of the Financial Institutions) (1980) *Report*, Cmnd. 7937, London: HMSO.

Winters, A. (1980) 'Aggregation in logarithmic models: some experiments with UK exports', *Oxford Bulletin of Economics and Statistics*, 42, February.

Working, H. (1960) 'Note on the correlation of first differences of averages in a random chain', *Econometrica*, 28: 916–18.

Wren-Lewis, S. (1986) 'An econometric model of UK manufacturing employment using survey data on expected output', *Journal of Applied Econometrics*, 1: 297–316.

Zellner, A. (1962) 'An efficient method of estimating seemingly unrelated regressions and tests for aggregation bias', *Journal of the American Statistical Association*, 57: 348–68.

(1966) 'On the aggregation problem: a new approach to a troublesome problem', in Fox, K.A. *et al.* (eds), *Economic models, estimation and risk programming: essays in honor of Gerhard Tintner*, Berlin: Springer-Verlag.

(1971) *An introduction to Bayesian-inference in econometrics*, New York: John Wiley.

(1988) 'Causality and causal laws in economics', *Journal of Econometrics*, 39: 7–21.

Index